The Neuropsychology of Consciousness

FOUNDATIONS OF NEUROPSYCHOLOGY

A Series of Textbooks, Monographs and Treatises

Series Editor

LAIRD S. CERMAK

*Memory Disorders Research Center, Boston Veterans Administration,
Medical Center, 150 South Huntington Avenue, Boston, MA 02130, USA*

The Neuropsychology of Consciousness

EDITED BY

A.D. Milner
&
M.D. Rugg

Department of Psychology
University of St Andrews
St Andrews
Fife KY16 9JU
Scotland

ACADEMIC PRESS
Harcourt Brace Jovanovich Publishers
London   San Diego   New York
Boston   Sydney   Tokyo   Toronto

ACADEMIC PRESS LIMITED
24/28 Oval Road,
London NW1 7DX

United States Edition published by
ACADEMIC PRESS INC.
San Diego, CA 92101

Copyright © 1992 by
ACADEMIC PRESS LIMITED

British Library Cataloguing in Publication Data

A catalogue record for this book is available from the British Library

ISBN 0-12-498045-7
0-12-498046-5 (pbk)

Typeset by MCS Ltd, Salisbury, Wiltshire
Printed and bound in Great Britain by
Hartnolls Ltd, Bodmin, Cornwall.

CONTENTS

List of contributors   vii

Preface   xi

1 Introduction: Dissociated Issues   1
   L. Weiskrantz

2 Reflections on Blindsight   11
   A. Cowey and P. Stoerig

3 Covert Processing in Different Visual Recognition
Systems   39
   G.W. Humphreys, T. Troscianko, M.J. Riddoch,
   M. Boucart, N. Donnelly and G.F.A. Harding

4 Face Recognition and Awareness after Brain Injury   69
   A.W. Young and E.H.F. De Haan

5 Attentional Mechanisms and Conscious Experience   91
   M.I. Posner and M.K. Rothbart

6 Understanding Consciousness: Clues from Unilateral
Neglect and Related Disorders   113
   E. Bisiach

7 Disorders of Perceptual Awareness—Commentary   139
   A.D. Milner

8 The Distinction Between Implicit and Explicit
Language Function: Evidence from Aphasia   159
   L.K. Tyler

9   Consciousness and Awareness in Memory and
Amnesia: Critical Issues   180

     D.L. Schacter

10   Unconscious Influences of Memory: Dissociations and
Automaticity   201

     L.L. Jacoby and C. Kelley

11   Automatic Memory Processes in Amnesia: How Are
They Mediated?   235

     A.R. Mayes

12   Conscious and Unconscious Processes in Language
and Memory—Commentary   263

     M.D. Rugg

Index   279

CONTRIBUTORS

E. Bisiach
Istituto di Clinica Neurologica, Ospedale Maggiore—Policlinico, Università di Milano, via Francesco Sforza, 35, Italy

M. Boucart
Laboratoire de Psychologie Expérimentale, Université René Descartes, 28 Rue Serpente, Paris F-75006, France

A. Cowey
Department of Experimental Psychology, University of Oxford, South Parks Road, Oxford OX1 3UD, England

N. Donnelly
Cognitive Science Research Centre, School of Psychology, University of Birmingham, Edgbaston, Birmingham B15 2TT, England

E.H.F. De Haan
MRC Neuropsychology Unit, Radcliffe Infirmary, Woodstock Road, Oxford OX2 6HE, England

G.F.A. Harding
Department of Vision Sciences, Aston University, Aston Triangle, Birmingham V4 7ET, England

G.W. Humphreys
Cognitive Science Research Centre, School of Psychology, University of Birmingham, Edgbaston, Birmingham B15 2TT, England

L.L. Jacoby
Department of Psychology, McMaster University, Hamilton, Ontario L8S 4K1, Canada

C.M. Kelley
Department of Psychology, Macalester College, 1600 Grand Avenue, St Paul, Minnesota 55105, USA

A.R. Mayes
Department of Psychology, University of Liverpool, Eleanor Rathbone Building, P.O. Box 147, Liverpool L69 3BX, England

A.D. Milner
Psychological Laboratory, University of St Andrews, St Andrews, Fife KY16 9JU, Scotland

M.I. Posner
Institute of Cognitive and Decision Sciences, University of Oregon, Eugene, Oregon 97403, USA

M.J. Riddoch
Cognitive Science Research Centre, School of Psychology, University of Birmingham, Edgbaston, Birmingham B15 2TT, England

M.K. Rothbart
Institute of Cognitive and Decision Sciences, University of Oregon, Eugene, Oregon 97403, USA

M.D. Rugg
Wellcome Brain Research Group, Department of Psychology, University of St Andrews, St Andrews, Fife KY16 9JU, Scotland

D.L. Schacter
Department of Psychology, Harvard University, Cambridge, MA 02138, USA

P. Stoerig
Institute of Medical Psychology, Ludwig–Maximilians–University of Munich, Munich, Germany

T. Troscianko
Perceptual Systems Research Centre, Department of Psychology, Bristol University, 8–10 Berkeley Square, Bristol BS8 8JB, England

L.K. Tyler
Department of Psychology, Birkbeck College, Malet Street, London WC1E 7HX, England

L. Weiskrantz
*Department of Experimental Psychology, University of Oxford,
South Parks Road, Oxford OX1 3UD, England*

A.W. Young
*Department of Psychology, Durham University, Science Laboratories,
South Road, Durham DH1 3LE, England*

PREFACE

In September 1990, with the support and encouragement of the Russell Trust, and with additional financial help from the Wellcome Trust, a symposium entitled 'Consciousness and Cognition: Neuropsychological Perspectives' was held at the University of St Andrews. The intention was to assemble a group of the major researchers at the forefront of this field. The meeting proved a great success, and we hope that the chapters of the present volume will help to explain why by conveying some of the excitement of current research and theory in the area.

The starting point for the symposium and for the book was the widespread realization that in several areas of human cognition (e.g. visual perception, memory, language comprehension, and attention), the severe and profound impairments due to brain damage that have been described over the past 150 years are often not absolute. In particular, the use of indirect methods of testing may reveal unsuspected preservation of capacities that are undetected by more traditional direct methods. Since such techniques reveal abilities of which the patient is unaware, these findings have sometimes proved as much a surprise for the patient as for the investigators, and have thrown questions about the relationship between cognition and consciousness into sharp relief. Lawrence Weiskrantz was a major pioneer in what are still the two most intensively investigated of the neurological deficits that give rise to dissociations between 'aware' and 'unaware' processing: amnesia, and 'cortical blindness'. Furthermore, his contributions since those early reports have continued to be highly influential. It is therefore particularly appropriate that he should provide the Introduction to the present volume.

We would like to express our thanks not only to the sponsors of the symposium, and to those contributors to it who are represented in this volume, but also to others whose contributions at the meeting undoubtedly, if covertly, helped shape the contents of the book. We particularly acknowledge the contributions of Daniel Bub, Andrew Ellis, Melvyn Goodale, Michael Kopelman and Patrick Rabbitt. Finally, we thank Andrew Carrick of Academic Press for his organizational help, and Nikki Jones for her untiring secretarial assistance; without them this book could not have been completed in so short a time.

A.D. MILNER
M.D. RUGG
St Andrews, April 1991

CHAPTER 1

Introduction: Dissociated Issues

Lawrence Weiskrantz

1.1. IMAGING AND EPIDEMIOLOGY

Every period in the relatively brief history of neuroscience has considered that it had a special, sometimes even ultimate, insight into the neural mechanisms of conscious awareness, offered against a sustained background hum of denials that the problem was real, or, if real, capable of being investigated within science. In the main, among those who accepted it as both real and of scientific interest, the approaches were largely large-scale correlational, e.g. changes in electrical activity during periods of heightened attention, or during stages of sleep, as in the reticular formation research, combined of course with supportive clinical and behavioural invasive research. Alternatively, they were theoretical and speculative, often depending upon an implicit assumption that awareness depends upon particular details of cortical activity, an assumption rooted in late nineteenth century thinking but extending into modern times.

While modern work is continuous with its past, the last 15–20 years has nevertheless seen two developments which make the period into which we are about to enter somewhat special and exciting, and a volume such as this one especially useful and topical. The first of these is the development of imaging techniques which, even now, strike one as so remarkable as to exude a flavour of science fiction. Combined with increasing sophistication of analysis of event-related potentials, they provide a heretofore totally inaccessible view of fine-grained patterns of brain activity that occur during ongoing cognitive activity. Even more significant for the present theme, and even more recent, they are being put to the service of those asking sophisticated experimental questions about the information processing aspects of those cognitive operations,

THE NEUROPSYCHOLOGY OF CONSCIOUSNESS
ISBN 0–12–498045–7

so well illustrated in the work of Michael Posner (see Chapter 5, this volume).

A second development, one that is unique to this age, is the virtual epidemic of dissociations discovered by neuropsychologists whereby residual processing occurs in the absence of acknowledged awareness. The first to be recognized, perhaps, was in the field of amnesia, where it is now widely agreed that amnesic patients show good retention for certain types of events even though the patients acknowledge no memory for them as such. But other examples have recently come to light, most of them also the subject of detailed treatment in this volume: blindsight, blind-touch, 'deaf hearing' (Michel, 1990), prosopagnosia and other forms of agnosia, dyslexia, unilateral neglect, and aphasia. A complementary condition, the denial of loss of a capacity (anosognosia), has also come under focused investigation. Potentially it seems possible that the dissociation between capacity and acknowledged awareness will emerge for every cognitive, and even non-cognitive, neuropsychological syndrome.

This epidemic of dissociations encouragingly has led to an increase in interest by philosophers of mind in empirical *evidence*; without experimental analysis none of the dissociates would be known. In addition, they have also interacted with, indeed often been the spur for uncovering, apparently similar evidence in the human experimental psychology of normal subjects. Capacity in the absence of, or independent of, explicit awareness has come under heavy scrutiny in such phenomena as repetition priming, backward central masking, lexical decision, stem-completion, picture completion, sentence arrangement, anomalous pictures/sentences, long-delayed forced-choice recognition, subliminal perception, skills, autonomic responses, and shadowing in dichotic listening.

Of course, there is a wealth of detail to consider and uncover, but in the context of a volume such as this a number of more general questions arise, and two of them arise straight away. The first is how well do the phenomena *within* either neuropsychology or *within* normal human experimental psychology map onto each other? A second is how well do these two domains map *onto each other*? An epidemic does not necessarily imply common mechanisms. How readily can one assume a parasitism of explanation for one category of effects on another; are there common generalizations?

1.2. LOGICAL POWERS AND LIMITATIONS OF DISSOCIATIONS

All of the neuropsychological evidence mentioned above depends on dissociations, i.e. different capacities being differently affected by different treatments. Further questions emerge from a consideration of the logical powers and limitations of dissociations. Evidence for distinctions between residual capacity and acknowledged awareness are often based on *single* dissociations, e.g. it is readily possible to demonstrate a loss of 'explicit' recognition without a loss of priming, but apparently not vice versa. Single dissociations are useful logically for drawing inferences about hierarchical control, but provide a very weak basis for arguments in favour of independent systems or processes, for which double dissociations are necessary (but not sufficient). Yet theories of independent systems or independent processes are not uncommon across the range of phenomena considered above, and have led to the drawing of a number of dichotomous contrasts. Which of the phenomena would we *expect* to be susceptible to double dissociations and for which would double dissociations be unexpected or even impossible?

Where double dissociations are found, as is the case in sub-species of blindsight, for example, inferences about independent visual processors or 'modules' readily emerge and are conveniently mapped onto physiological and anatomical evidence. However, even when such potentially independent processes are inferred, evidence of double dissociations tells one little or nothing about the *interactions* of such systems or processes. For this one needs a different type of enterprise, with theoretical underpinning.

Finally, many of the double dissociations inevitably are 'trend' (Shallice, 1988) or 'relative' (Weiskrantz, 1989) dissociations, i.e. not absolute or pure. Inferences of independence are still possible, but require qualifications based on, say, intermingling of anatomical pathways; but it is even possible that such 'trend' dissociations could be found in a 'lesioned' PDP network (see Shallice) where independent systems are, by definition, not available.

1.3. QUANTIFIED VALIDATION OF AWARENESS–NONAWARENESS DIFFERENCES

It is now becoming recognized, especially in the area of subliminal perception, that quantitative differences can be reliably measured between objective discriminative thresholds and the threshold for 'subjective awareness'. Moreover, Cheesman and Merikle (1986), having measured such a difference, also validated the difference in terms of converging evidence from differential stimulus control of another phenomenon, the effect of varying probability of congruent information in a Stroop-priming task. More recently, Kunimoto *et al.* unpublished data have subjected the difference between objective and subjective thresholds to a signal detection analysis by requiring a retrospective judgment of correctness after each trial. Their results yield a somewhat different outcome from Cheesman and Merikle, but they nevertheless found a small, but highly reliable, subliminal effect in colour identification by normal subjects.

Given this background, a number of questions arise in relation to both the neuropsychological evidence and that from human experimental psychology. How many of the phenomena from those domains could be quantified in this way? When quantified, could the difference in thresholds be shown to be qualitatively dissociable, i.e. how much converging evidence has been generated, or even could be generated? Is such a qualitative functional difference *necessary*? A further question arises in some neuropsychological domains: how can one deal quantitatively with the phenomenon of 'switched' or 'gut' awareness? For example GY, a blindsight subject, sometimes says (but this is not true of all blindsight nor of GY under all conditions) that he 'knows' that a stimulus has occurred, but insists that he definitely does not 'see'.

A final and deep question concerns whether it is possible to measure awareness/non-awareness differences in animals. The question is seen to be real when it is realized that some of the methods used to establish such a difference in human subjects can be mapped directly on 'gedanken' experiments with animals. For example, the method used by Kunimoto *et al.* (unpublished data) is logically closely similar to a suggestion for independent response alternatives for forced-choice discriminations, on the other hand, versus responses on each trial for 'seeing' and 'guessing', on the other, that could be used with monkeys (Weiskrantz, 1986, 1988; see also Cowey & Stoerig, Chapter 2, this volume).

1.4. DESCRIPTIVE CHARACTERIZATIONS

1.4.1. Dissociative Descriptions

Each of the neuropsychological domains within which awareness/non-awareness dissociations have been reported has generated domain-specific *dissociative* descriptions, e.g. in the memory field, implicit versus explicit, procedural versus declarative, semantic versus episodic; in vision, two-visual system distinctions between detection and identification, 'where' or 'whether' versus 'what'; in prosopagnosia, 'directed visual processing' versus 'face recognition', and in aphasia, 'on-line' versus 'off-line' processing.

Do these various dichotomous pairs have anything in common, other than that one in each is said to lack acknowledged awareness? Do we proceed among the set for analysis one-by-one, or are bolder generalizations possible? Given that some of the dichotomies emerge from single dissociations, and others from double dissociations, there is a prima-facie case for separate examination and, at the very least, a dichotomous classification of different dichotomies. At a more abstract level, a central but difficult question is whether one can distinguish between *disconnected* awareness and subtraction of a particular sub-system. For example, in amnesia can we account for residual function by subtraction of a system specialized for, say, episodic memory, or are we dealing with a disconnection from a central 'awareness' module? At this stage, there are no clear, sharp criteria for deciding between these two alternatives.

1.4.2. Graded Processes

In contrast to dissociative descriptions is an approach in terms of graded processes. Depth of processing, data-driven versus concept-driven processing, and transfer of procedures are all recent examples of attempts to explain the apparent disjunctions in human experimental psychology and neuropsychology in terms of continuously variable aspects of task demands and subjects' capacities (cf. Roediger *et al.*, 1989). A more traditional example in another domain is levels of vigilance as a concept in attention.

A question that naturally arises is whether there is any way to choose between dissociative and graded accounts. It is agreed that double dissociations are necessary but not sufficient to prove that independent and disjunctive processes or systems exist, and so what else is needed? It is also the case that, whether or not one's allegiance is to multiple systems or to graded processes, all relevant research starts from results using tasks that are impure for either type of category: there is no such creature as a 'pure task', and hence further dissection beyond a catalogue of tasks, as such, is mandatory (cf. Weiskrantz, 1989; Jacoby & Kelley, Chapter 10 this volume). Can we get beyond a show of hands? Given that the decision about independent systems or processes will be based, in part, on convergent evidence, what kind of pragmatic and convergent evidence is available? In neuropsychology we at least have independent evidence from neuroscience; e.g. for claims of independent varieties of blindsight, one can bolster one's case by reference to independent anatomical outputs from V1 to V2–V5, together with inputs from the superior colliculus and the lateral geniculate nucleus to V2–V5 that bypass V1, but what kinds of converging evidence within the domain of normal human experimental psychology are available to which a comparable appeal can be made?

1.5. MULTI-DOMAIN CHARACTERIZATIONS

Some theoretical approaches have assumed that there is a unified nature of 'conscious awareness' that warrants a general unified account in neurological or physical terms. Many dissent from such a position, on various grounds: philosophical, semantic, pragmatic, over-complexity and inhomogeneity even in folk-psychology discourse. Among those that find the question of *the* nature of conscious aware-ness viable, there are suggestions at widely different levels and different degrees of specification. A traditional view, given impetus by Sperry (1969), is that conscious awareness emerges directly as a function of complexity of the nervous system, but without specifying what it is about complexity that allows such a qualitative attribute to arise. Other views have tried to specify particular hypothetical arrangements within nervous systems, or computational systems, independent of whether some threshold level of complexity as such is a necessary condition. Johnson-Laird's (1988) view of parallel hierarchical systems might be an example of this. Another view, similarly placed within a hierarchical arrangement, characterizes systems with 'awareness' as those with par-allel monitoring circuits which, in turn, also have communicative links, especially with language, and have an effect on control systems (Weiskrantz, 1988). This in turn is consonant with philosophical views of awareness involving 'higher order thoughts', as advanced by Rosenthal (1986).

An account that was deliberately designed to assimilate neuropsycho-logical evidence of dissociations is the DICE ('dissociable interactions and conscious experience') schema of Schacter (1989), a box-and-arrow model which assumes the existence of a conscious awareness system with specific connections to knowledge modules and an episodic memory system (among others). It is a moot point whether the con-scious awareness system as such is necessary or whether multiple sub-systems will themselves be sufficient. But even if one assumes the latter, questions will continue to nag us as to what it is about particular sub-systems that enables one to attach an attribute of phenomenal aware-ness to their operation. Can one point to any stage or organizational property of such systems and say *that* is where, or how, the critical step takes place—or is this a pseudo-problem?

A quite different approach is that of Crick and Koch (1990) who link the question of awareness to the 'binding' problem, the problem of how the multiplicity of specialized visual neurons allows a single coherent visual image to emerge. Attentional mechanisms that selectively focus on different details of, say, visual inputs to V1 are assumed to be reflected in interactions among different widely dispersed neurons throughout the whole galaxy of specialized visual cortical areas. It is a theory that links awareness to selective attention and, it is assumed, also to short-term, 'working memory'. It may be that particular lesions will disenable specific forms of binding to take place, and hence lead to specific forms of 'unawareness'. It is a moot point whether patients with attenuated 'working memories' have attenuated consciousness, and also whether selective attention may or may not still operate in unaware vision in blindsight or in on-line semantic processing in aphasia or prosopagnosia, but the schema does lead to some clear testable predictions.

It is worth bearing in mind, in case we were allowed to forget them, some current popular accounts that take us into quite different ballparks, especially those based on quantum effects (Penrose, 1989) which, in turn, can lead to various species of interactionistic dualism (Eccles, 1987). These all assume that there is a problem of consciousness to be explained, but take it well outside any explanatory level that would link specific neural circuits with specific dissociations. Indeed, given the universality of quantum effects (actually given empirical underpinning in the limiting sensitivity of the retina), the question arises as to whether there are any parts of the nervous system (including the retina) that are *not* conscious.

Aside from the 'other ballparks' accounts of the last paragraph, the question is whether any of these approaches are any more than heuristic at the moment. All of them stimulate certain lines of enquiry and, in limited domains, testable predictions, but most are still at the level of 'points of view'. A further question that requires consideration is the relation of any of the accounts to executive control. In lay language, what is the relation of awareness to the question of determinants of action, e.g. 'free' or 'not free' will.

1.6. SUGGESTED NEURAL CORRELATES AND EMBODIMENTS

No one would claim that there are more than hints about embodiments at the moment, although there is an air of anticipation that we are on the verge. But among the various references to the r.n.s. (the real nervous system) one can note the prominence of the parietal lobe and frontal lobe — especially its medial aspect, the anterior cingulate — in connection with neglect and attention. There is much consideration, also, of the role of the midbrain, especially the superior colliculus, in mediating certain 'implicit' aspects of perception, as in blindsight, although the midbrain must be considered, for this example, in relation to specialized cortical areas beyond V1 to which the midbrain (but also the lateral geniculate nucleus) projects. This, in turn, leads to speculations that 'awareness' may require a convergence of both the midbrain and cortical inputs.

The approach through the 'binding' problem and selective serial attention of Crick and Koch (1990) draws heavily on observations of coherent, correlated oscillations, roughly at 40 Hz in the firing patterns of cells in the visual cortex. Finally, mention should be made of the various studies of Libet (1982) and his colleagues of the claim that awareness arises slowly in sensory systems, as compared with the control that such systems might exert on motor responses. It is not clear just what it is about the minimal 'on-time' that is necessary for awareness to arise, and just what happens during this period, but Libet is one of the few physiologists making an effort to investigate temporal aspects of conscious versus unconscious processing. In addition, of course, one must mention the large literature on average evoked potentials that are related to different aspects of cognitive processing, within which domain it ought to be possible in principle to separate overt from covert modes of processing.

1.7. WHAT IS IT FOR?

Discussion of the possible evolutionary value of conscious awareness has been continuous for over 100 years, at least among those that assume that it is a special attribute that both can evolve and can bestow benefits. One dominant theme is to attach its benefits to the benefits of active thought itself — in allowing the initiation of predictive strategies, in detaching the observer from an immediate dependence on current inputs, by allowing current inputs to be linked, with or without imagery, to other events distant either in space or time, and in allowing flexible rather than automatic processing. Certainly the neuropsychological patients who suffer from any of the syndromes that are discussed in this volume are deeply disabled: amnesic patients cannot survive on priming or conditioning alone, nor can prosopagnosic patients overcome their acute embarrassment in not recognizing their children, even though they may be able to process 'implicitly' their semantic status, nor can the blindsight subject avoid bumping into lamp-posts, even if they can guess their presence or absence in a forced-choice situation, nor can they compare their 'covert' detection with past visual experience. All of these subjects lack the ability to think about or to image the objects that they can respond to in another mode, or to inter-relate them in space and in time; and this deficiency can be crippling.

A sub-species of the evolutionary position considers the very special benefits in the social domain of being able to entertain a theory of 'other minds', i.e. to make predictions based on what the cognition of another being is inferred to be. This, in turn, leads one to consider the disadvantages, as well as the advantages, of conscious awareness, and to the view that paranoia is a uniquely species-specific attribute: only in the case of humans is existence potentially deeply distorted by attribution of devious motives to other beings. It is not clear, from this point of view, that when one considers the collective paranoia exhibited in certain unstable political arenas, the advantages always outweigh the disadvantages.

Finally, having drifted rather far from the main theme of the book, it is time to return: it is clear that the combination of rapidly developing imaging techniques plus the extraordinary epidemic of dissociations between 'overt' and 'covert' processes, both in neuropsychology as well as in the human experimental laboratory, will generate a new and important set of insights into the mechanisms underlying forms of awareness, both functionally speaking and in terms of neural events and circuits themselves. It is encouraging to witness not only the emergence of fresh directions within experimental psychology, neuropsychology, and their partners in neuroscience in a collective enterprise, with a sophisticated dissection of evidence, but also to provide philosophers of mind with material that by its very nature will remove them from a complete dependence upon the armchair. It will be for the future to see just how dissection and assimilation in the larger arena takes place.

REFERENCES

Cheesman, J. & Merikle, P.M. (1986). Distinguishing conscious from unconscious perceptual processes. *Canadian Journal of Psychology*, **40**, 343–367.

Crick, F. & Koch, C. (1990). Towards a neurobiological theory of consciousness. *Seminars in the Neurosciences*, **2**, 263–275.

Eccles, J. (1987). Brain and mind, two or one? In C. Blakemore and S. Greenfield (eds), *Mindwaves*. Oxford: Basil Blackwell.

Johnson-Laird, P.N. (1988). A computational analysis of consciousness. In A.J. Marcel and E. Bisiach (eds), *Consciousness in Contemporary Science*. Oxford: Oxford University Press.

Kunimoto, C., Miller, J. & Pashler, H. Perception without awareness confirmed: a bias-free procedure for determining awareness thresholds. Department of Psychology, University of California, San Diego (unpublished manuscript).

Libet, B. (1982). Brain stimulation in the study of neural functions for conscious sensory experiences. *Human Neurobiology*, **1**, 235–242.

Michel, F. (1990). Hemi-anacusia is usually unknown to the patient. Poster presented at Russell Trust symposium, St Andrews, Scotland, September 1990.

Penrose, R. (1989). *The Emperor's New Mind*. Oxford: Oxford University Press.

Roediger, H.L. III, Weldon, M.S. & Challis, B.H. (1989). Explaining dissociations between implicit and explicit measures of retention: a processing account. In H.L. Roediger, III and F.I.M. Craik (eds), *Varieties of Memory and Consciousness: Essays in Honour of Endel Tulving*. Hillsdale, NJ: Erlbaum.

Rosenthal, D.M. (1986). Two concepts of consciousness. *Philosophical Studies*, **49**, 329–359.

Schacter, D.L. (1989). On the relation between memory and consciousness: dissociable interactions and conscious experience. In H.L. Roediger, III and F.I.M. Craik (eds), *Varieties of Memory and Consciousness: Essays in Honour of Endel Tulving*. Hillsdale, NJ: Erlbaum.

Shallice, T. (1988). *From Neuropsychology to Mental Structure*. Cambridge: Cambridge University Press.

Sperry, R. (1969). A modified concept of consciousness. *Psychological Review*, **76**, 532–536.

Weiskrantz, L. (1986). *Blindsight. A Case Study and Implications*. Oxford: Oxford University Press.

Weiskrantz, L. (1988). Some contributions of neuropsychology of vision and memory to the problem of consciousness. In A.J. Marcel and E. Bisiach (eds), *Consciousness in Contemporary Science*. Oxford: Oxford University Press.

Weiskrantz, L. (1989). Remembering dissociations. In H.L. Roediger, III and F.I.M. Craik (eds), *Varieties of Memory and Consciousness: Essays in Honour of Endel Tulving*. Hillsdale, NJ: Erlbaum.

CHAPTER 2

Reflections on Blindsight

Alan Cowey and Petra Stoerig

2.1. INTRODUCTION

Although neurologists have often disagreed about the nature of visual disorders, they were for a century almost unanimous in agreeing that partial destruction or denervation of part of the striate cortex renders the patient clinically blind in the resulting visual field defect. The minority view, that some sensitivity remained or returned, was easily dismissed on the grounds that the visual cortex was merely damaged, not destroyed, or had partially recovered from damage. Despite the blindness, assessed by visual field perimetry, more recent investigations show that some patients with an apparently totally blind field defect, can detect and localize visual stimuli when persuaded to guess (Pöppel et al., 1973; Weiskrantz et al., 1974; Perenin & Jeannerod, 1978; Stoerig & Pöppel, 1986). Their high level of performance contrasts with their surprise when it is pointed out to them. Detection and discrimination of movement (Weiskrantz, 1986; Barbur et al., 1980; Magnusson & Mathiesen, 1989), flicker (Barbur et al., 1980; Weiskrantz, 1986; Blythe et al., 1987; Magnusson & Mathiesen, 1989) and orientation (Weiskrantz et al., 1974; Perenin, 1978; Weiskrantz, 1987) may also be present. Two patients asked to reach for solid objects, adjusted their grasp so that it matched the shape and size of the unseen objects. Even more surprisingly, they could use the meaning of unseen words flashed in their field defects in order to select between pairs of words subsequently presented in the intact visual field, i.e. they showed a priming effect (Marcel, 1983 a,b). These far-ranging residual visual capacities can be demonstrated even though the patients assert that they do not see anything in the field defects and are surprised when their often excellent performance is pointed out to them. This phenomenon has become known as 'blindsight' (Weiskrantz et al., 1974; Weiskrantz, 1986, 1990 for reviews) and has attracted the attention of philosophers, psychologists and neuroscientists because it highlights the nature of covert

THE NEUROPSYCHOLOGY OF CONSCIOUSNESS
ISBN 0–12–498045–7

vision, indicates that striate cortex is indispensible for visual awareness, and provides a means of studying the visual information carried by pathways other than the major route through striate cortex.

2.2. THE VISUAL PATHWAYS

The pathways from the eye to their first projection zones in the brain are shown schematically in Fig. 2.1. Although most texts on vision describe the massive retinal projection to the dorsal lateral geniculate nucleus (dLGN) and to the superior colliculus (SC) the others are rarely mentioned, despite the fact that many of them, as judged from electrophysiological recordings, transmit information about the position, size, and movement of visual stimuli (e.g. Simpson, 1984). Given that several of them appear to deal with reflexive non-cognitive responses, e.g. the ventral lateral geniculate nucleus in the detection of light levels and intensity discrimination (Legg & Cowey, 1977a,b) the olivary

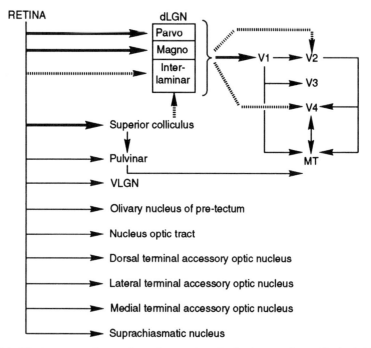

FIGURE 2.1. The known pathways from the eye into the brain, together with the initial further cortical projections. In the absence of the striate cortex (V1) it is possible for visual signals to reach secondary cortical visual areas. The dotted lines show pathways whose properties are particularly poorly documented but which could, in theory, provide signals to extrastriate cortex.

pretectum in the control of the pupil, or the three accessory optic nuclei together with the nucleus of the optic tract in the detection of self-motion and the subsequent postural adjustments to flow fields (see Simpson, 1984 for review) they might seem excellent candidates for at least some aspects of blindsight. For instance, the change in skin conductance that follows the sudden presentation of a light persists when the light appears in the blind field (Zihl *et al.*, 1980). The pupil continues to respond to changes in pattern and contrast, (Weiskrantz, 1990). And a patient with complete cortical blindness continued to follow a large moving striped display with his eyes, displaying optokinetic nystagmus, despite disclaiming any visual sensation that might have explained his visual tracking (Ter Braak *et al.*, 1971).

2.3. WHICH PATHWAYS MEDIATE BLINDSIGHT?

One reason why many of the pathways shown in Fig. 2.1 have not been seen as contributing to blindsight is that an experiment by Mohler and Wurtz (1977) indicated that they played a negligible role. They showed that monkeys in which a small part of the striate cortex had been removed could still detect a spot of light briefly presented within the resulting visual field defect and accurately move their eyes to that position, but that following subsequent removal of the retinotopically corresponding part of the SC, they now behaved as if totally insensitive within the field defect. However, even earlier Pasik and Pasik and their collaborators (see Pasik & Pasik, 1982 for review) demonstrated that the excellent ability of monkeys to discriminate between a lit and an unlit target after total removal of striate cortex was subsequently impaired much more by additional destruction or denervation of the lateral pretectum and the accessory optic system, than by removing the SC. They also showed that additional removal of parts of extra-striate visual cortex had the same effect, suggesting either that these regions were the important final target of the midbrain pathways, via the pulvinar nucleus of the thalamus, underlying residual vision or that the pre-striate cortical areas were involved via other visual inputs. The latter view leaves it unclear why Mohler and Wurtz (1977) found that striate plus collicular damage eliminates the detection of brief dim targets, unless collicular damage, with its well-known effects on visual attention, visual thresholds and eye movements even when the striate cortex is intact, renders brief and faint non-striate cortical signals sub-threshold. It is important to note that these experiments differ not only in what the monkeys are required to do, i.e. make a saccade, press a lever etc., but also in the extent of the lesion. The monkeys of Mohler and Wurtz (1977) had small unilateral lesions, whereas the monkeys of Pasik and Pasik (1982) had extensive bilateral lesions. It is not implausible that the delicate balance of the visual systems's excitatory and inhibitory functional connections are differentially affected by uni- and bilateral lesions, and that the effect of a larger striate cortical lesion may not simply be a more pronounced functional loss. An example is the 'Sprague' effect (Sprague, 1966) whereby the severity of the field defect caused by a unilateral visual cortical lesion in cats was *reduced* by subsequent ablation of the contralateral SC or simply by severing the intertectal commissure. The latter even reinstated visual sensitivity within a dense bilateral field defect caused by bilateral removal of visual cortex (Sherman, 1974). These effects are explicable in terms of excitatory projections from cortex to ipsilateral colliculus and the predominantly inhibitory connections between the colliculi and adjacent regions connected by axons travelling in the caudal collicular commissure (Wallace *et al.*, 1990). Although the pathways are somewhat differently organized in cat and monkey, it is known that the intercollicular pathways are also inhibitory in primates, that the corticotectal pathway which is derived from pyramidal cells probably uses glutamate as an excitatory neurotransmitter, and that interhemispheric interactions in patients with bilateral scotomata can best be interpreted within the same hypothetical framework (Pöppel & Richards, 1974).

Further evidence that all residual visual functions can not be attributed to the SC comes from the experiments of Schiller *et al.* (1990) who showed that visual sensitivity was abolished in the field defect caused by destruction of all layers of the dLGN, even though neurons in the retinotopically corresponding part of the SC retained their visual receptive fields. Furthermore, the visual properties of cells in the thalamic pulvinar nucleus to which the SC projects, remain almost unchanged even when the SC is removed (Bender, 1983). Bender's interpretation of his finding is that the pulvinar acquires the visual properties from the projection it receives from various cortical visual areas, but a contribution from the direct retinal projection to the pulvinar (Itaya & Van Hoesen, 1983) should not be discounted.

An additional reason for reconsidering other possible pathways as contributing to blindsight concerns the discrimination of colour or, strictly speaking, wavelength. There is no doubt that wavelength discrimination, normally one of the easiest discriminations for a monkey or human subject, becomes difficult in the residual vision of monkeys (Schilder *et al.*, 1972; Humphrey, 1974; Keating, 1979) and patients (Stoerig, 1987). Indeed, not all patients with blindsight for achromatic targets could discriminate red from green with peak wavelengths 150 nm apart. However, as genuine wavelength coding independent of luminosity has never been reported for the SC (Wolin *et al.*, 1966; Kadoya *et al.*, 1971) reports of colour discrimination in blindsight suggest that other pathways are involved. What might they be? To answer this question it is necessary to go back to the pathways from the eye.

2.4. RETINAL GANGLION CELLS AND THEIR SIGNALS

There are three broad morphological classes of retinal ganglion cell in primates, namely Pα, Pβ and Pγ cells (see Shapley & Perry, 1986 for review). The Pβ cells form about 80% of all retinal ganglion cells, and the Pα and Pγ cells each form about 10% (Perry *et al.*, 1984; Perry & Cowey, 1984). The Pα cells, also called A or M cells, project to the two magnocellular layers of the dLGN (Perry *et al.*, 1984) where their post-synaptic targets have spatially opponent but chromatically broad-band physiological properties. This means that they respond well to light–dark borders and poorly if at all to isoluminant coloured borders. In addition their contrast gain is high, i.e. they respond briskly to very small differences in luminosity, which means that they are very sensitive even to faint achromatic borders (Kaplan & Shapley, 1982). Their receptive field centres are also about two to three times larger than those of other types, implying that they are not as capable of transmitting information about fine spatial details (De Monasterio & Gouras, 1975). Some Pα cells also project to the midbrain (Leventhal *et al.*, 1981; Perry & Cowey, 1984). The only known projection area of the Pβ cells is the parvocellular zone of the dLGN (Perry *et al.*, 1984), where neurons are chromatically opponent, i.e. they can be excited or inhibited by light, depending on its wavelength. Most of them are also spatially opponent, for example the receptive field centre may be excitatory for long wavelengths and the surround inhibitory for medium wavelengths. The indispensable role in colour vision of the colour opponent Pβ cells has never been seriously questioned, and their small receptive field centres suggest an important role in the perception of fine spatial detail. Experiments in which either the parvocellular or magnocellular zones of the dLGN have been destroyed in monkeys support these conclusions. When visual targets were presented within the field defect caused by a magnocellular dLGN lesion, only the discrimination of flicker and motion were impaired, whereas the parvocellular lesion impaired or even prevented the processing of colour, texture, fine patterns and stereopsis)(Schiller *et al.*, 1990). The Pγ cells project to the midbrain, the pretectal area and the S-layers of the dLGN (Weber *et al.*, 1983; Perry & Cowey, 1984). They are physiologically heterogeneous, comprising motion-sensitive cells as well as cells lacking centre-surround organization (De Monasterio, 1978). Although genuine wavelength opponency seems to be absent (Schiller & Malpeli, 1977) many collicular cells show prominent wavelength bias (Kadoya *et al.*, 1971). Unfortunately we know little about the classes or proportions in primates that project to many of the sub-cortical targets shown in Fig. 2.1. Assuming that the organization in primates is similar to that in other mammals, especially the cat, the accessory optic system is probably innervated by Pγ cells. The retinorecipient zone of the ventral LGN consists of pale small cells whereas the corticorecipient outer zone that receives only scant retinal input consists of larger deeply staining cells (Hendrickson et al., 1970) suggesting that it is primarily small cells (Pβ, Pγ or both) that innervate this nucleus. The pulvinar also receives its retinal input from small ganglion cells (Bannister, 1990). Obviously, the classification of the secondary pathways with respect to their retinal input needs further investigation. Knowing the retinal input is important in considering the neuronal basis of different residual visual functions, and in understanding the effects of retrograde degeneration that occurs in the dLGN and in the retinal ganglion cell layer after striate cortical destruction.

2.5. RETROGRADE DEGENERATION AFTER DESTRUCTION OF STRIATE CORTEX

When part of the striate cortex is destroyed or undercut in primates the retinotopically corresponding region of the dLGN degenerates within weeks. Although some neurons survive it was assumed for many years that they were all interneurons, with no axon reaching the cortex. However, a few of these isolated cells resemble projection neurons (Mihailovic et al., 1971). One possible reason for their survival is that they depart from the otherwise strict point-to-point projection of the dLGN on the striate cortex, either by providing a sustaining collateral to striate cortex remote from the primary terminal zone or even by confining their terminals to an anomalous location in the retinotopic map, as indicated by cell a in Fig. 2.2. There is anatomical evidence for the first possibility in the striate cortex of monkeys (Blasdel & Lund, 1983; Danek et al., 1988; Freund et al., 1989), and its proposed role in residual vision within the field defects of monkeys and (by implication) blindsight in patients is not new (e.g. Weiskrantz & Cowey, 1970). Note however that no amount of divergence within the geniculo-striate projection system can explain residual visual sensitivity following total destruction of the striate cortex, because the latter destroys all overlap as well. Nevertheless, as some aspects of blindsight have only been demonstrated in patients with partial field defects these may be mediated via overlap in the geniculostriate pathway and the solitary surviving geniculate projection neurons may be its sign. This was specifically tested in monkeys by placing the retrograde tracer horse-radish peroxidase (HRP) in intact striate cortex immediately adjacent to the region in which the lateral striate cortex had been removed some years earlier (Cowey & Stoerig, 1989). Figure 2.3 shows that although neurons in the undamaged part of the dLGN adjacent to the degenerated sector are densely and profusely labelled, none of the surviving large neurons within the area of degeneration is labelled. This pattern was found in three monkeys, showing that any overlap that exists in the undamaged geniculostriate projection does not survive damage to the collaterals that probably underly it. Therefore it cannot explain residual vision and blindsight. Perhaps we should breathe a sigh of relief that it also frees us from the difficult job of trying to explain why visual detection via collaterals to intact striate cortex is blind. But if these anomalous surviving cells in the dLGN do not project to remaining striate cortex, what is their cortical target?

2.6. THE EXTRA-STRIATE PROJECTION

The dLGN of primates was believed to project only to the striate cortex until a series of papers showed that a few thousand of its thalamo-cortical neurons (less than 1%) projected to extra-striate visual cortex (Benevento & Yoshida, 1981; Fries, 1981; Yukie & Iwai, 1981; Bullier &

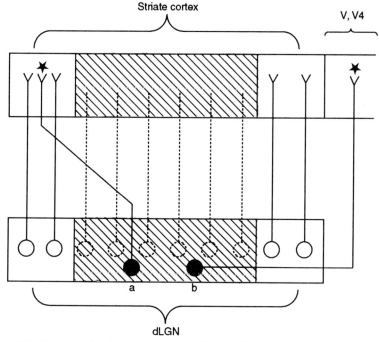

FIGURE 2.2. Diagram showing that neurons in the dorsal lateral geniculate nucleus (dLGN) project in a topographically orderly fashion to striate cortex. Consequently, local destruction of striate cortex (lined) causes almost complete retrograde degeneration of the corresponding region of the dLGN (lined). Rare projection neurons that survive may do so because (cell a) they project anomalously to the still intact regions of striate cortex, or (cell b) they project outside striate cortex. These two hypotheses were tested by placing a retrograde tracer (asterisk) in intact striate cortex or in extrastriate cortex. The result of doing so is shown in Fig. 2.3. Modified from Cowey & Stoerig (1991) with permission.

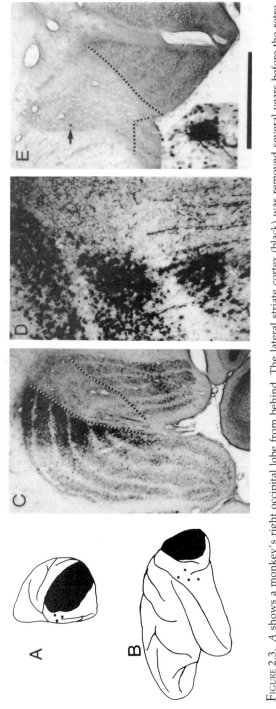

FIGURE 2.3. *A* shows a monkey's right occipital lobe from behind. The lateral striate cortex (black) was removed several years before the retrograde tracer HRP (stars) was placed in remaining dorsomedial striate cortex next to the ablation. The resulting pattern of labelling in the dLGN is shown in *C* and *D*. There are no labelled neurons in the degenerated region between the dashed lines; the dark elements are blood cells. The only isolated neurons are within a few microns of the intact region (arrow in *D*). *B* shows the other hemisphere, where HRP was placed in *V4*. Labelled neurons were scattered throughout the degenerated region e.g. arrowed cell in *E*, also shown inset. Scale: *C* and *E* = 2 mm, *D* = 0.5 mm. Modified from Cowey & Stoerig (1989) with permission.

Kennedy, 1983). Perhaps these neurons survive destruction of striate cortex and contribute to blindsight. This possibility was examined by placing HRP in extra-striate cortex, chiefly visual area V4 on the pre-lunate gyrus, following long-standing removal of part or all of the striate cortex in one hemisphere (Yukie and Iwai, 1981; Hendrickson & Dineen, 1982; Cowey & Stoerig, 1989). Up to 50% of the solitary neurons could be labelled (Cowey & Stoerig, 1989) and following striate cortical damage in infancy both their cell bodies and dendritic arrays were conspicuously larger than normal, suggesting an enlarged terminal zone in V4 and a greater retinal recipient zone in the dLGN (Hendrickson & Dineen, 1982). This could well be related to the frequent observation that cortical damage in infancy can have less serious permanent effects than apparently comparable damage in adults.

Is there any evidence that these surviving projection neurons in the dLGN receive either a direct visual input from the retina or an indirect one from other visual structures? This question was first addressed by Dineen *et al.*, (1982) who were able to identify both retinal and non-retinal synaptic terminals within the degenerated dLGN on the basis of ultrastructural criteria. Unfortunately it was not possible to establish whether the post-synaptic targets of these surviving terminals included either projection neurons or interneurons. We have recently re-examined this problem in a monkey in which the striate cortex of one hemisphere had been removed several years earlier and in which the dLGN showed the characteristic almost complete retrograde neuronal degeneration (Kisvarday *et al.*, 1990). Surviving projection neurons were retrogradely labelled by injections of HRP into visual area V4 and retino-thalamic terminals were anterogradely labelled by an intraocular injection of HRP. It was possible to identify retinogeniculate terminals both on the basis of their characteristic ultrastructure (Guillery, 1971) and additionally by the presence of HRP reaction product in the terminal boutons. On the normal side of the brain the great majority of retinal terminals were in direct synaptic contact with the dendrites of projection neurons. On the degenerated side every one of 184 identified retinal terminals was in contact with the dendrites of a GABA-immunopositive interneuron and it was these dendrites that were presynaptic to the surviving projection neurons. In other words there is anatomical evidence for a direct retinal input to a degenerated dGLN which could provide information to extra-striate visual cortex without involving any other thalamic or midbrain visual structures. However, we also found that the retrogradely labelled projection neurons additionally received direct synaptic input that was ultrastructurally characteristic of the projection from the SC (Wilson & Hendrickson, 1981). It seems that there is both a direct, GABA-immunopositive, and an indirect, GABA-immunonegative, route from the eye to a degenerated dLGN, and therefore to the extra-striate visual cortex.

2.7. PHYSIOLOGICAL PROPERTIES OF SURVIVING PATHWAYS

Is there any indication of the kind of information that may be transmitted via these routes and which could be related to the properties of blindsight? Here it is necessary to consider some well-known and some neglected properties of retinal ganglion cells. As already mentioned, the admittedly few electrophysiological studies of the retinal axons destined for the SC or their post-synaptic cells in the superficial layers (Wolin *et al.*, 1966; Kadoya *et al.*, 1971; Schiller & Koerner, 1971) indicate that the cells in this pathway are very sensitive to moving stimuli but indifferent to their colour in the sense that true colour opponency, whereby a cell can unambiguously signal formation about wavelength, seems to be absent. This pathway could mediate many of the well-known characteristics of blindsight, especially target position and sensitivity to movement. In this respect it is particularly interesting that about 50% of the neurons in the middle temporal (MT) cortical visual area, often referred to as the motion area because its cells are finely tuned to the direction and velocity of moving stimuli and are relatively indifferent to their size, shape and colour, retain their stimulus selectivity even when the striate cortex of the same hemisphere has been surgically removed or reversibly inactivated by cooling (Rodman *et al.*, 1989a). But when the SC is additionally removed, visual area MT can no longer be activated by the visual stimuli (Rodman *et al.*, 1989b). There is therefore good evidence that the midbrain may be involved in some aspects of blindsight. However, it would be premature to conclude that any involvement of visual area MT necessarily arises only via the projection of the SC to the pulvinar nucleus of the thalamus, and from there to MT, (see Standage & Benevento, 1983, for review). The SC also projects to the dLGN and although the latter does not project directly to area MT (Yoshida & Benevento, 1981) it does project to area V4 which provides projections to area MT (see Fig. 2.1, and Ungerleider & Desimone, 1986, for review).

What about the direct retinal projection to a degenerated dLGN? In the normal brain the parvocellular layers, innervated by the Pβ ganglion cells, are predominantly wavelength opponent and their properties are well suited to colour vision. In contrast the cells of the magnocellular layers are broad-band and cannot signal wavelength unambiguously. In a degenerated dLGN, surviving neurons are found in both the parvocellular and magnocellular portions, including the largely unexplored interlaminar layers. Whether their retinal input, via an inhibitory interneuron, is characteristic of their deceased neighbours is unknown. However, it is now clear that the retina which innervates them is highly unusual. It was first demonstrated in primates, including man, by Van Buren (1963) that there is extensive transneuronal retrograde degeneration of ganglion cells (up to 80%; Cowey, 1974) following destruction of striate cortex but it has only recently been shown that it is selective for a given type of ganglion cell. By placing HRP in the optic nerve of monkeys several years after the striate cortex of one hemisphere had been removed (see Fig. 2.4) it was shown that the Pα and P γ cells were apparently intact whereas up to 85% of the Pβ cells had degenerated in the central part of the affected hemi-retina (Cowey *et al.*, 1989). Instead

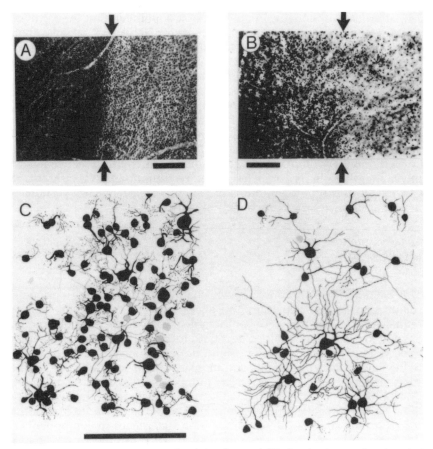

FIGURE 2.4. *A* is a photomicrograph of the flattened Nissl-stained central retina, just above the fovea, of the right eye of a macaque monkey 8 years after the left striate cortex was removed. Note the extensive loss of retinal ganglion cells to the right of the vertical meridian, indicated by arrows. *B* is the other eye of the same animal in which retinal ganglion cells are labelled by HRP deposited in the optic nerve. *C* and *D*, representing mirror image regions from the centre of the normal and degenerated areas shown in *B*, illustrate the huge reduction in the density of small colour opponent Pβ cells in the degenerated half. At least half of the small cells that remain are Pγ cells, projecting to the midbrain. The shaded cells were too poorly labelled to be characterized. Scale: *A*, 200 μm; *B*, 1 mm; and *D*, 200 mm. Modified from Cowey *et al.* (1989) with permission.

of outnumbering the Pα and Pγ cells by about 8 : 1 the 150 000 or so Pβ cells that survive removal of striate cortex in the monkey are only barely more common than Pα and P γ cells. The survival of this sub-population suggests that they have unusual functional connections. As their only known projection zone is the parvocellular dLGN, where fewer than 1% of the projection neurons have survived, the remaining Pβ cells must either project to these sparse survivors or they must innervate another of the retinal targets shown in Fig. 2.1 and whose precise retinal input is unknown. In either case it is possible that they provide visual signals to extra-striate visual cortex, including signals about colour to visual areas V2 and V4, where wavelength selective cells are particularly common (Zeki, 1983). Whether cells in these two areas can remain visually excitable in the absence of striate cortex is unknown. Under anaesthesia cells in the inferior temporal cortex, which is the major target zone of area V4, cannot be excited by visual stimulation in the absence of striate cortex (Rocha-Miranda et al., 1975), and V2 is similarly visually unresponsive when striate cortex is temporarily inactivated by cooling it (Girard & Bullier, 1989). Whether this would be true in alert monkeys and whether discrimination training is needed for physiological as it is for behavioural restitution (e.g. Weiskrantz & Cowey, 1970) is unknown, but is of particular relevance to questions of neuronal plasticity and functional rehabilitation.

2.8. WAVELENGTH SENSITIVITY AND DISCRIMINATION IN BLINDSIGHT

The Pβ cells form the only known channel that transmits opponent-colour signals. As, depending on age at and after the lesion and on retinal eccentricity, up to 80% of them degenerate following destruction of striate cortex, one would expect both form and colour discrimination to be seriously impaired in blindsight. Both functions have been studied in the field defects of patients and monkeys, with contradictory results. With respect to form, a large number of positive results (see Weiskrantz, 1986 for review) must be queried following the demonstration (Weiskrantz, 1987) that patient DB's apparent form discrimination rested on his ability to detect orientation differences in components of the forms. When these were eliminated, for example by presenting square versus rectangle, discrimination was poor. However, not all examples are easily explained in this way (e.g. Ptito et al., 1987) although all need additional examination.

Just how good is genuine wavelength discrimination after striate cortical damage? In monkeys with complete removal of striate cortex and extensive involvement of extra-striate visual areas, spectral sensitivity, measured by matching targets of different wavelengths for their brightness, was scotopic whatever the adaptation level (Leporé et al., 1975).

As scotopic sensitivity coincides with the absorption spectrum of retinal rod receptors, it was thought that residual vision, and by implication blindsight, was rod dominated and colour blind, like vision in near darkness. By contrast, when spectral sensitivity was recently tested in patients with much smaller field defects and by an increment threshold method, peak sensitivity shifted from short to medium wavelengths with the change from dark to light adaptation (the Purkinje shift). This is clear evidence for the involvement of retinal cones. Just as importantly, the photopic curve, measured under conditions that are optimal for colour-opponent channels, i.e. white photopic background, large target, long presentation time (Sperling & Harwerth, 1971; King-Smith & Carden, 1976; Snelgar *et al.*, 1987) showed the characteristic peaks and troughs whose position indicates colour-opponent interactions (Stoerig & Cowey, 1989b). On the basis of these spectral sensitivity curves, narrowband coloured stimuli were then matched for luminous efficiency at 0.5 log units above threshold, and two-alternative forced-choice discrimination was measured. Peak filter transmissivity was at 550 nm (green), 580 nm (yellow) and 600 nm (orange) and the stimuli were presented at the same retinal position previously used to determine spectral sensitivity in the blind field. One pair of stimuli was used in each testing session and the stimuli were presented singly in random sequence. Figure 2.5 shows results based on 2500 trials with each pair. Two patients could discriminate significantly better than expected by chance with all three pairs and although performance was never excellent it should be remembered that the stimuli were not far above detection threshold. These results are the most direct evidence for wavelength discrimination after striate cortical damage and confirm previous examples in monkeys (Schilder *et al.*, 1972; Keating, 1979).

Which cells and pathways transmit signals about wavelength in blindsight? The most obvious candidates are the surviving Pβ retinal ganglion cells, via their projections into the degenerated dLGN and thence to extra-striate areas like V2 and V4. Another possibility is that the remaining Pβ cells project to the retino-recipient zone of the pulvinar, whose retinal input has not yet been classified, and from there to extra-striate areas. A third possibility is that Pα cells, despite their broad-band spectral response, nevertheless transmit sufficient information about chromatic differences (see Cowey & Stoerig, 1991, for discussion). This is highly unlikely because these cells and the luminance channel they are believed to underlie have a single broad plateau of sensitivity (King-Smith & Carden, 1976) in the spectral range of our behavioural experiments. Furthermore, when *luminance* difference thresholds were measured in the patients' blind fields with the same coloured stimuli, discrimination was poor and not what one would expect of the highly contrast-sensitive Pα cell channel (Kaplan & Shapley, 1981). Finally, under conditions selected to optimize the

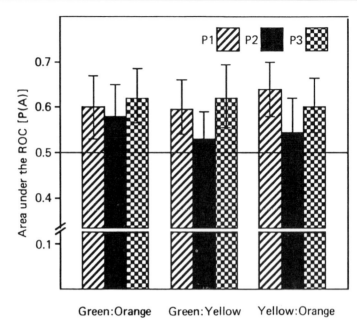

Green:Orange   Green:Yellow   Yellow:Orange

FIGURE 2.5. Wavelength discrimination in the visual field defects of three patients with blindsight. Stimuli were green (550 nm) yellow (580 nm) and orange (600 nm). Results are based on 2500 trials for each pair of colours, the presentation ratio within each pair being systematically varied in order to obtain receiver–operating–characteristic (ROC) curves (Stoerig & Pöppel, 1986). The histograms show the area under the ROC curve. Random guessing would yield a value of 0.5. Narrow band stimuli (116 arc minutes, 200 ms) were equated for luminous efficiency on the basis of the same patients' spectral sensitivity curves measured at the same retinal position under identical conditions. Two patients discriminated significantly with all three pairs, whereas patient 2 could only discriminate green from orange.

response of the broad-band channel at the expense of the opponent-colour channel (small test spot, no background, photopic levels) we could no longer demonstrate even red/green discrimination in blind fields.

Another, and at first sight unlikely, candidate for wavelength processing in blindsight is the $P\gamma$ cell channel. But it is generally supposed to have poor spectral tuning and no colour-opponency. However, although many cells in the retinorecipient layers of the SC in the squirrel monkey have broad-band responses and discharge briskly to white light, nearly as many show narrow tuning and fail to respond to white light (Kadoya et al., 1971). Cells responding to long but not to short or medium wavelengths were commonest. Unfortunately more conventional measures of opponency were not made because of the low spontaneous discharge of collicular cells. Nor was the wavelength-tuned input to the SC identified as retinal or cortical. Given these findings, the paucity of experiments on the SC of primates with respect to colour, and the fact that its homologue (the optic tectum) in fish and reptiles seems well equipped to mediate colour vision, the SC and its Pγ cell input may yet surprise us. In addition, the cytochrome oxidase-rich blobs in the supragranular layers of striate cortex, which contain the highest proportion of cells tuned to colour, receive a projection from the interlaminar layers of the dLGN (Livingstone & Hubel, 1982; Fitzpatrick *et al.*, 1983). In turn, the latter receive a retinal projection whose physiological properties are characteristic of Pγ cells (Irvin *et al.*, 1986) and a projection from the SC, which has a predominantly Pγ cell retinal input (see Fig. 2.1). When striate cortex is damaged it is predominantly projection neurons in the interlaminar layers of dLGN that survive, project to extra-striate cortex, and continue to receive visual input via retinal terminals onto nearby geniculate interneurons and via the SC (Kisvarday *et al.*, 1990).

2.9. THE LACK OF SIGHT IN BLINDSIGHT

From the very first reports on blindsight (Pöppel *et al.*, 1973; Richards, 1973; Weiskrantz *et al.*, 1974) several authors have stressed that the patients claim not to see the visual stimuli which they can nevertheless detect and discriminate. This denial of visual experience may be present even when the subject's detection or discrimination approaches 100% correct (Weiskrantz, 1986), or when localization of an unseen target is excellent (Perenin & Jeannerod, 1978), or when the threshold for detection is reduced by less than a log unit (Stoerig & Cowey, 1989b). Moreover it may be stable over many years. In many studies a non-visual cue, usually auditory, prompts the subject to attend and respond to visual stimuli in his field defect (e.g. Pöppel *et al.*, 1973; Stoerig & Cowey, 1989a,b). Often the patients must be cajoled into responding because they feel it is silly to guess about visual events they cannot see. Richards (1973, p. 335) described this demand an 'eccentric request'. To circumvent this uncomfortable problem some investigators have studied whether an unacknowledged and 'irrelevant' stimulus in the blind field influences the response to a seen stimulus in the normal visual field. For example, Marzi *et al.* (1986) showed that reaction time to a seen stimulus was altered by an unseen stimulus in the blind field. Although this effect may also occur in normal subjects, Rafal *et al.* (1990) found that the distracting effect of a stimulus in the normal field was confined to the patients. Similarly, Richards (1973) found that the presentation of a line stimulus in the blind field influenced judgements about the relative distance of targets presented in the normal field. And Pöppel (1986) reported that the colour of targets in the seeing field was affected by unseen colours in the scotoma.

It is of special interest that some patients do report occasional sensations, which may even be of a visual nature. Three of the nine patients studied by Richards (1973) described the visual stimuli in the blind field as 'pinprick', 'a prickling' or 'gunfire at a distance' (p. 338). Some investigators (Barbur *et al.*, 1980; Blythe *et al.*, 1987) refrain from using the term blindsight precisely because certain patients do report sensations, among them the extensively studied GY who 'feels' the presence of a moving stimulus in the blind field. Even hemidecorticated patients reported that although they could not see the form or size of the target they nevertheless felt 'that a quite bright light had been turned on' (Perenin & Jeannerod, 1978, p. 4). The factors determining whether some sort of conscious sensation is evoked by a visual stimulus in the blind field have not been systematically studied. But as N.K. Humphrey (unpublished manuscript) suggested long ago, retinal projections to polysensory sub-cortical targets, such as the deeper layers of the SC, could provoke non-visual sensations in the absence of confirmatory evidence from striate cortex. Indeed, Humphrey noted that the destriated monkey Helen, having learned to reach out and touch briefly presented visual targets, responded in the same way to brief tones, unlike a sighted monkey, and as if she confused them.

2.10. DO MONKEYS HAVE BLINDSIGHT?

Monkeys have an impressive range of residual visual abilities within field defects caused by removal of striate cortex; their performance is certainly not inferior to that of human patients. But do they experience themselves as blind within their field defects, as the patients do (see Cowey & Weiskrantz, 1963, for discussion)? Do they, like the patients, believe that they are only guessing? Or do they have degraded, amblyopic, vision in the field defects which, although it may be less sensitive and even qualitatively altered, is otherwise normal and accompanied by a conscious representation of the stimuli within the field defect? This problem has never been tackled experimentally, yet monkeys are often studied as a means of investigating the behavioural and neural basis of blindsight and we would feel more comfortable if we could be certain that the same phenomenon was being investigated. But how can one get a monkey to tell us that it does, or does not, *see* a visual stimulus that it can detect within a field defect? We think that this has never been attempted but here are three of several possibilities that we intend to try.

In the first method a normal monkey is trained to press a lever, A, when a visual stimulus of variable intensity is presented somewhere in the visual field at a fixed time, say 1 s, after a warning signal. Eye position is monitored so that the retinal position of the stimulus can be controlled. On other trials a non-visual stimulus is presented, e.g. a brief sound or odour or touch, in which case lever B should be pressed. On still other trials no target stimulus is presented, and the monkey must press lever C for its reward. By these means, the monkey is indicating whether it detected a light, or some other non-visual stimulus, or nothing at all. The crucial trials occur after part of the striate cortex is removed and the visual stimulus is directed into the field defect. If the monkey detects it in anything like the normal manner it should press lever A. If it detects it, but experiences it as a non-visual 'event' (c.f. Richards, 1973, with human blindsight patients) it should press lever B. If it presses lever C, the animal is telling us that no stimulus occurred. If at first it presses C on trials in which the target is presented in the field defect, then changes to B on such trials, this would confirm (albeit indirectly) that the animal can detect visual stimuli (as we know already) but that they are 'perceived' in a non-visual way. However, if initial responding to C was progressively replaced by A, this would indicate that the stimulus was initially so faint that it was overlooked but that with further training its visual nature was genuinely perceived.

The second method is more direct, more interesting, but possibly more difficult, for it attempts to reveal when the animal is guessing, as in human blindsight. It involves teaching a monkey to press lever A when a light (initially always conspicuous) is presented and to press lever B on trials when no light appears. The two types of trial occur at random. This procedure has been used before to demonstrate and plot field defects in monkeys (Cowey & Weiskrantz, 1963; Cowey, 1967). Then the light is made progressively dimmer until the animal scores no better than 50% correct overall, i.e. it cannot detect the light. The trick is to have a third lever C, which can be introduced by the experimenter and which will guarantee reward on 75% of trials, at random, if the monkey presses it in preference to A and B. To optimize reward the animal should press levers A or B when it is confident that the visual target is easily perceptible on those trials when it appears, but press C when the target is so dim that the choice between A and B is too difficult. In other words when the animal reverts to lever C it is saying 'I am just guessing'. The last twist is to produce a field defect. When the visual stimulus is consistently presented in the field defect will the monkey press lever C, indicating that it is just guessing in the way it has been trained to do when it cannot reliably detect light at threshold levels? And if it does press C, would it then nevertheless perform excellently with levers A and B if the guessing mode lever is withdrawn, leaving the animal with a two-alternative forced choice, as in blindsight?

Our third approach utilizes the facilitatory effect that an unseen light can have on the response to a seen target presented in the intact field, for example the shortening or lengthening of reaction times (Marzi *et al.*, 1986; Rafal *et al.*, 1990). We could apply this to our problem by training a monkey to fixate a VDU and to expect a visual stimulus, to which it must respond as fast as possible in order to obtain its preferred reward. On some trials two lights are presented, and either both can appear in the intact visual field or one of them is directed into the field defect. Will reaction time to the pair be different from that to the single stimulus, as it is in normal human vision and in blindsight, the sign and magnitude of the difference depending on the precise time relations between the two stimuli? On completely separate test sessions, whose difference is signalled in some way to the animal (e.g. by testing in a different room) one or two stimuli are again presented but the animal has to press A if 'one' and B if 'two'. If the monkey presses lever A when two lights are presented but one of them lies in the field defect, despite showing a reduced latency in the reaction time task, this would indicate that the animal is not seeing the light in the field defect even though it can influence some aspects of behaviour. We hope that experiments such as these will show whether monkeys, like blindsight patients, are experientially blind in their field defects. Knowing the answer will make our inferences about the anatomical and physiological basis of blindsight much more convincing.

2.11. WHY IS BLINDSIGHT BLIND?

Several suggestions have been, or can be made, to explain the lack of sight in blindsight. The commonest, which does little more than restate the problem, focuses on the fact that the patients have suffered destruction of the striate cortex or its afferents. But why should this render them incapable of forming a conscious representation of the stimuli even though they may be able to respond to them? Why should the remaining pathways from the eye (Fig. 2.1) be denied access to visual awareness? One possibility is that the important neural events behind blindsight are sub-cortical and that we are not aware of sub-cortical events. We say 'important' because at some stage, e.g. when making a voluntary movement to indicate a target or giving a verbal response, the cortex must be involved, even if it is the cortex of the other hemisphere in patients with hemispherectomy. But perhaps cortex is no longer involved in the analytical stage of visual processing (e.g. where is the target, is it horizontal or vertical?), which may now operate without access to the cortical mechanisms underlying perceptual awareness. This proposal has much to commend it. After all we are not aware of many of the neural events, and their outcomes, occurring in our brainstem and spinal cord, for example those events that allow us to remain standing without falling over. The signals underlying blindsight may be just like many others in the CNS, and the fact that patients can use them to guess astonishingly well does not necessarily set them apart. We simply do not know whether we could learn to respond to sub-cortical events but given that even single muscle fibres are conditionable we should not be surprised by our ability to learn to respond to 'inaccessible' events if we take the time to try. Furthermore, patients with stimulating electrodes implanted in their ventrobasal thalamus for the purpose of controlling severe pain that was uncontrollable by conventional methods were able to guess, using a forced choice paradigm, in which of two time intervals the stimulation was applied even though it never produced any sensation or consciously definable basis for the response (Libet, 1990b). However, there may be a crucial difference between this phenomenon and blindsight. In blindsight, the stimuli typically remain unseen despite all changes in stimulus parameters whereas the thalamic stimulation was consciously sensed under certain conditions (Libet, 1990a), possibly because the ventrobasal thalamus has access to its primary sensory cortical area. The findings are therefore in accordance with the notion of a privileged role for the primary sensory areas.

What about secondary cortical areas that receive direct input from sub-cortical structures? The difference in performance of patients with blindsight caused by visual cortical damage who can indicate the direction in which a target is moving (Barbur *et al.*, 1980; Blythe *et al.*, 1987) and of hemispherectomized patients who can detect movement but not its direction (Perenin, 1989; Ptito *et al.*, 1991) suggests that extra-striate cortex is involved in the former. This seems especially likely in view of the demonstration that direction and velocity tuning remain in cortical visual area MT after striate cortex is inactivated (Rodman *et al.*, 1989a,b). This evidence that cortex may be involved in processing visual information in blindsight is also in accordance with other examples of covert knowledge, such as correct recognition in amnesia, priming in attention, appropriate responses to stimuli whose presence is denied in cases of parietal neglect, and different response latencies or electrodermal responses to familiar and unfamiliar faces in prosopagnosic patients who deny any knowledge of their identity (see other chapters in this volume). It is possible that when cortex can participate in the processing of unacknowledged visual information the opportunity for eliciting some inappropriate sensation in response to a stimulus is better, and interestingly, the reports of such sensations in residual visual functions are most frequent when moving stimuli are used. However, not all patients with circumscribed striate cortical damage experience such sensations.

A further possible explanation is that the neural signals that reach extra-striate visual cortex are in some way too feeble on their own to elicit conscious perception. Any such ineffectiveness is unlikely to be based on small numbers of neurons because a substantial number of fibres, including the 150 000 or so to the SC, remain intact after striate cortical damage and should have indirect access to cortex via the thalamus. Furthermore, we can consciously perceive the colour of a brief tiny light that stimulates only a few cones in the eye at threshold intensity (Krauskopf, 1978). Its post-retinal effects may be multiplied by divergent connections, but the same should apply in blindsight. Finally, cortical microstimulation where the effective excitation is limited to a region about 85 μm from the tip of the microelectrode can influence what we assume to be conscious awareness. Applying such stimulation to neurons tuned to a particular direction of movement in area MT of the monkey influences the animal's responses to perceived movement in a task where the monkey is trained to signal whether a pattern is moving in one direction or the opposite direction (Salzman et al., 1990). Although Libet (1982) has shown in human subjects that for cortical microstimulation to be consciously appreciated it must last for up to 500 ms and may not be consciously registered even when it demonstrably affects neurons some distance away, additional evidence would be needed before concluding that the remaining visual projections that are still present after removal of striate cortex have unusual properties which make it impossible for them to provide either enduring or propagating neural signals. Although such evidence is sparse there are two results that point in this direction. First is the recent finding that the degenerated part of the retina following long-term striate cortical damage displays elevated GABA immunoreactivity, particularly in the inner plexiform layer, but also in optic axons themselves whose terminals are found in the degenerated dLGN (Kisvarday et al., 1990). If the functional effect is to intensify GABA-mediated inhibition then visual signals via this pathway may be unusual. Second is the change in balance of excitation and inhibition after cortical and sub-cortical lesions (Sprague, 1966; Sherman, 1974). If the balance between hemispheres is also disturbed following unilateral cortical damage, visual signals may be blocked at this level.

Enhancement of inhibition for whatever reason, may also influence the rate at which neural assemblies necessary for awareness are formed. Flohr (1991) suggests that this rate of assembly formation determines the presence or absence of phenomenal states: 'deficits in phenomenal consciousness occur if the rate of assembly formation falls below a critical threshold level. Whenever this level is surpassed, phenomenal states must necessarily occur' (p. 21). The phenomenon of assembly formation has seen an upsurge of interest since the intriguing reports of widespread oscillations in the cat's visual cortex (Gray et al., 1989; Gray & Singer, 1989). When the cat is viewing a particular stimulus, e.g. a moving bar at some particular orientation, widely separated cells that are tuned to that stimulus now show remarkable frequency and phase-locked oscillations. Such observations led Crick and Koch (1990) to propose that only when a large population of neurons dealing with some particular sensory stimulus showed correlated activity of this kind, is the observer aware of that stimulus. In this scheme consciousness and sensory computation are dissociable, as happens in blindsight and in other phenomena, such as selective attention and visual neglect, discussed elsewhere in this book.

But why should removing striate cortex irreversibly produce this dissociation? A recent study (Kammen *et al.*, 1991) demonstrates that in visual cortex frequency locking, especially between different visual areas, is difficult without feedback between areas that are connected. Removing striate cortex, with its massive reciprocal connections with several secondary cortical visual areas that are in turn further connected with each other and with additional visual areas, is likely to disrupt or even destroy this delicate phase locking.

All these hypotheses are at present speculative. They need not be mutually exclusive because the visual signals from the blind field may be predominantly sub-cortical, weak, inhibitory and incapable of yielding correlated cortical activity. Although many facets of this scheme are missing, its implications are testable. Does striate cortical damage, or better its reversible cooling, abolish frequency and phase locking in remaining cortical visual areas? Does it leave non-visual cortex unaffected? Is phase locking differentially disturbed after circumscribed extra-striate cortical lesions that produce functional deficits such as achromatopsia or neglect? Is it absent in other pathological conditions where performance and awareness are dissociated? Do subcortical structures oscillate as well, and if they do, as demonstrated in the dLGN (Ghose & Freeman, 1990), do they continue to do so, and if so at what frequency, when striate cortex is inactivated? Does neurotransmitter expression change in other visual structures, and in what way is their functional connectivity altered when striate cortex is removed? Does electrical stimulation of the extra-striate visual cortex of the hemisphere where striate cortex is decreased elicit the sensation of visual phosphenes as it does when striate cortex is intact (Penfield & Perot, 1963)? If it does, it would strengthen the proposal that the blindsight signals are too weak. If it does not, it would point to an indispensable role of striate cortex in forming conscious visual perceptions, and perhaps to that of all primary sensory areas in conscious perception. Unfeeling touch (Paillard *et al.*, 1983) and deaf hearing (Michel, 1990), which can follow damage to the primary somatosensory or auditory cortices respectively, may be analogous to blindsight.

ACKNOWLEDGEMENT

We thank the McDonnell-Pew Cognitive Neuroscience Centre (Oxford) and the Deutsche Forschungsgemeinschaft for continued support of our collaboration.

REFERENCES

Bannister, M.E. (1990). The Neurobiological Basis of Blindsight. MSc Thesis, University of Oxford.

Barbur, J.L., Ruddock, K.H. & Waterfield, V.A. (1980). Human visual responses in the absence of the geniculo-calcarine projection. *Brain*, **103**, 905–928.

Bender, D.B. (1983). Electrophysiological and behavioral experiments on the primate pulvinar. *Progress in Brain Research*, **75**, 55–65.

Benevento, L.A. & Yoshida, K. (1981). The afferent and efferent organization of the lateral geniculo-prestriate pathways in the macaque monkey. *Journal of Comparative Neurology*, **203**, 455–474.

Blasdel, G.G. & Lund, J.S. (1983). Termination of afferent axons in macaque striate cortex. *Journal of Neuroscience*, **3**, 1389–1413.

Blythe, I.M., Kennard, C. & Ruddock, K.H. (1987). Residual vision in patients with retrogeniculate lesions of the visual pathways. *Brain*, **110**, 887–905.

Bullier, J. & Kennedy, H. (1983). Projection of the lateral geniculate nucleus onto cortical area V2 in the macaque monkey. *Experimental Brain Research*, **53**, 168–172.

Cowey, A. (1967). Perimetric study of field defects in monkeys after cortical and retinal ablations. *Quarterly Journal of Experimental Psychology*, **19**, 232–245.

Cowey, A. (1974). Atrophy of retinal ganglion cells after removal of striate cortex in a rhesus monkey. *Perception*, **3**, 257–260.

Cowey, A. & Stoerig, P. (1989). Projection patterns of surviving neurons in the dorsal lateral geniculate nucleus following discrete lesions of striate cortex: Implications for residual vision. *Experimental Brain Research*, **75**, 631–638.

Cowey, A. & Stoerig, P. (1991). The neurobiology of blindsight. *Trends in Neurosciences*, **14**, 140–145.

Cowey, A. & Weiskrantz, L. (1963). A perimetric study of visual field defects in monkeys. *Quarterly Journal of Experimental Psychology*, **15**, 91–115.

Cowey, A., Stoerig, P. & Perry, V.H. (1989). Transneuronal retrograde degeneration of retinal ganglion cells after damage to striate cortex: Evidence for selective loss of Pβ cells. *Neuroscience*, **29**, 65–80.

Crick, F. & Koch, C. (1990). Towards a neurobiological theory of consciousness. *Seminars in the Neurosciences*, **2**, 263–276.

Danek, A., Faul, R. & Fries, W. (1988). Divergence of distal optic radiation fibres in the macaque. *European Neuroscience Association Abstracts*, **1988**, **158**.

De Monasterio, F.M. (1978). Properties of ganglion cells with atypical receptive field organization in retina of macaques. *Journal of Neurophysiology*, **41**, 1435–1449.

De Monasterio, F.M. & Gouras, P. (1975). Functional properties of ganglion cells in the rhesus monkey retina. *Journal of Physiology (London)*, **251**, 167–195.

Dineen, J., Hendrickson, A. & Keating, E.G. (1982). Alterations of retinal inputs following striate cortical removal in adult monkeys. *Experimental Brain Research*, **47**, 446–456.

Fitzpatrick, D. Itoh, K. & Diamond, I.T. (1983). The laminar organization of the lateral geniculate body and the striate cortex in the squirrel monkey (*Saimiri sciureus*). *Journal of Neuroscience*, **3**, 673–702.

Flohr, H. (1991). Brain processes and phenomenal consciousness: A new and specific hypothesis. *Theory and Psychology*, **1**, 245–262.

Freund, T.F., Martin, K.A.C., Soltesz, I., Somogyi, P. & Whitteridge, D. (1989). Arborization pattern and postsynaptic targets of physiologically identified thalamocortical afferents in striate cortex of the macaque monkey. *Journal of Comparative Neurology*, **289**, 315–336.

Fries, W. (1981). The projection from the lateral geniculate nucleus to the prestriate cortex of the macaque monkey. *Proceedings of the Royal Society,* **B213**, 73–80.

Ghose, G.M. & Freeman, R.D. (1990). Origins of oscillatory activity in the cat's visual cortex. *Society for Neuroscience Abstracts,* **16**, 1270.

Girard, P. & Bullier, J. (1989). Visual activity in area V2 during reversible inactivation of area 17 in the macaque monkey. *Journal of Neurophysiology,* **62**, 1287–1302.

Gray, C.M. & Singer, W. (1989). Stimulus specific neuronal oscillations in the orientation columns of cat visual cortex. *Proceedings of the National Academy of Science,* **86**, 1698–1702.

Gray, C.M. Konig, P., Engel A.K., & Singer, W. (1989). Oscillatory responses in cat visual cortex exhibit inter-columnar synchronization which reflects global stimulus properties. *Nature,* **338**, 334–337.

Guillery, R.W. (1971). Patterns of synaptic interconnections in the dorsal lateral geniculate nucleus of cat and monkey: a brief review. *Vision Research Supplement,* **3**, 211–227.

Hendrickson, A. & Dineen, J.T. (1982). Hypertrophy of neurons in the dorsal lateral geniculate nucleus following striate cortex lesions in infant monkeys. *Neuroscience Letters,* **30**, 217–222.

Hendrickson, A., Wilson, M.E. & Toyne, M.J. (1970). The distribution of optic nerve fibres in *Macaca mulatta. Brain Research,* **23**, 425–427.

Humphrey, N.K. (1974). Vision in a monkey without striate cortex: a case study. *Perception,* **3**, 241–255.

Irvin, G.E., Norton, T.T., Sesma, M.A. & Cassagrande, V.A. (1986). W-like properties of interlaminar zone cells in the lateral geniculate nucleus of a primate (*Galago crassicaudatus*). *Brain Research,* **362**, 254–270.

Itaya, S.K. & Van Hoesen, G.W. (1983). Retinal projections to the inferior and medial pulvinar nuclei in the old-world monkey. *Brain Research,* **269**, 223–230.

Kadoya, S., Wolin, L.R. & Massopust, L.C. (1971). Collicular unit responses to monochromatic stimulation in squirrel monkey. *Brain Research,* **32**, 251–254.

Kammen, D.M., Holmes, P.J. & Koch, C. (1991). Origin of synchronised oscillations in visual cortex: global feedback versus local coupling. *Proceedings of the National Academy of Science* (in press).

Kaplan, E. & Shapley, R.M. (1981). The primate retina contains two types of retinal ganglion cells, with high and low contrast sensitivity. *Proceedings of the National Academy of Science,* **83**, 2755–2757.

Kaplan, E. & Shapley, R.M. (1982). X and Y cells in the lateral geniculate nucleus of macaque monkeys. *Journal of Physiology (London),* **330**, 125–143.

Keating, E.G. (1979). Rudimentary color vision in the monkey after removal of striate and preoccipital cortex. *Brain Research,* **179**, 379–384.

King-Smith, P.F. & Carden, D. (1976). Luminance and opponent-colour contributions to visual detection and adaptation and to temporal and spatial integration. *Journal of the Optical Society of America,* **66**, 709–717.

Kisvarday, Z.F., Cowey, A., Stoerig, P. & Somogyi, P. (1990), Synaptic input of residual cells in the monkey lateral geniculate nucleus after striate cortex removal. *European Journal of Neuroscience,* Supplement 3, 245.

Krauskopf, J. (1978). On identifying detectors. In: J.C. Armington, L. Krauskopf and B.R. Wooren (eds), *Visual Psychophysics and Physiology.* New York: Academic Press.

Legg, C.R. & Cowey, A. (1977a). The role of the ventral lateral geniculate nucleus and posterior thalamus in intensity discrimination in rats. *Brain Research*, **123**, 261–273.

Legg, C.R. & Cowey, A. (1977b). Effects of sub-cortical lesions on visual intensity discriminations in rats. *Physiology and Behaviour*, **19**, 635–646.

Leporé, F., Cardu, B., Rasmussen, T. & Malmo, R.B. (1975) Rod and cone sensitivity in destriate monkeys. *Brain Research*, **93**, 203–221.

Leventhal, A.G., Rodiek, R.W. & Dreher, B. (1981). Retinal ganglion cell classes in old-world monkey: morphology and central projections. *Science*, **213**, 1139–1142.

Libet, B. (1982). Brain stimulation in the study of neuronal functions for conscious sensory experience. *Human Neurobiology*, **1**, 235–242.

Libet, B. (1990a). Cerebral processes that distinguish conscious experience from unconscious mental functions. In J.C. Eccles and O. Creutzfeldt (eds), *The Principles of Design and Operation of the Brain*. Experimental Brain Research Series, 21, pp. 185–202. Berlin: Springer-Verlag.

Libet, B. (1990b). Conscious subjective experience vs. unconscious mental functions: A theory of the mental processes involved. In R.M.J. Cotterill (ed.), *Models of Brain Function*. Cambridge: Cambridge University Press.

Livingstone, M. & Hubel, D. (1982). Thalamic inputs to cytochrome oxidase-rich regions in monkey visual cortex. *Proceedings of the National Academy of Science USA*, **71**, 6098–6101.

Magnusson, S. & Mathiesen, T. (1989). Detection of moving and stationary gratings in the absence of striate cortex. *Neuropsychologia*, **27**, 725–728.

Marcel, A.J. (1983a). Conscious and unconscious perception: experiments on visual masking and word perception. *Cognitive Psychology*, **15**, 197–237.

Marcel, A.J. (1983b). Conscious and unconscious perception; an approach to the relations between phenomenal experience and perceptual processes. *Cognitive Psychology*, **15**, 238–300.

Marzi, C.A., Tassinari, G., Aglioti, S. & Lutzemberger, L. (1986). Spatial summation across the vertical meridian in hemianopics: a test of blindsight. *Neuropsychologia*, **24**, 749–758.

Michel, F. (1990). Hemi-anacusia is usually unknown to the patient. Poster presented at the Russell Trust/Wellcome Trust Symposium, St Andrews, Sept. 1990.

Mihailovic, L.T., Cupic, D. & Dekleva, N. (1971). Changes in the number of neurons and glia cells in the lateral geniculate nucleus of the monkey during retrograde cell degeneration. *Journal of Comparative Neurology*, **142**, 223–230.

Mohler, C.W. & Wurtz, R.H. (1977). Role of striate cortex and superior colliculus in the guidance of saccadic eye movements in monkeys. *Journal of Neurophysiology*, **40**, 74–94.

Paillard, J., Michel, F. & Stelmach, G. (1983). Localization without content: a tactile analogue of 'blindsight'. *Archives of Neurology*, **40**, 548–551.

Pasik, P. & Pasik, T. (1982). Visual functions in monkeys after total removal of visual cerebral cortex. *Contributions to Sensory Physiology*, **7**, 147–200.

Penfield, W. & Perot, P. (1963). The brain's record of auditory and visual experience: a final summary and discussion. *Brain*, **86**, 595–696.

Perenin, M.T. (1978). Visual function within the hemianopic field following early cerebral hemidecortication in man. II. Pattern discrimination. *Neuropsychologia*, **16**, 697–708.

Perenin, M.T. (1989). Visual motion processing in perimetrically blind fields. *European Journal of Neuroscience* Suppl. 2, 295.

Perenin, M.T. & Jeannerod, M. (1978). Visual function within the hemianopic field following early cerebral hemidecortication in man. I. Spatial localization. *Neuropsychologia*, **16**, 1–13.

Perry, V.H. & Cowey, A. (1984). Retinal ganglion cells that project to the superior colliculus in the macaque monkey. *Neuroscience*, **12**, 1125–1137.

Perry, V.H., Oehler, R. & Cowey, A. (1984). Retinal ganglion cells that project to the dorsal lateral geniculate nucleus in the macaque monkey. *Neuroscience*, **12**, 1101–1123.

Pöppel, E. (1986). Long-range colour-generating interactions across the retina. *Nature*, **320**, 523–525.

Pöppel, E. & Richards, W. (1974). Light sensitivity in cortical scotomata contralateral to small islands of blindness. *Experimental Brain Research*, **21**, 125–130.

Pöppel, E., Held, R. & Frost, D. (1973). Residual visual functions after brain wounds involving the central visual pathways in man. *Nature*, **243**, 2295–2296.

Ptito, A., Lassonde, M., Leporé, F. & Ptito, M. (1987). Visual discrimination in hemispherectomized patients. *Neuropsychologia*, **25**, 869–879.

Ptito, A., Leporé, F., Ptito, M. & Lassonde, M. (1991). Target detection and movement discrimination in the blind field of hemispherectomized patients. *Brain*, **114**, 497–512.

Rafal, R., Smith, W., Krantz, J., Cohen, A. & Brennan, C. (1990). Extrageniculate vision in hemianopic humans: saccade inhibition by signals in the blind field. *Science*, **250**, 118–121.

Richards, W. (1973). Visual processing in scotomata. *Experimental Brain Research*, **17**, 333–347.

Rocha-Miranda, C.E., Bender, D.B., Gross, C.G. & Mishkin, M. (1975). Visual activation of neurons in inferotemporal cortex depends on striate cortex and forebrain commissures. *Journal of Neurophysiology*, **38**, 475–491.

Rodman, H.R., Gross, C.G. & Albright, T.D. (1989a). Afferent basis of visual response properties in area MT of the macaque. 1. Effects of striate cortex removal. *Journal of Neuroscience*, **9**, 2033–2050.

Rodman, H.R., Gross, C.G. & Albright, T.D. (1989b). Afferent basis of visual response properties in area MT of the macaque: II. Effects of superior colliculus removal. *Journal of Neuroscience*, **10**, 1154–1164.

Salzman, C.D., Britten, K.H. & Newsome, W.T. (1990). Cortical microstimulation influences perceptual judgements of motion direction. *Nature*, **346**, 174–177.

Schilder, P., Pasik, P. & Pasik, T. (1972). Extrageniculostriate vision in the monkey. III. Circle vs. triangle and 'red vs. green' discrimination. *Experimental Brain Research*, **14**, 436–448.

Schiller, P.H. & Koerner, F. (1971). Discharge characteristics of single units in superior colliculus of the alert rhesus monkey. *Journal of Neurophysiology*, **36**, 920–936.

Schiller, P.H. & Malpeli, J.G. (1977). Properties and retinal projections of monkey retinal ganglion cells. *Journal of Neurophysiology*, **40**, 428–445.

Schiller, P.H., Logothetis, N. & Charles, E. (1990). Functions of the colour-opponent and broad-band channels of the visual system. *Nature*, **343**, 68–70.

Shapley, R. & Perry, V.H. (1986). Cat and monkey retinal ganglion cells and their visual functional roles. *Trends in Neuroscience*, **9**, 229–235.

Sherman, S.M. (1974). Visual fields of cats with cortical and tectal lesions. *Science*, **185**, 355–357.

Simpson, J.I. (1984). The accessory optic system. *Annual Review of Neuroscience,* **7,** 13–41.

Snelgar, R.S., Foster, D.H. & Scase, M.O. (1987). Isolation of colour-opponent mechanisms at increment threshold. *Vision Research,* **27,** 1017–1027.

Sperling, H.G. & Harwerth, P. (1971). Red-green cone interactions in the increment-threshold spectral sensitivity of primates. *Science,* **172,** 180–184.

Sprague, J.M. (1966). Interaction of cortex and superior colliculus in mediation of visually guided behavior in the cat. *Science,* **153,** 1544.

Standage, G.P. & Benevento, L.A. (1983). The organization of the connections between the pulvinar and visual area MT in the macaque monkey. *Brain Research,* **262,** 288–294.

Stoerig, P. (1987). Chromaticity and achromaticity. Evidence for a functional differentiation in visual field defects. *Brain,* **110,** 869–886.

Stoerig, P. & Cowey, A. (1989a). Residual target detection as a function of stimulus size. *Brain,* **112,** 1123–1139.

Stoerig, P. & Cowey, A. (1989b). Spectral sensitivity in blindsight. *Nature,* **342,** 916–918.

Stoerig, P. & Pöppel, E. (1986). Eccentricity-dependent residual target detection in visual field defects. *Experimental Brain Research,* **64,** 469–475.

Ter Braak, J.W., Schenk, V.W.D. & Van Vliet, A.G.M. (1971). Visual reactions in a case of long-lasting cortical blindness. *Journal of Neurology, Neurosurgery and Psychiatry,* **34,** 140–147.

Ungerleider, L.G. & Desimone, R. (1986). Cortical connections of visual area MT in the macaque. *Journal of Comparative Neurology,* **248,** 190–222.

Van Buren, J.M. (1963). Trans-synaptic retrograde degeneration in the visual system of primates. *Journal of Neurology, Neurosurgery and Psychiatry,* **26,** 402–409.

Wallace, S.F., Rosenquist, A.C. & Sprague, J.M. (1990). Ibotenic acid lesions of the lateral substantia nigra restore visual orientation behavior in the hemianopic cat. *Journal of Comparative Neurology,* **296,** 222–252.

Weber, J.T., Huerta, M.F., Kaas, J.H. & Harting, J.K. (1983). The projections of the lateral geniculate nucleus of the squirrel monkey: Studies of the interlaminar zones and 's' layers. *Journal of Comparative Neurology,* **213,** 135–145.

Weiskrantz, L. (1986). *Blindsight: a Case Study and Implications.* Oxford: Clarendon Press.

Weiskrantz, L. (1987). Residual vision in a scotoma. A follow-up study of form discrimination. *Brain,* **110,** 77–92.

Weiskrantz, L. (1990). Outlooks for blindsight: explicit methodologies for implicit processes. *Proceedings of the Royal Society,* **B239,** 247–278.

Weiskrantz, L. & Cowey, A. (1970). Filling in the scotoma: A study of residual vision after striate cortex lesions in monkeys. In E. Stellar and J.M. Sprague (eds), *Progress in Physiological Psychology,* Vol. 3, pp. 237–260. New York: Academic Press.

Weiskrantz, L., Warrington, E.K., Sanders, M.D. & Marshall, J. (1974). Visual capacity in the hemianopic field following a restricted cortical ablation. *Brain,* **97,** 709–728.

Wilson, J.R. & Hendrickson, A.E. (1981). Neuronal and synaptic structure of the dorsal lateral geniculate nucleus in normal and monocularly deprived macaque monkeys. *Journal of Comparative Neurology,* **197,** 517–539.

Wolin, L.R., Massopust, L.C. & Meder, J. (1966). Differential color responses from the superior colliculus of squirrel monkeys. *Vision Research,* **6,** 637–644.

Yoshida, K. & Benevento, L.A. (1981). The projection from the dorsal lateral geniculate nucleus of the thalamus to extrastriate visual association cortex in the macaque monkey. *Neuroscience Letters*, **22**, 103–108.

Yukie, M. & Iwai, E. (1981). Direct projection from the dorsal lateral geniculate nucleus to the prestriate cortex in the macaque monkey. *Journal of Comparative Neurology*, **201**, 81–97.

Zeki, S.M. (1983). The distribution of wavelength and orientation cells in different areas of monkey visual cortex. *Proceedings of the Royal Society*, **B217**, 449–470.

Zihl, J., Tretter, F. & Singer, W. (1980). Phasic electrodermal responses in patients with cerebral blindness. *Behavioural Brain Research*, **1**, 197–203.

CHAPTER 3

Covert Processing in Different Visual Recognition Systems

Glyn W. Humphreys, Tom Troscianko,
M. Jane Riddoch, Muriel Boucart,
Nick Donnelly, and Graham F.A. Harding

3.1. INTRODUCTION

Our concern in this chapter is with covert visual processing in patients. By the term covert processing, we mean that patients can show above chance, and even possibly normal, discrimination of information for which they have no conscious experience. For instance, blindsight patients appear to have no conscious experience of the presence of stimuli which they can nevertheless discriminate (Cowey & Stoerig, Chapter 2, this volume). Our usage of the term is thus distinct from the idea that covert processing is tied to indirect as opposed to direct tests of perception (e.g. Humphreys, 1981; Reingold & Merikle, 1990). This of course opens up the question of how we define conscious and unconscious processes, and how we conceptualize consciousness, once we are prised away from the notion that unconscious processes are revealed only by indirect tests. We turn to these difficult issues in Section 3.6.

3.1.1. Covert Visual Processing: 'Blindsight' and Prosopagnosia

Studies of covert visual processing have concentrated largely on two issues: the processing of visual information in areas of apparently blind visual field (in cases of 'blindsight'; Weiskrantz, 1986; Cowey & Stoerig, this volume), and the processing of familiar faces in cases of prosopagnosia (e.g. Bauer, 1984; Young & De Haan, 1990, and Chapter 4, this volume).

Patients who exhibit blindsight typically have lesions of their primary visual (striate) cortex, rendering them consciously blind to light in parts of the visual field topographically linked to the lesioned cortex. Despite this, the patients can show remarkably good discrimination of various properties of visual stimuli presented to the now blind areas of field. For instance, patients have been shown to be able to discriminate stimulus location, movement direction and velocity, size, orientation and possibly even colour (e.g. Weiskrantz, 1986, 1987; Stoerig & Cowey, 1989a,b; Cowey & Stoerig, Chapter 2, this volume). The patients do not show similar discriminations to stimuli presented to the blindspot within their intact field, so the discriminations are unlikely to reflect light scatter from the impaired into the intact field (see Weiskrantz, 1986). One account of blindsight is in terms of a neurophysiological model in which the patients lack the primary retinogeniculostriate pathway necessary for conscious perception, but have intact the midbrain visual pathway (projecting to the superior colliculus). In blindsight, we witness the properties of this midbrain pathway, plus possibly also those of other extra-striate visual pathways (e.g. from the retina to the thalamus to extra-striate cortex in cases of residual colour vision; see Stoerig & Cowey, 1989b). Cowey and Stoerig (Chapter 2, this volume) further speculate that intact striate cortex is *necessary* for conscious visual perception because consciousness is dependent on phase-locked temporal oscillation in reciprocally connected cortical neurons (see also Crick & Koch, 1990).

Studies of covert processing in prosopagnosia have shown that, despite the patients having no conscious experience of familiarity for a known face, they can apparently discriminate familiar from unfamiliar faces (see Young & De Haan, Chapter 4, this volume). This has been demonstrated mainly using indirect tests of face recognition, in which patients are not required to make a purposeful response on the basis of facial identity or even familiarity. Example demonstrations of covert face recognition include: faster matching of familiar relative to unfamiliar faces; semantic interference effects from familiar faces paired to incorrect but associated names; faster learning of correct relative to incorrect face-name pairings (see De Haan *et al.*, 1987a,b; Young & De Haan, 1988), and raised galvanic skin responses for familiar relative to unfamiliar faces (Tranel & Damasio, 1985). Interestingly, covert processing via these indirect tests can be demonstrated even in cases where patients fail to perform above chance on some forced-choice discriminations of face familiarity (e.g. Young & De Haan, 1988). This is unlike many of the patients manifesting blindsight, where blindsight is shown by above chance discrimination in forced-choice tasks, despite the patients having no conscious experience of the stimuli presented. We return to this point in Section 3.6. Such cases of prosopagnosia may be accounted for in terms of a psychological processing model (e.g. Bruce & Young, 1986), in which faces activate stored recognition units, but in which there is impaired output from these recognition units, disconnecting them from other parts of the processing system which presumably mediate conscious face recognition (e.g. De Haan *et al.*, 1987a).

3.1.2. On Using Tests of Covert Processing to Distinguish Separable Disorders

Not all prosopagnostic patients manifest covert face recognition (e.g. Newcombe *et al.*, 1989; Sergent & Villemure, 1989; Young & Ellis, 1989). One proposal is that covert recognition is not found in patients whose prosopagnosia results from a perceptual impairment (e.g. a failure to derive an appropriate input description of faces, which may be used to activate stored face recognition units); covert recognition is found only in cases where there is a mnestic problem, affecting either the stored recognition units themselves or output from these units to other parts of the face processing system (e.g. Newcombe *et al.*, 1989; see also De Renzi, 1986, for further discussion of the perceptual versus mnestic distinction in prosopagnosia). Note that even if the alignment of covert recognition with mnestic rather than perceptual causes of prosopagnosia turns out not to be the whole story (e.g. see McNeil & Warrington, 1991), the data suggest that studies of covert visual processing may provide one way to distinguish between different types of prosopagnosia, and hence between different components of the face processing system.

3.1.3. The Separation of Visual Processing Systems

Over the past 15 years, there has been increasing evidence for the separate processing of different properties of visual stimuli. Physiological evidence suggests that there are at least 20 different cortical areas concerned with visual processing, many of which have contrasting functional specializations (e.g. Van Essen, 1985). Several attempts have been made to characterize these functional specializations; these include the dichotomy between the processing of colour, texture, shape and fine stereopsis, and the processing of motion and flicker (e.g. Mollon, 1990; Schiller *et al.*, 1990); the tripartite distinction between the processing of colour (conducted by cells in the 'blob' regions of the striate cortex), the processing of shape (by cells in the 'interblob' regions of the striate cortex), and the processing of movement, depth and figure–ground relations (by cells in the magnocellular cortical pathway) (e.g. Livingstone & Hubel, 1987); and the dichotomy between the processing of 'object' and of 'spatial' information (e.g. Ungerleider & Mishkin, 1982; Desimone & Ungerleider, 1989). Of particular interest to our present concern is the distinction between the processing of colour and of shape information, both of which seem to occur within the 'object' processing system in Ungerleider and Mishkin's terms.

According to Livingstone and Hubel (1987), fine shape and colour information are optimally conveyed by different neurons within the retinogeniculocortical visual pathway. In the striate cortex, cells in layers 2 and 3 are subdivided into blob and interblob regions which are distinct in terms of their physiological properties, local interconnectivities and forward and backwards projections. Livingstone and Hubel propose that fine shape details are coded by cells in the interblob regions, whilst colour is coded in cells in the blob regions. Cells in the blob regions subsequently project to area V4, where cells respond selectively to colour and can display colour constancy (e.g. Zeki, 1980, 1981). Shape processing, perhaps supported by inputs from cells in the interblob regions, may similarly be mediated by cells in V4, but also by cells in other higher visual areas, including V3 (cf. Livingstone & Hubel, 1987).

This physiological work suggests the separate processing of colour and shape information. Neuropsychological evidence can also be found to support this distinction. For instance, patients with marked problems in discriminating between shapes matched for area can nevertheless show good colour discrimination and naming (e.g. Benson & Greenberg, 1969; Efron, 1968); in contrast, patients with poor colour discrimination following a brain lesion ('cerebral achromatopsia') can show good shape discrimination (e.g. Heywood et al., 1987). However, in many cases colour-processing deficits are accompanied by deficits in shape processing, and vice versa, perhaps because the lesion disrupts the separate processes concerned with colour and shape information (cf. Meadows, 1974).

Given the pattern of co-occurrence between shape and colour processing disorders, we may need to look to other ways to try and separate these processes using neuropsychological evidence. We have suggested above that one way to tease apart components of the visual processing system is to examine covert processing in patients with deficits in overt discrimination tasks. In particular, consider the case of a patient with apparently associated deficits in overt tests of visual processing of colour and shape. It is possible that there may be covert processing of one but not both types of information. This would then support the argument for the functional and anatomical separation of processes specialized for these different types of information.

3.1.4. The Present Work: The Separation of Covert Processing of Colour and Form

In this Chapter, we summarize evidence on a visual agnosic patient, HJA, whose problems in object and face recognition have been previously documented (e.g. Humphreys & Riddoch, 1987a,b; Riddoch & Humphreys, 1987; Humphreys *et al.*, 1991a). In this previous work, it has been argued that HJA's agnosia reflects an impairment in his form perception such that he fails to derive a correctly structured input description of objects. HJA also reports that he no longer has conscious experience of colours, even though premorbidly he apparently had normal colour vision and indeed his job involved advising clients on the installation of coloured glass to prevent the effects of light deterioration on fine art. We compare HJA's processing of colour relative to his processing of form. The data show that HJA does not manifest covert object or face recognition, but does demonstrate residual covert processing of colour. This covert processing of colour is manifested providing tasks do not require access to stored knowledge about colours (colour identification). It is also affected by masking by dynamic luminance noise and by high contrast levels. These last results would not be expected were the residual colour processing taking place solely in the primary 'blob' colour system. We suggest instead that residual colour processing may operate in processing systems other than the primary colour system, but it then fails to support either colour identification or conscious colour perception. The relations between covert colour perception and both blindsight and prosopagnosia are discussed.

3.2. THE CASE

Full details on HJA's case history are reported by Riddoch and Humphreys (1987). In brief, HJA suffered a stroke in 1981 which produced a bilateral lesion in the occipital cortex. Subsequently he presented with a superior altitudinal field defect (for both his left and right visual fields). Saccadic and smooth pursuit eye movements, and corrected visual acuity, were normal. He had a marked visual object agnosia, typically identifying only about 60–70% of common real objects and 30–40% of line drawings of the same objects. In addition to this he was profoundly prosopagnosic, failing to identify visually any familiar faces that he was presented with (Humphreys *et al.*, 1991a). He had topographical problems in negotiating his everyday environment, and impaired reading, with word identification initially depending upon a letter-by-letter strategy. He also complained of having no colour vision and only seeing the world in terms of 'blacks, whites and greys'.

In regular testing since his lesion, HJA's performance has remained very stable. He remains markedly agnosic for both objects and faces. He continues to have problems finding his way, and reading remains slow and effortful. The world continues to be consciously perceived as being without colour.

The tests reported here were conducted at various times since his lesion. Tests of his covert processing of objects and faces were carried out between January 1988 and July 1990. Tests of colour processing were carried out between September 1981 and December 1990 (see Humphreys *et al.*, in preparation). Repeat tests were always administered in cases where comparisons would otherwise have been made across widely separated time periods.

3.3. TESTS OF COVERT OBJECT PROCESSING

3.3.1. Matching Using Fragmented Forms

In an initial set of tests we were concerned with whether HJA showed covert recognition of drawings of objects, using a matching task which provides various indirect tests of object processing. Full details of these tests are given in Boucart and Humphreys (1991).

Subjects were presented with a sequence of two stimuli on a trial. The first stimulus served as a reference that had to be matched with one of two subsequent probe stimuli. The task required the subject to judge which of the two probe stimuli had the same global shape as the reference stimulus. In the experiments reported here, the target was an outline drawing, and the probes fragmented figures (see Fig. 3.1). The use of fragmented figures provided us with one test of covert object recognition. Fragmented forms could be one of two types. 'Well structured' forms were composed of fragments which allowed the real boundaries of the objects (as defined in line drawings of the same stimuli) to be derived on the basis of collinearity and closure between the fragments. In a pre-test, 73.7% of these 'well structured' forms could be named by control subjects when the forms were presented for 150 ms at the centre of a computer screen. A second set of 'poorly structured' forms was then derived so that the 'well' and 'poorly structured' versions of the same form were matched in terms of their global shape and the location of the local densities of the fragments, but the fragments in the 'poorly structured' forms lacked collinearity and closure. Examples of the 'well' and 'poorly structured' forms are given in Fig. 3.2. In the pre-test, control subjects were able to identify only 13.3% of the 'poorly structured' forms. The reference stimulus appeared for 150 ms at the centre of a computer monitor, followed by a 500 ms interval, and the probe display for 150 ms. Probe items were centred 3° to the left and right of fixation.

The normal pattern of performance is given in Fig. 3.3. There are three ways in which covert processing can be demonstrated in this experiment. The first depends on the contrast between the matching of 'well' and 'poorly structured' forms. When normal subjects match non-identical reference and probe stimuli on the basis of their global shape (e.g. in conditions SS and GS, see below for details), performance can be better with 'poorly structured' than with 'well structured' forms (see

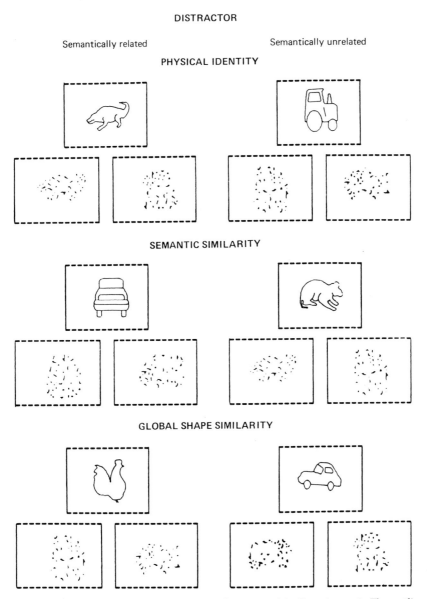

FIGURE 3.1. Example of the presentation conditions used in Experiment 1. The outline drawing was presented first on each trial, as a reference figure; the two fragmented forms were presented subsequently (see text for details).

Fig. 3.3). One factor here is that, with 'well structured' forms, subjects have to match two stimuli which will have different identities, and this mismatching identity information slows responses. However, since 'poorly structured' forms tend not to be identified, there is no conflicting identity information, and matching proceeds efficiently. In HJA covert recognition could be manifest via slowed matching of 'well' relative to 'poorly structured' forms.

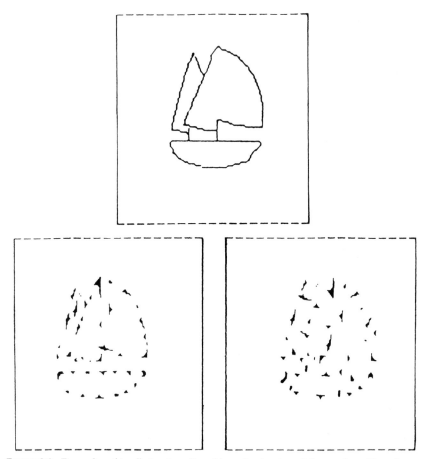

FIGURE 3.2. Examples of 'well structured' and 'poorly structured' figures from Experiment 1. On the top is an outline figure, used to derive both types of fragmented form. The form on the left is 'well structured', having collinearity and closure between its elements. The form on the right is 'poorly structured'. It is matched in global shape to the 'well structured' form, but the fragments lack collinearity and closure. The 'well structured' form also tends to have a greater degree of overlap between its fragments and the contours in the outline drawing.

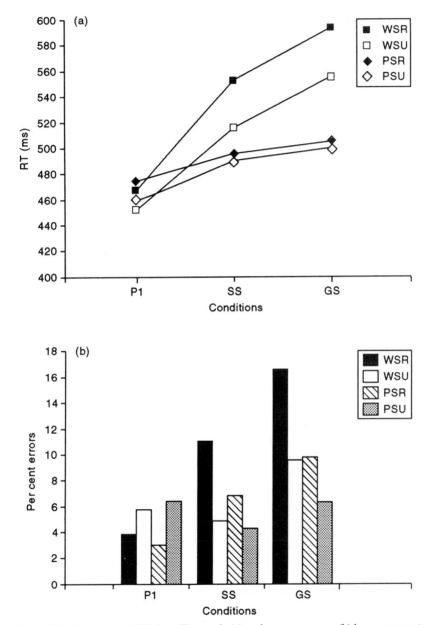

FIGURE 3.3. Mean correct RTs in milliseconds (a) and per cent errors (b) by young control subjects in Experiment 1. WSR corresponds to well structured target, semantically related distractor; WSU to well structured target, semantically unrelated distractor; PSR to poorly structured target, semantically related distractor; PSU to poorly structured target, semantically unrelated distractor. The three test conditions employed are illustrated in Fig. 3.1.

The second test of covert processing is based on the relation between the reference and the to-be-matched probe stimulus. These stimuli could be: (a) derived from the same stimulus (the physically identical condition, PI); (b) drawn from the same category (the semantically similar condition, SS); or (c) drawn from different categories (the globally similar condition, GS). Normally, matching in condition PI is faster than in either of the other two conditions, and matching in condition SS is faster than in condition GS (Fig. 3.3). The advantage for condition PI is to be expected, since subjects can then match on the basis of a very similar physical representation of the reference and probe stimuli; in the other two conditions matching must be based only on non-identical global shapes (see also Posner & Mitchell, 1967; Rosch, 1975). However, the advantage for condition SS over condition GS suggests that global shape matching can be facilitated by matching semantic information when stimuli are from the same category. Note that the SS versus GS difference cannot be attributed to greater physical similarity between same- relative to different-category items (in SS relative to GS), since the difference only occurs with 'well structured' forms; it does not occur with 'poorly structured' forms for which the global shape similarity between the reference and probe stimuli is closely matched (Fig. 3.3). Hence covert recognition may be shown via faster matching in condition SS relative to condition GS, particularly if this occurs only with 'well structured' forms.

The final test of covert processing is based on the relation between the two probes on each trial. In one condition, the target and distractor probes were from the same category; in the other they were from different categories. Normal subjects are slowed when the target and distractors are from the same category, at least when matching cannot be based on identical global representations (i.e. there is semantic interference in conditions SS and GS but not in condition PI). Again this can be attributed to semantic rather than physical similarity because the effect occurs with 'well structured' forms but not with their physically-matched 'poorly structured' partners (Fig. 3.3). Semantically-related distractors slow matching to targets. Such semantic interference would also indicate covert object recognition in a patient unable to show overt recognition of the same figures.

In a test of overt recognition, picture naming, HJA identified 38.4% of the outline drawings used for reference stimuli, and 19.2% of the 'well structured' fragmented forms, using a lenient scoring criterion in which basic category names as well as exact names were taken as correct (indeed HJA was only able to identify one of 12 items used in the experiment using the correct specific name). When this lenient scoring procedure is applied to control subjects, performance reaches ceiling. HJA is impaired at overt identification of the drawings. His problem is one of recognition rather than naming, in that he displays no semantic knowledge of the objects he misidentifies and his errors are always visually based (see also Riddoch & Humphreys, 1987).

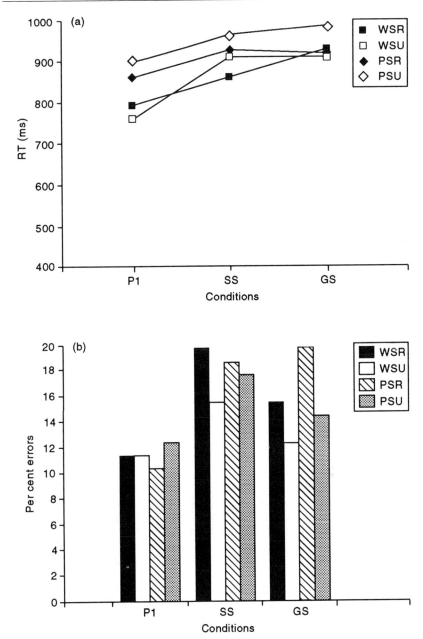

FIGURE 3.4. Mean correct RTs in milliseconds (a) and per cent errors (b) by HJA in Experiment 1. WSR corresponds to well structured target, semantically related distractor; WSU to well structured target, semantically unrelated distractor; PSR to poorly structured target, semantically related distractor; PSU to poorly structured target, semantically unrelated distractor. The three test conditions employed are illustrated in Fig. 3.1.

Mean correct reaction times (RTs) and percentage errors for HJA in the matching task are shown in Fig. 3.4. HJA was slower overall than control subjects; moreover, he produced a qualitatively different pattern of performance, and there was no evidence for covert recognition. First, apart from in condition PI (which we return to consider below), there was no difference between 'well' and 'poorly structured' forms, and certainly no indication of an advantage for 'poorly structured' forms, as found in conditions SS and GS with the control subjects (Fig. 3.3) (The trend for a RT advantage for 'well structured' forms in condition SS was not significant, and RTs in that condition were also associated with the highest error rate.) Second, there was no facilitation for matching non-identical forms from the same category relative to those from different categories (i.e. there was no advantage for condition SS over condition GS). Third, there was no effect of the nature of the distractor (i.e. there was no semantic interference when the distractor belonged to the same category as the target relative to when they came from different categories). In all three respects these results differ from those of control subjects.

The one result that matched the control data was the advantage for condition PI relative to conditions SS and GS; like control subjects, HJA was sensitive to the overall similarity between reference and probe shapes. However, HJA also showed a RT advantage for 'well structured' over 'poorly structured' forms in condition PI (Fig. 3.4). Control subjects were not affected by the structural characteristics of the fragmented forms in condition PI, and indeed showed an opposite advantage (for 'poorly structured' forms) in conditions SS and GS (Fig. 3.3). The advantage for 'well structured' forms suggests that HJA is strongly affected by the degree of contour overlap between the reference and the to-be-matched probe stimulus — the amount of overlap being higher for 'well' relative to 'poorly structured' forms in condition PI. Control subjects are not so affected by absolute levels of contour overlap between identical stimuli, perhaps because they can use the reference outline to help structure all matching fragmented forms (i.e. 'poorly structured' in addition to 'well structured' forms). HJA seems unable to structure forms in this way. Thus HJA's performance in condition PI suggests that he uses somewhat impoverished (unstructured) visual descriptions to perform the matching task, consistent with there being an early perceptual locus to his agnosia (Riddoch & Humphreys, 1987).

3.3.2. Learning Object–Name Associations

The above experiments indicate that HJA manifests neither intact overt or covert recognition for fragmented figures. However, this might simply reflect a particular problem with fragmented figures, and it should not be taken to imply a general failure of covert recognition for objects. To assess HJA's covert processing of objects more generally, we conducted an object–name learning experiment. HJA was asked to learn associations between object names and line drawings of objects he was consistently unable to identify. Half of the names were correct for the objects, half were incorrect. Using similar procedures with face–name learning in a prosopagnosic patient, De Haan *et al.* (1987a) argued that covert recognition could be demonstrated by better learning of correct relative to incorrect stimulus–name pairings.

Two versions of the learning test were run, one using object–name associations, and a second control version using name–name associations. The name–name version was included to verify that the objects and names were associated for HJA, in which case correct name–name associations should be learned more easily than incorrect name–name associations.

The line drawings were taken from Snodgrass and Vanderwart's (1980) norms. Eight drawings were used: dog, cow, lion, bear, donkey, horse, camel, rabbit[1]. In pre-tests with these drawings, HJA was unable to identify correctly any item, describing them all as 'only animals'. Each animal was given an associate name (dog–kennel, cow–milk, lion–pride, donkey–Eeyore, camel–pyramid, bear–Pooh, horse–Arkle, rabbit–warren)[2]. For four animals the drawing was paired with the correct name (dog, cow, camel, rabbit), and for the other four there were incorrect drawing–name pairings (lion–Pooh, donkey–Arkle, bear–pride, horse–Eeyore). HJA was given each line drawing for 5 s, and the to-be-learned name was read aloud by the experimenter. Following the presentation of the full set of drawings, HJA was presented with all eight drawings together, and a name was read aloud again; HJA was required to point to the appropriate picture for the name. When incorrect he was given the correct name. The procedure was then repeated. There was a cycle of 10 learning sequences, at the end of which HJA had learned all the object–name associations.

In a subsequent session, the procedure was repeated except that the names of each animal were read aloud on each trial, and in the testing sequence HJA was presented with the eight written names of the animals. Also, in the name–name version the correct and

---

1 All drawings were of animals because HJA is considerably better at picture–word matching than at picture identification, and he only makes picture–word matching errors when targets and distractors are drawn from categories with many visually similar exemplars (see Riddoch & Humphreys, 1987). Hence it was felt that all items needed visually similar partners in the set to prevent HJA from using the name to help identify the object in a top-down fashion. The set of animals was chosen so that all items came from a category with many visually similar exemplars, and so that each item in the set had a visually similar partner.

2 Eeyore and Pooh are characters from A.A. Milne's *Winnie the Pooh* stories; Arkle was a famous English racing horse. All these facts were known by HJA.

TABLE 3.1
Number of correct associations made by HJA per learning trial for object–name
and name–name associations

Trial	1	2	3	4	5	6	7	8	9	10
Object–name associations										
Correct pairing	2	1	2	1	2	2	2	3	4	4
Incorrect pairing	0	1	1	2	1	2	3	3	3	4
Name–name associations										
Correct pairing	2	3	3	4	3	3	4	4	4	4
Incorrect pairing	0	0	1	1	2	2	2	3	3	2

incorrect pairings were changed from the object–name version
(in the name–name version the incorrect pairings were: dog–warren,
rabbit–kennel, camel–milk, cow–pyramid).

The number of correct associations made per learning sequence, for
correct and incorrect object–name associations, is given in Table 3.1.
There was no difference between HJA's ability to learn correct and
incorrect object–naming pairings ($P = 0.688$, sign test). In contrast,
there was a clear advantage for correct relative to incorrect name–name
pairings ($P < 0.001$, sign test).

The data support the argument made from the matching task with
fragmented figures: HJA shows no covert recognition for objects he fails
to identify overtly.

3.4. TESTS OF COVERT FACE PROCESSING

In addition to having a marked visual object agnosia, HJA is profoundly
prosopagnosic. In numerous tests of face identification conducted since
his lesion, he has failed to identify any faces correctly. He is also
impaired at identifying sex and emotional expression from static faces
(interestingly, he is not impaired on these judgements when given
moving faces; Humphreys et al., 1991b). As with his visual object
agnosia, there are grounds for proposing a perceptual locus to his prosopagnosia since his face-matching abilities are strongly affected by the
complexity and orientation of faces, and (unlike normal subjects) he is
unable to use configural information in faces to facilitate the identification of facial features (Humphreys et al., 1991a). However, given the
potential of tests of covert processing for teasing apart perceptual processes, we also need to assess HJA's covert face processing abilities. In
particular, if HJA shows covert recognition of faces but not objects,
there would be evidence that face and object processing are functionally
independent.

3.4.1. Learning Face–Name and Face–Occupation Associations

Adopting the learning procedure used with line drawings, HJA was required to learn either correct and incorrect face–name associations, or correct and incorrect face–occupation associations. In both tasks HJA was presented with photographs of the faces of four British politicians and four British television presenters that he was able to identify pre-morbidly. Half were assigned the correct face–name and face–occupation pairings, half were assigned incorrect pairings. The procedure was otherwise the same as for the object–name learning task, except that 12 trials were needed for learning to criterion.

The number of correct associations made by HJA for face–name and face–occupation learning are given in Table 3.2. There was no advantage for learning correct over incorrect associations.

3.4.2. Face Matching

Further evidence confirming the lack of covert face processing is provided by HJA's performance on the 'external/internal' features matching task used to test covert face recognition by De Haan *et al.* (1987a). This task advances studies of covert recognition using simple learning procedures, because it manipulates the configural information which seems important for recognizing familiar faces. For instance, in normal subjects, the internal features of faces seem to play a relatively more important role in the recognition of familiar faces than the external features (e.g. Ellis *et al.*, 1979; Endo *et al.*, 1984); this is not the case for unfamiliar faces. Thus in tasks requiring subjects to match either external or internal features to full faces, normal subjects show an effect of familiarity on matching internal but not external features (Young *et al.*, 1985). It follows that patients who show an equivalent effect (of

TABLE 3.2
Number of correct pairings reported by HJA on each learning trial for face–name and face–occupation associations

Trial	1	2	3	4	5	6	7	8	9	10	11	12
Face–name associations												
Correct pairing	2	2	1	2	1	2	3	3	3	4	3	4
Incorrect pairing	2	2	1	2	2	3	3	3	4	4	4	4
Face–occupation associations												
Correct pairing	1	1	0	2	2	3	2	2	3	2	3	4
Incorrect pairing	2	2	2	1	2	2	3	2	3	2	4	4

face familiarity on matching internal but not external features) appear to utilize normal perceptual processes; in such cases covert recognition does not seem to operate using some qualitatively different recognition procedure to those employed in normal subjects.

In the external-features task, HJA had to match a full photograph of a familiar or unfamiliar face with a photograph showing only the external features of the same or a different face. In the internal-features task, the full face had to be matched with a photograph showing only the internal features (nose, eyes and mouth). In both tasks, the full face and the features were taken from different viewpoints even on matching trials. The mean correct RTs and percentage correct responses made by HJA are given in Table 3.3.

HJA performed very poorly. His RTs were extremely long, and he was at chance at matching in the internal features task. There were both RT and accuracy advantages for matching external over internal features, but no effects of face familiarity on either matching task. These results have been replicated using similar stimuli but in which there was no viewpoint change between the part and whole faces (Humphreys et al., 1991).

Again, HJA's pattern of performance is qualitatively different from normal in this task, since, with familiar faces, he performs better at matching external relative to internal features. There is no evidence that HJA is able to recognize familiar faces covertly, or even that he is able to derive useful configural information from photographs of faces.

3.4.3. Summary of Covert Object and Face Processing

HJA does not manifest covert recognition of objects and faces. There are also indications that his deficits in object and face processing are perceptual in nature. For instance, his matching of fragmented figures seems affected by the percentage overlap between stimuli, and not by structural properties such as collinearity and closure between the fragments.

TABLE 3.3

The percentage (and number) of correct responses and correct RTs (in seconds) for HJA matching full and part faces differing in orientation

	Internal-features		External-features	
	Familiar	Unfamiliar	Familiar	Unfamiliar
RT	9.43	9.50	8.64	8.42
SD	3.62	3.40	2.88	2.83
% Correct	53.75	51.25	76.25	70.0
No. Correct	43/80	41/80	61/80	56/80

Also, he is unable to match internal features with full photographs of faces, at least when there is a small change in viewpoint between the photographs. The results are consistent with the proposal that covert recognition is minimized in cases where a recognition impairment has a perceptual locus (e.g. Newcombe *et al.*, 1989).

3.5. COLOUR PROCESSING

Since the time of his lesion, HJA has reported a complete loss of colour vision (see Humphreys & Riddoch, 1987a). However, detailed data on his processing of colour information have not been reported. We now summarize tests of his colour processing, paying particular attention to the contrast between direct and indirect measures of performance, and the possibility that HJA may manifest covert colour processing. First, a number of tests were undertaken, each of which can be said to provide a direct test of colour perception, in that HJA had to respond directly to colour information. These direct tests are described in Sections 3.5.1 and 3.5.2.

3.5.1. Colour Naming, Pointing and Matching

Between November 1981 and December 1990, HJA's ability to match and name colours was tested on a number of occasions, with consistent results. When given patches of standard colour widely separated across the colour spectrum, he typically named about 40–50% correctly. This is not due to anomia; for instance, HJA was unable to make any correct associations to the colours he misnamed (e.g. he misnamed blue as brown, and said it was the colour of a tree trunk, rather than (for example) the colour of the sea). Adding static luminance noise (adding 20% luminance contrast differences to the colour patches) impaired his colour naming, reducing it to a level of about 19% correct.

Asked to point to a named colour patch, HJA scored similarly to his naming level (around 50%; chance 6.3%), and this again reduced under static luminance noise conditions (31% correct).

Colour matching was tested by having HJA point to one of 20 colour patches to match the colour pointed to by the examiner (in a second set of 20 patches). With widely separated colours, he scored 60% correct (chance = 5%). We were interested that, when performing the colour matching test, HJA often reported that he was guessing when he was correct; contrastingly, he sometimes reported that he was confident that a response was correct when it was incorrect. We assessed this more formally by asking him to rate (using a 4-point scale) how sure he was that his matching responses were correct. Table 3.4a shows the number of correct and incorrect matching responses broken down as a function of the confidence with which he made the response. There was little difference between his confidence ratings on correct and incorrect responses (e.g. he was sure or very sure of 50% of both his correct and incorrect responses). This is not because HJA cannot use a rating scale; when asked to rate his confidence when naming pictures of objects, HJA is more confident of his correct responses than his errors (Humphreys & Riddoch, unpublished; Table 3.4b). The result suggests that HJA does not have subjective experience of the colour information he apparently uses for colour-matching judgements.

We went on to examine HJA's confidence ratings on colour judgments by making the colour matching test harder in two different ways;

TABLE 3.4

(a) Number of responses in each confidence rating category as a function of correct or incorrect colour matching by HJA

Rating	Very sure	Sure	Unsure	Very unsure
Correct	2	4	3	3
Incorrect	1	3	2	2

(b) Number of responses in each rating category as a function of correct or incorrect object identification by HJA (Humphreys & Riddoch, unpublished data) (20 line drawings of objects presented)

Rating	Very sure	Sure	Unsure	Very unsure
Correct	3	4	2	0
Incorrect	0	0	4	7

(c) Number of responses in each confidence rating category as a function of correct or incorrect matching of colours with similar hues

Rating	Very sure	Sure	Unsure	Very unsure
Correct	1	3	3	1
Incorrect	1	5	4	2

(d) Number of responses in each confidence rating category as a function of correct and incorrect matching of colours with static luminance noise

Rating	Very sure	Sure	Unsure	Very unsure
Correct	1	2	5	5
Incorrect	0	2	3	2

by using colours more closely grouped in the colour spectrum, and by adding 20% static luminance noise to the patches. With closely grouped colours, HJA's colour matching decreased to 40% correct; however, the proportion of sure responses remained the same as with the widely separated colours (Table 3.4c). With luminance noise added to the widely separated colour patches, HJA's matching performance did not decrease (65% correct), but the proportion of unsure responses did (Table 3.4d).

These results point to an interesting difference between HJA's colour matching and his confidence ratings. Colour matching is affected by the degree of separation between colours in the colour spectrum but not by (at least small levels of) static luminance noise. In contrast, HJA's confidence ratings are not affected by the degree of separation in the colour spectrum but are by luminance noise. The effects of luminance noise on HJA's confidence ratings also parallel the effects on his colour naming and his pointing to named colours. The data suggest that HJA matches using colour information, but his colour identification (when required to name or point to named colours), and his confidence ratings, are both affected by luminance rather than by colour. The confidence ratings indicate that HJA is unable to judge when his colour-based judgements are correct or erroneous.

3.5.2. Farnsworth–Munsell 100-Hue Test and Matching at Isoluminance

Though we have suggested that HJA uses colour information when matching colour patches, he is clearly far from normal at doing this. He matches even widely separated colours with only around 60% accuracy. Figure 3.5 gives his profile on the Farnsworth–Munsell 100-Hue test, in which the patient is required to order 'swatches' in terms of their colour. Normal performance should be reflected by a pattern of responses close to the central circle. HJA's error scores are in fact over three times the age matched norm. Nevertheless, there is some suggestion that discriminations in the purple range of the spectrum (hue numbers 63–84) are rather better than elsewhere.

A yet more rigorous test is to examine colour matching under isoluminance conditions, where brightness differences between to-be-matched colours are eliminated. We have examined HJA's colour matching at isoluminance under a number of conditions, varying the colour difference from red–green to yellow–green, the brightness of the boundary between the to-be-matched colours (a 1° bright white strip), and the presence of static and dynamic luminance noise at temporal frequencies of 0, 6 and 25 Hz. HJA performed well above chance across all conditions which had colour differences between the fields to be discriminated. He was better at matching such patches differing in

colour relative to patches differing in luminance alone, providing the
luminance contrast between differing patches was relatively low
(⩽30%); at 50% contrast, however, performance was optimal for both
colour and luminance-defined patterns, at all temporal frequencies
used. Colour-defined (isoluminant) patterns—having 0% contrast on the
R/G graphs shown in Fig. 3.6—gave chance performance when static
luminance noise (of 50% contrast) was present. Similar results were
obtained for 6 Hz noise; with 25 Hz noise, on the other hand, they were
seen almost perfectly. Thus, increasing the temporal frequency of the

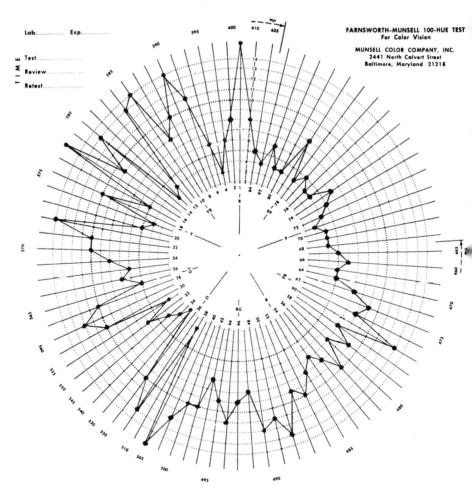

FIGURE 3.5. The results of the Farnsworth–Munsell 100-Hue Test. Errors are plotted
radially and positions on the circumference represent points along a continuum of hue.

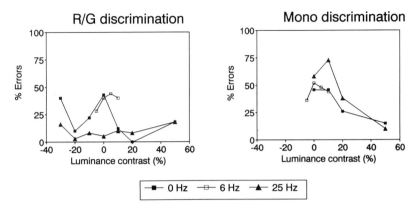

FIGURE 3.6. HJA's performance on two-interval forced-choice discrimination between patches either differing in monochromatic illumination (Mono) or red–green colour (R/G), as a function of the contrast difference between the patches. Luminance noise of 50% contrast was added at three temporal frequencies as indicated.

luminance noise improves performance for chromatic stimuli, while having no such effect for monochromatic stimuli.

That HJA is above chance at matching colours presented under isoluminant conditions indicates that he does have residual ability to discriminate colour. However, this ability is far from normal, as shown by his poor colour matching and poor performance on the Farnsworth –Munsell 100-Hue test. HJA may be able to tell that there is some difference between red and green fields, but is unable to make fine colour judgements.

What kind of neural mechanism allows HJA to have this residual (and unconscious) ability to discriminate colour? There are two theoretical possibilities. The first is that the information passes through the normal, *parvocellular* (Livingstone & Hubel, 1987) system, e.g. cells in the blob region of the striate cortex, which respond poorly with low luminance contrast and are increasingly insensitive as temporal frequency is increased. Thus, the random luminance noise would be seen well at 0 Hz, less at 6 Hz, and not at all at 25 Hz. The results show that, as the noise is less well coded by the parvo cells, so performance with coloured stimuli improves. This suggests that it is the parvo cells which are contributing the colour information.

This pattern of results tends to rule out the second possibility, namely that the colour information is encoded by the *magnocellular* ('transient') system. This is frequently thought of as being colour-blind (e.g. Livingstone, 1988) and is thought not to have strong colour-opponent responses. However, many cells within this pathway show some ability to respond under isoluminant conditions (Derrington *et al.*, 1984; Saito *et al.*, 1989). Our results suggest that HJA's colour-discrimination performance is unlikely to be based on such activity, since adding more 'jamming noise' to the system does not impair colour discrimination.

3.5.3. Indirect Tests of Colour Perception

The direct tests of colour processing showed that HJA has residual colour perception, but that he has little subjective knowledge about this, given the lack of correspondence between his confidence ratings and his objective performance on colour-matching tasks. That is, his residual colour processing is covert. We have also confirmed the presence of residual colour perception using indirect tests, in which responses to the colour information were not required, although it could be used to facilitate task performance.

First, HJA was given the Ishihara colour plates, and asked to identify the numbers present. When first given this test 1 month after his stroke, HJA was unable to identify any numbers present. However, on more recent retesting (in November, 1989 and July, 1990), he was able to identify 17/26 numbers (summing over the two test occasions). In a modified version of the test, where the numbers were defined by contrast rather than colour he scored 20/26. Apparently HJA could respond to the colour differences defining the numbers in the colour test; his identification failures were of a different kind, seemingly due to problems in perceptual integration. These problems were present when he had to discriminate the figure against the background of visual noise, and arose irrespective of whether the numbers were defined by contrast or colour. Poor performance when the test was initially administered was probably because of severe difficulties in perceptual integration at that time. A spared ability to identify letters in the Ishihara test has been noted in other achromatopsic patients (e.g. Mollon *et al.*, 1980; Victor *et al.*, 1989; Heywood *et al.*, 1991). However, unlike at least some cases, HJA did not have to view the Ishihara plates from a distance in order to be able to identify them. We return to review the relations between HJA and other achromatopsic patients in the General Discussion.

In a second indirect test, we measured evoked potentials to black–white and to red–green checkerboard patterns: a comparison that may be considered akin to the tests of autonomic responses to familiar and unfamiliar faces in prosopagnosic patients (e.g. Bauer, 1984). Black–White checkerboards had 70% contrast; red–green checkerboards had less than 10% luminance contrast. The average latency of the P100 response to black–white patterns, used as a clinical measure of cortical responsivity to pattern (Harding & Wright, 1986), was 122 ms to black–white patterns whilst to red–green patterns it was 123 ms. The null effect of the change from black–white to red–green pattern on the latency of the P100 response suggests that the response to red–green patterns was based on colour rather than luminance — were it based on luminance the P100 response would have been delayed because of the reduced contrast for red–green patterns. The evoked response data confirm that there is residual colour processing.

The third indirect test of colour processing assessed the effects of colour on object identification. Price and Humphreys (1989) found that normal subjects correctly identified coloured drawings more easily than black and white drawings, and incorrectly coloured drawings were identified worst. When given stimuli from the same set, HJA named 18/60 of the black and white drawings, 27/60 of the correctly coloured drawings, and 28/60 of the incorrectly coloured drawings. The benefit for correctly coloured drawings is not because they are correctly coloured, since incorrectly coloured drawings were also advantaged relative to black and white drawings. Rather, there is an effect of colouring surfaces (whether the colouring itself is correct or incorrect). This effect probably occurs because either colour, or the brightness contrasts introduced by colouring the surfaces of drawings, helps HJA segment objects correctly into their parts, and this in turn aids object identification. It is not because there is covert identification of colour. Indeed, in other experiments we have given HJA learning tasks where he has to learn pairings between colour patches and names (either colour names or the names of colour associates such as blue–sky, pink–salmon, yellow–canary). As in the studies of object–name and face–name learning, half the pairings were correct, half incorrect. For neither colour–name nor colour–associate pairings were correct pairings learned more easily than incorrect pairings. Taken together these indirect tests of colour perception confirm that HJA has residual processing of colour, but there is no evidence of covert colour identification.

3.6. GENERAL DISCUSSION

We have presented a broad set of results on object, face and colour processing in the agnosic patient HJA. The results on object and face processing unanimously show that HJA fails to manifest covert recognition for objects and faces. There are no advantages for learning correct over incorrect name- and associate- pairings, for either objects or names. There are also no differences between the matching of familiar and unfamiliar faces, and no effects of associate pairings on object matching. HJA's agnosia and prosopagnosia seem to be such that normal visual access to stored knowledge about objects and faces fails to take place, and this holds whether he is tested for 'overt' or 'covert' recognition, using direct and indirect tests of object and face processing. Interestingly, HJA's memory for the visual characteristics of objects and faces remains relatively good. He is able to draw objects from memory that he no longer recognizes visually (Riddoch & Humphreys, 1987), and he is good at forced choice questions concerning visual characteristics of glasses; Humphreys et al., 1991a). In his case it seems unlikely that the lack of covert recognition is due to impaired stored visual representations of objects or faces.

Also using both direct and indirect tests, HJA can be shown to have residual colour processing. Yet, this residual colour processing seems to operate covertly, without HJA having conscious experience of colour; in particular, he is unable to judge whether his colour matches are correct or not, and seems to base such judgements on luminance contrasts. On the other hand, he is able to judge accurately when he is correct at form identification tasks, so the problem with confidence judgements is specific to colour. Because of the covert nature of HJA's colour processing, he cannot be deemed to have a colour agnosia in which he has conscious colour perception along with no access to categorical colour information.

Nevertheless, the data do show a clear distinction between HJA's performance when he has to detect colour differences and his performance when colour information needs to be identified (i.e. assigned to a known colour category). When responses can be based on colour-defined surface or boundary differences (e.g. in matching colour patches; in matching at isoluminance; in naming numbers on the Ishihara plates; in tests of colour evoked responses) HJA can be shown to use colour information; however, there is no evidence that this information can be identified. HJA is poor at colour naming and at pointing to named colours; he cannot use colour information to help identify objects and he does not learn correct colour–name or colour–associate pairings any better than incorrect pairings. Indeed, colour naming and pointing seem to be performed using brightness rather than colour information, since these tasks are impaired when static luminance noise is added to the colour patches (unlike colour matching).

We suggest then that there is residual colour processing without colour identification. This distinction is not as clear cut as one might hope, since even his use of (uncategorized) colour boundary or surface information is impaired. Even so, HJA is not able to use the residual colour information he has for purposes of identification.

At first glance, the contrast between HJA's residual covert processing of colour, and his lack of covert processing of faces and objects, fits with the evidence indicating the functional separation of colour and shape processing in vision. This conclusion should be cautious, however. Our evidence is in fact consistent with the proposal that HJA's residual colour processing may be based on the normal colour pathway but in a very weak form not accessible to conscious perception. We base this on the relationship between performance and the temporal frequency of the luminance noise in the display. The conclusion also fits with HJA's relatively preserved motion perception (e.g. see Humphreys et al., 1991b). Indeed, HJA's inability to identify colours, both consciously and unconsciously, implies that weak parvocellular function is not by itself sufficient to do anything except detect colour change, conveying no information about the identity of the colours present.

Residual colour processing has also been observed in other achromatopsic patients, whose colour matching and ordering ability is markedly impaired. Mollon *et al.* (1980) found that their patient was able to identify letters in the Ishihara plates, from a distance; Heywood *et al.* (1991) have also shown that the same patient remained above chance at colour matching at isoluminance. Victor *et al.* (1989) further showed that their achromatopsic patient produced visual-evoked responses to isoluminant gratings. These data mesh with our findings with HJA. In all of these cases, it was also reported that the patients had no conscious colour appreciation. There are similarities in the data. Heywood *et al.*'s patient was poor at matching colours at isoluminance when the colours were separated by a small achromatic boundary. This was also true of HJA, who remained at chance at discriminating between isoluminant colours separated by both a black and a white boundary with static luminance noise present. Also, HJA could identify numbers on the Ishihara plates from a normal viewing distance. Heywood *et al.* suggest that their patient detected chromatic borders without being able to adduce the nature of the hues. The patient was impaired by the introduction of an achromatic border between to-be-matched colours since hue-differences between the colour patches and the achromatic borders were a less reliable signal of a colour difference than hue-differences between the borders of the colours when spatially aligned. Similarly, when seen close up, luminance differences between the dots in the Ishihara plates might overwhelm the computation of borders based on hue differences. Seen from afar, the luminance differences between the dots will not be resolvable; the chromatic boundaries will then be most apparent, allowing the numbers to be identified (also see Mollon *et al.*, 1980).

HJA was not affected so dramatically by achromatic boundaries or by viewing distance to the Ishihara plates. This may mean either that he is better able to use chromatic boundary information than Heywood *et al.*'s patient, or that there remain processes sensitive to surface colour (and not just colour boundaries), possibly mediated by the blob region of the parvocellular pathway.

3.6.1. Covert Processing and Direct Versus Indirect Tests of Performance

The distinction between residual covert colour processing and colour identification cuts across the task-based distinction between direct and indirect tests of perception. In HJA the residual processing of colour can be observed via either direct or indirect tests (e.g. in both forced-choice colour matching at isoluminance and the naming of Ishihara plates and colour evoked responses). The lack of colour identification can similarly be observed using both test types (e.g. in both colour naming when there is luminance noise and in learning colour–name and associate pairings). Nevertheless, we propose that HJA's residual colour processing is covert. HJA reports no conscious experience of colour. Also, his confidence ratings fail to discriminate correctly matched from incorrectly matched colours (unlike his confidence ratings in object identification).

How are we then to understand the relations between direct and indirect tests of visual processing and the distinction between overt and covert recognition? The distinction between direct and indirect tests of processing lends itself most easily to a disconnection account of unconscious perception. Using direct measures, subjects apparently fail to perceive a stimulus because perceptual processes are disconnected from the systems that modulate conscious recognition (cf. the account of covert face recognition in prosopagnosia given in the Introduction; see also Young & De Haan, Chapter 4, this volume). A disconnected perceptual system may nevertheless influence systems other than those modulating conscious recognition, to which it remains connected. Indirect measures can thus show unconscious perception providing the measures tap the still-connected secondary systems. However, with respect to HJA's colour perception, and also in cases of blindsight, there is evidence of residual processing in direct tests, yet the patients deny the presence of the stimulus properties that they are sensitive to. In such cases it can also be proposed that the residual processing reflects pathways other than those normally responsible for conscious visual perception of form and colour—namely the blob and interblob pathways in the striate cortex. The unconscious nature of these residual processes would then fit the speculation that conscious visual perception depends on phase-locked firing within a reciprocally connected oscillatory cortical network, of which the blob and interblob pathways are an integral part (cf. Crick & Koch, 1990). However, even when these pathways are impaired, they may support the residual processing of certain stimulus properties (e.g. motion, the computation of colour boundaries and surfaces). Outputs from such impaired pathways can be directly responded to, but they do not lead to conscious visual perception.

But now a problem arises; if conscious visual perception depends on phase-locked firing within a reciprocally connected cortical network, how might problems due to disconnection occur? One possibility is that cells within one region of the network are activated relatively normally from external input, but are prevented from passing on this activation or from becoming phase-locked in the normal way into the network supporting conscious perception. Whether the patients can respond unconsciously to a direct test on a given stimulus would then depend either on whether there exist enough signals that can give discriminatory responses to the stimulus (as we have suggested for the residual colour processing in HJA) or whether even partial activation can be passed on to other parts of the network (when it may be detected by means of indirect tests). In the case of low level vision, separate pathways are likely to be involved in coding different aspects of an image, making residual processing a possibility. For higher-level tasks, such as face recognition, separate pathways are a less distinct possibility, so increasing the likelihood that unconscious effects are demonstrated only through indirect tests. Note though that even in cases of covert recognition in prosopagnosia, recent evidence suggests residual recognition can be revealed in direct tests, providing the tests are suitably constrained. For instance, Sergent and Poncet (1990) report the case of a prosopagnosic who could not distinguish familiar from unfamiliar faces, and who had no conscious familiarity for faces, but who performed better than chance when forced to choose between a correct and an incorrect name for each face (see also Young & De Haan, Chapter 4, this volume). Apparently this constrained version of the task enabled the patient to respond directly to partial information (possibly because the face–name pairings raised the level of partial activation). The data suggest that we would be wise to be cautious in thinking that only indirect tasks provide a window on to unconscious processes.

Our final point is methodological. Our argument for HJA showing residual covert colour perception is based in large part on the lack of correspondence between his objective matching performance and his subjective ratings of how well he is performing. The use of ratings maps on to recent attempts in experimental psychology to define unconscious perception in terms of subjective judgements of whether a stimulus has occurred (e.g. Cheesman & Merikle, 1985), and attempts to show that perceptual discriminations can still be made even when subjects cannot judge whether their responses are incorrect or correct (Kunimoto *et al.*, 1991). The collection of subjective ratings may be easily incorporated into neuropsychological studies, and can provide a useful methodological link with attempts to define unconscious perception in normality.

ACKNOWLEDGEMENTS

The work reported in this paper was supported by grants from the Medical Research Council and the Wolfson Foundation to the first and third authors, a grant from the Ministry of Defence to the second author, and by a grant from the Fyssen Foundation to the fourth author. Our thanks to IA and HJA for all their patience in carrying out the experiments reported, to Dr Mary Hill and Dr John Patten for their referral of HJA, to Mike Harris for comments on an earlier version of the paper, and to Andy Young for loan of the face stimuli for the internal–external features matching test.

REFERENCES

Bauer, R.M. (1984). Autonomic recognition of names and faces in prosopagnosia: A neuropsychological application of the Guilty Knowledge test. *Neuropsychologia*, **22**, 457–469.

Benson, D.F. & Greenberg, J.P. (1969). Visual form agnosia. *Archives of Neurology*, **20**, 82–89.

Boucart, M. & Humphreys, G.W. (1991). Global shape cannot be attended without object identification. *Journal of Experimental Psychology: Human Perception and Performance*, in press.

Bruce, V. & Young, A.W. (1986). Understanding face recognition. *British Journal of Psychology*, **77**, 305–327.

Cheesman, J. & Merikle, P.M. (1985). Word recognition and consciousness. In D. Besner, T.G. Waller & G.E. MacKinnon (eds), *Reading Research: Advances in Theory and in Practice*, Vol. 5. New York: Academic Press.

Crick, F. & Koch, C. (1990). Towards a neurobiological theory of consciousness. *Seminars in the Neurosciences*, **2**, 263–275.

De Haan, E.H.F., Young, A.W. & Newcombe, F. (1987a). Face recognition without awareness. *Cognitive Neuropsychology*, **4**, 385–415.

De Haan, E.H.F., Young, A.W. & Newcombe, F. (1987b). Faces interfere with name classification in a prosopagnosic patient. *Cortex*, **23**, 309–316.

De Renzi, E. (1986). Current issues in prosopagnosia. In H.D. Ellis, M.A. Jeeves, F. Newcombe & A.W. Young (eds), *Aspects of Face Processing*. Dordrecht: Martinus Nijhoff.

Derrington, A.M., Krauskopf, J. & Lennie, P. (1984). Chromatic mechanisms in lateral geniculate nucleus of macaque. *Journal of Physiology*, **357**, 241–265.

Desimone, R. & Ungerleider, L.G. (1989). Neural mechanisms of visual processing in monkeys. In F. Boller & J. Grafman (eds), *Handbook of Neuropsychology*, Vol. 2. Amsterdam: Elsevier Science.

Efron, R. (1968). *What is Perception?* Boston Studies in the Philosophy of Science. New York: Humanities Press.

Ellis, H.D., Shepherd, J.W. & Davies, G.M. (1979). Identification of familiar and unfamiliar faces from internal and external features: Some implications for theories of face recognition. *Perception*, **8**, 431–439.

Endo, M., Takahashi, K. & Maruyama, K. (1984). Effects of observer's attitude on the familiarity of race: Using the difference in cue value between central and peripheral facial elements as an index of familiarity. *Tohoku Psychologia Folia*, **43**, 23–34.

Harding, G.F.A. & Wright, C.E. (1986). Visual evoked potentials in acute optic neuritis. In R.F. Hess & G.T. Plant (eds), *Optic Neuritis*. Cambridge: Cambridge University Press.

Heywood, C.A., Wilson, B. & Cowey, A. (1987). A case study of cortical colour 'blindness' with relatively intact achromatic discrimination. *Journal of Neurology, Neurosurgery and Psychiatry*, **50**, 22–29.

Heywood, C.A., Cowey, A. & Newcombe, F. (1991). Chromatic discrimination in a cortically colour blind observer. *European Journal of Neuroscience*, **3**, 802–812.

Humphreys, G.W. (1981). Direct vs. indirect tests of the information available from masked displays: What visual masking does and does not prevent. *British Journal of Psychology*, **72**, 323–330.

Humphreys, G.W. & Riddoch, M.J. (1987a). *To See but Not to See: a Case Study of Visual Agnosia.* London: Erlbaum.

Humphreys, G.W. & Riddoch, M.J. (1987b). The fractionation of visual agnosia. In G.W. Humphreys & M.J. Riddoch (eds) *Visual Object Processing: A Cognitive Neuropsychological Approach.* London: Erlbaum.

Humphreys, G.W., Donnelly, N. & Riddoch, M.J. (1991a). Face processing in visual agnosia, submitted.

Humphreys, G.W., Donnelly, N. & Riddoch, M.J. (1991b). Expression is computed separately from facial identity, and it is computed separately for moving and static faces: neuropsychological evidence, submitted.

Humphreys, G.W., Troscianko, T., Riddoch, M.J. & Harding, G.F.A. Overt and covert colour processing in cerebral achromatopsia, in preparation.

Kunimoto, C., Miller J. & Pashler, H. (1991). Perception without awareness confirmed: A bias-free procedure for determining awareness thresholds. Unpublished manuscript.

Livingstone, M.S. (1988). Art, illusion and the visual system. *Scientific American*, **258**, (January), 68–75.

Livingstone, M.S. & Hubel, D.H. (1987). Psychophysical evidence for separate channels for the perception of form, color, movement and depth. *Journal of Neuroscience*, **7**, 3416–3468.

McNeil, J.E. & Warrington, E.K. (1991). Prosopagnosia—a reclassification. *Quarterly Journal of Experimental Psychology*, **43A**, 267–287.

Meadows, J.C. (1974). Disturbed perception of colours associated with localised cerebral lesions. *Brain*, **97**, 615–632.

Mollon, J.D. (1990). The club-sandwich mystery. *Nature*, **343**, 16–17.

Mollon, J.D., Newcombe, F., Polden, P.G. & Ratcliff, G. (1980). On the presence of three cone mechanisms in a case of total achromatopsia. In G. Verriest (ed.), *Colour Vision Deficiencies.* Bristol: A. Hilger.

Newcombe, F., Young, A.W. & De Haan, E.H.F. (1989). Prosopagnosia and object agnosia without covert recognition. *Neuropsychologia*, **27**, 179–191.

Posner, M.I. & Mitchell, R. (1967). Chronometric analysis of classification. *Psychological Review*, **74**, 392–409.

Price, C.J. & Humphreys, G.W. (1989). The effects of surface detail on object categorization and naming. *Quarterly Journal of Experimental Psychology*, **41A**, 797–828.

Reingold, E.M. & Merikle, P.M. (1990). On the inter-relatedness of theory and measurement in the study of unconscious processes. *Mind and Language*, **5**, 9–28.

Riddoch, M.J. & Humphreys, G.W. (1987). A case of integrative visual agnosia. *Brain*, **110**, 1431–1462.

Rosch, E. (1975). Cognitive representations of semantic categories. *Journal of Experimental Psychology: General*, **104**, 192–233.

Saito, H., Tanaka, K., Isono, H., Yasuda, M. & Mikami, A. (1989). Directionally selective response of cells in the middle temporal area (MT) of the macaque monkey to the movement of equiluminous opponent colour stimuli. *Experimental Brain Research*, **75**, 1–14.

Schiller, P.H., Logothetis, N.K. & Charles, E.R. (1990). Functions of the colour-opponent and broad-band channels of the visual system. *Nature*, **343**, 68–70.

Sergent, J. & Poncet, M. (1990). From covert to overt recognition of faces in a prosopagnosic patient. *Brain*, **113**, 989–1004.

Sergent, J. & Villemure, J. (1989). Prosopagnosia in a right hemispherectomized patient. *Brain*, **112**, 975–995.

Snodgrass, J.G. & Vanderwart, M.A. (1980). Standardized set of 280 pictures: norms for name agreement, image agreement, familiarity and visual complexity. *Journal of Experimental Psychology: Human Learning and Memory*, **6**, 174–215.

Stoerig, P. & Cowey, A. (1989a). Residual target detection as a function of stimulus size. *Brain*, **112**, 1123–1139.

Stoerig, P. & Cowey, A. (1989b). Wavelength sensitivity in blindsight. *Nature*, **342**, 916–917

Tranel, D. & Damasio, A.R. (1985). Knowledge without awareness: An autonomic index of facial recognition by prosopagnosics. *Science*, **228**, 1453–1454.

Ungerleider, L.G. & Mishkin, M. (1982). Two cortical visual systems. In D.J. Ingle, M.A. Goodale & R.J.W. Mansfield (eds) *Analysis of Visual Behavior*. Cambridge, MA: MIT Press.

Van Essen, D.C. (1985). Functional organization of the primate visual cortex. In E.G. Jones & A.A. Peters (eds), *Cerebral Cortex*. Vol. 3. New York: Plenum Press.

Victor, J.D., Maiese, K., Shapley, R., Sidtis, J. & Gazzaniga, M. (1989). Acquired central dyschromatopsia: Analysis of a case with preservation of color discrimination. *Clinical Vision Science*, **4**, 183–196.

Weiskrantz, L. (1986). *Blindsight: A Case Study and Implications*. Oxford: Oxford University Press.

Weiskrantz, L. (1987). Residual vision in a scotoma: A follow-up study of 'form' discrimination. *Brain*, **110**, 77–92.

Young, A.W. & De Haan, E.H.F. (1988). Boundaries of covert recognition in prosopagnosia. *Cognitive Neuropsychology*, **5**, 317–336.

Young, A.W. & De Haan, E.H.F. (1990). Impairments of visual awareness. *Mind and Language*, **5**, 29–48.

Young, A.W. & Ellis, H.D. (1989). Childhood prosopagnosia. *Brain and Cognition*, **9**, 16–47.

Young, A.W., Hay, D.C., McWeeny, K.H., Flude, B.M. & Ellis, A.W. (1985). Matching familiar and unfamiliar faces on internal and external features. *Perception*, **14**, 737–746.

Zeki, S.M. (1980). The representation of colours in the cerebral cortex. *Nature*, **284**, 412–418.

Zeki, S.M. (1981). The mapping of visual functions in the cerebral cortex. In Y. Katsuki, R. Norgren & M. Sato (eds), *Brain Mechanisms of Sensation*. New York: Wiley.

CHAPTER 4

Face Recognition and Awareness After Brain Injury

Andrew W. Young and
Edward H.F. De Haan

4.1. INTRODUCTION

When you look at a familiar face, recognition seems automatic. You can't look at a face and *decide* not to recognize it. This is not to say that face recognition never goes wrong. There are many occasions in everyday life when mistakes can happen (Young *et al.*, 1985a), but these mistakes mostly occur outside our conscious control.

The apparent ease with which we recognize faces can be deceptive. Searle (1984, p. 52) used face recognition as an example of an ability that happens 'quite effortlessly' and which he considered may not require complex computation. Instead, he argued that it could be 'as simple and automatic as making footprints in the sand'. We have pointed out elsewhere some of the problems with this view, not the least of which is that there is no evidence that sand can *recognize* your footprints (Ellis *et al.*, 1987).

In fact, studies of everyday difficulties and errors show that recognition of a familiar face is not a unitary phenomenon, since many of them reflect breakdown at different levels of recognition (Young *et al.*, 1985a). For example:

(1) We may completely fail to recognize a familiar face, and mistakenly think that the person is unfamiliar.
(2) We may recognize the face as familiar, but be unable to bring to mind any other details about the person, such as her or his occupation or name.
(3) We may recognize the face as familiar and remember appropriate semantic information about the person, whilst failing to remember her or his name.

THE NEUROPSYCHOLOGY OF CONSCIOUSNESS
ISBN 0–12–498045–7

The orderliness of these types of everyday error suggests that the face recognition system itself uses some form of sequential access to different types of information, in the order familiarity then semantics then name retrieval. Experiments with normal subjects have given strong support to this suggestion (for reviews see Bruce & Young, 1986; Bruce, 1988; Young & Ellis, 1989a). Additional confirmation has come from studies of errors made under laboratory conditions, and the types of cue needed to resolve them (Hanley & Cowell, 1988; Hay *et al.*, 1991). These studies can eliminate reporting biases, yet still find *only* the types of error predicted by the sequential access view.

Each of the three types of error we have mentioned can also arise after neuropsychological impairment. In such cases, a brain-injured patient will make her or his characteristic error to many or almost all seen faces. In prosopagnosia, for example, known faces seem unfamiliar (Hécaen & Angelergues, 1962; Meadows, 1974), which corresponds to error type 1. We have recently reported a case in which known faces were familiar only (De Haan *et al.*, 1991), corresponding to error type 2. In anomia, name retrieval known to faces may become problematic even though semantic information can be properly accessed (Flude *et al.*, 1989), as in error type 3.

We thus have converging evidence from studies of everyday errors, laboratory errors, experiments, and neuropsychological case studies indicating that the functional organization of the face recognition system involves sequential access to different types of information. Hay and Young (1982) first suggested this view, and it has since been more fully developed by Bruce and Young (1986) and partially implemented in the form of an interactive activation model of the recognition of face and name inputs by Burton *et al.* (1990). The Burton *et al.* (1990) implementation is particularly important, since it can account for a number of effects reported in the literature with very few assumptions. At present, though, the Burton *et al.* (1990) implementation only deals with part of the Bruce and Young (1986) model, and does not yet encompass name retrieval from seen faces (though it does deal with the recognition of name inputs).

Although there is evidence of sequential access within the face *recognition* system, other types of facial information (such as emotional expression) may be determined independently from identity (Bruce & Young, 1986; Parry *et al.*, 1991). It is not necessary to analyse the facial expression before a person's identity can be known, or vice versa; there are *parallel* systems for extracting these different types of information from seen faces. Again, both studies of normal subjects and people with brain injuries support this conclusion (for reviews, see Bruce & Young, 1986; Young and Bruce, 1991).

So far, so good. We have been able to piece together much of the functional organization of the face processing system, and there is every indication that future work will continue to increase the precision and explanatory power of the models proposed (Bruce & Young, 1986; Ellis, 1986; Bruce, 1988; Burton *et al.*, 1990). However, there are also neuro-psychological findings which are not so easily incorporated into this general picture. In particular, the issue of *awareness* in relation to recognition impairments poses problems of interpretation. Recent studies with brain-injured patients have described face recognition problems which involve awareness as a central feature, including both awareness of recognition and awareness of impairment. Our knowledge of these impairments is still limited, but it is clear that they will require extensive exploration. What we present here is a progress report, not a solution.

4.2. PROSOPAGNOSIA

The neurological symptom of prosopagnosia will feature prominently in our discussions, so it is worth saying a few words about it at this point. The essential feature of prosopagnosia is that a brain-injured patient who is still able to see loses the ability to recognize the faces of familiar people that she or he can still recognize from non-facial cues, such as voice or name. Notice that this rules out as possible causes of the face recognition impairment both blindness (the patient can still see, and in many published cases can see quite well) and general intellectual impairment (people are still recognized from non-facial cues). Yet even the most familiar faces may go unrecognized; famous people, friends, family, and the patient's own face when seen in a mirror (Bodamer, 1947; Hécaen & Angelergues, 1962; Meadows, 1974). In contrast, other aspects of face processing, such as the ability to interpret facial expressions, or to match views of unfamiliar faces, can remain remarkably intact in some (though by no means all) cases (e.g. Bruyer *et al.*, 1983). The ability to recognize visual objects other than faces may also remain good, and many prosopagnosic patients are able to read without difficulty.

Much of the existing neuropsychological literature on prosopagnosia has concentrated on the issues of whether the deficit is specific to face recognition, and the location of the lesions (Meadows, 1974; Hécaen, 1981; Damasio *et al.*, 1982; Jeeves, 1984; Ellis & Young, 1989). These are important questions, but they have sometimes tended to take attention away from equally central issues concerning the functional nature of the deficit. Findings of covert recognition in prosopagnosia have returned these to prominence.

4.3. FACE RECOGNITION WITHOUT AWARENESS

The phenomenon of covert recognition of familiar faces after brain injury was first reported by Bruyer *et al.* (1983). Although well acquainted with this aspect of Bruyer *et al.*'s (1983) report, however, we failed to grasp its significance until the more dramatic demonstration by Bauer (1984), who studied the prosopagnosic patient LF's autonomic responses to familiar faces.

Bauer (1984) made use of the Guilty Knowledge Test, a technique sometimes used in criminal investigations, which is based on the view that a guilty person will show some involuntary physiological response to stimuli related to the crime. He showed the prosopagnosic patient LF photographs of familiar faces for 90 s, accompanied by five different names, one of which was the correct name. Maximal skin conductance responses to the correct name were found on 61% of trials, a figure well above the chance level of 20%. Yet when LF was asked to *choose* which name was correct for each face, he was at chance level (22% correct).

Bauer's (1984) study showed compellingly a difference between *overt* recognition, which is at chance level for LF, and some form of preserved *covert* recognition, as evidenced by his skin conductance responses. This finding profoundly affects our conception of the nature of prosopagnosia, since it shows that it is inadequate to think of it as simply involving loss of recognition mechanisms. Instead, at least some degree of recognition does take place; what LF has lost is *awareness of recognition*.

Later studies by Tranel and Damasio (1985, 1988) confirmed Bauer's (1984) findings with a somewhat different procedure, and further work by Rizzo *et al.* (1987) and Renault *et al.* (1989) has revealed comparable covert recognition effects in eye movement patterns and evoked potentials.

Our own approach has been to draw on techniques of experimental psychology. We have made a detailed investigation of the patient PH (De Haan *et al.*, 1987a,b; Young & De Haan, 1988; Young *et al.*, 1988), for whom we have shown covert recognition using matching, interference, associative priming, and learning paradigms.

PH suffered a severe closed-head injury in a road accident in 1982, when he was knocked off his motorcycle at the age of 19. His visual acuity is normal for his right eye, but impaired for his left eye, probably because of an untreated squint. There is some loss of contrast sensitivity for spatial frequencies greater than 1.5 cycles per degree, but this is no more serious than that observed in many brain-injured patients who have no problems with face recognition (Newcombe *et al.* 1989b). PH's language abilities are well preserved, and he has normal short-term memory, but shows poor performance on long-term memory tasks and on some visuospatial tasks. He can read, and can recognize many (not all) seen objects, but is profoundly impaired at recognizing familiar faces. Most faces he simply says are unfamiliar, though there are about a dozen faces (from the hundreds he has been shown) that he has recognized occasionally. The only face we have noticed being fairly consistently recognized is Mrs Thatcher's.

On formal tests, PH recognized 0/20 highly familiar faces, and was at chance level (18/36 correct) at deciding whether faces were familiar (De Haan *et al.*, 1987b). Even in a forced-choice task in which he was only asked to pick which one of two simultaneously presented faces (one familiar, one unfamiliar) was the familiar person, PH was at chance level (65/128 correct), yet he was much more accurate (118/128 correct) on a parallel task involving those people's names (Young & De Haan, 1988), showing that he has not forgotten who they are.

Although PH's ability to recognize faces overtly is so badly impaired, we have found considerable evidence of covert recognition. In matching tasks, PH showed faster matching (as same or different) of pairs of photographs of familiar faces than of unfamiliar faces, which indicates that some information about known faces as familiar visual patterns is preserved, even if he is unaware of it (De Haan *et al.*, 1987b). As for normal subjects (Young *et al.*, 1985b), PH was only faster at matching photographs of familiar than unfamiliar faces when matches had to be based on the faces' internal (eyes, nose, mouth) rather than external (hair, face shape, chin) features (De Haan *et al.*, 1987b). This normal pattern of responses to familiar and unfamiliar faces was found despite PH's inability to identify the familiar faces overtly.

By using interference tasks, De Haan *et al.* (1987a,b) also showed that information about the semantic category to which a face belonged was accessed covertly by PH. In these tasks PH was asked to classify printed *names* as those of politicians or non-politicians. His reaction times for name classification were longer when the names were accompanied by distractor faces drawn from the opposite semantic category than when a distractor face was not present, or when the distractor face came from the same semantic category. The same pattern of interference of faces on name classification is found for normal subjects (Young *et al.*, 1986). Unlike normal subjects, though, PH could not usually achieve accurate overt classification as politicians or non-politicians of the distractor faces used. For example, in the second of the interference tasks described by De Haan *et al* (1987b, Task 4), PH was only 55.5% correct at classifying the faces used into one of two semantic categories (politicians or television personalities; chance performance = 50% correct), yet he showed interference from the semantic categories of face distractors when asked to classify printed names.

Perhaps the most interesting results of all have been obtained with associative priming (Young *et al.*, 1988). Associative priming tasks examine the influence of one stimulus on the recognition of a related stimulus; for instance, the effect of seeing Prince Charles's face on recognition of Princess Diana's name. Recognition of a target stimulus is facilitated by an immediately preceding prime stimulus which is a close associate of the target (Bruce & Valentine 1986). PH shows associative priming from faces he does not recognize. Table 4.1 shows his mean correct reaction times for classification of target names as

TABLE 4.1

Reaction times (in milliseconds) for PH's correct responses to target names of familiar people preceded by related, neutral, or unrelated face or name primes (data from Young et al., 1988)

	Related	Neutral	Unrelated
Face primes	1016	1080	1117
Name primes	945	1032	1048

familiar when they are preceded by face or name primes (reaction times to unfamiliar names are not shown). The data are taken from Young et al. (1988), who presented primes to PH for 450 ms each, with a 50-ms inter-stimulus interval before onset of the target name. Three types of prime were used: related (for example, Prince Charles as a prime for the target name 'Princess Diana'), neutral (an unfamiliar prime with a familiar target name), or unrelated (for example, John Lennon as a prime for the target name 'Princess Diana').

As the data in Table 4.1 show, PH recognized familiar target names more quickly when they were preceded by related face primes than when they were preceded by neutral or by unrelated face primes. Hence he shows associative priming from faces he does not recognize overtly (in a separate post-test given immediately after the experiment, PH could only recognize 2/20 of the familiar faces used). The nature of the associative priming for PH is that thought by Posner and Snyder (1975) to characterize a purely automatic effect, since there is facilitation of responses to related targets (related < neutral) without inhibition of responses to unrelated targets (neutral = unrelated). Moreover, it is possible to compare the size of the priming effect onto name targets, across face primes (which PH doesn't recognize overtly) and printed name primes (which he recognizes without difficulty). These are exactly equivalent; the possibility of overt recognition of name primes makes no additional contribution to the associative priming effect.

We adapted the use of learning tasks to show covert recognition from the work of Bruyer et al. (1983). Bruyer et al. (1983) found that their prosopagnosic patient learnt 'true' pairings of faces and names more readily than he learnt 'untrue' combinations. That is, when shown a particular face he could learn to associate the correct name to it more easily than someone else's name. This was also true for PH, and it even applied to faces of people who had only become known to PH since his accident (we used photographs of our own faces). This shows that his recognition system has continued to build up representations of faces of the people he meets, even though he does not recognize them overtly (De Haan et al. 1987b).

4.4. PRESENCE AND ABSENCE OF COVERT RECOGNITION

We have seen that for PH there is a striking difference between his inability to recognize faces overtly and the evidence of preserved, covert recognition. A question which thus arises concerns whether such findings will hold for all patients with severely impaired overt face recognition ability. The answer is that they do not; patients who fail to show covert recognition have been described (Bauer, 1986; Newcombe *et al.*, 1989a; Sergent & Villemure, 1989; Young & Ellis, 1989b; Humphreys *et al.*, Chapter 3, this volume).

To illustrate this point, we will consider the patient MS (Newcombe *et al.*, 1989a), who has been tested with most of the procedures used with PH. MS is a former police cadet who contracted a febrile illness in 1970, at the age of 23. He has normal visual acuity, but experiences severe problems in object recognition, and is completely unable to recognize familiar faces. Previous studies of his object recognition impairment reached the conclusion that even though MS can make accurate copies of drawings of objects which he cannot recognize, he suffers a form of higher-order perceptual impairment which interferes with the construction of object-centred representations (Newcombe & Ratcliff, 1974; Ratcliff & Newcombe, 1982).

Table 4.2 shows a comparison of MS, PH, and a patient we will discuss later, BD, on forced-choice familiarity decision tasks in which the patients are asked to choose which of two faces (one familiar, one unfamiliar) or which of two names (one familiar, one unfamiliar) is familiar. As can be seen, MS's overt face recognition abilities are as badly impaired as those of PH yet, like PH, MS remains able to recognize familiar names.

Unlike PH, however, MS shows no evidence of covert recognition of familiar faces. Table 4.3 shows MS's reaction times to familiar name targets preceded by related, neutral, or unrelated face or name primes

TABLE 4.2

Forced-choice familiarity decision to faces and names by MS (Newcombe *et al.*, 1989a), PH (Young & De Haan, 1988), and BD (Hanley *et al.*, 1989)

	Faces	Names
MS	67/128	116/128
PH	65/128	118/128
BD	97/128	101/128

TABLE 4.3

Reaction times (in milliseconds) for MS's correct responses to target names of familiar people preceded by related, neutral, or unrelated face or name primes (data from Newcombe *et al.*, 1989a)

	Related	Neutral	Unrelated
Face primes	1260	1276	1264
Name primes	1178	1370	1439

(Newcombe *et al.*, 1989a). Only the name primes, which MS can recognize overtly, produced any facilitation of his responses. Similarly, in learning tasks MS showed no facilitation in the learning of true as compared to untrue names to faces, either for faces known to him before or since his illness.

Evidently, then, there are different forms of prosopagnosia. This has been pointed out before (Meadows, 1974; Hécaen, 1981; Jeeves, 1984), but investigations of covert recognition have been useful in confirming the suggestion. Patients like MS show clear signs of higher-order perceptual impairment (Ratcliff & Newcombe, 1982), which probably affects the structural encoding of faces sufficiently to prevent any form of recognition. This is consistent with the distinction between perceptual and mnestic forms of prosopagnosia emphasized in some clinical studies (Hécaen, 1981; Jeeves, 1984; De Renzi, 1986a).

Some of the other cases of prosopagnosia without covert recognition reported to date (Bauer, 1986; Sergent & Villemure, 1989; Young & Ellis, 1989b; Humphreys *et al.*, Chapter 3, this volume) have also involved higher-order perceptual impairment. However, it has become clear from recent work by Etcoff *et al.* (1991) and McNeil and Warrington (1991) that the perceptual versus mnestic distinction is insufficient to account for the full range of findings on presence or absence of covert recognition, since Etcoff *et al.*'s (1991) patient did *not* show covert recognition despite having many well-preserved perceptual abilities, and McNeil and Warrington (1991) found evidence of less intact perception for their cases with covert recognition. Both Etcoff *et al.* (1991) and McNeil and Warrington (1991) conclude that brain injury can selectively eliminate stored information about the appearance of familiar faces; in Bruce and Young's (1986) terms this would be equivalent to loss of the face recognition units.

4.5. DIRECT AND INDIRECT TESTS

With the benefit of hindsight, findings of covert recognition in prosopagnosia need not have been so unexpected. There is a clear parallel with the findings of implicit memory from studies of amnesia (Warrington & Weiskrantz, 1968, 1970; Schacter, 1987), and there are also related findings from other types of visual impairment, ranging from blindsight (Weiskrantz *et al.*, 1974; Weiskrantz, 1986) to visual neglect (Marshall & Halligan, 1988). These have been reviewed by Schacter *et al.* (1988) and Young and De Haan (1990).

In order to provide some form of common general account of these phenomena, which are related in that they all involve the breakdown of different aspects of awareness after brain injury, much use has been made of constrasts between 'overt' and 'covert', and 'explicit' and 'implicit'. These contrasts can be useful, but they also pose problems. One of these is a danger that 'overt' is beginning to be seen as interchangeable with 'explicit', and 'covert' as interchangeable with 'implicit'. We had found that we were starting to do this ourselves, but now recognize that there are important distinctions to be drawn.

A key distinction is between the nature of the tasks used and patients' *insight* into their abilities. Here, we have used 'overt' and 'covert' to refer to patients' *insight* into their recognition abilities. Overt abilities are ones that the patient knows she or he possesses, whereas covert abilities are found in the absence of acknowledged awareness.

To classify tasks, we will use the terms 'direct' and 'indirect' (Humphreys, 1981; Reingold & Merikle, 1988, 1990). A task intended as a direct test will directly enquire about the ability of interest ('Whose face is this?' 'Which is familiar?', etc.), whereas in an indirect test the ability in question is introduced as an incidental feature of a task that ostensibly measures something else (effects of familiarity on face matching, effects of different types of face prime on *name* recognition, etc.).

In terms of the findings we have discussed so far, PH shows a neat pattern of preserved covert recognition of familiar faces on indirect tests, whilst failing all direct tests. For some time, we were convinced that this would hold quite generally, and were willing to equate covert recognition with the use of indirect tests. However, we now know that there are important exceptions.

The first exception is that not all indirect tests produce evidence of covert recognition. We will discuss this point in more detail in Section 4.6 of this chapter. All that we need to mention at the moment is that whether PH shows better learning of true than untrue pairings in learning tasks is critically dependent on the type of material to be learnt to each face (Young & De Haan, 1988). For learning of full names and general occupational categories there is better performance to true pairings, indicating covert recognition, but for first names and quite 'precise' semantic information (such as a politician's specific party) untrue pairings can be learnt with no more difficulty than true pairings. Hence characterizing a task as indirect is not in itself sufficient to produce evidence of covert recognition.

The second exception is that not all direct tests are performed at chance level. Our attention was first drawn to this by the work of Sergent and Poncet (1990). They asked their prosopagnosic patient, PV, to choose which of two names (one correct, the other a distractor belonging to a person of the same sex and occupation) went with a particular face. Her performance (40/48 correct) was well above chance, though below that of control subjects (who made no errors). We find that PH also performs this task at an overall level which is well above chance, though obviously impaired (30/40, 27/40, 26/40, and 27/40 correct in four separate runs; De Haan et al., in press).

In our terms, this forced-choice decision between two alternative names for a face is a direct test, because it asks about identity ('Which name is correct for the face?'). An important issue, however, concerns whether it elicits covert or overt face recognition abilities. Sergent and Poncet (1990) argue that overt recognition is not involved, because PV did not know when she had chosen correctly or incorrectly, and was usually just as ready to make a choice between two names even when these were both incorrect for the face shown. Our findings with PH are the same (De Haan et al., in press). It seems that even though the test is direct, it allows the patient to utilize covert recognition abilities in some way.

We conclude that while contrasts between direct and indirect tests, and overt versus covert abilities, can play an important role in helping us initially to characterize patterns of intact and deficient performance, they are not in themselves an explanation. Instead, we must now move to adopt explanations couched in terms of functional models. One promising way of achieving this is to look more carefully at the levels to which covert processing can be achieved.

4.6. PRESERVED COVERT PROCESSING AT DIFFERENT LEVELS OF RECOGNITION

We have found learning tasks particularly useful in examining preserved covert processing at different levels of recognition. The particular advantage of the learning paradigm for this purpose is that it is easy to vary the type of material to be learnt. Table 4.4 shows the results of doing this with PH (De Haan et al., 1987b; Young & De Haan, 1988). The point of interest is that whether PH shows better learning of true than untrue pairings is dependent on the type of material to be learnt to the familiar faces. Better learning of true pairings was found for full names and for occupational categories ('politician', 'actor', etc.), but was not found for first names ('Jim', 'Bob', etc.) or for relatively detailed, 'precise' semantic information (such as the political parties and backgrounds associated with a group of politicians, or the specific sports associated with a group of sportsmen).

TABLE 4.4

Summary of results of learning tasks for PH (De Haan *et al.*, 1987b; Young & De Haan, 1988) and BD (Hanley *et al.*, 1989)

Type of material to be associated with unrecognized stimulus	Better learning of true than untrue pairings	
	PH	BD
Full names	Yes	Yes
Occupational categories	Yes	Yes
'Precise' semantic information	No	Yes
First names	No	No

Our interpretation of these findings is that the system responsible for covert face recognition by PH only operates at a certain, limited level of recognition. In particular, it does not encompass name retrieval, since PH does not learn true pairings of faces and peoples' first names any better than untrue pairings, and it only includes limited access to semantic category information, since PH shows no benefit from precise semantic information in these learning tasks. We think that the better learning of true pairings of faces and occupations, and faces and full names, can be attributed to some form of limited interaction between the recognition systems that handle face and name inputs (Young & De Haan, 1988).

One of the defining characteristics of prosopagnosia is that recognition of familiar people by non-facial means remains relatively intact. However, we have also had the opportunity to study a post-encephalitic patient, BD, who is poor at recognizing familiar people from face, name, or voice (Hanley *et al.*, 1989). BD is a right-handed man, born in 1929, who suffered herpes simplex encephalitis in 1974. He complains of problems in finding his way around, and difficulties in identifying people other than his wife, immediate family, and close friends. We must emphasize that BD should not be considered prosopagnosic, since he is also unable to recognize many familiar people from non-facial cues. Instead, it is probably more useful to consider his problems as involving a form of semantic memory impairment (Hanley *et al.*, 1989).

Table 4.2 showed BD's ability to recognize faces and names in forced-choice familiarity decision tasks. Notice that he is impaired for both faces and names, but that the impairment for faces is not as severe as that experienced by MS or PH, and he remains able to recognize overtly a proportion of familiar people. This makes it relatively tricky to investigate covert recognition, but we were able to investigate BD's performance in learning tasks using faces or names of people he failed to identify in initial screening tests. Better learning of true than untrue pairings of faces and full names was found even when both the face and the name were overtly unfamiliar to BD at the start of the experiment.

The most interesting feature of BD's learning task performance, however, is that unlike PH he did show better learning of true than untrue combinations of faces and precise semantic information. Similarly, he also showed better learning of true than untrue combinations of names and precise semantic information (Hanley *et al.*, 1989).

This pattern is perhaps as one might expect on the view that, since BD's impairment affects faces, voices, and names, it must be sited more 'deeply' in the recognition system than PH's, at a point where domain-specific representations are no longer involved. In this respect it is interesting that BD does not show evidence of covert name retrieval from faces in face + first name learning tasks.

The contrast between BD and PH, then, shows that awareness of recognition can break down at different levels. This point about the importance of the level of breakdown is also seen in a more dramatic form in cases where patients are unaware of their impaired ability to recognize faces overtly.

4.7. UNAWARENESS OF IMPAIRED FACE RECOGNITION

One of the most striking effects of brain injury involves patients who are unaware of their impairments and thus may fail to comprehend or even actively deny their problems. This is called anosognosia. A wide range of types of impairment can be subject to anosognosia; here we consider unawareness of impaired face recognition.

A review of studies of unawareness of deficits in neuropsychological conditions has been made by McGlynn and Schacter (1989). It is clear that the patients who show unawareness of impairment are not necessarily demented, and experience no global change of consciousness. Conversely, patients who are disoriented and confused may none the less continue to achieve insight into their cognitive impairments (Parkin *et al.*, 1987). Thus there is evidence for a double dissociation between anosognosias and more general impairments of consciousness.

The view that unawareness of impairment cannot be attributed to global changes in consciousness is strengthened by the important observation that patients with more than one deficit may be unaware of one impairment yet perfectly well aware of others. Von Monakow (1885), for instance, noted that a patient who had been left almost blind after extensive bilateral brain lesions complained of other problems, even though he was not aware of his visual impairment. Anton (1899) made similar observations, and suggested that unawareness of impairment of a particular function is caused by a disorder at the highest levels of organization of *that* function. This position has been further developed by Bisiach *et al.* (1986), who demonstrated dissociations between anosognosia for hemiplegia and anosognosia for hemianopia. Bisiach *et al.* (1986, p. 480) conclude that 'monitoring of the internal working is not secured in the nervous system by a general, superordinate organ, but is decentralized and apportioned to the different functional blocks to which it refers'. There is evidence, then, to suggest that unawareness of impairment does not result from any general change in the patient's state of consciousness, but can be specific to particular disabilities.

Patients with severe face recognition problems are often very concerned and frustrated by them (see, for example, Newcombe, 1979, p. 318; De Renzi, 1986b, Case 1, p. 172), but unawareness of face recognition problems has also been previously reported. Kertesz (1979) described a closed head injury patient with memory problems, alexia, object agnosia and prosopagnosia, who never complained of visual difficulty, and if asked directly denied it or gave a confabulatory response. Landis *et al.* (1986) reported six cases of prosopagnosia, four of whom showed unconcern or denial of their face recognition problems. Sergent and Villemure's (1988) right hemispherectomy patient with prosopagnosia also showed no awareness of her deficit.

One of the most interesting reports of unawareness of face recognition problems is that of Levine (1978), whose patient had object and face recognition impairments, and admitted some blurring of vision and problems in object recognition, yet denied having difficulties with faces. Levine's (1978) case thus suggests that a degree of deficit-specificity may also be possible in cases of unawareness of impaired face recognition. This is strongly supported by the patient we were able to investigate, SP (Young *et al.*, 1990).

SP was a right-handed woman who suffered a sub-arachnoid haemorrhage from a right middle cerebral artery aneurysm. She performed poorly on several face processing tasks, including perception of facial expressions, unfamiliar face matching, and identification of familiar faces. Table 4.5 shows her performance of a variety of face processing tasks at different dates.

Identification of familiar people from non-facial cues (names) remained relatively well preserved for SP, but severe problems were evident for face recognition. Her errors mostly involved either failures to find a face familiar at all, or misidentification as another familiar person. In face–name learning tasks, there was evidence of covert recognition of faces SP failed to recognize overtly.

SPs face processing impairment remained stable across a 20-month period of investigation (see Table 4.5), during which one of the most striking features was her complete lack of insight into her face recognition difficulties. She was not distressed by her inability to recognize many familiar faces, and maintained that she recognized faces 'as well as before'. Her denials of her face recognition impairment were made

TABLE 4.5

SP's performance of face processing tasks at different dates (data from Young et al., 1990)

Face processing task	SP			Controls		
	June 1986	September 1986	February 1988	Mean	SD	n
Mooney faces	18/40	—	17/40	31.3	5.8	32
Benton test	32/54	30/54	34/54	44.4	3.0	38
Expression matching	—	11/18	11/18	16.3	1.7	34
Expression labelling	—	15/24	13/24	21.1	1.7	34
Famous face recognition	—	3/20	4/20	15.4	3.6	11

in a polite, somewhat detached, matter-of-fact way, with occasional expressions of mild surprise or disbelief if we continued to suggest that there might be any problem. She maintained that she had no problem in recognizing faces in everyday life, in paintings, on the television, in newspapers or magazines.

When directly confronted with her failure to recognize photographs of familiar faces, SP could only offer the suggestion that the photograph was a 'poor likeness', or that she had 'no recollection of having seen that person before'. She had been a talented amateur artist, specializing in portraiture. After her illness, though, she could only recognize the portraits she had painted by careful deduction from the sitter's age, sex, background details, etc. When asked about her inability spontaneously to recognize her own paintings, she commented only that she 'had recognized them', and did not seem to think that there was anything unusual about the laborious method she used to achieve this. As Anton (1899) had noted, anosognosic patients are not only unaware of their impairment, but seem also to have lost all knowledge of what it was like to have the relevant ability.

In contrast to her lack of insight into her face recognition impairment, SP showed adequate insight into other physical and cognitive impairments produced by her illness, including poor memory, hemiplegia, and hemianopia. Thus SP did not suffer any general lack of insight into her problems; yet throughout the period of investigation she showed no awareness of her difficulties in recognizing faces.

These findings bear out the point that unawareness of impairment does not result from any general change in the patient's state of consciousness, but can be specific to particular disabilities; SP's lack of insight into her face recognition impairment involved a deficit-specific anosognosia. Like Bisiach et al. (1986), we consider that such deficit-specific anosognosias reflect the existence of the need to monitor our own performance in everyday life. Monitoring is necessary to correct errors we sometimes make, and also because different types of information must sometimes be intentionally combined and evaluated.

Young *et al.* (1985a), for instance, give several examples of everyday face recognition problems involving decision processes, such as being unsure whether or not a seen person really is person 'X'. The point is neatly illustrated by Thomson (1986), who asked the daughter of an Australian couple to stand outside a London hotel when her parents thought she was in Australia. They recognized their daughter, but when she (deliberately) did not respond, her father apologized; 'I am terribly sorry, I thought you were someone else'. Decision processes have also been implicated in delusional misidentification syndromes found in neuropsychiatric conditions (Ellis & Young, 1990; Young *et al.*, 1990).

Impairment of such monitoring and decision processes is, in our view, what causes anosognosias. In this respect, it is interesting that a number of SP's errors in recognizing familiar people involved frank misidentifications of one familiar person for another. Although common in everyday errors (but usually quickly corrected; see Young *et al.*, 1985), this is a phenomenon we had not encountered before in our investigations of face recognition impairments caused by brain injury. We draw attention to it here because it is consistent with the idea that SP's monitoring and decision processes were defective, since such errors are usually quickly corrected by normal people.

As Bisiach *et al.* (1986) point out, the existence of deficit-specific anosognosias suggests that this monitoring does not involve a common central monitoring mechanism, but is to some degree decentralized.

4.8. EXPLAINING BREAKDOWNS OF AWARENESS

We have seen that even for what might be considered a circumscribed skill, face recognition, awareness can break down in different ways following brain injury. Patients like PH continue to show covert recognition of faces that are not recognized overtly, whereas patients like MS show neither overt nor covert recognition. Even when covert effects are found, they do not encompass all aspects of face recognition. For example, there was no evidence of covert name retrieval to familiar faces in the learning tasks used with PH. There are also indications, as in the contrast between PH and BD, that covert recognition may proceed to different levels, depending on the nature of the overt recognition impairment. Finally, there is also a type of impairment which affects the patient's ability to monitor her or his own face recognition abilities, leading to unawareness of impaired face recognition in SP.

In all these cases, there is no global alteration of consciousness, but specific aspects of awareness of recognition of familiar faces can be lost. It is clear that recognition and awareness of recognition are not the same thing, and hence that awareness is not integral to the operation of perceptual mechanisms in the way that has often been supposed (see Marcel, 1983).

Can we achieve more precise accounts of these breakdowns of awareness? There are some existing theories which seek to explain covert recognition in prosopagnosia. We have already discussed the widely used implicit versus explicit distinction, and explained our view that although the distinction is an important one it is now being asked to do too much theoretical work. What other explanations are possible?

The most detailed account of covert recognition was given in the original paper by Bauer (1984). Bauer (1984) proposed that neurologically dissociable information processing routes are involved in overt recognition and in orienting responses to emotionally salient stimuli. This proposal is elegant, and useful in that it can potentially be extended to provide an account of other conditions such as Capgras' syndrome (Ellis & Young, 1990), but it suffers from the limitation that covert recognition effects can be found in cases of prosopagnosia even to faces of people who seem to have little emotional importance to the patient.

Tranel and Damasio (1985) suggested that covert recognition arises when 'facial templates' are intact, but the processes required for the 'activation of multimodal associations' from the face are defective. This does seem to capture part of the problem, but it is insufficiently detailed to provide a satisfying account. For example, the findings of Bruyer et al. (1983), De Haan et al. (1987a,b), Young et al. (1988), and Young and De Haan (1988), which we summarized here, all imply that some multimodal associations are implicated in covert recognition, since in all these reports a salient characteristic of covert face recognition was its ability to influence name processing.

Recent investigations of covert recognition in prosopagnosia have made the point that for cases like PII (De Haan et al., 1987b) or LF (Bauer, 1984) what seems to be preserved are those aspects of recognition whose operation is automatic, and does not require conscious initiation (Schacter et al., 1988; Young, 1988; Young & De Haan, 1990). Hence we have argued that covert recognition effects in prosopagnosia reflect the operation of a partially isolated face recognition system, whose outputs are disconnected from systems responsible for awareness but remain able to interact in a limited way with other input recognition systems (Young & De Haan, 1988). The parallel with other types of neuropsychological impairment that can also be seen as involving different types of defective access to consciousness is an intriguing one that we are keen to pursue (Schacter et al., 1988; Young, 1988; Young & De Haan, 1990).

A contrast could be made between this type of account, which postulates that part of the recognition system has become disconnected, and accounts which emphasize *damage* to the recognition system itself. Damage to the recognition system might, for instance, lead to the

patient only experiencing weak degrees of recognition. We have preferred to emphasize the disconnection hypothesis as an account of PH's
difficulties because we are impressed that the *pattern* of PH's responses
in many indirect face recognition tasks is so close to normal, whereas
we would have expected damage to the recognition system to attenuate
or distort this pattern. It is true, though, that PH's reaction times are
often longer than those of normal people of comparable age. However,
we attribute this to a generalized slowing consequent on his closed-
head injury, since his responses are slow even to tasks which do not
involve faces (such as name recognition with name primes; see Table
4.1).

Although we favour a disconnection explanation, this does not
necessarily mean that the problem has to be absolute and insuperable.
This has recently been demonstrated in a remarkable manner by Sergent
and Poncet (1990), who also offer an explanation of the disconnection
type.

Sergent and Poncet (1990) found that if they presented together eight
faces which were members of the same semantic (occupational) category, their prosopagnosic patient PV was able to recognize overtly the
faces from two of the four occupational categories used. This happened
only if she could determine the appropriate category herself. For the
two categories PV could not determine, she continued to fail to recognize the faces overtly even when the occupational category was pointed
out to her. When the same faces were later presented one at a time in
random order, PV was again unable to recognize any of them, including those she had recognized when they were placed in appropriate
category groupings.

We have been able to replicate this phenomenon of overt recognition
provoked by presentation of multiple exemplars of a semantic category
with PH (De Haan *et al.*, in press). Table 4.6 shows data from a task
in which PH was asked to recognize faces from three broadly defined
semantic categories (politicians, television presenters, and comedians)
and three narrowly defined categories (the television soap operas
'Neighbours', 'Eastenders', and 'Coronation Street'). There were eight
faces from each category. It can be seen that there was a marked
improvement in his ability to recognize the 'Eastenders' faces when
these were all presented simultaneously (the Category Presentation
condition), and that (in contrast to Sergent & Poncet's (1990) findings)
this improvement generalized to an Immediate Post-test with the faces
presented one at a time in pseudo-random order. The improvement
did, though, dissipate across a 2-month interval (Delayed Post-test).

Sergent and Poncet (1990) suggest that their demonstration shows
that 'neither the facial representations nor the semantic information
were critically disturbed in PV, and her prosopagnosia must thus reflect
faulty connections between faces and their memories, perhaps
characterized by a heightened threshold of activation of the information

TABLE 4.6
Number (max = 8) of correct (+) and incorrect (−) overt identifications by PH in the different conditions of a category presentation task. These involved a Pre-test with the faces in pseudo-random order, simultaneous presentation of all 8 faces from a particular Category, and an Immediate Post-test and Delayed Post-test (after a 2-month interval) with pseudo-random ordering

					Post-test			
		Category						
	Pre-test		presentation		Immediate		Delayed	
	+	−	+	−	+	−	+	−
Broad categories								
Politicians	0	0	0	0	0	0	0	0
TV presenters	0	0	0	0	0	4	0	1
Comedians	2	2	1	0	2	2	1	0
Narrow categories								
'Neighbours'	0	0	1	0	1	0	0	0
'Eastenders'	1	0	6	0	5	0	1	0
'Coronation St'	0	0	1	0	1	1	0	0

that underlies conscious recognition'. They hypothesize that the simultaneous presentation of several members of the same category may have temporarily raised the activation level above the appropriate threshold.

The disruption of overt face recognition in prosopagnosia is usually so complete that findings of covert recognition have been a considerable surprise. One cannot fail to be even more impressed by the finding that overt recognition can be provoked under certain conditions, at least for some patients (and some faces). This not only enhances our understanding of the underlying deficit (or one of its forms, at any rate) but offers the hope that, given sufficient ingenuity, we may be able to find ways to help at least some of the people who suffer these very disabling conditions.

ACKNOWLEDGEMENTS

Our work on recognition impairments is supported by MRC grant G 890469N to Edward De Haan and Andy Young, MRC grant PG 7301443 to Freda Newcombe and John Marshall, and by ESRC grant R 000231922 to Andy Young, Rick Hanley and Freda Newcombe. We are grateful to the Press Association and the Lancashire Evening Post for help in finding suitable photographs for use as stimuli.

REFERENCES

Anton, G. (1899). Ueber die Selbstwahrnemung der Herderkrankungen des Gehirns durch den Kranken bei Rindenblindheit und Rindentaubheit. *Archiv für Psychiatrie und Nervenkrankheiten*, **32**, 86–127.

Bauer, R.M. (1984). Autonomic recognition of names and faces in prosopagnosia: a neuropsychological application of the guilty knowledge test. *Neuropsychologia*, **22**, 457–469.

Bauer, R.M. (1986). The cognitive psychophysiology of prosopagnosia. In H.D. Ellis, M.A. Jeeves, F. Newcombe and A. Young (eds), *Aspects of Face Processing*. Dordrecht: Martinus Nijhoff.

Bisiach, E., Vallar, G., Perani, D., Papagno, C. & Berti, A. (1986). Unawareness of disease following lesions of the right hemisphere: anosognosia for hemiplegia and anosognosia for hemianopia. *Neuropsychologia*, **24**, 471–482.

Bodamer, J. (1947). Die Prosop-Agnosie. *Archiv für Psychiatrie und Nervenkrankheiten*, **179**, 6–53.

Bruce, V. (1988). *Recognising Faces*. London: Lawrence Erlbaum.

Bruce, V. & Valentine, T. (1986). Semantic priming of familiar faces. *Quarterly Journal of Experimental Psychology*, **38A**, 125–150.

Bruce, V. & Young, A. (1986). Understanding face recognition. *British Journal of Psychology*, **77**, 305–327.

Bruyer, R., Laterre, C., Seron, X., Feyereisen, P., Strypstein, E., Pierrard, E. & Rectem, D. (1983). A case of prosopagnosia with some preserved covert remembrance of familiar faces. *Brain and Cognition*, **2**, 257–284.

Burton, A.M., Bruce, V. & Johnston, R.A. (1990). Understanding face recognition with an interactive activation model. *British Journal of Psychology*, **81**, 361–380.

Damasio, A.R., Damasio, H. & Van Hoesen, G.W. (1982). Prosopagnosia: anatomic basis and behavioral mechanisms. *Neurology*, **32**, 331–341.

De Haan, E.H.F., Young, A. & Newcombe, F. (1987a). Faces interfere with name classification in a prosopagnosic patient. *Cortex*, **23**, 309–316.

De Haan, E.H.F., Young, A. & Newcombe, F. (1987b). Face recognition without awareness. *Cognitive Neuropsychology*, **4**, 385–415.

De Haan, E.H.F., Young, A.W. & Newcombe, F. (1991). A dissociation between the sense of familiarity and access to semantic information concerning familiar people. *European Journal of Cognitive Psychology*, **3**, 51–67.

De Haan, E.H.F., Young, A.W. & Newcombe, F. Covert and overt recognition in prosopagnosia. *Brain*, in press.

De Renzi, E. (1986a). Current issues in prosopagnosia. In H.D. Ellis, M.A. Jeeves, F. Newcombe and A. Young (eds) *Aspects of Face Processing*, Dordrecht: Martinus Nijhoff.

De Renzi, E. (1986b). Slowly progressive visual agnosia or apraxia without dementia. *Cortex*, **22**, 171–180.

Ellis, A.W., Young, A.W. & Hay, D.C. (1987). Modelling the recognition of faces and words. In P.E. Morris (ed.), *Modelling Cognition*. Chichester: Wiley.

Ellis, H.D. (1986). Processes underlying face recognition. In R. Bruyer (ed.). *The Neuropsychology of Face Perception and Facial Expression*. New Jersey: Erlbaum.

Ellis, H.D. & Young, A.W. (1989). Are faces special? In A.W. Young and H.D. Ellis (eds), *Handbook of Research on Face Processing*. Amsterdam: North Holland.

Ellis, H.D. & Young, A.W. (1990). Accounting for delusional misidentifications. *British Journal of Psychiatry*, **157**, 239–248.

Etcoff, N.L., Freeman, R. & Cave, K.R. (1991). Can we lose memories of faces? Content specificity and awareness in a prosopagnosic. *Journal of Cognitive Neuroscience*, **3**, 25–41.

Flude, B.M., Ellis, A.W. & Kay, J. (1989). Face processing and name retrieval in an anomic aphasic: names are stored separately from semantic information about familiar people. *Brain and Cognition*, **11**, 60–72.

Hanley, J.R. & Cowell, E.S. (1988). The effects of different types of retrieval cues on the recall of names of famous faces. *Memory and Cognition*, **16**, 545–555.

Hanley, J.R. Young, A.W. & Pearson, N. (1989). Defective recognition of familiar people. *Cognitive Neuropsychology*, **6**, 179–210.

Hay, D.C. & Young, A.W. (1982). The human face. In A.W. Ellis (ed.), *Normality and Pathology in Cognitive Functions*. London: Academic Press.

Hay, D.C., Young, A.W. & Ellis, A.W. (1991). Routes through the face recognition system. *Quarterly Journal of Experimental Psychology*, in press.

Hécaen, H. (1981). The neuropsychology of face recognition. In G. Davies, H. Ellis and J. Shepherd (eds), *Perceiving and Remembering Faces*. London: Academic Press.

Hécaen, H. & Angelergues, R. (1962). Agnosia for faces (prosopagnosia). *Archives of Neurology*, **7**, 92–100.

Humphreys, G.W. (1981). Direct vs. indirect tests of the information available from masked displays: what visual masking does and does not prevent. *British Journal of Psychology*, **72**, 323–330.

Jeeves, M.A. (1984). The historical roots and recurring issues of neurobiological studies of face perception. *Human Neurobiology*, **3**, 191–196.

Kertesz, A. (1979). Visual agnosia: the dual deficit of perception and recognition. *Cortex*, **15**, 403–419.

Landis, T., Cummings, J.L. Christen, L., Bogen, J.E. & Imhof, H-G. (1986). Are unilateral right posterior cerebral lesions sufficient to cause prosopagnosia? Clinical and radiological findings in six additional patients. *Cortex*, **22**, 243–252.

Levine, D.N. (1978). Prosopagnosia and visual object agnosia: a behavioral study. *Brain and Language*, **5**, 341–365.

McGlynn, S. & Schacter, D.L. (1989). Unawareness of deficits in neuropsychological syndromes. *Journal of Clinical and Experimental Neuropsychology*, **11**, 143–205.

McNeil, J.E. & Warrington, E.K. (1991). Prosopagnosia: a reclassification. *Quarterly Journal of Experimental Psychology*, **43A**, 267–287.

Marcel, A.J. (1983). Conscious and unconscious perception: an approach to the relations between phenomenal experience and perceptual processes. *Cognitive Psychology*, **15**, 238–300.

Marshall, J.C. & Halligan, P.W. (1988). Blindsight and insight in visuo-spatial neglect. *Nature*, **336**, 766–767.

Meadows, J.C. (1974). The anatomical basis of prosopagnosia. *Journal of Neurology, Neurosurgery, and Psychiatry*, **37**, 489–501.

Newcombe, F. (1979). The processing of visual information in prosopagnosia and acquired dyslexia: functional versus physiological interpretation. In D.J. Oborne, M.M. Gruneberg and J.R. Eiser (eds), *Research in Psychology and Medicine*, Vol 1. London: Academic Press.

Newcombe, F. & Ratcliff, G. (1974). Agnosia: a disorder of object recognition. In F. Michel and B. Schott (eds). *Les Syndromes de Disconnexion Calleuse Chez l'Homme*. Lyon: Colloque Internationale de Lyon.

Newcombe, F., Young, A.W. & De Haan, E.H.F. (1989a). Prosopagnosia and object agnosia without covert recognition. *Neuropsychologia*, **27**, 179–191.

Newcombe, F., De Haan, E.H.F., Ross, J. & Young, A.W. (1989b). Face processing, laterality, and contrast sensitivity. *Neuropsychologia*, **27**, 523–538.

Parkin, A.J., Miller, J. & Vincent, R. (1987). Multiple neuropsychological deficits due to anoxic encephalopathy: a case study. *Cortex*, **23**, 655–665.

Parry, F.M., Young, A.W., Saul, J.S.M. & Moss, A. (1991) Dissociable face processing impairments after brain injury. *Journal of Clinical and Experimental Neuropsychology*, **13**, 545–558.

Posner, M.I. & Snyder, C.R.R. (1975). Facilitation and inhibition in the processing of signals. In P.M.A. Rabbitt and S. Dornic (eds), *Attention and Performance*, V, pp. 669–682. London: Academic Press.

Ratcliff, G. & Newcombe, F. (1982). Object recognition: Some deductions from the clinical evidence. In A. W. Ellis (ed.), *Normality and Pathology in Cognitive Functions*, pp. 147–171. London: Academic Press.

Reingold, E.M. & Merikle, P.M. (1988). Using direct and indirect measures to study perception without awareness. *Perception and Psychophysics*, **44**, 563–575.

Reingold, E.M. & Merikle, P.M. (1990). On the inter-relatedness of theory and measurement in the study of unconscious processes. *Mind and Language*, **5**, 9–28.

Renault, B., Signoret, J.L., Debruille, B., Breton, F. & Bolgert, F. (1989). Brain potentials reveal covert facial recognition in prosopagnosia. *Neuropsychologia*, **27**, 905–912.

Rizzo, M., Hurtig, R. & Damasio, A.R. (1987). The role of scanpaths in facial recognition and learning. *Annals of Neurology*, **22**, 41–45.

Schacter, D.L. (1987). Implicit memory: history and current status. *Journal of Experimental Psychology: Learning, Memory and Cognition*, **13**, 501–518.

Schacter, D.L., McAndrews, M.P. & Moscovitch, M. (1988). Access to consciousness: dissociations between implicit and explicit knowledge in neuropsychological syndromes. In L. Weiskrantz (ed.), *Thought Without Language* . Oxford: Oxford University Press.

Searle, J. (1984). *Minds, Brains and Science: the 1984 Reith Lectures*. London: British Broadcasting Corporation.

Sergent, J. & Poncet, M. (1990). From covert to overt recognition of faces in a prosopagnosic patient. *Brain*, **113**, 989–1004.

Sergent, J. & Villemure, J-G. (1989). Prosopagnosia in a right hemispherectomized patient. *Brain*, **112**, 975–995.

Thomson, D.M. (1986). Face recognition: more than a feeling of familiarity? in H.D. Ellis, M.A. Jeeves, F. Newcombe and A. Young (eds), *Aspects of Face Processing*. Dordrecht: Martinus Nijhoff.

Tranel, D. & Damasio, A.R. (1985). Knowledge without awareness: an autonomic index of facial recognition by prosopagnosics. *Science*, **228**, 1453–1454.

Tranel, D. & Damasio, A.R. (1988). Non-conscious face recognition in patients with face agnosia. *Behavioural Brain Research*, **30**, 235–249.

Von Monakow, C. (1885). Experimentelle und pathologisch-anatomische Untersuchungen über die Beziehungen der sogenannten Sehsphäre zu den infracorticalen Opticuscentren und zum N. opticus. *Archiv für Psychiatrie und Nervenkrankheiten*, **16**, 151–199.

Warrington, E.K. & Weiskrantz, L. (1968). New method of testing long-term retention with special reference to amnesic patients. *Nature*, **217**, 972–974.

Warrington, E.K. & Weiskrantz, L. (1970). Amnesia: consolidation or retrieval? *Nature*, **228**, 628–630.

Weiskrantz, L. (1986). *Blindsight: a Case Study and Implications*. Oxford: Oxford University Press.

Weiskrantz, L., Warrington, E.K., Sanders, M.D. & Marshall, J. (1974). Visual capacity in the hemianopic field following a restricted occipital ablation. *Brain*, **97**, 709–728.

Young, A.W. (1988). Functional organization of visual recognition. In L. Weiskrantz (ed.), *Thought Without Language*. Oxford: Oxford University Press.

Young, A.W. & Bruce, V. (1991). Perceptual categories and the computation of 'grandmother'. *European Journal of Cognitive Psychology*, **3**, 5–49.

Young, A.W. & De Haan, E.H.F. (1988). Boundaries of covert recognition in prosopagnosia. *Cognitive Neuropsychology*, **5**, 317–336.

Young, A.W. & De Haan, E.H.F. (1990). Impairments of visual awareness. *Mind and Language*, **5**, 29–48.

Young, A.W. & Ellis, H.D. (1989a). Semantic processing. In A.W. Young and H.D. Ellis (eds), *Handbook of Research on Face Processing*. Amsterdam: North Holland.

Young, A.W. & Ellis, H.D (1989b). Childhood prosopagnosia. *Brain and Cognition*, **9**, 16–47.

Young, A.W., Hay, D.C. & Ellis, A.W. (1985a). The faces that launched a thousand slips: everyday difficulties and errors in recognizing people. *British Journal of Psychology*, **76**, 495–523.

Young, A.W., Hay, D.C., McWeeny, K.H., Flude, B.M. & Ellis, A.W. (1985b). Matching familiar and unfamiliar faces on internal and external features. *Perception*, **14**, 737–746.

Young, A.W., Ellis, A.W., Flude, B.M. McWeeny, K.H. & Hay, D.C. (1986). Face–name interference. *Journal of Experimental Psychology: Human Perception and Performance*, **12**, 466–475.

Young, A.W., Hellawell, D. & De Haan, E.H.F. (1988). Cross-domain semantic priming in normal subjects and a prosopagnosic patient. *Quarterly Journal of Experimental Psychology*, **40A**, 561–580.

Young, A.W., De Haan, E.H.F., & Newcombe, F. (1990). Unawareness of impaired face recognition. *Brain and Cognition*, **14**, 1–18.

Young, A.W., Ellis, H.D., Szulecka, T.K. & De Pauw, K.W. (1990). Face processing impairments and delusional misidentification. *Behavioural Neurology*, **3**, 153–168.

CHAPTER 5

Attentional Mechanisms and Conscious Experience

Michael I. Posner and Mary K. Rothbart

5.1. INTRODUCTION

What is the relationship between the study of attention and the under-standing of consciousness? We begin our inquiry into this question by briefly reviewing evidence for the existence of three networks involved in selective attention: the posterior and anterior attention systems and the vigilance system. Although these three networks are neither mutu-ally exclusive nor exhaustive of all aspects of attention, they provide a starting place for reviewing what is currently known about the struc-tures of the human brain's attentional system. We then consider the role of these three networks in awareness and control. We argue that the functions of orienting associated with the operations of the posterior network are relatively easily dissociated from conscious processing, whereas it appears possible that the output of the anterior network pro-vides the content of awareness. The vigilance network appears to influ-ence both the anterior and posterior networks, by increasing the efficiency of orienting by the posterior system and suppressing ongoing activity in the anterior system. This combination produces a subjective state of readiness that is both alert and free of conscious content, which we refer to as the 'clearing of consciousness'.

In the last two sections of this chapter, we relate awareness and con-scious control to issues of development and psychopathology. Although awareness as the output of the anterior system is likely to be present very early in life, aspects of conscious control, including selec-tion and integration of the output of data processing modules and the emergence of verbal control, are important developments in the early years of life. In the final section, we provide examples of the ways in which failures of these aspects of awareness and control are related to psychopathology.

THE NEUROPSYCHOLOGY OF CONSCIOUSNESS
ISBN 0–12–498045–7

5.2. STRUCTURES AND FUNCTIONS OF SELECTIVE ATTENTION

The last 5 years has seen a tremendous increase in our understanding of three networks involved in selective attention (see Posner & Petersen, 1990 for a review). These networks are indicated in Fig. 5.1. Each is involved in the selective aspects of attention in somewhat different ways. Writers on awareness have usually agreed that awareness is selective and that only a relatively narrow range of events is at its focus. It seems reasonable to suppose that the brain systems performing selection produce as an output this focal awareness. This hypothesis would mean that the brain's attentional system produces the contents of awareness in the same way that its visual system organizes the way the visual world is perceived. To develop this hypothesis, we begin by considering the posterior, anterior and vigilance attentional networks.

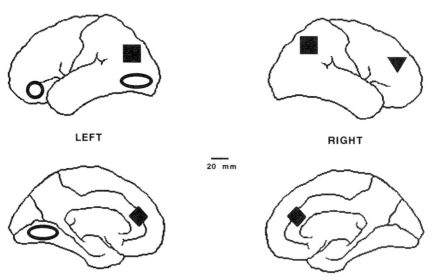

FIGURE 5.1.
This figure illustrates the cortical projections of the attentional networks described in the chapter. The data are mainly from PET studies. The attentional networks are shown by solid shapes on the lateral and medial surfaces of the right and left hemisphere. Squares are the posterior attention network (parietal lobes), triangles, the vigilance network (right frontal) and diamonds, the anterior attention network (anterior cingulate, supplementary motor area). The open shapes refer to word processing systems (Ellipse = visual word form), (circle = semantic associates) that have been shown to relate to the posterior and anterior attention systems respectively.

5.2.1. The Posterior Attention Network

Anatomically, the posterior attention network involves at least portions of the parietal cortex, associated thalamic areas of the pulvinar and reticular nuclei and parts of the midbrain's superior colliculus. These areas co-operate in performing the operations needed to bring attention to a location in space. The posterior system also has close anatomical connections to anterior attention networks and to arousal or vigilance systems (Posner & Petersen, 1990).

The posterior attention network is involved in orienting to sensory stimuli. Most is known about visual attention, but similar systems are available for the other modalities as well (Posner, 1990). The posterior network is involved in directing attention to relevant locations as in visual search, in binding information to spatial locations to produce object perception, and in selecting a relevant scale for examining visual input. The metaphor of a zoom lens has been useful in guiding research on this system. The popularity of lens and spotlight metaphors, despite their obvious inadequacy in detail, reflects the idea that selection is necessary because of the limited capacity of attentional systems. The reason for this limited capacity may lie in the importance of integrating separable features into objects and co-ordinating actions so that behaviour can maintain coherence, rather than in an intrinsic limitation in the neural systems. However, at an empirical level, interference between signals can be used as an indicator of this capacity limitation.

When one attends to a location in visual space, not only is information at that location increased in processing efficiency, but information at other locations is reduced over what it would be if attention had not been paid to the selected location (Posner & Presti, 1987). This basic selective property of attention has been demonstrated for the posterior network by cellular recording, electrical recording from the scalp, detection of near-threshold stimuli and reaction time. There is evidence that injury to the posterior attention system is closely related to specific deficits in the ability to make selections from information contralateral to the lesion (Bisiach, Chapter 6, this volume).

5.2.2. The Anterior Attention Network

A second attention network involves areas of the midprefrontal cortex (including the anterior cingulate gyrus and the closely related but more superior supplementary motor area) that together appear to be active in a wide variety of situations involving the detection of events (Posner & Petersen, 1990). In human adults, this detection is often signalled by a verbal response, but we take this verbalization as evidence that the person has a subjective experience of the target that allows performance of any one of a set of arbitrary detection responses to these targets.

These responses can involve key presses or merely noting or storing the presence of the target for later actions.

Detection plays a special role in the production of interference. People can monitor many input channels at once with little or no interference, but if a target on any one channel is detected, the probability of detection on other channels is greatly restricted (Duncan, 1980). A source of evidence favouring an anterior attention network comes from studying the activity of brain systems during target detection. The degree of activation of the anterior attention system during detection tasks appears to be related not to the number of events presented, but rather to the number of targets presented (Posner et al., 1988). The anterior attention system is also much more active during conflict blocks of the Stroop task than during non conflict blocks (Pardo et al., 1990). Finally, the anterior attention system is active during all tasks requiring subjects to detect target visual stimuli, whether the targets are defined by colour, form, motion, or word semantics (Corbetta et al., 1990; Petersen et al., 1990).

There is a great deal of cognitive evidence on the functional role of attention in relation to word association. We have known for 15 years, for example, that words can have relatively automatic input to their semantic associations, at least under some conditions (Posner, 1978). However, attending to words can modify that effect. If one attends to one meaning of a word, activation of other meanings, at least within the left hemisphere (Burgess & Simpson, 1988), is suppressed. Attending to a word meaning also reduces the ability of unrelated words to be detected. That is, attending to a semantic category retards the speed at which words in other categories are detected. These effects are similar to the enhancements described previously by the posterior attention system when a visual location is attended. We do not have direct evidence that these enhancements require activation of the anterior cingulate, but our interpretation of extant data suggests that they are caused by anterior cingulate interaction with the lateral frontal areas.

There is experimental evidence on the effects of lesions of the anterior cingulate on performance. Bilateral lesions in this area can cause akinetic mutism (Damasio & van Hoesen, 1983), but the presence of recovery of function from lesions in this area and the relatively benign effect of cingulotomy for psychiatric disorders suggest that this area may not be alone in mediating attentional affects. We return to this pathological evidence later in this chapter. Even our Positron Emission Tomography (PET) tasks suggest a whole band of areas involved in attention effects on language, as inferior as the anterior cingulate or as superior as the supplementary motor area (Petersen et al., 1989). The more closely the task is related to actual motor output, the more superior the location of the activation.

The structure of the anterior cingulate in non-human primates is consistent with its role in humans of relating to both semantics and control of the posterior attention network. Research labelling cells in this area shows that alternate columns are connected to the lateral prefrontal cortex (involved in semantic processing in humans) and to the posterior parietal cortex (posterior attention network; Goldman-Rakic, 1988). We now consider the relation between anterior and posterior attention networks.

5.2.3. Relation Between Posterior and Anterior Networks

There are strong anatomical connections between the anterior cingulate and the posterior parietal lobe, at least in the monkey (Goldman-Rakic, 1988). The obvious fact that we can command orienting via high level cognitive strategies requires that there be some connection between the two networks, and this is also suggested by the anatomy. None the less, cognitive studies suggest that they also maintain considerable independence. It is also important that there is a considerable degree of independence in the development and function of the two systems, as we shall see later in this chapter.

A number of recent studies have tried to examine the ability of peripheral and central cues to produce orienting (i.e. to activate the posterior attention system) when the subject is processing another task that would be likely to tie up the anterior attention system (Jonides, 1981; Posner, 1988; Posner *et al.*, 1989; Pashler, 1991). These studies have found some independence between the two systems. The degree of independence appears to depend upon the amount of on-line mental activity required of the primary task. Pashler (1991) showed that a level of primary task activity sufficient to produce interference in several tasks had little effect on shifts of visual attention. However, a study using a more demanding shadowing task showed that the shift of visual attention in response to a cue could be delayed, but not eliminated, by performing the primary task (Posner *et al.*, 1989). There was a large effect on overall reaction time (RT) and a smaller effect on the speed with which subjects were able to shift attention.

5.2.4. The Vigilance Network

Another close connection between awareness, control and the anterior cingulate arises from its relation to the third network of attentional areas that we have labelled the vigilance system (Posner & Petersen, 1990). We believe that this system involves locus coeruleus norepinephrine input to the cortex (see Harley, 1987 for a review). When subjects are required to maintain the alert state in the foreperiod of a reaction time task or when they attend to a source of signals while waiting for an infrequent target to occur (vigilance), there is strong activity in this system (see Posner & Petersen, 1990, for a review of this evidence). This activity shows up in PET scans in the right lateral frontal lobe (see Fig. 5.1). When lesioned, this area gives rise to deficits in the ability to develop and maintain the alert state.

Lateralization of a network for alerting may seem puzzling: both hemispheres need to maintain alertness, and the function seems so basic and simple that there would be little reason for lateral asymmetries. We (Rothbart *et al.*, 1990) believe lateralization of this system to the right hemisphere may reflect its close involvement with regulation of the heart. Heart rate as well as other autonomic systems intimately reflects the attentional state. The heart is asymmetric and there is evidence connecting heart rate changes to the left stellate ganglion which in turn is controlled by the right cerebral cortex. There is much reason to believe that the right hemisphere develops earlier in infancy than does the left, possibly reflecting the need to replace the rapid shifts between sleep and wakefulness in newborns with sustained periods of alertness as the infant develops. The ability to control the alert state in this way is what is called 'vigilance' in adults, where it is indexed by marked slowing of the heart. We speculate that the asymmetric control of the heart produces the asymmetry found in the cortical control of vigilance.

Cohen *et al.* (1988) found an area of the right lateral midfrontal cortex that appears to be the most active during an auditory vigilance task. Of special interest in this report is that the higher metabolic activation was accompanied by reduced activation of the anterior cingulate. If one views the anterior cingulate as related to target detection, this makes sense. In tasks where one needs to suspend activity while waiting for low probability signals, it is important not to interfere with detecting the external event. Subjectively, one feels empty headed, trying to avoid any stray thoughts that might detract from detection of the signal. Objectively, this suspended state has been shown to be effective in reducing loss of information in short-term memory (Reitman, 1971) and in producing a widespread inhibitory effect that includes not only cortical activity but also sympathetically controlled autonomic activity (Kahneman, 1973).

In addition to its effect on the anterior attention system, vigilance also has a clear effect on the posterior attention system. It appears to tune the posterior system so that its interaction with accumulating information in object recognition systems is faster (Posner, 1978). Anatomically it is known that the locus coeruleus (lc) has its primary norepinephrine input to the areas of the posterior attention system, including the parietal, pulvinar and collicular systems (Morrison & Foote, 1986). Within these systems the receptive field sizes of cells can be altered by the simultaneous activity of lc cells. Cognitively, this means that during vigilant states the posterior attention network can interact more efficiently with the object recognition system of the ventral occipital lobe. Thus in highly alert states it is found that responses are faster, with more anticipatory reactions and higher error rates (Posner, 1978).

The operations of the brain's attentional system boost signals within various brain areas. For example, attention to a visual dimension increases blood flow and electrical activity in prestriate areas, and attention to semantic associations boosts activity in lateralized frontal areas. What is the effect of this increase in signal strength? Objectively, it increases the probability of being able to detect the relevant signal. That objective fact is based on the increased probability of being aware or having the subjective experience of the signal. In this sense attention selects the content for our current awareness. But how direct is this control? To examine this issue we turn next to efforts to dissociate awareness and attention.

5.3. AWARENESS AND THE ATTENTIONAL NETWORKS

There is little reason to connect closely the operation of the posterior network in itself to awareness. We have relatively little awareness of guiding our eyes to locations, or it would not have been necessary to conduct experiments showing that covert attention can be dissociated from eye position (Posner, 1980). Eye movements are also poorly represented in consciousness. The eyes move about as we concentrate on semantic or verbal information, and this movement is not readily available to awareness.

When the posterior attention network is oriented toward a location, it boosts the activity of stimuli that occur at that location. This increased signal strength can be shown by reductions in the threshold for detection or by increases in the electrical activity produced by the signal. The impact of a target that occurs at the attended location is thus enhanced with respect to targets at other locations. This is clearly selection. Damage to the posterior attention system produces dramatic effects on our ability to become aware of signals contralateral to the damaged hemisphere. Under conditions where the posterior attention system is drawn to a visual location in an ipsilesional direction, a contralesional target is simply undetected and the patient unaware that it has been presented. However, it is not the posterior network itself that produces awareness of the signal, as can be demonstrated by studies that clearly dissociate orienting to signals from their detection.

A model for dissociating orienting from awareness has arisen in the study of blindsight (Weiskrantz, 1986; Cowey & Stoerig, Chapter 2, this volume). Here there appears to be evidence that at least a crude form of orienting can take place without any awareness of its target. If operations of the posterior attention network were directly related to the output of consciousness, such dissociations would not be possible.

The anterior attention network seems to be much more directly related to awareness than the posterior network, as has been indicated by the PET studies cited previously. The use of subjective experience as evidence for a brain process related to consciousness has been criticized by many authors. However, we note that the evidence for the activation of the anterior cingulate is entirely objective; it does not rest upon any subjective report. Nevertheless, if one defines consciousness in terms of awareness, it is necessary to show evidence that the anterior attention network is related to phenomenal reports in a systematic way. In this section, we note five points, each of which appears to relate subjective experience to activation of the anterior attention system. First, the degree of activation of this network increases as indexed by PET with the number of targets presented in a semantic monitoring task and decreases with the amount of practice in the task. At first one might suppose that target detection is confounded with task difficulty. But in our semantic monitoring task the same semantic decision must be made irrespective of the number of actual targets. In our tasks no storage or counting of targets was needed. Thus we effectively dissociated target detection from task difficulty. None the less anterior cingulate activation was related to number of targets presented. The increase in activation with number of targets and reduction in such activation with practice corresponds to the common finding in cognitive studies that conscious attention is involved in target detection and is required to a greater degree early in practice (Fitts & Posner, 1967). As practice proceeds, feelings of effort and continuous attention diminish, and details of performance drop out of subjective experience.

Second, the anterior system appears to be active during tasks requiring the subject to detect visual stimuli, when the targets require discrimination of colour, form, motion, or word semantics (Petersen et al., 1989; Corbetta et al., 1990).

Third, the anterior attention system is activated when listening passively to words, but not when watching those words. This finding appears to correspond to the subjectively intrusive nature of auditory words to consciousness when they are presented in a quiet background. They seem to capture awareness. Reading does not have this intrusive character. For a visual word to dominate awareness, an act of visual orienting is needed to boost its signal strength.

Fourth, the anterior attention system is more active during conflict blocks of the Stroop test than during non-conflict blocks (Pardo et al., 1990). This is consistent with the commonly held idea that conflict between word name and ink colour produces a strong conscious effort to inhibit saying the written word (Posner, 1978). Finally, there is a relation between the vigilance system and awareness. When one attends to a source of sensory input in order to detect an infrequent target, the subjective feeling is of emptying the head of thoughts or feelings. This subjective 'clearing of consciousness' appears to be accompanied by an increase in activation of the right frontal lobe vigilance network and a reduction in the anterior cingulate. Just as feelings of effort associated with target detection or inhibiting prepotent responses are accompanied by evidence of cingulate activation, so the clearing of thought is accompanied by evidence of cingulate inhibition.

The distinction between the anterior and posterior attention systems may be very important for understanding dissociations between attention and awareness. It has become commonplace to believe that attention can be dissociated from complex information processing. Studies of semantic priming, blindsight, amnesia and implicit learning discussed in this volume have all revealed that complex forms of information processing and storage can take place without the subject attending to or being aware of them. If one believes in a separate attention system as outlined above, the ability of other information processing systems to carry on some of their computations without the involvement of attention seems quite reasonable. Thus, evidence that lexical items can contact semantics without attention, or that simple linear sequences can be learned when one is not attending, appears consonant with this fundamental separation.

Nor should it be particularly surprising that there are limits to what can be computed in the absence of conscious attention. Thus, while it is frequently reported that lexical semantics can be accessed without attention, it is rare that sentences are integrated into their constituent meanings without attention (Posner, 1978). While simple linear sequences seem to be learned without attention, when hierarchical structures or new associations are involved, this becomes impossible (Cohen *et al.*, 1990). Nor should we expect that the boundary between what can be learned with and without conscious attention will be fixed for every person or at every age. Rather, just as for attentive learning, we should expect individual differences based on constitutional abilities and prior learning.

An approach that stresses the potential independence of the posterior and anterior systems is important for evaluating claims that attention and awareness are dissociable. Most studies in the literature do not distinguish between posterior and anterior networks. Thus, we have to interpret whether or not they represent a puzzle for our hypothesis. Currently, the most interesting demonstration of a dissociation between attention and awareness in normal subjects is in the studies of sequence learning by Bullemer and Nissen (see Nissen & Bullemer, 1987; Bullemer & Nissen, 1990; Cohen *et al.*, 1990). In this task, subjects press keys when lights appear. Usually following a few random sequences, a repeating sequence is introduced. Subjects show they have learned the repeating sequence by their improved speed on this sequence in comparison with subjects who continue to practice random sequences, and because they are greatly slowed when a random list is presented. Many of these subjects, however, show no awareness of the repeating list. This can be shown either by protocol analysis, or by giving the subject the opportunity to generate the next item in the sequence following each light. If subjects deny they are aware of the sequence and are at chance in generating items, one can conclude they are unaware. The probability of getting subjects to be unaware of the sequence is increased if amnesic subjects are used, if explicit memory is blocked by scopolamine or if a divided attention task is employed in conjunction with the sequence learning task (Nissen & Bullemer, 1987; Cohen et al., 1990).

From her work, Nissen concluded that attention, but not awareness, is necessary for sequence learning. That is, subjects who were unaware of the sequence could learn it implicitly, but they could not accomplish this when attention was directed elsewhere. Cohen et al. (1990) qualified the Nissen conclusion by showing that sequences with simple associative structures could be learned without attention or awareness, for example, under divided attention conditions. Although these results are extremely interesting, they require no major dissociation between attention and awareness. Subjects may learn without awareness and even without attention under some conditions. If subjects attend to performance aspects of the task, they might or might not have become aware of the sequence of events. Whether or not they became aware, they could still learn, since learning often proceeds implicitly. There are many examples where subjects appear to attend to some aspects of the task but may not be aware of many of the components or details of the task. We all implicitly show evidence of knowing grammar or spelling without necessarily being able to report the rules we use. These examples indicate that we may not be able to report the underlying reasons for our behaviour, a finding well documented in the literature.

Recently, however, Bullemer and Nissen (1990) have shown a crucial distinction between awareness and attention. They measured attention by the reaction time of subjects to events that occurred out of sequence. If subjects had learned to respond to spatial location 4 following a spatial location 3, but on this trial the light at location 2 was illuminated, they were not only slowed, but they took longer to respond than if it had been a random series. According to the cost-benefit approach, this kind of inhibition is a sign of attention. That is, when subjects attend to the wrong item, they will show a cost in switching attention to the item that actually occurs. If they had not attended to the wrong item, but merely had it activated passively as an associate, no such cost should occur.

Suppose for the purpose of argument, one maintains the view that cost means attention to the learned item. If there is a direct association between awareness and attention, subjects who attend to the next item should also be aware of what it is and be able to report that they know that item. However, some subjects cannot generate the sequence and, more importantly, the amount of cost is the same for those subjects who are aware and who are not aware of the sequence. This dissociation appears on the surface to serve as remarkable evidence for the separation between attention and awareness, and to undermine the simple hypothesis that the output of the attentional system is available to our awareness so that it can be reported in a variety of ways.

Although the Bullemer and Nissen research appears at first to suggest that awareness is dissociated from attention, we argued above that attention in the sense of orienting (posterior network) *can* be dissociated from detection by the anterior attention network. The learning subjects demonstrate can be viewed as a program for successive orienting of the posterior attention network, rather than the operation of the anterior attention network that we associate with awareness and control. We examine evidence below that learning of expectancies of the type studied by Bullemer and Nissen can occur at about 4 months in conjunction with the development of posterior attention system. Even in adults, integration of information between posterior and anterior attention remains incomplete. This dissociation between attention systems corresponds to the more general idea emerging from cognitive studies of the human personality as a federation of minds, a view that emphasizes the difficulty humans have in becoming aware of the operations of their own mental sub-components.

5.3.1. Control and Attention

A second important aspect of consciousness is its function in the control of thought and behaviour. We know that our conscious behaviour can be accompanied by feelings of conscious control or volition. Allport (1988) notes the feeling of consciousness that accompanies much voluntary behaviour, but argues that this feeling does not in itself provide a basis for a formal definition of consciousness. He argues that we need to consider three broad criteria which would constitute the necessary and sufficient conditions for assessing an internal state of consciousness or volition. The first is that the person could choose an appropriate course of direct action upon the situation. The second is that the person could subsequently recall the situation. The third is that the person could confidently testify as to his or her awareness of the situation.

These criteria are not always associated. Thus, subjects in the implicit learning task described earlier may show they know the sequence by their ability to orient to the next item, but not show awareness in terms of the behaviour that would be needed to describe or generate the sequence. Similarly, subjects may show a galvanic skin response indicating that they recognize a word or face, while failing to be able to report that the word was presented or to show evidence of recognizing the face (Tranel & Damasio, 1988).

Because of these naturally occurring dissociations, Allport argues that coming to understand processes that provide coherence or integration to actions will yield us as good an understanding of consciousness as we might be able to achieve. One of these processes he calls 'selection for action', but we think of this process more broadly as selection for *thought* as well as action. As outlined previously, we identify the operation of the anterior attention network with the level of selection for thought that provides the basis for voluntary actions in adults (Posner *et al.*, 1988).

What requirements would be necessary for a mechanism that allows integration between different systems that act on a given input? Surely, any such mechanism would have to share input from many information sources. It should also have close relationships to motor systems, but be able to maintain its separation from them. Anatomically, the anterior cingulate has close relationships to the basal ganglia, which provide rich dopamine innervation from the ventral tegmental area. The anterior cingulate lies adjacent to and has close interconnections with the supplementary motor area. Indeed, our studies of activation of midline frontal areas in humans suggest that the more motoric the task, the more likely activation will be in the supplementary motor area in addition to, or rather than, the cingulate gyrus (Petersen *et al.*, 1989). It should have available a memory capacity to maintain a goal state while activating processes involved in integration. The anterior cingulate has rich connections to areas of the lateral cortical surface known to be important in holding information in temporary storage and to the hippocampus, which is involved in the formation of more permanent memories. It is also the cortical outflow of the limbic system and thus allows for close integration with emotional systems (Buck, 1988). The anterior attention network therefore appears to be well suited to provide integration of thought and behaviour.

Recently, Edelman (1989) has put forward a somewhat similar analysis to our own of the relationship between consciousness and attention. The initial ideas for Edelman's inquiry and the kinds of evidence he uses are quite different from those used in this chapter. Yet the questions he poses, the issues he raises and even some of the solutions he proposes appear to have remarkable similarity to our position. Edelman begins his analysis from the standpoint of neuronal groups rather than from the idea of anatomically organized attentional networks. However, as in our analysis, he believes that attention serves to boost activity within neuronal ensembles formed to compute specific cognitive functions. He further indicates that these attentional functions come under the control of conscious intentions. Thus he sees consciousness and attention as separate. However, the neural basis of consciousness appears to involve much of what we call the anterior attention system. He identifies it in figure 9.1 in his book, with a system that includes the septum, hippocampus and cingulate cortex and is involved in the comparison of exteroceptive stimuli with internal states.

Edelman's idea of conscious processing as controlling attention appears similar to our idea of an attentional system, the anterior portion of which is involved in executive control of behaviour. In one sense Edelman appears to see attention as involving the site of enhancement of signals, while he views consciousness as involved with the source of the attentional processes that boost input signals. Thus, our distinction between site and source of attention may differ from his distinction between consciousness and attention in only a rather trivial way. The Edelman ideas are based on rather general properties of the brain as a neural network and are not as closely tied to specific experiments as ours, so that it is often difficult for us to know how to make the translation from one analysis to another. However, it would be remarkable if the two views starting from such different points do indeed converge on common issues.

Both Edelman's (1989) and our own analysis suggest that the integration of computational units is at the heart of the problem of consciousness. According to a number of views, this co-ordination does not require a part of the brain that holds within its anatomy the information which is to be integrated. It is possible instead to argue that parts of the brain are responsible for acting upon codes that are anatomically quite separate (Damasio, 1989; Edelman, 1989; Crick & Koch, 1990). Our argument for a separate attentional system (Posner & Petersen, 1990) can be seen as suggesting the anatomy of the parts of the brain that are the source of this co-ordination. The findings using PET suggest that the attentional systems can be seen as a source of activation in many brain areas (e.g. pre-striate cortex) that are co-ordinated in tasks such as visual search and semantic monitoring. How does this co-ordination develop? We turn to an analysis of the development of voluntary control mechanisms and sensory integration as a way of studying consciousness in the preverbal organism.

5.4. DEVELOPMENT OF ATTENTIONAL NETWORKS

One of the important aspects of regarding attention as a neural system with its own anatomy is that one can ask quite specific questions about its development (Johnson, 1990; Rothbart *et al.*, 1990). We have been exploring the way in which the posterior attention network develops over the first year of life in conjunction with what is known about the laminar development of the visual system. We have used the method of marker tasks to connect the maturation of brain systems to behaviour. These are tasks which have been shown in adults to involve specific aspects of attention. Thus, it has been shown that the superior colliculus carries out a computation that reduces the probability of reorienting attention to an already examined visual location (inhibition of return; Posner, 1988). We have studied this function in infants from 3 to 12 months, and shown that it is not present at 3 months, but appears to be at the same level as in adults by 6 months (Clohessy *et al.*, 1991; Rothbart *et al.*, 1990).

We have also examined other forms of attention shift that may well be properties of the posterior attention network, including the ability to disengage from a stimulus and the ability to develop an expectation of the location of a stimulus from an arbitrary prior event (Johnson *et al.*, 1991). These aspects of attention also show development in the period from 3 to 6 months. The infant of 4 months is capable of learning that an arbitrary stimulus means the next event is likely to occur to the left rather than to the right (Johnson *et al.*, 1991), but there are obvious difficulties in ascertaining how conscious of the expectation the baby is.

One of the most striking aspects of running 4-month olds in visual orienting experiments is the degree to which, once locked on to stimulus events, their attention can be moved to various events at the will of the experimenter. They appear almost to be little looking machines, until distress or fatigue overtakes them. The 4-month old is so cooperative in orienting studies that she or he is often the subject of choice in infant research. Thus, Rose and Ruff (1987) conclude that, 'The work in auditory–visual matching tends to stand as a monolithic investigation of abilities of the 4-month old'. This contrasts with the laboratory behaviour of 12-month olds, who appear to have an agenda of their own. They will look for a while, but appear to have other activities pressing upon them and may quickly turn to them. Thus at 4–6 months there is evidence of selection in terms of orienting to stimuli, even orienting based on clearly learned expectations. However, the behavioural evidence suggests that further development is needed for control aspects of the anterior attentional network. Much of this development appears to occur late in the first year.

Even though the 4–6-month old shows efficient visual orienting and a degree of understanding of object constancy, motion, number and identity, this knowledge appears to be part of visual knowledge, and is not generally available as the basis for making a wide range of arbitrary responses. Our studies (Clohessy *et al.*, 1991; Vecera *et al.*, 1991) and those of other researchers (Baillargeon, 1987) document a shift during the second 6 months of postnatal development in a more formal way. Six-month old infants, like adults, tend to avoid returning their eyes or attention to already inspected locations (inhibition of return). This is one example of a preference for novelty that is strong in some forms of looking patterns almost from birth. Another form of alternation is the tendency to avoid repeating the same motor pattern in successive trials (spontaneous alternation). This tendency to alternate movements is found in rats and other mammals (Douglas, 1989). In our studies, infants at 6 months of age do not show spontaneous alternation in their reaching movements, although they show inhibition of return in their eye movements.

More generally, it has been found using habituation of looking patterns that infants of 4 months can indicate they are aware of the qualities of an object hidden from view (Baillargeon, 1987), even though their motor activity towards the objects suggests that they do not yet know that they maintain existence when hidden from view (Piaget, 1952). When does the ability to co-ordinate these elementary forms of orienting and action come into play? Several signs point to the importance of a period around 9 months.

Recently Lalonde and Werker (1990) studied three seemingly quite separate tasks said to involve mental co-ordination, two of which are the ability to search for a hidden object, and the ability to recognize the correlation between features of a visual object. These abilities become highly correlated at 9 months when infants tend to pass both tests or neither of them. The period of from 7 to 12 months also marks the ability of the infant to reach in a direction different from the line of sight (Diamond, 1991). In some ways, exercising this ability is the initial form of Stroop-type conflict. In adults, the conflict condition in naming the ink colour of coloured words (Stroop effect) has been shown to activate the anterior attention network (Pardo *et al.*, 1990). Thus, it seems reasonable to suppose that the anterior attention network is involved in these co-ordinative activities developing in the period around 9 months.

Nine months is also about the time that infants begin to use words. The PET data suggest that the semantic association among words involves a left lateral frontal area very close to the area thought to be related to reaching. Indeed the early use of words is very closely related to gestures towards objects by the infant (Dore *et al.*, 1976). Gesturing is also frequently used to aid in the development of word use by language delayed children (Pien & Klein, 1989).

The period from 7 to 9 months has been identified by Emde and his colleagues (Emde *et al.*, 1976) as a period of biobehavioural shift, characterized by changes in wariness to novelty and the onset of stranger fearfulness concurrent with changes in sleep-state organization. Kagan (1979) has also reviewed evidence for a similar change which he relates to the development of the ability to retrieve information from memory with minimal environmental cues, and the ability to maintain a representation of past or present events in working memory. Finally, McCall (1979) has reviewed research indicating the presence of a shift between 7 and 13 months in infants' means–ends competences, their co-ordination of action schemes upon an object, their motor and vocal imitation, and the beginnings of response uncertainty (wariness). McCall summarizes the changes in this way:

> At approximately 7 months of age, the child's cognitive development first permits the separation of means from ends and infant from environment. Whereas previously the infant's response and its consequences were unitary, now their separation introduces an element of response uncertainty—either, 'will this response have a desired consequence?' and/or 'which of several responses shall I make?' (McCall, 1979, p. 207).

There is evidence of dissociations between awareness and control in adults. Consider the difference between the waking and dreaming states. In dreaming, awareness is clearly present, but the ability to regulate one's own thought and behaviour is limited (Mamelak & Hobson, 1989). In the Nissen task, some adults show they are able to orient to a learned expected event (as do our 4-month olds), but they are not aware in a more general sense that guides other forms of behaviour in an integrated way. Their awareness seems to be locked into an individual system and not yet broadcast more generally so as to be available for the integration of other forms of behaviour. Following Allport (1988), we are using integrative ability as a marker in nonverbal organisms of the level of processing related to consciousness and to the formation of voluntary control that develops slowly in infancy.

Thus, 9 months seems crucial for the development of co-ordination between cues and responses in a number of domains. If one follows Allport in the conviction that such integration is a behavioural sign of conscious control, this may be a very important time in attentional development. The aspect of consciousness that seems to be most related to this development at 9 months appears to be control or volition. Put in popular terms, the infant has developed a mind of its own, in the sense of having an internal agenda that controls behaviour. That mind is also linked to its expression to others, and communication emerges in co-ordinated gesture and language.

Why should the control aspect of consciousness develop so late in infancy? Why should it not be specified at birth? We believe that the controls of behaviour must be open to influence by the culture in which the infant is raised. This view was championed by Luria (1973), who argued that the orienting system (the posterior attention system in our terms) was biological and was fully developed in early infancy. Our studies certainly support this view. However, he also argued, following Vygotsky (1962), that higher forms of attention (what he called voluntary attention) are primarily cultural and can only emerge in close connection to the caregivers. Although we support a biological basis for the origin of both of these systems, the arguments above certainly emphasize the strongly social character of the development of the anterior network.

5.5. PATHOLOGIES OF ATTENTION

Another approach to the study of volition in adults involves its breakdown in nervous and mental disorders. We would argue that the study of schizophrenia, attention deficit disorder and akinetic mutism all provide some support to the idea that disorders involving the anterior cingulate reflect a loss of conscious control.

Severe disorders of the cingulate gyrus can produce akinetic mutism.

This involves a complete loss of spontaneous behaviour in all domains with some preservation of the ability to orient and maintain the alert state. Although much of this behaviour may recover, there are reports of continued disruption of control (Eslinger & Damasio, 1985).

However, bilateral anterior cingulotomies performed for intractable depression usually have not produced evidence for severe deficits in cognition. A recent case (Janer & Pardo, 1991) suggests that this operation does produce impaired performance in just those high level tasks found to activate the region in PET scans (e.g. the Stroop task and the generation of uses). We are only beginning to have the tools to evaluate in more detail the exact role of such lesions on attention.

At a more moderate level, unilateral lesions of the anterior cingulate and supplementary motor area can produce a symptom complex called the alien hand sign (Goldberg, 1981; Goldberg & Bloom, 1991). In this complex, patients regard the hand contralateral to the lesion as not being controlled by them. It is as if the hand belonged to someone else. We can contrast the alien hand sign found with lesions of the anterior attention system to a somewhat similar effect of lesions of the posterior attention system. In severe lesions of the posterior parietal lobe, patients with neglect may deny that a hand or arm belongs to them (see Bisiach, Chapter 6, this volume). With the anterior lesion they know it is their hand, but believe that some other person or thing is in control of it. These findings and many other aspects of neglect from anterior and posterior lesions suggest that the two attentional systems share much in common, but that the posterior system is more related to location in space whereas the anterior system is more related to feelings of volition and control.

These data support the close relation of this midfrontal area to feelings of volition and control, but the recovery that takes place over the course of a year suggests the importance of other areas. Goldberg and Bloom (1991) argue for a close reciprocal relation between midfrontal and lateral frontal areas in the control of voluntary movements. Patients suffering from the alien hand sign due to lesions often produce speech similar to that found in schizophrenia and indeed, the alien hand sign may also accompany schizophrenia.

We have argued that schizophrenia involves a dysfunction of the anterior cingulate due to alteration of dopamine input from the ventral tegmental area (Early *et al.*, 1989). It is striking that this disorder produces a loss of control of verbal association, difficulty in orienting attention rightward and frequently the conviction that the person's own thought and action are controlled externally. The first and last are central features of conscious control, while the orienting problem appears to connect the disorder to the posterior attention system as well.

Finally, we have recently found evidence that attention deficit disorder may involve a specific deficit in the attentional network subserving vigilance (Rothlind *et al.*, 1991; Swanson *et al.*, 1991). Given the anatomy of this network (see Fig. 5.1), this deficit would suggest a right frontal abnormality. If this abnormality prevents the child from executing inhibitory control over the anterior cingulate, as would be suggested from the connections between the vigilance network and the anterior attention system, one might be able to appreciate the difficulty such children have in maintaining a quiet attentive state in school settings, where the clearing of consciousness is required frequently over the course of the day. While the study of these clinical syndromes is still incomplete, they provide another source of data that may aid our understanding of the cognitive and anatomical nature of awareness and control.

We believe that the study of attention is fundamental to understanding conscious processing. As the anatomical basis and cognitive operations of the attentional networks become clearer, the extent of the relationship should be further clarified. We recognize that the hypothesis outlined in this chapter is controversial. Most authors would probably conclude with Bisiach (Chapter 6, this volume) that the concept of consciousness involves such a highly distributed system that the specification of its anatomical basis is not a meaningful exercise. A similar view would have been tenable in the study of word reading a few years ago. However, recent PET studies seem to have shown that although reading or listening involves much of the brain, the specifiable computations that compose the task of processing its major constituents are very localized (Posner *et al.*, 1988). It seems likely that a similar resolution between distribution and localization will be possible in the study of consciousness. We hope this chapter serves as a contribution to understanding the relation between the brain's attention networks and our conscious experience.

ACKNOWLEDGEMENTS

The research reported here was supported in part by ONR Contract N 0014–89–J3013 and NIMH grant 43361 and by the Center for Cognitive Neuroscience of Attention supported by the Pew Charitable Trusts & James S. McDonnell Foundation. The paper has greatly benefited by Tom Carr's critical comments on an earlier version, and we thank him for his help.

REFERENCES

Allport, A. (1988). What concept of consciousness? In A.J. Marcel and E. Bisiach (eds), *Consciousness in Contemporary Science*. London: Clarendon Press.

Baillargoen, R. (1987). Object permanence in 3.5 and 4.5 month old infants. *Developmental Psychology*, **23**, 655–664.

Buck, R. (1988). *Human Motivation and Emotion*. New York: Wiley.

Bullemer, P. & Nissen, M.J. (1990). Attentional orienting in the expression of procedural knowledge. Paper presented to the Psychonomic Society, New Orleans.

Burgess, C. & Simpson, G.B. (1988). Cerebral hemispheric mechanisms in the retrieval of ambiguous word meanings. *Brain and Language*, **33**, 86–103.

Clohessy, A.B., Posner, M.I. & Rothbart, M.K. (1991). The development of inhibition of return in early infancy. *Journal of Cognitive Neuroscience*, in press.

Cohen, A., Ivry, R.I. & Keele, S.W. (1990). Attention and structure in sequence learning. *Journal of Experimental Psychology: Learning, Memory and Cognition*, **16**, 17–30.

Cohen, R.M., Semple, W.E., Gross, M., Holcomb, H.J., Dowling, S.M. & Nordahl, T.E. (1988). Functional localization of sustained attention. *Neuropsychiatry, Neuropsychology and Behavioral Neurology*, **1**, 3–20.

Corbetta, M., Meizen, F.M., Dobmeyer, S., Shulman, G.L. & Petersen, S.E. (1990). Selective attention modulates neural processing of shape, color and velocity in humans. *Science*, **248**, 1556–1559.

Crick, F. & Koch, C. (1990). Towards a neurobiological theory of consciousness. *Seminars in Neurosciences*, **2**, 263–275.

Damasio, A.R. (1989). Time-locked multiregional retroactivation: a systems level proposal for the neural substrate of recall and recognition. *Cognition*, **33**, 25–62.

Damasio, A.R. & Van Hoesen, G.W. (1983). Emotional disturbances associated with focal lesions of the limbic frontal lobe. In K. Heilman and P. Satz (eds), *Neuropsychology of Human Emotion*. New York: Guilford Press.

Diamond, A. Retrieval of an object from an open box: The development of visual-tactile control of reaching in the first year of life. *Child Development Monographs*, in press.

Dore, J., Franklin, M.B., Miller, R.T. & Ramer, A.L.H. (1976). Transitional phenomena in early language acquisition. *Journal of Child Language*, **3**, 13–27.

Douglas, R.J. (1989). Spontaneous alternation and the brain. In W.N. Dember and C.L. Richman (eds), *Spontaneous Alternation Behavior*, pp. 27–85. New York: Springer-Verlag.

Duncan, J. (1980). The locus of interference in the perception of simultaneous stimuli. *Psychological Review*, **87**, 272–300.

Early, T.S., Posner, M.I., Reiman, E.M. & Raichle, M.E. (1989). Hyperactivity of the left striato-pallidal projections: I Lower level theory, II Phenomenology and thought disorder. *Psychiatric Developments*, **2**, 85–108.

Edelman, G.M. (1989). *The Remembered Present*. New York: Basic Books.

Emde, R.N., Gaensbauer, T.J. & Harmon, R.J. (1976). Emotion expression in infancy. *Psychological Issues*, Monograph No. 37.

Eslinger, P.J. & Damasio, A.R. (1985). Severe disturbance of higher cognition after bilateral frontal lobe ablation. *Neurology*, **35**, 1731–1741.

Fitts, P.M. & Posner, M.I. (1967). *Human Performance*. Belmont, California: Brooks/Cole.

Goldberg, G. (1981). Medial frontal cortex infarction and the alien hand sign. *Neurology*, **38**, 683–686.

Goldberg, G. & Bloom, K. (1991). The alien hand sign. Localization, lateralization and recovery. *American Journal of Physical Medicine and Rehabilitation,* in press.

Goldman-Rakic, P.S. (1988). Topography of cognition: parallel distributed networks in primate association cortex. *Annual Review of Neuroscience,* **11**, 137–156.

Harley, C.W. (1987). A role for norepinephrine in arousal, emotion and learning: limbic modulation by norepinephrine and the key hypothesis. *Progress in Neuro-Pharmacology and Biological Psychiatry,* **11**, 419–458.

Janer, K.W. & Pardo, J.V. (1991). Deficits in selective attention following bilateral anterior cingulotomy. *Journal of Cognitive Neuroscience,* **3**, 231–241.

Johnson, M. (1990). Cortical maturation and the development of visual attention in early infancy. *Journal of Cognitive Neuroscience,* **2**, 81–95.

Johnson, M.H., Posner, M.I. & Rothbart, M.K. (1991). Components of visual orienting in early infancy: contingency learning, anticipatory looking and disengaging. *Journal of Cognitive Neuroscience,* in press.

Jonides, J. (1981). Voluntary versus automatic control over the mind's eye. In J. Long and A.D. Baddeley (eds), *Attention and Performance IX.* Hillsdale, NJ: Erlbaum.

Kagan, J. (1979). Structure and process in the human infant: The ontogeny of mental representation. In M.H. Bornstein and William Kessen (eds), *Psychological Development from Infancy.* Hillsdale, NJ: Erlbaum.

Kahneman, D. (1973). *Attention and Effort.* Englewood Cliffs: Prentice Hall.

Lalonde, C.E. & Werker, J.F. (1990). Cognitive/perceptual integration of three skills at 9 months. Paper presented at the 7th International Conference on Infancy Studies, Montreal, April, 1990.

Luria, A.R. (1973). *The Working Brain: an Introduction to Neuropsychology.* New York: Basic Books.

Mamelak, A.N. & Hobson, J.A. (1989). Dream bizarreness as the cognitive correlate of altered neural behavior in REM sleep. *Journal of Cognitive Neuroscience,* **3**, 201–222.

McCall, R.B. (1979). Qualitative transitions in behavioural development in the first two years of life. In M.H. Bornstein and William Kessen (eds), *Psychological Development from Infancy.* Hillsdale, NJ: Erlbaum.

Morrison, J.H. & Foote, S.L. (1986). Noradrenergic and serotonergic innervation of cortical, thalamic and tectal structures in old and new world monkeys. *Journal of Comparative Neurology,* **143**, 117–118.

Nissen, M.J. & Bullemer, P.H. (1987). Attentional requirements of learning: evidence from performance measures. *Cognitive Psychology,* **19**, 1–32.

Pardo, J.V., Pardo, P.J., Janer, K.W. & Raichle, M.E. (1990). The anterior cingulate cortex mediates processing selection in the stroop attentional conflict paradigm. *Proceedings of the National Academy of Sciences,* **87**, 256–259.

Pashler, H. (1991). Dual task interference and elementary psychological mechanisms. *Attention and Performance XIV,* in press.

Petersen, S.E., Fox, P.T., Posner, M.I., Mintum, M. & Raichle, M.E. (1989). Positron emission tomographic studies of the processing of single words. *Journal of Cognitive Neuroscience,* **1**, 153–170.

Petersen, S.E., Fox, P.T., Snyder, A.Z. & Raichle, M.E. (1990). Activation of extrastriate and frontal cortical areas by visual words and word like stimuli. *Science,* **249**, 1041–1044.

Piaget, J. (1952). *The Origins of Intelligence in Children*. (M. Cook, trans.) New York: International University Press.

Pien, D. & Klein, J.M. (1989). *Gestures: The Missing Link to Language*. Seattle: University of Washington.

Posner, M.I. (1978). *Chronometric Explorations of Mind*. Hillsdale, NJ: Erlbaum.

Posner, M.I. (1980). Orienting of attention. *Quarterly Journal of Experimental Psychology*, **32**, 3–25.

Posner, M.I. (1988). Structures and functions of selective attention. In T. Boll and B. Bryant (eds), *Master Lectures in Clinical Neuropsychology and Brain Function: Research, Measurements, and Practice*, pp. 173–206. Washington DC: American Psychological Association.

Posner, M.I. (1990). Hierarchical distributed networks in the neuropsychology of selective attention. In A. Caramazza (ed.), *Cognitive Neuropsychology and Neurolinguistics: Advances in Models of Cognitive Function and Impairment*, pp. 187–210. New York: Plenum.

Posner, M.I. & Petersen, S.E. (1990). The attention system of the human brain. *Annual Review of Neuroscience*, **13**, 25–42.

Posner, M.I. & Presti, D. (1987). Selective attention and cognitive control. *Trends in Neuroscience*, **10**, 12–17.

Posner, M.I., Inhoff, A., Friedrich, F.J. & Cohen, A. (1987). Isolating attentional systems: a cognitive-anatomical analysis. *Psychobiology*, **15**, 107–121.

Posner, M.I., Petersen, S.E., Fox, P.T. & Raichle, M.E. (1988). Localization of cognitive functions in the human brain. *Science*, **240**, 1627–1631.

Posner, M.I., Sandson, J., Dhawan, M. & Shulman, G.L. (1989). Is word recognition automatic? A cognitive anatomical approach. *Journal of Cognitive Neuroscience*, **1**, 50–60.

Reitman, J. (1971). Mechanisms of forgetting in short term memory. *Cognitive Psychology*, **2**, 131–157.

Rose, S.A. & Ruff, H.A. (1987). Cross-modal abilities in human infants. In J.D. Osofsky (ed.), *Handbook of Infant Development*, 2nd edn, pp. 318–362. New York: Wiley.

Rothbart, M.K., Posner, M.I. & Boylan, A. (1990). Regulatory mechanisms in infant temperament. In J. Enns (ed.), *The Development of Attention: Research and Theory*, pp. 47–66. Amsterdam: North Holland.

Rothlind, J., Posner, M.I. & Schaughency, E. (1991). Lateralized control of eye movements in attention deficit hyperactivity disorder. *Journal of Cognitive Neuroscience*, in press.

Swanson, J.M., Posner, M.I., Potkin, S., Bonforte, S., Youpa, D., Cantwell, D. & Crinella, F. (1991). Activating tasks for the study of visual-spatial attention in ADHD children: a cognitive anatomical approach. *Child Neurology*, in press.

Tranel, D. & Damasio, A.R. (1988). Non-conscious face recognition in patients with face agnosia. *Behavioural Brain Research*, **30**, 235–249.

Vecera, S., Rothbart, M.K. & Posner, M.I. (1991). The development of spontaneous alternation in human infants. *Journal of Cognitive Neuroscience*, in press.

Vygotsky, L.S. (1962). *Thought and Language*. New York: John Wiley.

Weiskrantz, L. (1986). *Blindsight: A Case Study and Implications*. Oxford: Oxford University Press.

CHAPTER 6

Understanding Consciousness: Clues from Unilateral Neglect and Related Disorders

Edoardo Bisiach

> '... *if we did not have phenomenal experience we would not have a concept of consciousness at all.*'
>
> Anthony J. Marcel (1988)

6.1. INTRODUCTION

Suspicion about consciousness as an object of scientific inquiry is rooted in the cultural prejudice due to which we regard physics as the paradigm of science *par excellence*. This prejudice may lead us to legislate away subjective experience from the scientific domain—a solution with which I have formerly sympathized (Bisiach, 1988)—or vice versa (e.g. Nagel, 1974), depending on where the emphasis is laid. Alternatively, it may induce outright denial of the subjectivity of consciousness, as exemplified by Rorty's statement, 'The problem is not to take account of the special difficulty raised by the "inside"-character of consciousness, but to convince people that there is no reason to grant that persons have more of an inside than particles' (Rorty, 1982, p. 183).

Not many people, I surmise, are likely to be persuaded by Rorty. In fact, although I would hardly describe myself as having inside experience of the particles that constitute the complex physical system I am, I strongly oppose defining as 'fictional' or 'eliminable' the inside experience inherent in some states and processes of that system. This does not imply regarding that experience as a mysterious non-physical accompaniment of those states and processes. That experience is *my*

THE NEUROPSYCHOLOGY OF CONSCIOUSNESS
ISBN 0–12–498045–7

'point of view'. That's the way it is. The bat, I presume has its own (Nagel, 1974). Why on earth should they be 'eliminated'?

People who resist programmatic repudiation of their own consciousness may legitimately develop a specific scientific interest in it. They may enquire as to how phenomenal experience is structured; what distinguishes conscious from nonconscious states and processes *besides* subjective experience, i.e. in neural and/or information processing terms; what conditions determine access to, and recess from, that experience; how conscious and nonconscious states and processes interact; etc. The case of blindsight (Weiskrantz, 1986) has been very instrumental in disciplining the urge and clarifying the scope of scientific inquiry on consciousness.

Recognizing consciousness as a proper object of scientific inquiry entails extending the paradigm of science beyond the standards of traditional physics. So what? It has often been claimed that the study of the mind is an 'immature' discipline, but it would be more accurate to view it as the most problematic and least explored frontier of science, and it is probably our general conception of science that needs further maturation.

6.2. METHODOLOGICAL ISSUES

After having sanctioned, at least in principle, the project of studying one's own consciousness empirically, something should be said about tactics, expectations and boundary conditions, while bearing in mind that it would be a mistake to be too prescriptive and exacting at the start. The only method I can envisage is the ascription of *phenomenal experience* to an observed individual, by analogy with the phenomenal experience of the observer. Commonplace as it might appear at first sight, this move is exceptional in science: what it affords, indeed, is neither an anthropomorphic metaphor nor a theoretical construct. It is not a metaphor because what is ascribed is meant to apply literally to the recipient. It is not a theoretical construct because the *observer's* consciousness is not such, and to the extent that the ascription of phenomenal experience to the observed individual *is not simply intended to explain his or her behaviour*. What the move consists in, is the *hypothetical ascription* to another individual of a property, that the observer asserts to be real of him- or herself on the basis of inside information. This is the first step one must make in an attempt to gain insight into *one's own* conscious mentality and, secondarily, into that of other people. The transaction may be reversed, as it were, in the sense of the observer's hypothetical self-ascription of the behaviour displayed by the observed individual, so that the question becomes what would it be like to be me, if I displayed such behaviour. An advantage of this reversal of perspective is that it tallies with the condition in which I would *directly* learn about my consciousness if I were a subject, for example, of Marcel's (1983) experiments on nonconscious priming. While this condition can be realized, granting phenomenal experience to other people is the only possibility we are given to learn *indirectly* about consciousness when we study the consequences of brain lesions (unless we were *ourselves* suffering from dysfunctions such as blindsight or unilateral neglect). Trying to figure out what it would be like to be the person whose behaviour we are studying, is not the 'first step in the operationalist sleight of hand' (Searle, 1980, p. 451). On the contrary, it prevents that step and its unavoidable consequence, namely, the replacement of consciousness by a conventional, impoverished, and more or less rigid substitute such as a piece of behaviour or some putative functional components of the cognitive machinery (see Shallice, 1988, p. 401, for a catalogue of proposals for such components, as well as for his own account). On the other hand, no matter how problematic and tricky it might be, reference to the observer's phenomenal experience obviates the need for the 'objective' criteria in the absence of which sceptical conclusions are drawn about consciousness as a proper object of empirical investigation (e.g. by Allport, 1988).

The move I am advocating has obvious disadvantages. First of all, it could be claimed that it misses 'the real thing', i.e. what it would actually be like to be the observed individual (or what it would actually be like to be oneself as subject of the observed behaviour). To the extent to which it is qualia-related, this claim is a truism with which it would be otiose to bother, because it misses the point altogether. There is no way in which a natural science of consciousness could have anything to do with qualia. Whatever experimental manipulations of his own brain processes a gifted bat could devise, they would not tell him the whole story about why being a bat is like what it is. There cannot be a science of those aspects of phenomenal experience that are manipulated in thought experiments such as qualia inversion. Our problem is to understand what, *besides* such aspects, distinguishes conscious activities of a system, in themselves and with respect to any other activity of the same system.

A more serious disadvantage of the move at issue is its being based, as it were, upon introspection by proxy. This is a severe handicap, considering the halo of disrepute surrounding direct introspection itself. For those who are not frightened away from the outset, this means investing a great deal of labour in an intricate trigonometry of the mind while still not being in a position to form a correct estimate of the validity of its results; it also requires the utmost caution in assessing such results. 'Introspection', to make things worse, is a potentially misleading term. On the one hand, it may induce questionable linguistic constructs (such as 'consciousness of consciousness' or 'reflexive consciousness') that suggest an enigmatic higher order consciousness rather than the mundane act of conscious thinking about conscious experience. On the other hand, it may be misused or misunderstood as meaning (fallible) self-interpretation. I use the term 'introspection' in the sense of bona fide self-witnessing and I think that what can first of all be expected from a scientific approach to consciousness is a closer view of what is being witnessed and a better estimate of the veridicality of its report.

6.3. THE GENERAL CONTENT OF CONSCIOUSNESS AND ITS SPATIO-TEMPORAL STRUCTURE

As regards what is self-witnessed, we must make a distinction between externally driven (i.e. perceptual) and internally driven phenomenal experience, such as mental images and thought. The first kind of experience is strictly constrained by, and anchored to, the properties of the perceived environment. The second is conceivably inherent in the largely parallel activities of a network of 'fuzzy-jittery' neuronal assemblies whose surfacing in consciousness is _enthymematic_, in the sense that it leaves out a great deal of what gives meaning to what we are aware of. This is what makes internally driven experience almost impossible to describe except when we endeavour to entertain a relatively stable mental image or crystallize an idea into the format of inner speech. The notion of _fuzzy-jittery cell assemblies_ is an admittedly vague expansion of Hebb's (1949) seminal proposal. Roughly, the term is intended to capture and combine four ideas:

(1) The huge expanse of the busy neural network in which representational activity is implemented and which is beyond any realistic hope of panoramic assessment by neurophysiological means.
(2) The imprecise correspondence of a cell assembly involved in thinking about a certain object to the cell assembly activated during perception of that object.
(3) The co-occurrence of different cell assemblies, some of which may have segments of the relevant circuitry in common.
(4) The instability of endogenous clusters of neural representational activity.

Phenomenal correlates of points 1–4 are suggested to be the sketchiness and possible overlap of the fleeting conscious experiences resulting from endogenous neural activity at any given instant. As an explanatory construct, the notion of fuzzy-jittery cell assemblies has the obvious problem of being too versatile. It is hoped that its main virtue may be that of warning against some models of the brain's representational activities, offered by AI-inspired theorists, that are often too clear-cut and rationalistic inasmuch as they relate more to the final product, than to the process of thought.

Both kinds of phenomenal experience, perceptual and internally driven, are spatio-temporal. They are spatial in two senses: *phenomenological* and *information processing*. In the phenomenological sense, their sensory or sensory-like content extends in an egocentric space; a space that is likely to be represented by the brain in an analogue medium (Bisiach & Berti, 1987). Within this space, consciousness may either be focal or (borrowing the term from Kinsbourne, 1988) panoramic, or focal with a panoramic periphery. In the information processing sense, phenomenal experience has spatial structure in so far as it is most likely to be assembled from activities distributed among centralized processors. These processors work more or less in parallel, following a complex interactive schedule by which, no matter how stabilized it might appear in a short interval of time, the content of consciousness is continually restructured.

In saying that conscious experience is the result of processing distributed in neural space, I do not simply refer to the horizontal separation of the various sensory modalities, nor to the fact that, within single modalities, there are spatially organized neural maps conforming to spatial and even to non-spatial features of environmental stimuli (see, e.g. Merzenich & Kaas, 1980, as regards the distribution of intensity- and pitch-sensitive cells in the auditory cortex). I refer in particular to the vertical organization along the input–output axis that offers the possibility of sensory–premotor interaction in the generation of conscious experience. The dependence of consciousness on such an interaction is theoretically most significant and is suggested, by way of example, by the effect of response modality on awareness of sensory stimuli. This effect may give rise to phenomena that, unlike other phenomena of interference such as backward masking, are not explicable in terms of a modulation of incoming information at a response-independent preconscious level, and therefore, question any pre-theoretical intuition of consciousness as a flat interface dividing efferent from afferent processes.

Neuropsychological investigation offers several examples of such an effect. In right brain-damaged patients, awareness of contralesional visual stimuli may to a variable extent be impaired by damage to visual pathways or due to the dysfunction(s) underlying unilateral neglect of space. So far, it is often impossible to assess the contribution of each of these factors to the disorder. However, it has been found that awareness of contralesional stimuli may appear more impaired if manual choice-reactions, rather than verbal responses, are used to monitor detection (Bisiach *et al.*, 1989). In our tachistoscopic experiment patients had to react to elementary visual stimuli—200-ms illumination of a single diode in either hemifield, or of two diodes, one in each hemifield—either by verbally reporting the number of stimuli, or by pressing a key if they had perceived a single stimulus, witholding their response to double stimuli and on blank trials. Whatever may be the correct explanation of the reduced rate of detection of contralesional stimuli we recorded in right brain-damaged patients—both in conditions of single and in conditions of double simultaneous stimulation—when a manual as opposed to verbal response was required, this result shows that the different ways in which sensory information has to be processed in order to result in different kinds of intentional activity may differently affect access to consciousness.

A further example is provided by another experiment in right brain-damaged subjects suffering from unilateral neglect (Bisiach *et al.*, 1990a). It is well-known that such patients usually bisect horizontal lines to the right of the objective midpoint. In our experiment, we asked patients to execute the task by means of a pulley device operating in two different conditions: a congruent (canonical) condition in which a pointer was *directly* moved from either end of the line to its subjective midpoint, and a non-congruent condition in which the pointer was *indirectly* moved along the line by a hand movement *in the opposite direction*. The amount of the rightward bisection error was found to decrease, to an extent varying among patients, in the non-congruent as opposed to the congruent condition. We interpreted the result as revealing two different factors of neglect, respectively related to input analysis and premotor programming. The latter corresponds to Watson *et al.*'s (1978) concept of 'directional hypokinesia', i.e. reluctance to carry out actions towards the contralesional side of egocentric space. More precisely, we concluded that in the congruent condition of the task perceptual and premotor factors contributed to displacing the subjective midpoint in the same direction, i.e. rightwards, whereas in the non-congruent condition the rightward displacement of the subjective midpoint resulting from faulty perceptual analysis was to a variable degree counteracted by the inertness of the leftward hand-movement required to move the pointer rightwards. Here too, phenomenal experience appears to be influenced by variables that relate to premotor programming of intentional actions, i.e. to a stage traditionally conceived to be later than the representation in consciousness of sensory information on the basis of which actions are initiated. We found the premotor component of the dysfunction to be relatively more pronounced in patients whose lesions extended to the frontal lobe, or to sub-cortical structures held to have motor functions, than in patients with exclusively retrorolandic lesions. As regards neglect, this is in agreement with a distinction conjectured by Watson *et al.* (1978) and Mesulam (1981). As regards consciousness, this differentiation affords a glimpse of the anatomical arrangement of the distributed mechanism by which input and output stages of information processing interactively frame perceptual judgements.

A dependence of perceptual awareness on response mechanisms is also suggested by the results of a recent investigation by Tegnér and Levander (1991). Eighteen patients with left neglect were asked to execute a variant of Albert's (1973) cancellation task in which the subject has to cross out with a pencil a number of short lines drawn on a sheet of paper. Patients had to perform first in the canonical condition, and then in a condition in which the visual array was left-to-right inverted by means of a 90° mirror device, while direct view of their hand and of the sheet of paper was prevented by a bench. In this condition, the subject's hand must operate on the left side of the sheet of paper to cross out the lines he sees on the right side of the visual display, and vice versa. In the canonical condition, as usual, the patients only crossed out lines lying on the right side. The inverted condition revealed three different patterns of behaviour. Ten patients only crossed out the lines they could *see* on their right; to do that their (right) hand had to cross the midline and work on the left side of the sheet of paper. Their neglect was therefore interpreted as being due to *perceptual* factors. Four patients, on the contrary, only crossed out lines lying on the right of the sheet of paper (as they had done in the canonical condition), although those lines were seen through the mirror as lying on the left side. In these patients neglect appeared thus to be due to a (broadly conceived) *premotor* dysfunction. The remaining four patients, in the mirror-inverted condition, only crossed out the lines in the middle. Their performance was interpreted by the authors as being caused both by perceptual and premotor factors of neglect. In agreement with our results, Tegnér and Levander found evidence of 'directional hypokinesia' only in patients whose lesion involved the frontal lobe or the basal ganglia.

Perhaps 'directional hypokinesia' is also responsible for the fact, observed by Halligan and Marshall (unpublished; cited by Allport, 1988), that a neglect patient may seem unaware of the full extent of the horizontal line he is asked to bisect, whereas he seems to be aware of it when he has to use that same line as the base of an imaginary square of which he is asked to draw the right-hand (vertical) side.

There are still other examples of the role of response mechanisms in gating access to consciousness in patients with unilateral neglect. Joanette *et al.* (1986) and Halligan and Marshall (1989) described patients whose ability to detect left-side stimuli was more impaired when they had to respond with their right hand than when they had to respond with their left.

Finally, an impressive demonstration of the influence of response factors on reports of visual stimuli in blindsight has been given by Zihl and Von Cramon (1980). Their study was replicated and expanded both in blindsight and normal subjects by Marcel (1990). In his Experiment 2, Marcel asked his patient GY to react either by blinking or by pressing a button with his right forefinger, or by saying 'yes' when he 'felt' that a light had come on in his blind field. Blink responses were found to be more sensitive than finger responses; verbal responses were least sensitive. Similar results were obtained in two normal subjects by using near-threshold visual stimuli. [1]

The data so far reviewed suggest that conscious experience of external stimuli cannot be separated from, and is affected by, the whole situation in which they are perceived, including any response to such stimuli (no matter whether spontaneous or, as in most experimental conditions, complying with instructions). If so, we must conclude that the mechanisms by which conscious experience of a relatively complex situation is achieved are indeed widely distributed in neural space and subdivided into several processors. None of these, so far as we know from observation of brain-damaged subjects, centralizes in itself the role of conscious homunculus.

The division of preconscious labour among several processors with no sole gate-way to consciousness entails a relativity of the timing of consciousness as well as the possibility of ongoing rearrangement of what is being experienced. In normal people, a rearrangement of this kind is suggested by the results of an unpublished experiment by Cumming, cited by Allport (1988). In that experiment, a row of five letters was presented to the subjects. The letters flashed one after another in rapid sequence and in a spatio-temporal order such as to produce masking of the letters in the second and fourth locations in the row. Subjects had to press one key if a target letter was present and another key if it was not. Under time pressure, when the target letter was in a masked position subjects on some occasions correctly responded by pressing the 'present' key and then apologized for what they believed was an error. The phenomenon is similar to the abortive movement which, under conditions of double simultaneous stimulation, I observed some brain-damaged patients to make towards the stimulus undergoing extinction before indicating the location of the antagonist stimulus. In both cases, however, the problem arises as to whether the subjects had responded on the basis of a fleeting sensory experience or had produced a nonconsciously triggered reaction.

The kind of problems arising from the diachronic structure of conscious experience is illustrated by the following example. In an experiment done some years ago (Bisiach et al., 1985), patients with left hemineglect had to react to single 200-ms illuminations of red or green diodes in either visual hemifield by pressing a lit response-key of the same colour with their right forefinger. There were four response keys, one red and one green on each side of the apparatus which lay in front of the patient. On each trial, two keys of different colours, one on the left and one on the right, came on simultaneously with the flash of light and remained lit until one of them was pressed. Stimuli were flashed during visual fixation on the centre of the frontal panel of the apparatus; after their appearance, the patient was free to move his eyes in any direction. There were four stimulus–response conditions, two spatially uncrossed and two crossed, with 16 trials for each of them (left-side stimuli requiring left-side response; left-side stimuli requiring right-side response; etc). Catch trials in which the response keys were turned on in the absence of any stimulus were interspersed among regular trials. The rate of correct reactions to left (contralesional) stimuli was found to be more severely reduced when the response was required on the left-side key than when required on the right-side key. Reactions to stimuli appearing in the right visual hemifield (i.e. in the hemifield unaffected by the brain lesion) were almost errorless when the response was required on the right side; when it was required on the left side, however, the patients made many errors. The latter were mainly due to an erroneous ipsilateral response, either to the unlit key of the correct colour or to the lit key of the incorrect colour, but in several instances the patients gave no response at all, as if they had not perceived the stimulus in the *intact* visual field.

This paradoxical phenomenon was most evident in patient FS, who had a lesion involving the frontal lobe and anterior sub-cortical structures. Whereas his performance was errorless on trials in which right-side stimuli required responses to the right, on the 16 trials on which he should have reacted to the same type of stimuli by pressing the left key, FS gave only one correct response. On several such occasions he asserted, as he did on catch trials, that no stimulus had appeared. Given his correct performance on trials with right-hand stimuli requiring responses to the right side of the panel, it is plausible to assert that he had been phenomenally aware of those stimuli, at least for a brief interval, also when he denied the occurrence of some of them in trials requiring responses to the left side. What is not possible to say is whether any trace of phenomenal experience persisted at the moment when he uttered his denial. Perhaps, all conscious memory of the stimulus had been suppressed by inhibitory processes caused by not having found the appropriate response-key on the preferred side. Alternatively, his denial could have been confabulated, as suggested by Shallice (1988, p. 398) over a preserved phenomenal experience of the stimulus. It is worth noting that a paradoxical denial of stimuli present on the *ipsilesional* side of egocentric space has also been found by Tegnér and Levander in the above mentioned study. Those of their patients who showed 'directional hypokinesia', after having crossed out in the mirror-inverted condition only the lines which lay on their right but were seen on their left, denied the presence of further lines, thus ignoring those which were present on the right side of the visual array.

If one considers these puzzling data, Allport's (1988) doubts about the possibility of giving a full answer to some questions about consciousness appear justified. Nevertheless, it is evident that this sceptical conclusion is drawn from data that tell us a great deal about what phenomenal experience consists of.

6.4. UNITY AND DISUNITY OF CONSCIOUSNESS

One may still feel inclined to play down the import of the distributed origin of phenomenal experience suggested by the data reviewed above and claim that what really matters is the coherence of that experience. However, the unity that at first glance distinguishes most of everyday phenomenal experience breaks down progressively if we take into consideration the transition from illusions to delusions and other more dramatic dissociations, some of which, though of marginal occurrence, are not of a pathological nature. A touch of dissociation is already present in common perceptual illusions, where phenomenal experience may peacefully coexist with the conscious belief in its lack of veridicality. The dissociation becomes much more impressive when an illusion overwhelms a belief of which the rationality is still acknowledged by the subject. I have two favourite examples. One is the patient mentioned by Hécaen (1972), who remarked on her inability to be convinced by her own sight that the upper limb joined to the left side of her body belonged to her. The other is LA-O, a patient of mine. Shortly after the onset of a right-hemisphere lesion, while taking for granted the ownership of her left shoulder, she inferred that the left upper arm was also hers (because it was attached to her left shoulder), but was unsure about her elbow and lower arm and firmly refused to admit that the left hand was part of her body. During recovery, she seemed to entertain contemporaneously opposing doxastic attitudes towards the same proposition, as can be observed in patients recovering from schizophrenia: averments of true and false beliefs about the ownership of her left upper limb appeared in close temporal proximity and were equally suffixed, as it were, with a short-lived look of tense puzzlement.

It might be objected that what occurs in such instances is not a split of phenomenal awareness but an alternation of normal and abnormal experiences which does not undermine the notion of the unity of consciousness. There are, however, situations in which the dissociability of phenomenal experience seems undeniable. Dreams, indeed, are sometimes experienced as real and unreal at the same time, as happens when one finds solace in the *arrière-pensée* that the terrifying event one is involved in is in fact a dream. A double awareness, in dreaming, may sometimes be likened to two different characters on the stage. This is exemplified by the following personal anecdote. I once dreamt that I was being told by my teacher Alexsandr Romanovich Luria that a certain patient had undergone an intracarotid sodium amytal test a few days earlier at the Burdenko Neurosurgical Institute. 'Which side?', I asked. Alexsandr Romanovich hesitated an instant and then answered, somewhat dryly: 'Both sides, of course'. On which I felt ashamed of my silly question: *of course*, I 'remembered' patients always undergo sodium amytal injection on both sides when a test is required.

The above example, however, demonstrated that, even when under particular circumstances the content of awareness reveals the disunity of its source, a great deal of integration may be achieved through mechanisms we are still very far from knowing. In my dream, a mechanism of some sort had done the job of the playwright, giving coherence to incompatible pieces of cognitive activity through the expedient of dramatization, i.e. by meaningfully dividing between two individuals what would have been incoherent in one. In an old-time party game, a haphazard cluster of words may directly combine or be edited into surrealist prose such as '*Le cadavre exquis goûtera le vin nouveau*'. Likewise, when the elements of what is going to be the content of phenomenal experience swarm from the endogenous activity of the nervous system in a disorderly way, they might be integrated by the intervention, as it were, of the brain's editorial staff. In the awareness of the external world, the coherence of phenomenal experience largely reflects the coherence of the environment; a slight amount of retouching is evident in phenomena such as the visual completion occurring in the blind spot, the phoneme restoration effect (Warren, 1970), or intriguing illusions (reviewed by Dennett & Kinsbourne, 1991) such as the colour changes during illusory movement or the 'cutaneous rabbit' phenomenon. In the case of internally generated experiences, on the other hand, coherence is probably achieved with reference to a model set by previous exposure to the environment and through induction; this leaves much room for inventiveness but imposes constraints, vestiges of which are retained even in dreaming and schizophrenia. Conformity with such a model is likely to require a great deal of pruning and readjusting of preconscious activity, whereas it may admit nonveridical intrusions in the recollection of previous experiences. At any rate, the process of coherent cross-integration of phenomenal experience does not require a mind within the mind—let alone a mind above the mind —any more than a resident architect is required for the shaping of a cluster of H_2O molecules into a snow crystal. The result of this process may be a more or less complete temporary relaxation achieved through a distributed conterbalance of different competing representations arising within the expanse of the neural network. The fact that in wakefulness thought processes are radically different from those occurring in dreaming suggests that there are progressive levels of cross-integration. This, however, does not imply the endorsement of an intelligent homunculus responsible for the highest level: (relative) rationality may still be conceived to result from a virtual machine distributed across a vast expanse of the cerebral cortex.

6.5. LEVELS OF PROCESSING OF CONSCIOUS REPRESENTATIONS

The foregoing attempt to clarify what it means for phenomenal experience to have spatio-temporal structure and to dispel homuncular preconceptions still leaves unanswered the question as to what level of processing characterizes the representation of individual contents of consciousness. This aspect of the problem has been discussed at length by Jackendoff (1987). If I understand it correctly, his *Intermediate-Level Theory of Consciousness* states that: (a) the contents of phenomenal experience are sensory-specific; (b) as regards perceptual awareness, their structure is neither an unelaborated neural reproduction of the most peripheral stimulation pattern, nor a 'central' (categorical and amodal) interpretation of that same pattern. In other words, the contents of phenomenal experience consist of parsed and selected information preserving the instant, modality-specific properties of objects in a singular, definite orientation with respect to the sensory surface. Thus, for example, phenomenal awareness of a word is held by Jackendoff to correspond to the phonological structure of that word, rather than to its acoustic spectrum or to its meaning, and phenomenal awareness of a visual object to Marr's concept of '$2\frac{1}{2}$-D sketch' of that object, rather than to a '3-D model' of the latter. I largely subscribe to Jackendoff's views, to which, however, I will add a few comments.

It is true that, in the normal case, we are not separately conscious of, for example, the intermediate product of the dedicated processors that in the case of vision analyse in parallel single features of objects such as shape, location, colour and motion. However, when damage to all but one of such processors leaves a single feature being processed, awareness of that isolated feature is still possible, as for example in patient BRA, studied by Warrington (1985, and personal communication). While being severely impaired as regards visual acuity, shape perception and visual location due to brain infarctions incurred during open-heart surgery, BRA was fully aware of the colour of an object though unable to attribute definite shape or location to that 'feeling' of colour.

As regards the lack of any phenomenal experience of more abstract structures such as types or categories, even within single sensory domains, this might be due to the fact that such conceptual entities, as opposed to tokens, have no existence in the brain, except as procedures available to *catalogue* or *generate*, when required, modality-specific instances of any category through activation of determinate cell assemblies. The application of procedures of this kind to incoming sensory information might underlie capabilities such as perceptual constancies and intersensory matching. Their endogenous activation might give rise to mental images, dreams and hallucinations. Jackendoff argues that if phenomenal experience of a *perceived* token went beyond the intermediate-level structure (which, in the case of vision, would be something like Marr's '$2\frac{1}{2}$-D sketch') we would not be conscious of a seen cube as something different from a felt cube. But this might be due to the fact that, whatever might be the ultimate structural level of conscious percepts, our being conscious of a seen cube as something different from a felt cube depends on lower-level structures being organized into, *but not superseded by*, higher-level structures. On the other hand, there is no earmark left by earlier sensory processing upon the contents of phenomenal awareness, on the basis of which to explain why an imagined or hallucinated cube is experienced as seen or felt rather than amodal. Activities of the mind underlying uninstantiated concepts such as 'cubeness' do not figure, *per se*, among the contents of phenomenal experience. We may know them, as it were, by *our own* description, rather than by acquaintance. This is why I would qualify such activities as 'abstracting' (rather than 'abstract') and 'generative', and call them 'procedures' involved in the construction of the contents of phenomenal experience, rather than 'structures' (in order to avoid confusion with that which is being constructed).

Finally, granted that what Jackendoff calls 'intermediate-level structure' is the skeleton of what we experience, the question remains open as to the extent to which such a structure can be teased apart from what goes beyond it, that is from the unavoidable experiential halo aroused by associations of any kind. As soon as I happen to hear 'If' played by Art Tatum, my experience differs in important respects from what it would be if I were born in the 1960s.

Within the specific scope of this chapter, however, the main problem is whether reaching an 'intermediate-level structure' is a sufficient condition for access to consciousness or, if it is not, what else is needed. Do 'nonconscious' masked primes in experiments such as those of Marcel (1983) and Allport *et al.* (1985) fail to access consciousness despite having been processed up to an intermediate-level structure or do they immediately recede from it, without leaving any trace, as a consequence of backward masking? To what extent are neglect patients nonconscious of stimuli lying on the side of space contralateral to their lesioned hemisphere when their behaviour shows that such stimuli are processed up to the level at issue?

My patient EB, who suffered from right brain damage, was apparently unaware of the left side of written words and pronounceable nonwords, so that, for example, she read STAGIONE (season) or RAGIONE (reason) or CARNAGIONE (complexion); yet she would correctly name the letters composing the left side of unpronounceable nonwords such as XRTMNGIONE, although stimuli belonging to the three categories were randomly interleaved (Bisiach *et al.*, 1990b). Did the left side of words and pronounceable nonwords have short-lived permanence in consciousness, or did they have no access to it at all? These questions seem to take for granted that access to consciousness is an all-or-nothing step. Probably it is not. In the case of EB we had an observable input, i.e. the written word, and an observable output, i.e. the spoken word. What was in between is conjectural. Earlier stages of visual processing were evidently unimpaired, as demonstrated by her ability to react differently to pronounceable and unpronounceable strings of letters. Yet, when she read real words and pronounceable nonwords the output did not match the input. A possible explanation of EB's behaviour is that what occurred in her head was the wrong construction of an incremental hypothesis about the input. Due to the dysfunction underlying her hemineglect, that hypothesis was eventually dominated by the right side of the input, thus giving rise to phenomena of neglect or completion, unless an interrupt was brought about by the strangeness of an unpronounceable string of letters. However, given the data, we cannot say anything definite about EB's phenomenal experience during the process leading up to the output, all the more so because there is no reason to believe that processes of that kind are linear. All we can say is that, as in the case of nonconscious priming, information that has reached a relatively advanced stage of cognitive processing may not have access to (or permanence in) consciousness.

In unilateral neglect a dissociation between graphemic and word awareness may even be found. Whereas we have no definite evidence about conscious experience of the content of the graphemic buffer as regards EB's neglect and completion dyslexia, RB, a neglect patient described by Hillis and Caramazza (1990), was at least temporarily aware of graphemes in the word-segment undergoing neglect or completion; invited to read words (e.g. VILLAGE), he would first spell them correctly and, immediately after, make a neglect or completion error in reporting the whole word (MILEAGE).

Patients suffering from unilateral neglect may provide further evidence about the possible lack of consciousness of visual information the processing of which has reached what Jackendoff calls 'intermediate level'. This evidence comes from simple experiments in which two drawings are shown, one above the other, differing in a conspicuous detail on the left (neglected) side. When it is established that the patient is unable to detect that difference, he is invited to indicate his preference for one of the two drawings. If he objects to the silliness of being asked to opt for one of two identical drawings, it is necessary to induce him to choose. The preference test is repeated a number of times, with one of the two drawings placed at random above or below the other. In the original experiment by Marshall and Halligan (1988), the drawings were outlines of two houses, of which one had bright red flames on the left side; asked which house she would prefer to live in, the patient, despite having found the two pictures identical, consistently chose the non-burning house. We attempted to replicate Marshall and Halligan's results in four patients, with three additional pairs of drawings (Bisiach & Rusconi, 1990, see Fig. 6.1). The preference test was not always possible, either because some patients were able to indicate the relevant difference in a pair, or because they were not able to identify some of the drawings. When it was possible, the result was not always in agreement with that obtained by Marshall and Halligan. Of the three patients who were asked to show their preference for one of the two houses, one gave inconsistent responses and two consistently preferred the burning

FIGURE 6.1. (From Bisiach & Rusconi, 1990).

house. On the contrary, the unbroken glass was consistently preferred by the two patients who could be tested with that pair. The pot containing flowers was also preferred in all trials by the only patient to whom that test could be given. Our patients offered spontaneous comments on their choices, which appeared in some instances to be made on the basis of real (though negligible) differences on the right side of two paired drawings. In other instances, however, the alleged difference was clearly confabulated. The extent of the confabulation was impressive when it referred, for example, to the different number of windows or the different layout of the two houses. Taken together, the results suggest that information about a prominent detail, the presence of which is not acknowledged by the patient, may influence his appraisal of the configuration in which that detail is located. In some instances, information about that detail appears to be processed up to the level at which meaning is captured.

6.6. BREAKDOWN OF AWARENESS OF STIMULI IN CENTRAL VISION

Our replication of Marshall and Halligan's (1988) study was supplemented by a very elementary task from which we obtained unexpected results. In an attempt to force the patients to find the relevant difference existing between the two drawings of each pair, we asked them to trace the contour of each drawing with the tip of their right forefinger. Altogether, we were able to collect the results of 10 administrations of this tracing task. In one instance, the procedure was effective in revealing the differing detail to the patient; its effectiveness was dubious in two, but in the remaining seven the correct execution of the task was of no help. Hard to believe as it might appear, a patient could slide his fingertip through the flames without noticing them, or trace the contour of the left side of the broken glass without realizing that it was broken.

The phenomenon we observed on the tracing task is most significant because it reveals a severe disorder in the very area to which the patient's gaze is directed. The patients never lost sight of the path their finger had to follow; not even when that path was half concealed, as was the case with the drawing in which flames were superimposed on the outline of the house. Nevertheless, they seemed unaware of the leftside differences they came across in tracing the contour of the drawings, even when—as in the case of the two houses or of the two flowerpots—such differences lay, for an interval of time, to the *right* of the moving fingertip. This finding suggests that neglect, in some instances may be related to the (observer-relative) left side of a visual object, rather than to retinotopic co-ordinates, or other self-centred co-ordinates, independent of the content of the visual field.

It is well known that people can engender variable gradients of spatial attention independent of the line of their gaze. Therefore, and in agreement with Kinsbourne's theory (1987), neglect patients' *covert* attention is likely to be polarized towards the ipsilesional side of the visual field and to decrease—with a more or less continuous gradient—towards the fixation point and beyond, reaching its minimum in the most contralesional area. Some experiments by Posner and associates (Posner *et al.*, 1982) indeed suggest that in unilateral neglect covert attention cannot easily be disengaged from the ipsilesional side when conative attention should be addressed to a more contralesional area. In left hemineglect, this may explain the paradoxical extinction of a parafoveal stimulus in the right (unaffected) half-field, when a more peripheral (i.e. rightward) stimulus is simultaneously presented in *that* half-field (Bisiach & Geminiani, 1991). Accordingly, it may be conjectured that an inability to disengage covert attention from the right side of a drawing might cause extinction-like phenomena as regards leftside details even when such details come into central vision. Obviously, however, an extinction hypothesis cannot explain the patients' failure to discover any leftside difference in a pair of drawings even when the difference lies in a contour they are able to trace. On the other hand, the failure can hardly be interpreted as being due to a faulty comparison depending on a disorder of visual memory restricted to contralesional space: in the pictures of the burning house, the broken glass and the torn banknote, indeed, the differing details were anomalies worthy of attention in their own right.

Although what we have learned from blindsight warns against forming rash opinions as regards the amount of phenomenal experience of sensory information guiding willed movements, it would seem preposterous to assert that an unfamiliar outline could be traced by the patient's finger with no perceptual awareness of the edge along which the finger has to proceed. It seems more reasonable to suggest that *mindful* processing of the right side of a visual object shaded, in our patients, into *absent-minded* processing of the left side, where sensory information would fail to achieve integration into a fully fledged conscious representation. This might also be the case when the object is the patient's own body. A common explanation would thus apply to our findings relative to the tracing task and to the puzzling instances in which neglect patients deny their hemiplegia even when they look at the examiner's demonstration of its presence.

A similar phenomenon is likely to affect perception of the whole environment. This is strongly suggested by what Crowne *et al.* (1981) found in the monkey after unilateral frontal eye-field ablation. Before fully recovering from the effects of the operation, the monkeys reacted to menacing stimuli approaching from either side by retreating to the opposite side of the cage. However, if two such stimuli were simultaneously presented, one on each side, the avoidance reaction appeared only to the ipsilesional stimulus, so that the animal retreated near to the contralesional. (Preoperatively, double stimulation caused double avoidance and the monkey would retreat to the middle of the cage.) 'Frequently', the authors reported, 'the operated monkeys would turn their heads briefly to look at the proximate threat object, but immediately returned to regard the distal threat. These contralateral-gaze glances were not accompanied by shifts in position in the cage.' (p. 179). This is all the more significant because when the monkey looked at the contralesional threat the ipsilesional was out of sight, thus ruling out any explanation in terms of *sensory* competition. Evidently, however, the ipsilesional threat was not out of mind, otherwise the monkeys would have reacted to the contralesional as they would if it had been presented alone. Full awareness of the contralesional threat thus appeared to be barred by competition at a higher representational level.

6.7. UNILATERAL DISTORTION OF THE CONTENT OF SUBJECTIVE EXPERIENCE

The contralesional disorder of representational activity appearing as a consequence of damage to crucial areas of one side of the brain may not only manifest itself in the form of the more or less complete eclipse from consciousness of one side of egocentric space (within one or more domains of representational content) that characterizes unilateral neglect in the strict acceptance of the term. Productive phenomena such as pathological completion, confabulation and somatoparaphrenia (Gerstmann, 1942) may also emerge. For reasons that are still unknown, such productive phenomena are most infrequent as regards the content of far extrapersonal space, although some patients claim, for example, that the side opposite to the hospital environment they correctly perceive on their right belongs to their home and behave in accordance with this claim (e.g. by calling for members of the family they assume to be there). In near extrapersonal space, pathological completion of one side of perceived words and drawings is much more frequent, but the imported portion is, as a rule, totally compatible with what is correctly reported from the other side. It is worth noting that in this case the phenomenon seems to be the result, as it were, of conceptual confabulation rather than of sensory completion; this, at least, is the impression one gets from the reading disorders of my patient EB and patient RB of Hillis and Caramazza (1990). Processes of a different kind are likely to underlie the paradoxical leftward displacement of the subjective midpoint observed in neglect patients when they bisect very short lines (Halligan & Marshall, 1988; Tegnér *et al.*, 1990). One of these patients reported seeing a 'shadow-line' extending leftwards from the line he had to bisect (Tégner, personal communication).

Productive misrepresentation of the contralesional side is much more frequent in bodily space. Its implications for the study of neural correlates of consciousness have been discussed elsewhere (Bisiach & Geminiani, 1991) and I will not deal with them here, except to attenuate my former opposition to a psychodynamic interpretation of unawareness and denial of neurological disorders such as hemiplegia and hemianopia, and to make a cursory remark on the impetus, as it were, of contents that are gated from consciousness in these pathological conditions.

I still believe that at the root of unawareness or denial of hemiplegia and hemianopia lies a dysfunction of the brain's representational activity circumscribed to one side of the body, rather than the concealment of extremely disturbing evidence. However, I agree that, at least as regards denial of hemiplegia and disavowal of the paralysed limbs, part of the patient's behaviour reflects the need to come to terms with the pathological representation of one side of their body. That is to say that the contents of the patient's consciousness corresponding to manifestations ranging from 'personification' of the paralysed limbs (Critchley, 1955) to the most abstruse forms of somatoparaphrenia are likely to combine active and reactive components; the former being the direct product of the lesion of a critical area of the neural network, the latter issuing from the spared areas of that same network.

An issue that has so far been neglected is whether and to what extent the phenomenal experience and the behaviour of the patients who are oblivious of neurological disorders, or utterly deny them, is influenced by contents that find no access to conscious representation. Although its assessment requires further data and reflection, this issue is worth attention, given the results of investigations in normal subjects that demonstrate different utilization of sensory input depending on whether or not its content reaches consciousness (Marcel, 1980). Contents held in incommunicado might still influence phenomenal experience in patients showing unilateral neglect and related disorders. Such nonconscious contents, rather than an (originally) content-free emotional attitude caused by the lesion, might be responsible for the phenomena of laevophobia that can sometimes be observed in patients with left hemineglect and/or misrepresentation. Misoplegia (Critchley, 1953), i.e. hatred for the paralysed limbs, is a well-known instance of laevophobia. The latter, however, can also manifest itself in regard to the extrapersonal environment, e.g. when the patients assert a dislike for things on their left, or simply behave as if they felt such a dislike.

6.8. CONCLUSIONS

In this chapter, I have argued—against the Cartesian tradition (Fig. 6.2) —that there is no definite brain centre for conscious experience (Sections 6.3 and 6.4). Clinical and experimental data collected in patients suffering from unilateral spatial neglect and related disorders, indeed, suggest that conscious experience rests entirely on a virtual mechanism distributed over brain circuits that are still very poorly understood. This distribution, however, seems to be both horizontal (across and within sensory modalities) and vertical, in so far as conscious experience

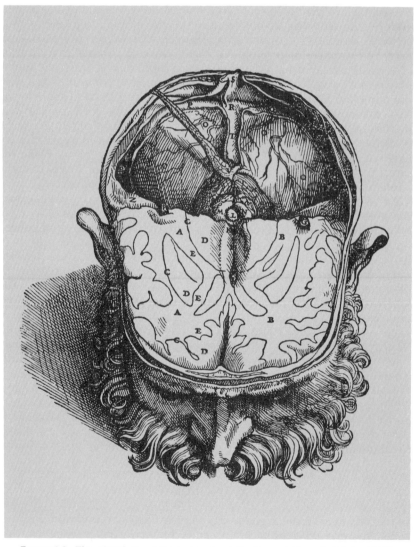

FIGURE 6.2. The pineal gland (L) in Vesalius' *De Humani Corporis Fabrica* (1543).

appears to be shaped not only by afferent occurrences but also by the kinds of actions that happen to be undertaken on the basis of such occurrences. The spread of such mechanisms in neural space entails the possibility of local failures and the dissociability of conscious experience into contrasting states. Clinical neurology provides dramatic examples of both kinds of disorder: the former is evident in the (cognitively irremediable) lack of awareness of one side of space or of the consequences of a brain lesion; among those most suggestive of the latter are the mirror-reversal of the lack of awareness of one side of visual space found by Tegnér and Levander and the doxastic doubleness that may affect particular beliefs on a background of normal cognitive activities (Bisiach & Geminiani, 1991).

In Section 6.5, I touched on the issue of the level of processing and representational contents (as regards the conscious/nonconscious dichotomy) and argued that patients may be apparently unaware of what lies on the side opposite to the brain lesion despite its having been processed up to a high level, even to the level, perhaps, at which meaning is captured. It might be objected that neglect and pathological completion of the contralesional side of visual stimuli could be the result of a false revision of earlier conscious veridical percepts, as suggested by the correct reading of the left side of unpronounceable nonwords by my patient EB; an 'Orwellian' revision, as Dennett (1991) would put it. The validity of this conjecture, however, is seriously questioned by the finding that neglect patients may adequately react to features of stimuli of which they seem to be totally unaware even *while* they focus attention on those features: such patients may in fact be quite consistent in 'liking' the drawing of an unbroken glass better than that of a broken one while being unable to tell the difference between the two of them even when they trace the contour of the broken edge (Section 6.6). All in all, there seem to be at present no available data about the precise way in which conscious and nonconscious representational structures might differ.

Finally, I raised (without even attempting to answer it) the question as to whether anomalous experiences about the contents of the contralesional side of personal and extrapersonal space might be an effect of nonconsciously processed features of such contents (Section 6.7). This, I believe, is one of the main tasks left for future investigation.

Another fundamental task for future investigation is to ascertain to what extent the failure underlying unilateral neglect and misrepresentation is due to structural unavailability (or subversion, or disconnection) of the representational medium, to withdrawal of processing resources from it, or to its inhibition by competing brain processes. Firmer grounds will be available for comprehensive theories of the brain mechanisms of conscious representation, in proportion to the development of our knowledge of the mechanisms underlying neglect and related disorders, as well as those that underlie their compensation.

Let us now turn to the crucial issue (Section 6.2). To what extent do the data reviewed in this chapter contribute to an understanding of consciousness? If we select each time just one of the possible operational definitions of consciousness (e.g. the ability to report verbally the contents of our mental processes), then it is clear that such data tell us a great deal. Conflicting conclusions, however, seem to be reached if we refer to different operational definitions, since we have confronted instances in which what is verbally reported fails to be witnessed by nonverbal responses (Bisiach *et al.*, 1989) and instances in which the opposite is true (e.g. Marcel, 1990). But here indeed seems to lie the main moral we can draw from the corpus of empirical data so far collected: any intuition to the contrary notwithstanding, consciousness is far from being unitary.

The aim stated at the beginning of the chapter, however, was somewhat more ambitious. It made explicit reference to the understanding of phenomenal experience, rather than of an operationalized consciousness. Now there are, as we have seen, extreme instances in which trying to make inferences about the phenomenal experience of a patient may seem to be hopeless, given the degree of incoherence of the observed behaviour. Such is the case, for example, as regards the delayed denial of visual stimuli in the unaffected field by patient FS (Bisiach *et al.*, 1985), or the denial of lines lying in the unaffected visual field by Tegnér and Levander's patients showing 'directional hypokinesia'. There is much less difficulty as regards the different rates of perceptual report that characterize different kinds of response. Here, the observed behaviour may be quite similar to that of normal subjects tested with near-threshold stimuli. In this case, the evaluation of data in terms of phenomenal experience is much safer and any residual doubt could be cleared up by first-person experience. Between these two extremes lies an area of uncertainty where reference to phenomenal experience, no matter how utopian in its aims, might at least guide retreat to an intelligent, non-eliminative operationalism.

FOOTNOTE

1. It must be noted that Marcel used *simple* nonverbal reactions, whereas we (Bisiach *et al.*, 1989) used *choice* nonverbal responses. This may explain why nonverbal indicators of perceptual awareness were more sensitive than verbal indicators in his experiments and less sensitive in ours (cf. the interpretation we gave in our paper).

ACKNOWLEDGEMENTS

The preparation of this chapter has greatly benefited from my participation in the workshop on Human Consciousness and the Brain. I gratefully acknowledge my debt to Dan Dennett who organized the workshop, the small group of participants who contributed in making it productive and pleasurable, and the Rockefeller Foundation, who gave us magnificent hospitality at the Villa Serbelloni in Bellagio at the end of March, 1990. David Milner, Mick Rugg and the Russell Trust/Wellcome Trust Symposium gave me the incentive to lay down, for what they are worth, some of the ideas that have grown out of my work with brain-damaged patients. Joe Bogen, Ray Jackendoff and Tony Marcel made very valuable comments on a preliminary draft; I hope I have not misinterpreted them in the final version.

REFERENCES

Albert, M.L. (1973). A simple test of visual neglect. *Neurology*, **23**, 658–664.

Allport, A. (1988). What concept of consciousness? In A.J. Marcel and E. Bisiach (eds), *Consciousness in Contemporary Science*. Oxford: Clarendon Press.

Allport, D.A., Tipper, S.P. & Chmiel, N.R.J. (1985). Perceptual integration and postcategorical filtering. In M.I. Posner and O.S.M. Marin (eds), *Attention and Performance XI*. Hillsdale NJ: Erlbaum.

Bisiach, E. (1988). The (haunted) brain and consciousness. In A.J. Marcel and E. Bisiach (eds), *Consciousness in Contemporary Science*. Oxford: Clarendon Press.

Bisiach, E. & Berti, A. (1987). Dyschiria. An attempt at its systemic explanation. In M. Jeannerod (ed.), *Neurophysiological and Neuropsychological Aspects of Spatial Neglect*, Amsterdam: North-Holland.

Bisiach, E., & Geminiani, G. (1991). Anosognosia related to hemiplegia and hemianopia. In G.P. Prigatano and D.L. Schacter (eds), *Awareness of Deficit after Brain Injury*, pp. 17–39. New York: Oxford University Press.

Bisiach, E. & Rusconi, M.L. (1990). Break-down of perceptual awareness in unilateral neglect. *Cortex*, **26**, 643–649.

Bisiach, E., Berti, A. & Vallar, G. (1985). Analogical and logical disorders underlying unilateral neglect of space. In M.I. Posner and O.S.M. Marin (eds), *Attention and Performance XI*. Hillsdale NJ: Erlbaum.

Bisiach, E., Vallar, G. & Geminiani, G. (1989). Influence of response modality on perceptual awareness of contralesional visual stimuli. *Brain*, **112**, 1627–1636.

Bisiach, E., Geminiani, G., Berti, A. & Rusconi, M.L. (1990a). Perceptual and premotor factors of unilateral neglect. *Neurology*, **40**, 1278–1281.

Bisiach, E., Meregalli, S. & Berti, A. (1990b). Mechanisms of production control and belief fixation in human visuospatial processing: clinical evidence from unilateral neglect and misrepresentation. In M.L. Commons, R.J. Herrnstein, S.M. Kosslyn and D.B. Mumford (eds), *Quantitative Analyses of Behavior. Vol. IX: Computational and Clinical Approaches to Pattern Recognition and Concept Formation*. Hillsdale NJ: Erlbaum.

Critchley, M. (1953). *The Parietal Lobes*. London: Hafner Press.

Critchley, M. (1955). Personification of paralyzed limbs in hemiplegics. *British Medical Journal*, **2**, 284–286.

Crowne, D.P., Yeo, C.H. & Steele Russell, I. (1981). The effects of unilateral frontal eye field lesions in the monkey: Visual-motor guidance and avoidance behaviour. *Behavioural Brain Research*, **2**, 165–187.

Dennett, D. (1991). *Consciousness Explained*. Boston: Little, Brown.

Dennett, D. & Kinsbourne, M. (1991). Time and the observer. *Behavioral and Brain Sciences*, in press.

Gerstmann, J. (1942). Problems of imperception of disease and of impaired body territories with organic lesions. *Archives of Neurology and Psychiatry*, **48**, 890–913.

Halligan, P.W. & Marshall, J.C. (1988). How long is a piece of string? A study of line bisection in a case of neglect. *Cortex*, **24**, 321–328.

Halligan, P.W. & Marshall, J.C. (1989). Laterality of motor response in visuo-spatial neglect: A case study. *Neuropsychologia*, **27**, 1301–1307.

Hebb, D.O. (1949). *Organization of Behavior*. New York: Wiley.

Hécaen, H. (1972). *Introduction à la Neuropsychologie*. Paris: Larousse.

Hillis, A. & Caramazza, A. (1990). The effects of attentional deficits on reading and spelling. In A. Caramazza (ed.), *Cognitive Neuropsychology and Neurolinguistics: Advances in Models of Cognitive Function and Impairment*. Hillsdale NJ: Erlbaum.

Jackendoff, R. (1987). *Consciousness and the Computational Mind*. Cambridge MA: MIT Press.

Joanette, Y., Brouchon, M., Gauthier, L. & Samson, M. (1986). Pointing with left vs right hand in left visual field neglect. *Neuropsychologia*, **24**, 391–396.

Kinsbourne, M. (1987). Mechanisms of unilateral neglect. In M. Jeannerod (ed.), *Neurophysiological and Neuropsychological Aspects of Spatial Neglect*. Amsterdam: North-Holland.

Kinsbourne, M. (1988). Integrated field theory of consciousness. In A.J. Marcel and E. Bisiach (eds), *Consciousness in Contemporary Science*. Oxford: Clarendon Press.

Marcel, A.J. (1980). Conscious and preconscious recognition of polysemous words: Locating the selective effects of prior verbal context. In R.S. Nickerson (ed.), *Attention and Performance VIII*. Hillsdale NJ: Erlbaum.

Marcel, A.J. (1983). Conscious and unconscious perception: Experiments on visual masking and word recognition. *Cognitive Psychology*, **15**, 197–237.

Marcel, A.J. (1988). Phenomenal experience and functionalism. In A.J. Marcel and E. Bisiach (eds), *Consciousness in Contemporary Science*. Oxford: Clarendon Press.

Marcel, A.J. (1990). Slippage in the unity of consciousness, or, to what do perceptual speech acts refer? Poster presented at Russell Trust Symposium, St Andrews, Scotland, September 1990.

Marshall, J.C. & Halligan, P.W. (1988). Blindsight and insight in visuo-spatial neglect. *Nature*, **336**, 766–767.

Mesulam, M.-M. (1981). A cortical network for directed attention and unilateral neglect. *Annals of Neurology*, **10**, 309–325.

Merzenich, M.M. & Kaas, J.H. (1980). Principles of organization of sensori-perceptual systems in mammals. *Progress in Psychobiology and Physiological Psychology*, **9**, 1–41.

Nagel, T. (1974). What is it like to be a bat? *Philosophical Review*, **83**, 435–450.

Posner, N.I., Cohen, Y. & Rafal, R.D. (1982). Neural systems control of spatial orienting. *Philosophical Transactions of the Royal Society. B*, **298**, 187–198.

Rorty, R. (1982). Comments on Dennett. *Synthese*, **53**, 181–187.

Searle, J.R. (1980). Minds, brains and programs. *Behavioral and Brain Sciences*, **3**, 417–457.

Shallice, T. (1988). *From Neuropsychology to Mental Structure*. New York: Cambridge University Press.

Tegnér, R. & Levander, M. (1991). Through a looking glass. A new technique to demonstrate directional hypokinesia in unilateral neglect. *Brain*, in press.

Tegnér, R., Levander, M. & Caneman, G. (1990). Apparent right neglect in patients with left visual neglect. *Cortex*, **26**, 455–458.

Vesalius, A. (1543). *De Humani Corporis Fabrica*. Basel: J. Oporinus.

Warren, R.M. (1970). Perceptual restoration of missing speech sounds. *Science*, **167**, 392–393.

Warrington, E.K. (1985). Visual deficits associated with occipital lobe lesions in man. *Pontificiae Academiae Scientiarum Scripta Varia*, **54**, 247–261.

Watson, R.T., Miller, B.D. & Heilman, K.M. (1978). Nonsensory neglect. *Annals of Neurology*, **3**, 505–508.

Weiskrantz, L. (1986). *Blindsight. A Case Study and Implications*. Oxford: Clarendon Press.

Zihl, J. & Von Cramon, D. (1980). Registration of light stimuli in the cortically blind hemifield and its effect on localization. *Behavioural Brain Research*, **1**, 287–298.

CHAPTER 7

Disorders of Perceptual Awareness—Commentary

A. David Milner

7.1. CRITERIA FOR CONSCIOUSNESS

A major part of the research that stimulated this book (and the symposium in St Andrews in September, 1990 that was associated with it) concerns demonstrations or claims of 'unconscious' or 'implicit' or 'covert'
perception, particularly in cases of brain damage. These terms are in
need of some terminological hygiene (see Section 7.2 below), but they
are all used to denote cases where the processing of perceptual information appears to proceed to a high level despite the absence of
acknowledged awareness of the results of this processing.

At first sight the concept of perceptual awareness seems unproblem-
atic, even if methods for operationalizing it are not. Furthermore, most
people would accept (with William James) the axiom that all of what we
attend to, and only what we attend to, is present in our consciousness.
In so far as these contents of our consciousness are directly determined
by events in the outside world, then they constitute our perceptual
awareness of that world. According to this commonsense view, we can
perfectly reasonably ask about normal subjects how and to what extent
nonconscious events (nonconscious either because non-attended, or
because below some suitably-defined threshold) can affect *behaviour*. If
these events affect behaviour in a qualitatively different way from consciously perceived events, then we have strong grounds for arguing
further that a beginning is being made on determining what particular
processes, or characteristics of perceptual processes, are associated with
the conscious/unconscious distinction (e.g. Cheesman & Merikle, 1986).

Neuropsychology adds new dimensions to these questions, in that
brain damage may result in dissociations that are either not apparent or
not so starkly apparent in normal individuals. Most modern neuropsychologists, at least tacitly, share Head's (1926) assumption that

'through injury or disease, normal function is laid bare' i.e. that aspects of normal function can be uncovered by brain damage. Moreover, the logic remains essentially the same: thus one can ask about the possible effects *on behaviour* of unacknowledged stimuli in a hemianopic field or in a neglected hemispace; and at a higher level one can ask whether and how agnosic patients may express *through their behaviour* visually derived information about unrecognized objects or faces.

As Allport (1988) points out, however, adoption of this commonsense view requires that we be able to delineate when a person is or is not aware of some stimulus. Unfortunately, as is abundantly clear from Bisiach's discussion (Chapter, 6 this volume), things are not that simple, especially in neurological disease. Thus in neglect a patient may reveal a less severe impairment in detecting lights when using the left than the right hand, or when using a verbal rather than a manual response mode (Duhamel & Brouchon, 1990; Bisiach, Chapter 6, this volume; but see also Halligan *et al.*, 1991). The patient apparently *sees* more stimuli under one response condition than under the other. Paradoxically a cortically blind patient may do *less* well in a detection task when responding verbally than manually (note however that in this case the difference is in responses made to stimuli *none* of which the patient consciously sees; Marcel, 1990).

The commonsense understanding of visual consciousness as unitary thus encounters the greatest and most dramatic problems in neurological conditions like neglect, blindsight, and agnosia. In contrast, in experiments on normal individuals it is generally assumed unquestioningly that any voluntary 'detection response', whether made verbally or manually, will equally reflect awareness of an event, and thus should be perfectly correlated. But once it is clear that such a correlation can be imperfect in cases of brain damage, the commonsense view has to be questioned in normal subjects too. Empirical evidence comes from an experiment by Cumming (unpublished research cited by Allport, 1988) in which, under speed stress, normal subjects sometimes made 'correct' manual responses to masked alphabetic stimuli but then verbally repudiated those responses. Thus it seems not to be the case simply that something is or is not present in consciousness; it all depends on how consciousness is operationally defined. Consciousness is not a single indivisible attribute, even in normal subjects.

Consequently, there are substantive problems in assessing whether an example of 'unconscious perception' actually is unconscious: it may be necessary to apply several criteria to ensure this. But equally challenging is the need to address the data that *make* this a problem. That is, it is important to neuropsychology and to psychology in general to understand not just dissociations between conscious and unconscious processes in perception, but also dissociations between different unconscious processes and even, perhaps, different *conscious* processes. (For example many people would accept that two distinct conscious processes may co-exist in a commissurotomized patient, though most such patients can only talk about one of them. It would thus be thinkable to take the further step and accept that such duality could [sometimes] happen within an undivided brain: cf. Puccetti, 1981.)

It should also be noted that the Jamesian assumption that to attend to X is to be aware of X has now to be questioned. Thus Posner and Rothbart (Chapter 5, this volume) argue that the two can be dissociated even in normal subjects. Again this kind of dissociation may be thrown into relief in instances of brain damage, such as cortical blindness: it is not implausible to suppose that Weiskrantz's patient DB may be attending to visual events of which he is unaware, when he successfully points to their location. One way of seeking evidence on this might be to test whether his performance of such a task would interfere with another concurrent task. Any such further support for instances of 'attention without awareness' would greatly strengthen Posner and Rothbart's theoretical proposal that shifts of attention can be governed by a posterior brain system that is partially independent of a separate frontal system that determines the contents of awareness.

7.2. TERMINOLOGY

The essence of many experiments held to demonstrate 'implicit knowledge' in neurological disorders is the *indirectness* of the testing procedures used in them. For example in the case of a visual disorder, a patient's behavioural acts could be examined for evidence that they are visually guided. However the examination of visuomotor acts is not *necessarily* an indirect test. Thus in the classic demonstrations of blindsight, the patient was not asked to say what he or she saw, but was instead asked to do things, such as to move the eyes or to point the hand. Nonetheless this was a *direct* test of visual localization, since the patient was specifically being asked to direct his eye or hand in space. Even more obviously direct tests used to demonstrate blindsight are where patients are asked to 'guess' the nature of visual stimuli about which they have no direct visual experience, as when Weiskrantz *et al.* (1974) found above-chance forced-choice guessing in DB about simple shapes presented in his field defect. In contrast such direct methods tend to be relatively unsuccessful in uncovering implicit visual abilities in agnosia (see Young & De Haan, Chapter 4, Humphreys *et al.*, Chapter 3, this volume). For example, patients with covert recognition abilities on indirect testing (e.g. priming) fail when tested on forced-choice familiar/unfamiliar face discrimination (Young & De Haan, Chapter 4, this volume).

A now well-established instance of successful direct testing is the demonstration of colour discrimination in cortical blindness (Cowey & Stoerig, Chapter 2, this volume); typically patients have to make direct judgements about the stimuli, even though in doing so they may feel that they are guessing. According to some viewpoints, if indirect methods are unable to provide confirmatory evidence, this might make us less ready to accept that such instances of 'covert' perception are really *qualitatively* different from normal kinds of visual perception. However, as Cowey and Stoerig (Chapter 2, this volume) point out, blindsight *can* be demonstrated by highly indirect methods. Thus Marzi *et al.* (1986) and Corbetta *et al.* (1990) have shown that in most 'blind-sight' patients (though *not* in most cortically blind patients), manual reaction times to stimuli in the intact hemifield are facilitated when an additional light is presented in the scotomatous field. Thus it may be that indirect techniques could demonstrate colour discrimination in scotomata if tried (e.g. perhaps the Marzi facilitatory effect is stronger for pairs of lights of similar wavelength; cf. Pöppel, 1986).

It seems now to be generally accepted that in describing *tasks*, the use of terms like 'covert' or 'implicit' is inappropriate: as discussed by Young and De Haan and by Jacoby and Kelley (Chapters 4 and 10, this volume) these are better reserved to refer to the nature of the *processing* that may or may not occur in response to tasks of different types. In the domain of memory studies, where theoretical developments have advanced furthest, the term 'implicit' is now widely (though by no means universally: see Jacoby and Kelley, Chapter 10 and Mayes, Chapter 11, this volume) used in referring to memory processing where retrieval is unconscious in the sense of being effortless and automatized (e.g. Richardson-Klavehn & Bjork, 1988). 'Covert' on the other hand is preferred by many authors in the perceptual domain (e.g. Cowey & Stoerig, Humphreys *et al.*, and Young & De Haan, Chapters 2, 3 and 4, this volume). This term has the possible drawback that it is also used in a more literal sense in the context of attention shifts that involve no overt act of behavioural orienting (e.g. Posner & Rothbart, Chapter 5, this volume). It also does not tally with the accepted usage in other domains of 'unconscious cognition'; however this could be a distinct advantage if quite different explanatory principles turn out to apply in the different domains. Indeed it may be that 'implicit' is best reserved for *knowledge* that a person possesses unknown to herself or himself (though an empiricist stance requires that this has itself ultimately to be gained through perceptual processes, which in turn will generally have been largely *conscious*). According to this distinction, one might perhaps talk of *covert* perception (i.e. where the products of perceptual analysis are not available to awareness), but *implicit* recognition (see Section 7.6). It would however be invidious to impose a particular terminology upon other authors.

One potentially confusing usage that has crept in to the fringes of the literature is the apparently self-contradictory phrase 'covert awareness'. This phrase probably arises from the ambiguity in the word 'aware': we can be aware of many things (e.g. that Oslo is the capital of Norway) without necessarily being conscious of them at a given time; in this sense, to be aware of something is simply to know it. Thus 'covert awareness' could be synonymous with covert knowledge. However things are confusing enough in this field without making them more so by using the word 'aware' in these two different ways. 'Covert awareness' is best avoided.

7.3. THE FUNCTIONS OF PERCEPTION

A comparative approach leads to a different view of perception from that traditionally held by philosophers, by the layman, and indeed by most visual scientists. The simplest visual systems seem to have evolved as necessary adjuncts to the efficient performance of motor acts; these would include prey catching and predator avoidance, escape, exploration, and manoeuvring around obstacles. Different visual sub-systems seem often to be associated with different behavioural activities; indeed at least to a first approximation they are more usefully thought of as separate *visuomotor* sub-systems (Goodale, 1983, 1988). Once one begins to apply such a functional viewpoint to higher as well as to lower vertebrates, the traditional assumption that the purpose of perceptual processing is to construct a unitary internal picture can be seen to be potentially counterproductive. The fact that we as humans happen to have a vivid and apparently unified visual experience most of the time, does not mean that this internal representation is there to guide behaviour, let alone that it constitutes the *only* way in which vision guides behaviour. The multiplicity of visual pathways apparent in lower vertebrates is retained and expanded in higher mammals (e.g. see Cowey & Stoerig, Chapter 2, this volume), in which indeed it has diversified enormously at the cortical level (e.g. Van Essen, 1985).

The discovery of blindsight and its subsequent refinement and exploration (Weiskrantz, 1986, 1987, 1990; Cowey and Stoerig, Chapter 2, this volume) provides behavioural evidence that multiple visual routes to action exist in man as well as other animals. It seems that in many 'cortically blind' patients visuomotor acts such as directing gaze toward a peripheral object can be accurately accomplished in the absence of awareness of the object, probably by virtue of much the same midbrain visuomotor system as mediates prey catching in frogs and orienting reactions in rats and monkeys (Weiskrantz, 1986). Once one has accepted this idea it becomes easy to regard the rich contents of our visual awareness as unnecessary for the execution of oculomotor and other visually guided acts in normal individuals as well. 'Blindsight' has caught the popular imagination mainly because it seems to constitute a variety of unconscious perception; but the alternative perspective is to regard it instead as evidence for a modular visual processing architecture in the brain. It seems reasonable to suppose that some modules will be (normally) consciously monitored, whilst others will not be; and dissociations between conscious and unconcious modules will be especially conspicuous. This fact renders blindsight (and various analogous dissociations in normal subjects: e.g. Bridgeman *et al.*, 1979; Goodale *et al.*, 1986; Meeres & Graves, 1990) striking, but not necessarily of greater theoretical import than other dissociations.

A new example of such a dissociation has come to light recently in the course of investigations of a case of 'visual form agnosia' (Benson & Greenberg, 1969). In this condition, a patient is severely impaired in the recognition of objects, faces, and other visual configurations, apparently because of a difficulty in telling apart even simple shapes such as squares and rectangles (Efron, 1969) or differently oriented gratings (Campion & Latto, 1985). In one particular patient, DF, these difficulties co-exist with good visual acuity and satisfactory colour discrimination (Milner *et al.*, 1991). (N.B. Some writers, e.g. Farah, 1990, would categorize DF as a typical apperceptive agnosic, while others, e.g. McCarthy & Warrington, 1990, would call her pseudo-agnosic.) Such patients allow one to examine whether visual attributes of an object other than its location (e.g. its size, shape, orientation, and motion) can unconsciously influence the movements of a hand as it is extended towards the object. It has been found that DF reaches accurately towards a slot, whose orientation she cannot judge verbally or manually, inclining the hand (or a hand-held card) in early anticipation of its final correct orientation (Milner *et al.*, 1991; Goodale *et al.*, 1991a). Furthermore DF behaves like normal subjects (Jeannerod, 1981; Jakobson & Goodale, 1991) in the course of reaching out to grasp solid objects of different dimensions, her finger-thumb grip varying lawfully as a function of the width, although she is unable to make width *judgements* of the same objects (Goodale *et al.*, 1991a). In both the orientation and the width domains, DF betrays severely impaired conscious perception whether this is tapped verbally or manually (e.g. by pantomime matching); there is therefore no evidence here for a dissociation between these two response modes, as has been reported in other visual disorders (Bisiach *et al.*, 1989; Marcel, 1990).

Thus at least some of the object properties important in organizing visuomotor prehension operate well in a patient who is unaware of those properties; it may be that other attributes that are difficult for her to perceive (e.g. global motion, and luminance contrast at low spatial frequencies) could likewise be used competently by her in appropriate circumstances. It is interesting that in cases of optic ataxia an opposite dissociation is seen. In these patients, the shape and location of objects can be *judged* with some accuracy, while visuomotor action directed at those objects is grossly impaired (Perenin & Vighetto, 1988). Yet the defect is often restricted to a single visual hemifield, ruling out a simple motor impairment (Rondot, 1989). The focus of damage in these cases lies in the superior parietal region (Perenin & Vighetto, 1988), dorsal to the focus for unilateral neglect (Vallar & Perani, 1986).

It is argued elsewhere (Goodale & Milner, 1991; see also Ettlinger, 1990) that there is a dorsal cortical system primarily dedicated to visuomotor co-ordination in both human and nonhuman primates, which is distinct from the dorsal visuospatial system proposed by Ungerleider and Mishkin (1982). There is growing physiological evidence for systems in area 7 of the parietal lobe not just for guiding arm movements through space (Andersen, 1987) but also for the visual control of concomitant grasping movements (Taira *et al.*, 1990). Neurons that are closely associated with reaching and grasping acts are also found in the inferior part of premotor cortex (area 6) in monkeys, to which area 7 sends heavy projections (Gentilucci & Rizzolatti, 1990).

Thus we may have multiple visuomotor systems operating in parallel with one another, only some of which may yield conscious visual experience; brain damage may act to preserve some at the expense of others. The result may be 'unconscious vision' as in DF and in blindsight, or it may be the reverse, where 'unconscious' visual skills are precisely what is lost, as in optic ataxia. And once the mystic sway that a 'single visual representation' has over our everyday and our scientific thinking has been done away with, it no longer seems surprising that different behavioural criteria for 'visual awareness' may sometimes disagree, any more than that purely behavioural measures may fail to be perfectly correlated. It is admittedly rare among claims for covert or implicit function that one can point to a converse case (double dissociation). Accordingly, optic ataxia provides a useful counter-example to the argument that, in general, damage to a brain system impairs the most 'controlled' aspects of its functioning, leaving relatively intact the most 'automatized' ones. (There are of course other neurological examples of visually guided acts that can be affected without necessarily impairing perceptual experience, such as disturbances in eye movements or in gait or posture.)

If in our patient DF a dorsal visuomotor processing system is operating without intrinsic visual awareness, the question arises as to whether this system might mediate other kinds of unaware vision, for instance in blindsight. Rodman *et al.*, (1989), for instance, note that the most neurons in the middle temporal (MT) area retain their sensitivity for visual motion despite the removal of striate cortex; and they suggest that it might play a role in the covert sensitivity to motion and flicker that has been observed in blindsight (Blythe *et al.*, 1987). Where striate cortex is lost, the dorsal system might have to depend for visual information upon its inputs from the retino-tecto-pulvinar route (see Cowey & Stoerig, Chapter 2, this volume).

7.4. SPACE AND ATTENTION

Although optic ataxia seems to have a different (superior parietal) focus from neglect (inferior parietal), the two disorders are frequently linked together as 'spatial impairments': a convenient simplification that helped lead to the 'two cortical visual systems' dichotomy in which an occipitoparietal stream of processing is often identified with spatial perception in general (Ungerleider & Mishkin, 1982). Of course after large parietal lesions, in monkeys as well as in man, a constellation of impairments (often also including deficits in tactile stereognosis), most of which can be called 'spatial', often co-occur. This does not however mean that they have a common cause. Even within the 'neglect syndrome' there are numerous reports of dissociations between component symptoms (e.g. Barbieri & De Renzi, 1989). In one study, it was found that ipsiversive errors in line bisection, frequently used as a measure of neglect severity, was unrelated to other conventional indices of neglect (Schenkenberg *et al.*, 1980).

A particularly stark departure from the view that neglect is primarily understandable as a disorder of spatial perception has stemmed from the influential writings of Heilman and his colleagues (e.g. Heilman & Valenstein, 1979). These authors proposed that the various symptoms of neglect (including disordered line bisection) could be attributed to a motor bias: a 'directional hypokinesia' in which contraversive actions are difficult to initiate. And as Bisiach (Chapter 6, this volume) describes, a net ipsiversive bias of this kind does seem to contribute to line-bisection errors, especially in certain patients. One patient even responded rightwardly in an 'incongruent' task arranged such that the result of his action was a *leftwardly* erroneous bisection of the line (Bisiach *et al.*, 1990). However this type of output bias seems mainly to underlie bisection errors in patients with frontal or striatal, rather than posterior cerebral lesions. The dual contribution of broadly separable 'motor/preparatory' and 'perceptual/attentional' factors in the symptomatology of neglect is further supported by the recent reports of Tegner and Levander (1991) and Coslett *et al.* (1990). Many neglect patients appear to suffer from a combination of the two.

However 'frontal' neglect is not easily dismissible simply as a motor bias, and is in fact extremely puzzling. It seems from both the work of Tegner and Levander (1991) and of Bisiach *et al.* (1990), that the directional hypokinesia can *over-ride* the perpetual feedback that the patient receives. Thus the above-mentioned patient of Bisiach *et al.*, apparently perceived his *leftward* bisection mark as correct in the 'incongruent' task (i.e. having responded rightwards), although of course a *rightward* bisection was performed under normal congruent conditions. In other words, in two contexts where a similarly oriented action was performed, oppositely erring bisections were *perceived* as being correct. Bisiach (Chapter 6, this volume) takes this as further evidence that response mode can somehow modulate the content of perceptual awareness. Yet in fact the response is not dissimilar in the two cases. Rather it would seem that the contents of the patient's awareness are largely determined by a monitoring of his intended action (intended to be centrally directed though actually rightwardly biased in both cases); it is as though the bottom-up sensory information is underweighted by comparison. Such a reduced sensory component of awareness could perhaps be attributed to damage to the 'anterior consciousness system' proposed by Posner and Rothbart (Chapter 5, this volume).

This idea may also contribute to an understanding of other paradoxical dissociations. Thus a neglect patient (FS) with a right frontal/ striatal lesion, was found to verbally deny seeing a stimulus even when it appeared on the *right*, in a task where manual detection responses had to be made towards the left (Bisiach, Chapter 6, this volume). Yet identical stimuli were readily detected verbally when a *rightward* manual response had to be made. Bisiach conjectures that FS must always have seen the stimulus when it appeared on the right, at least fleetingly, but that the leftward response set might somehow have cancelled out the percept. It is relevant here to note that physiological studies have demonstrated attentional gating of neuronal activity in the primate occipitotemporal 'identification' system, as well as in the parietal cortex. Thus it was reported in 1985 by Moran and Desimone that many cells in area V4 of the pre-striate cortex are modulated during discrimination tasks requiring selective attention to the form or colour of a stimulus. The gating seems to involve active inhibition; and as noted by Posner and Petersen (1990), there are examples where it takes around 90 ms for a cell's response to be 'shut off' (Wise & Desimone, 1988). It is as though such a neuron will initially respond even to the behaviourally unimportant item, but then be 'censored'. Thus it is conceivable that short-lived neural activity of the kind observed by Wise and Desimone could in some circumstances lead to a manual response (perhaps especially where a failsafe system for ensuring self-consistency between perception and action is disrupted due to brain damage). Yet Wise and Desimone's monkey might be 'unaware' of the unattended stimulus, if the perceptual system was activated too briefly to reach some awareness threshold. This idea is reminiscent of the 'unconscious perception' that can evidently occur in normal subjects despite backward masking of the stimulus cutting short processing that would otherwise yield awareness (e.g. Marcel, 1983a; Cheesman & Merikle, 1986; Kunimoto *et al.*, 1991). In the light of these considerations we might therefore speculate that under the circumstances described, Bisiach's patient FS might be briefly activated by a stimulus on his ipsilesional ('good') side but because of a 'censorship' of it when the response can not be made appropriately, this activation does not reach consciousness at all.

7.5. COVERT KNOWLEDGE IN A NEGLECTED HEMISPACE?

Given the dissociations that can exist within the neglect syndrome, it would not be surprising if 'implicit knowledge' of stimuli in the neglected space could be demonstrated. One anecdotal claim in the case of line bisection, for example, indicates that a horizontal line may be misjudged in bisection but then correctly judged when drawing a matching vertical line (Allport, 1988). On the other hand, Tegner (1990) has reported that five out of his nine neglect patients under-estimated the length of a 20-cm horizontal line in drawing a vertical copy, whilst only one of 12 control patients did. This casts doubt on the generality of the observation cited by Allport.

Hard evidence for covert knowledge about neglected stimuli is in fact sparse, and what there is is not entirely convincing. There are published data showing that matching between the left and right hemifield can be highly accurate despite the patient's failing to identify many of the left-field stimuli (Volpe et al., 1979; Karnath & Hartje, 1987). However as Farah et al. (1991) have recently argued, this difference could be due simply to a greater need for detailed visual information in the identification task, while partial or degraded information might suffice for the matching task. Farah et al., buttressed this claim by showing that normal subjects will show a similar 'dissociation' in conditions where one visual hemifield is artificially degraded. They further showed that patients with (mild) neglect were able to identify contralesional stimuli in a *forced-choice* paradigm just as well as they were able to make same/different between-field judgements, even though their identification of the stimuli was impaired as tested by report.

A more indirect test for covert knowledge in neglect has been devised recently by Marshall and Halligan (1988). They described a right-hemisphere-damaged patient who judged that a pair of similar stimuli (drawings of a house) were alike despite the presence of a conspicuously unattractive element (fire) on the left side of one of them. Yet the patient consistently chose the intact house when asked for a preference judgement. However as Farah et al. (1991) have pointed out, the patient might fasten on to a trivial or irrelevant difference between the drawings when forced to make a preference judgement, and adhere to that in order to be consistent, despite having ignored this detail in making same/different judgements. In other words a consistent preference choice need not imply that she was able to process the major difference on the neglected side; it would indeed be predicted that any consistent preference might go either way. This sceptical interpretation is strengthened by the verbatim reports of further patients tested on this and similar pairs of stimuli by Bisiach (Bisiach & Rusconi, 1990; and Chapter 6, this volume): their patients specifically mentioned minor details that differentiated some of the comparison stimuli. Furthermore in three out of eight instances they failed to make consistent preference choices. Most revealingly, when the patients were consistent they chose the *unattractive* almost as often as the *attractive* alternative (two versus three instances).

At present therefore it may be concluded that the Scottish verdict of 'not proven' has to be returned on claims of implicit perceptual identification in a neglected hemispace. However, one possibility that has not yet been investigated is that certain visually guided motor behaviours might still be able to function adequately in a patient's neglected hemispace. For example, it may be possible to demonstrate intact size scaling of hand grip in reaching to grasp a solid object, despite a patient's having an illusory percept of the object as being smaller than a similar one in the intact hemispace (Gainotti & Tiacci, 1971). If recruiting a separate visuomotor system is necessary for covert function to be revealed, such methodology might be expected to succeed where other techniques have failed to convince.

7.6. PERCEPTION

The dorsal stream of visual processing in the cortex (Maunsell & Newsome, 1987), which derives its visual input mainly from the broad-band magnocellular retino-geniculate system, has not as yet been shown to have any cells in it that are colour-*selective*. No such cells have been reported in areas MT or medial superior temporal (MST), let alone in parietal or frontal cortex. None the less not all dorsal lateral geniculate nucleus (LGNd) cells that feed the magnocellular stream are 'silenced' at equiluminance (Logothetis *et al.*, 1990). Indeed there is now known to be some parvocellular input to MT (Maunsell *et al.*, 1990), as well as two-way connections between V4 and MT. Thus, although an MT cell may not be able to signal colour, it may be able to signal colour differences, and detect boundaries between isoluminant colours (Saito *et al.*, 1989). This could account for most of the evidence for 'covert colour vision' that has been reported in the achromatopsic and agnosic patient HJA, such as his success with the Ishihara plates and the Farnsworth–Munsell 100-Hues test, and the normal-latency event-related potentials recorded to red/green gratings, as suggested by Humphreys *et al.* (Chapter 3, this volume). However it is unclear that it could account for all of HJA's colour performance, such as his relatively successful ability to point to colours that match a distant sample, even in the presence of luminance noise. Furthermore, Schiller *et al.* (1990) found no evidence for above-chance colour discrimination in monkeys that had been subjected to selective lesions within the parvocellular layers of the LGNd. (The contrasting success of some 'blind-sight' patients does not contradict this, if we assume, with Cowey & Stoerig, [Chapter 2, this volume], that their brains retain some direct thalamocortical inputs from the parvocellular LGNd to extra-striate cortex).

In contrast to their 'colour-blindness', the cells projecting into the dorsal stream from V1 and V2 are highly specialized to handle motion, depth, and low spatial frequency information; and by virtue of further processing (whereby eye-position is taken into account and the pooling of receptive field information can occur) one may add to this the ability to code accurate spatial location independent of gaze direction (Andersen, 1987, 1989). These 'dorsal stream' properties are all visual attributes that are essential for visuomotor acts such as reaching and grasping. One might speculate that colour identity and fine visual detail or texture would be less essential, though not irrelevant. On the other hand where the processing goal is object identification rather than object use, clearly colour and detail are likely to be highly pertinent. It is probably however an over-simplification to map this functional distinction onto Marr's (1982) distinction between the needs for object-centred versus viewer-centred descriptions; certainly Marr did not envisage parallel and differently informed processing streams in the achievement of these two ends. None the less, viewer-centred information is paramount for the visual guidance of hand movements, whilst it would be of limited use in the identification of an object (Goodale & Milner, 1992).

It may be instructive in this context to contrast our patient DF with 'cortically blind' subjects. Although densely agnosic, she does carry out a variety of visuomotor acts confidently and accurately; but she also is rather good at detecting fine detail (Milner et al., 1991) and at discriminating colour (though not achromatic differences: Milner & Heywood, 1989). Thus she has some residual function in the ventral as well as the dorsal system. Yet, although she has no acknowledged awareness of those visual qualities of size and orientation that can guide her actions, she does have clear experiences of colour and visual texture. (Happily for her, this allows her to identify, if not fully to enjoy, many trees and flowers.) She thus has lost visual awareness for some object properties (shape in particular) that are linked to the occipitotemporal system, but not all: she is acutely conscious of colour. (Indeed despite being unable to discriminate the orientation of gratings, DF shows a strong McCollough effect, an orientation-contingent colour after-effect: Humphrey et al., 1991. This may be mediated by her largely intact striate cortex.)

In contrast, cortically blind patients never retain more than *covert* processing capacity for colour. The elegant series of studies presented by Cowey and Stoerig (Chapter 2, this volume) indicates that this colour processing may be mediated by a direct pathway from the LGNd to cortical area V4. This area is well known from the pioneering work of Zeki (1973) to be greatly concerned with colour and indeed may mediate colour constancy (Zeki, 1983). Yet the presumably intact V4 and associated occipito-temporal areas concerned with object identification (Desimone & Ungerleider, 1989) evidently are not sufficient to provide *visual experience* in Cowey and Stoerig's patients. Their inability to perceive the colours that they could discriminate suggests that they lack something that DF in large part retains: a something that is *sine qua non* for the experience of colour. This something seems to be traceable to the striate cortex, as discussed at some length by Cowey and Stoerig. (Posner & Rothbart, Chapter 5, this volume, identify a frontal area as important in giving us awareness; but if visual information can reach extra-striate visual areas after striate cortical damage, it is difficult to see why it would fail to access the frontal lobe also.) On the other hand, some cortically blind patients may rival DF in their visual reaching ability, and perform above chance in other visuomotor skills (Marcel, 1983b). At least some of these capacities thus appear able to survive the loss of V1, and appear not to need visual awareness.

Yet at the same time V1 alone is not enough; it seems uncontestable, for example, that some patients with achromatopsia have an intact striate cortex, and yet they may have no awareness of colour (see Zeki, 1990). Presumably in these cases wavelength is processed in normal fashion up to the level of V1: this may allow such patients to have *covert* colour discrimination. Indeed, there is evidence that some achromatopsics can perceive the digits in the Ishihara colour plates (e.g. Humphreys *et al.*, Chapter 3, this volume), despite there being luminance noise to over-ride lightness differences between the colours in the plates. Likewise, although V1 seems to be largely intact in DF, she has no *awareness* of form. It may therefore be generally true that visual awareness requires a combination of activity in *both* striate cortex *and* in appropriate extrastriate areas, such as V4.

7.7. RECOGNITION

In agnosia, the defining defect is not one of detection or discrimination but one of assigning an input configuration to a particular semantic category ('recognition'). This assignment process can of course break down at a number of different points (Humphreys & Riddoch, 1987). In addition to this objectively measurable definition of recognition, however, our experience of recognition may be associated with a feeling of 'familiarity'. These two aspects are partially dissociable in everyday life: one can see a face as familiar without being able to categorize it. Indeed, feelings of *déjà vu* may be totally detached from real recognition memory.

In agnosia, both aspects of recognition are absent when direct tests are used. However in those cases of prosopagnosia where implicit knowledge of faces is demonstrable, a partial dissociation is obtained by the use of indirect tests, such that categorical information can be accessed in the absence of familiarity. The evidence from Young and his colleagues (Young & De Haan, Chapter 4, this volume) indicates that patient PH has visual access from faces to some of the 'semantic' information relating to familiar people, though not to their full identity. It should be added that perceptual awareness of faces is not lost in prosopagnosia, though in some patients it may be distorted; in those individuals in whom implicit knowledge has been demonstrated, it seems to be normal. That is, faces look like faces, but like the faces of unfamiliar people. Thus this type of prosopagnosia seems to be more closely akin to amnesia than to a perceptual impairment, although unlike amnesia, prosopagnosia yields evidence for implicit knowledge only in a minority of cases. Interestingly, Jacoby and Kelley (Chapter 10, this volume) are finding it fruitful to apply dissociation methodology, initially devised to separate explicit and implicit memory by setting the two in opposition, to perception above and below the subjective threshold in normal subjects. It will be interesting to see whether these and other techniques can be adapted from the memory domain to help elucidate implicit processes in patients with visual agnosias.

A major puzzle in cases such as PH (Young & De Haan, Chapter 4, this volume) is why the partial activation of facial 'semantic' representations cannot be exploited by the patient to permit above-chance discrimination of familiar versus unfamiliar people from photographs. This seems particularly surprising given the success achieved with PH using the technique of Sergent and Poncet (1990), in which members of one cognate group of individuals were recognized overtly, presumably through mutual facilitation. It may be that other more sensitive direct procedures could be introduced to bring out residual capacities, e.g. by the use of confidence ratings (cf. Kunimoto et al., 1991). It might also be of interest to test whether prosopagnosics might have available a 'fluency' cue when presented with familiar versus unfamiliar faces, which they for some reason incorrectly construe as perceptual clarity rather than familiarity (see Jacoby & Kelley, Chapter 10, this volume). If so, they should be trainable to use that cue, even if they have a persisting failure to experience familiarity.

There has not as yet been any comparable demonstration of implicit knowledge in a case of object agnosia: cases MS (Young & De Haan, Chapter 4, this volume) and HJA (Humphreys et al., Chapter 3, this volume) do not show priming or paired-associate learning effects using pictures of objects. However such patients do not appear to have been tested systematically with actual solid objects. For example, can they correctly distinguish between food and nonfood objects when given a choice as opposed to a recognition test? It may be that a good deal of implicit knowledge is present in associative object agnosias, and could be accessed by appropriately constructed visuomotor tests. Conversely, it will be of interest to see whether cases of visual form agnosia, such as our patient DF, can reveal covert knowledge of visual shapes through priming or paired-associate tests of the kind that have been used with associative agnosics. However it should be noted in passing that there seems to be a general rule that adding richness to object representations, in the form of surface colours, texture, and three-dimensionality, can improve performance substantially in visually impaired patients (Ptito *et al.*, 1987; Goodale *et al.*, 1991b; Humphreys *et al.*, Chapter 3, this volume). (Improvements occur in normal subjects also, but only in speed of identification.)

7.8. CONCLUDING COMMENTS

The evidence for lack of awareness in most instances of 'covert' perception is based firmly upon verbal report. As pointed out by Rugg (Chapter 12, this volume), we are highly reliant on verbal criteria (including confidence ratings, etc.) in assessing whether someone is or is not conscious of a given stimulus. Rightly or wrongly, the verbal criteria are generally taken as providing more reliable indices of awareness. Yet as Rugg points out, there are well-known instances of dissociations where we are ready to abandon this assumption. In particular, when a commissurotomized patient can make a manual response to discriminate between stimuli in the left visual hemifield, but yet is unable to acknowledge those stimuli verbally, we do not thereby infer that he is unaware of them. Most people indeed (though not all: see Eccles, 1973) have followed Sperry in believing that the patient *is* aware of such stimuli, though because of the surgical disconnection he or she is unable to speak about them. So is the only reason why we do not postulate a disconnection between visual awareness and verbal commentary in blindsight merely one of anatomical implausibility? I suspect that another reason why we are more ready to ascribe awareness on the strength of verbal than of motor responses is their generally (or potentially) greater richness. In some commissurotomy experiments, motor responses are able to convey far more than just the binary information in a single keypress and indeed they may provide evidence of functioning that is similar in character to that evident in the verbal left hemisphere. Furthermore, where a motor response can convey a confidence rating in respect of some perceptual judgement we may feel safer about ascribing awareness (see Allport, 1988; Kunimoto *et al,*. 1991). None the less, it seems inescapable that the attribution of consciousness must remain a conjecture in all cases where the verbal commentary is not available, and this includes a disconnected right hemisphere. It is furthermore a conjecture that seems intuitively far more hazardous than the one we always have to make when attributing awareness to people other than ourselves.

I have taken the line in this chapter, as predominantly have other contributors in the foregoing chapters, that what Schacter (Chapter 9, this volume) calls a 'second-order' account would seem to offer a ready understanding of covert visual capacities in blindsight and form agnosia, and of dissociation phenomena in neglect. That is, I have argued for parallel visual/visuomotor channels, rather than for different modes of action of a more unitary system (which may be none the less highly plausible in the memory domain). I would regard a detailed examination of these putative channels, both behaviourally and physiologically, as being of the greatest concern for the immediate future, and would advocate postponing questions of their association with awareness until we have a clearer picture of their operating properties and constraints.

ACKNOWLEDGEMENTS

The author is indebted to David Carey, Mel Goodale, Lorna Jakobson, and M.D. Rugg, for their comments on a draft of this chapter, and to the Wellcome Trust and William Ramsay Henderson Trust for their financial support.

REFERENCES

Allport, A. (1988). What concept of consciousness? In A.J. Marcel and E. Bisiach (eds), *Consciousness in Contemporary Science*. Oxford: Clarendon Press.

Andersen R.A. (1987). Inferior parietal lobule function in spatial perception and visuomotor integration. In V.B. Mountcastle, F. Plum and S.R. Geiger (eds), *Handbook of Physiology, Section 1: The Nervous System, Vol. V: Higher Functions of the Brain, Part 2*. Bethesda, MD: American Physiological Association.

Andersen, R.A. (1989). Visual and eye movement functions of the posterior parietal cortex. *Annual Review of Neuroscience*, **12**, 377–403.

Barbieri, C. & De Renzi, E. (1989). Patterns of neglect dissociation. *Behavioural Neurology*, **2**, 13–24.

Benson, D.F. & Greenberg, J.P. (1969). Visual form agnosia. A specific defect in visual discrimination. *Archives of Neurology*, **20**, 82–89.

Bisiach, E. & Rusconi, M.L. (1990). Break-down of perceptual awareness in unilateral neglect. *Cortex*, **26**, 643–649.

Bisiach, E., Vallar, G. & Geminiani, G. (1989). Influence of response modality on perceptual awareness of contralesional visual stimuli. *Brain*, **112**, 1627–1636.

Bisiach, E., Geminiani, G., Berti, A. & Rusconi, M.L. (1990). Perceptual and premotor factors of unilateral neglect. *Neurology*, **40**, 1278–1281.

Blythe, I.M., Kennard, C. & Ruddock, K.H. (1987). Residual vision in patients with retrogeniculate lesions of the visual pathways. *Brain*, **110**, 887–905.

Bridgeman, B., Lewis, S., Heit, G. & Nagle, M. (1979). Relation between cognitive and motor-oriented systems of visual position perception. *Journal of Experimental Psychology: Human Perception and Performance*, **5**, 692–700.

Campion, J. & Latto, R. (1985). Apperceptive agnosia due to carbon monoxide poisoning. An interpretation based on critical band masking from disseminated lesions. *Behavioural Brain Research*, **15**, 227–240.

Cheesman, J. & Merikle, P.M. (1986). Distinguishing conscious from unconscious perceptual processes. *Canadian Journal of Psychology*, **40**, 343–367.

Corbetta, M., Marzi, C.A., Tassinari, G. & Aglioti, S. (1990). Effectiveness of different task paradigms in revealing blindsight. *Brain*, **113**, 603–616.

Coslett, H.B., Bowers, D., Fitzpatrick, E., Haws, B. & Heilman, K.M. (1990). Directional hypokinesia and hemispatial inattention in neglect. *Brain*, **113**, 475–486.

Desimone, R. & Ungerleider, L.G. (1989). Neural mechanisms of visual processing in monkeys. In F. Boller and J. Grafman (eds), *Handbook of Neuropsychology*, Vol. 2. Amsterdam: Elsevier.

Duhamel, J.-R. & Brouchon, M. (1990). Sensorimotor aspects of unilateral neglect: a single case analysis. *Cognitive Neuropsychology*, **7**, 57–74.

Eccles, J.C. (1973). Brain, speech and consciousness. *Die Naturwissenschaften*, **60**, 167–176.

Efron, R., (1969). What is Perception? *Boston Studies in the Philosophy of Science*, **4**, 137–173.

Ettlinger, G. (1990). 'Object vision' and 'spatial vision': the neuropsychological evidence for the distinction. *Cortex*, **26**, 319–341.

Farah, M. (1990). *Visual Agnosia*. Cambridge, MA: MIT Press.

Farah, M.J., Monheit, M.A., Brunn, J.L. & Wallace, M.A. (1991). Unconscious perception of 'extinguished' visual stimuli: reassessing the evidence. *Neuropsychologia*, in press.

Gainotti, G. & Tiacci, C. (1971). The relationships between disorders of visual perception and unilateral spatial neglect. *Neuropsychologia*, **9**, 451–458.

Gentilucci, M. & Rizzolatti, G. (1990). Cortical motor control of arm and hand movements. In M.A. Goodale (ed.), *Vision and Action: The Control of Grasping*. Norwood, NJ: Ablex.

Goodale, M.A. (1983). Vision as a sensorimotor system. In T.E. Robinson (ed.), *Behavioural Approaches to Brain Research*. New York: Oxford University Press.

Goodale, M.A. (1988). Modularity in visuomotor control: from input to output. In Z.W. Pylyshyn (ed.), *Computational Processes in Human Vision: an Interdisciplinary Perspective*. Norwood, NJ: Ablex.

Goodale, M.A. & Milner, A.D. (1992). Separate visual pathways for perception and action. *Trends in Neurosciences*, in press.

Goodale, M.A., Pelisson, D. & Prablanc, C. (1986). Large adjustments in visually guided reaching do not depend on vision of the hand or perception of target displacement. *Nature*, **320**, 748–750.

Goodale, M.A., Milner, A.D., Jakobson, L.S. & Carey, D.P. (1991a). A neurological dissociation between perceiving objects and grasping them. *Nature*, **349**, 154–156.

Goodale, M.A., Humphrey, G.K., Milner, A.D., Jakobson, L.S., Servos, P. & Carey, D.P. (1991b). Object versus picture identification in a patient with visual form agnosia. *Invest Ophthal. Vis. Sci.* **32** (suppl.), 1181.

Halligan, P.W., Manning, L. & Marshall, J.C. (1991). Hemispheric activation vs spatio-motor cueing in visual neglect: a case study. *Neuropsychologia*, **29**, 165–176.

Head, H. (1926). *Aphasia and Kindred Disorders of Speech*. Cambridge: Cambridge University Press.

Heilman, K.M. & Valenstein, E. (1979). Mechanisms underlying hemispatial neglect. *Annals of Neurology*, **5**, 166–170.

Humphrey, G.K., Goodale, M.A. & Gurnsey, R. (1991). Orientation discrimination in a visual form agnosic: evidence from the McCollough effect. *Psychological Science*, in press.

Humphreys, G.W. & Riddoch, M.J. (1987). The fractionation of visual agnosia. In G.W. Humphreys and M.J. Riddoch (eds), *Visual Object Processing: A Cognitive Neuropsychological Approach*. London: Erlbaum.

Jakobson, L.S. & Goodale, M.A. (1991). Factors affecting high-order movement planning: a kinematic analysis of human prehension. *Experimental Brain Research*, **86**, 199–208.

Jeannerod, M. (1981). Intersegmental coordination during reaching at natural visual objects. In J. Long and A. Baddeley (eds), *Attention and Performance IX*. Hillsdale, NJ: Erlbaum.

Karnath, H.-O & Hartje, W. (1987). Residual information processing in the neglected visual half-field. *Journal of Neurology*, **234**, 180–184.

Kunimoto, C., Miller, J. & Pashler, H. (1991). Perception without awareness confirmed: a bias-free procedure for determining awareness thresholds. Unpublished Manuscript.

Logothetis, N.K., Schiller, P.H., Charles, E.R. & Hurlbert, A.C. (1990). Perceptual deficits and the activity of the color-opponent and broad-band pathways at isoluminance. *Science*, **247**, 214–217.

McCarthy R.A. & Warrington E.K. (1990). *Cognitive Neuropsychology*. New York: Academic Press.

Marcel, A.J. (1983a). Conscious and unconscious perception: experiments on visual masking and word perception. *Cognitive Psychology*, **15**, 197–237.

Marcel, A.J. (1983b). Conscious and unconscious perception; an approach to the relations between phenomenal experience and perceptual processes. *Cognitive Psychology*, **15**, 238–300.

Marcel, A.J. (1990). Slippage in the unity of consciousness, or, To what do perceptual speech acts refer? Poster presented at Russell Trust/Wellcome Trust symposium, St Andrews, September 1990.

Marr, D. (1982). *Vision*. San Francisco, CA: Freeman.

Marshall, J.C. & Halligan, P.W. (1988). Blindsight and insight in visuo-spatial neglect. *Nature*, **336**, 766–767.

Marzi, C.A., Tassinari, G., Aglioti, S. & Lutzemberger, L. (1986). Spatial summation across the vertical meridian in hemianopics: A test of blindsight. *Neuropsychologia*, **24**, 749–758.

Maunsell, J.H.R. & Newsome, W.T. (1987). Visual processing in monkey extrastriate cortex. *Annual Review of Neuroscience*, **10**, 363–401.

Maunsell, J.H.R., Nealey, T.A. & De Priest, D.D. (1990). Magnocellular and parvocellular contributions to responses in the middle temporal visual area (MT) of the macaque monkey. *Journal of Neuroscience*, **10**, 3323–3334.

Meeres, S.L. & Graves, R.E. (1990). Localization of unseen visual stimuli by humans with normal vision. *Neuropsychologia*, **28**, 1231–1237.

Milner, A.D. & Heywood, C.A. (1989). A disorder of lightness discrimination in a case of visual form agnosia. *Cortex*, **25**, 489–494.

Milner, A.D., Perrett, D.I., Johnston, R.S., Benson, P.J., Jordan, T.R., Heeley, D.W. *et al.*, (1991). Perception and action in visual form agnosia. *Brain*, **114**, 405–428.

Moran, J. & Desimone, R. (1985). Selective attention gates visual processing in the extrastriate cortex. *Science*, **229**, 782–784.

Perenin, M.-T. & Vighetto, A. (1988). Optic ataxia: a specific disruption in visuomotor mechanisms. *Brain*, **111**, 643–674.

Pöppel, E. (1986). Long-range colour-generating interactions across the retina. *Nature*, **320**, 523–525.

Posner, M.I. & Petersen, S.E. (1990). The attention system of the human brain. *Annual Review of Neuroscience*, **13**, 25–42.

Pitito, A., Lassonde, M., Lepore, F. & Pitito, M. (1987). Visual discrimination in hemispherectomized patients. *Neuropsychologia*, **25**, 869–879.

Puccetti, R. (1981). The case for mental duality: evidence from split-brain data and other considerations. *Behavioral and Brain Sciences*, **4**, 93–123.

Richardson-Klavehn, A. & Bjork, R.A. (1988). Measures of memory. *Annual Review of Psychology*, **39**, 475–543.

Rodman, H.R., Gross, C.G. & Albright, T.D. (1989). Afferent basis of visual response in area MT of the macaque. 1. Effects of striate cortex removal. *Journal of Neuroscience*, **9**, 2033–2050.

Rondot, P. (1989). Visuomotor ataxia. In J.W. Brown (ed.) *Neuropsychology of Visual Perception*. Hillsdale, NJ: Erlbaum.

Saito, H., Tanaka, K., Isono, H., Yasuda, M. & Mikami, A. (1989). Directionally selective response of cells in the middle temporal area (MT) of the macaque monkey to the movement of equiluminous opponent colour stimuli. *Experimental Brain Research*, **75**, 1–14.

Schenkenberg, T., Bradford, D.C. & Ajax, E.T. (1980). Line bisection and unilateral visual neglect in patients with neurological impairments. *Neurology*, **30**, 509–517.

Schiller, P.H., Logothetis, N.K. & Charles, E. (1990). Role of the color-opponent and broad-band channels in vision. *Visual Neuroscience*, **5**, 321–346.

Sergent, J & Poncet, M. (1990). From covert to overt recognition of faces in a prosopagnosic patient. *Brain*, **113**, 989–1004.

Taira M., Mine, S., Georgopoulos, A.P., Murata, A., & Sakata, H. (1990). Parietal cortex neurons of the monkey related to the visual guidance of hand movement. *Experimental Brain Research*, **83**, 29–36.

Tegner, R. (1990). Line bisection: more line than bisection. Poster presented at Russell Trust/Wellcome Trust symposium, St Andrews, September 1990.

Tegner, R. & Levander, M. (1991). Through a looking glass. A new technique to demonstrate directional hypokinesia in unilateral neglect. *Brain*, in press.

Ungerleider, L.G. & Mishkin, M. (1982). Two cortical visual systems. In D.J. Ingle, M.A. Goodale and R.J.W. Mansfield (eds), *Analysis of Visual Behavior*. Cambridge, MA: MIT Press.

Vallar, G. & Perani, D. (1986). The anatomy of unilateral neglect after right-hemisphere stroke lesions. A clinical/CT-scan correlation study in man *Neuropsychologia*, **24**, 609–622.

Van Essen, D.C. (1985). Functional organization of the primate visual cortex. In E.G. Jones & A.A. Peters (eds), *Cerebral Cortex*, Vol. 3. New York: Plenum Press.

Volpe, B.T., Ledoux, J.E. & Gazzaniga, M.S. (1979). Information processing of visual stimuli in an 'extinguished' field. *Nature*, **282**, 722–724.

Weiskrantz, L. (1986). *Blindsight. A Case Study and Implications*. Oxford: Oxford University Press.

Weiskrantz, L. (1987). Residual vision in a scotoma. A follow-up study of form discrimination. *Brain,* **110**, 77–92.

Weiskrantz, L. (1990). Outlooks for blindsight: explicit methodologies for implicit processes. *Proceedings of the Royal Society of London,* **B239**, 247–278.

Weiskrantz, L., Warrington, E.K., Sanders, M.D. & Marshall, J. (1974). Visual capacity in the hemianopic field following a restricted cortical ablation. *Brain,* **97**, 709–728.

Wise, S.P. & Desimone, R. (1988). Behavioral neurophysiology: insights into seeing and grasping. *Science,* **242**, 736–741.

Zeki, S.M. (1973). Colour coding in rhesus monkey prestriate cortex. *Brain Research,* **53**, 422–427.

Zeki, S.M. (1983). Colour coding in the cerebral cortex: the reaction of cells in monkey visual cortex to wavelengths and colours. *Neuroscience,* **9**, 741–765.

Zeki, S.M. (1990). A century of cerebral achromatopsia. *Brain,* **113**, 1721–1777.

CHAPTER 8

The Distinction Between Implicit and Explicit Language Function: Evidence from Aphasia

Lorraine K. Tyler

8.1. INTRODUCTION

The relationship between knowledge representations and the different ways in which they can be accessed underlies much of the current interest in explicit versus implicit access to mental representations. In a variety of cognitive domains (e.g. reading, face recognition, memory; see the other chapters in this volume), it has been repeatedly observed that implicit access to knowledge can be dissociated from explicit access. Some of the evidence comes from experimental studies with normal subjects (e.g. Marcel, 1983), but an increasingly impressive body of evidence comes from the study of patients with selective brain damage (e.g. Cohen & Squire, 1980; Graf & Schacter, 1985). The neuropsychological evidence takes the form of patients who show normal (or above chance) cognitive function when performance is measured by an *implicit task* but abnormal function when assessed by means of an *explicit task*. An implicit task is one which attempts to access internally represented knowledge without requiring the subject to become consciously aware of that knowledge. In contrast, an explicit task is one which requires the subject consciously to access particular types of knowledge in the process of carrying out the task.

Although the dissociation has been reported occasionally in the domain of language comprehension (e.g. Milberg & Blumstein, 1981), the distinction between explicit and implicit tasks and, more important, between explicit and implicit mental representations and what they

THE NEUROPSYCHOLOGY OF CONSCIOUSNESS
ISBN 0–12–498045–7

reveal both about a patient's deficit and about the structure of the language comprehension system, has been largely ignored. In this chapter, I will discuss a number of patients who show a pattern of deficits consistent with such a distinction between explicit and implicit mental representations and consider the implications of these data for the structure of the language comprehension system.

8.2. TASKS AND REPRESENTATIONS

Data relevant to the implicit/explicit distinction in language comprehension are very sparse. The two studies which have been most influential are those of Milberg and Blumstein (1981) and Linebarger *et al.* (1983). Milberg and Blumstein (1981) found Wernicke patients with severe comprehension deficits who showed significant semantic priming effects in a lexical decision task. The patients (just like normal subjects) showed faster lexical decision latencies to a target word (e.g. 'money') when it was preceded by a semantically related word ('bank') than when it was preceded by an unrelated word ('tree'). The lexical decision task, used in this way, *implicitly* tapped into semantic knowledge representations, in that the relationship between the primes and targets was not relevant to the task which the subject's attention was directed towards. These same patients, however, performed very poorly (and consistent with their original diagnosis as suffering from a severe comprehension deficit) when they were asked to judge overtly whether the same words were semantically related. This semantic judgement task required them to access explicitly their semantic knowledge in evaluating the relationships between the words (but see Hagoort, 1989).

Other research (e.g. Andreewsky & Seron, 1975; Linebarger *et al.*, 1983) has been interpreted (Schacter *et al.*, 1988) as being relevant to this issue, but it does not provide clear support for the distinction between implicit and explicit access to linguistic knowledge.

The data reported in Linebarger *et al.* (1983), for example, has been taken as evidence of the dissociation in that they have 'agrammatic' patients (as diagnosed on the basis of their disorder of speech production) who perform very well on a grammaticality judgement task but very poorly on a sentence–picture matching task (Schwartz *et al.*, 1980). Linebarger *et al.* (1983) claim that the sentence–picture matching task taps linguistic knowledge as it is used in the normal process of comprehending an utterance, whereas the grammaticality test taps into the patient's explicit access to that knowledge. My reservation in accepting this study as evidence of the implicit/explicit distinction lies in the lack of a task analysis which distinguishes between the sentence–picture matching and grammaticality tasks. I do indeed believe that these tasks tap different aspects of the comprehension process but, as I will argue later, I believe that they are both explicit tasks. Where they differ is in the way in which they reflect conscious awareness on the part of the subject. Since there is no such task analysis in the Linebarger *et al.* (1983) paper, it does not provide an adequate basis for assuming that one task implicitly taps language function whereas the other task taps into it explicitly.

However, the Linebarger *et al.* (1983) study is important in that it draws attention to an important related issue. This is the issue of what aspect of the comprehension process is being tapped by different types of task. Just as we can think of tasks in terms of whether they involve implicit or explicit properties, we can also think of mental representations in a similar way. That is, we can think of them in terms of whether they can, in principle, become available for conscious awareness. However, it is only possible to do this with respect to a specific model of the language comprehension process which distinguishes between different kinds of representations.

One such model has been developed by William Marslen-Wilson, myself and our colleagues over the past 15 years (Marslen-Wilson, 1973, 1975, 1987; Marslen-Wilson & Tyler, 1975, 1980; Marslen-Wilson, & Welsh, 1978; Tyler & Wessels, 1983, 1985). The model is based entirely upon data on the comprehension of *spoken* language. It specifies the processes and representations involved in mapping the speech input onto representations of the phonological form of a word, and accessing its semantic and syntactic content (Marslen-Wilson & Welsh, 1978; Tyler & Wessels, 1983; Warren & Marslen-Wilson, 1989; Marslen-Wilson & Zwitserlood, 1989; Lahiri & Marslen-Wilson, 1991). It also specifies the basic structure of higher-level processing, stating that higher-level representations are constructed incrementally as each word of the utterance is heard, and that both syntactic and semantic information are used immediately in the construction of higher-level representations (Marslen-Wilson & Tyler, 1975, 1980, 1987).

The model distinguishes between *intermediate* and *final* representations of a spoken utterance. In the process of interpreting the speech input, a set of processes operate to construct different types of *intermediate* representations, word-by-word as the speech input is heard. We can think of this as a set of layers with each layer corresponding to a different type of representation, and the top layer being the *final* representation. The processes involved in constructing these representations are automatic, not under voluntary control, nor are they available to conscious awareness. Similarly, the intermediate representations themselves are not normally available to conscious awareness. When listeners hear an utterance spoken in their native language, they cannot choose to hear it as anything other than a meaningful utterance of their language, although for this to happen, the utterance will have undergone a complex sequence of transformations: the acoustic–phonetic properties of the speech signal will have been encoded into individual words; the semantic and syntactic properties of those words will have been combined into syntactically and semantically well-formed phrases, etc. However, listeners cannot normally gain access to these intermediate representations. They do not 'hear' the utterance as a string of separate words, just as they do not hear it as a string of grammatical formatives. What they 'hear' is the final representation—a pragmatically coherent utterance in which the details of the intermediate representations have been lost. It is only this final representation which listeners can, in principle, gain conscious access to. This implies that the intermediate representations are qualitatively different from the final propositional representation (cf. Marcel, 1983, 1988). [1]

If it is indeed the case that the intermediate representations are not available to conscious awareness, any task which requires the listener to make some type of explicit response about properties of the utterance will, necessarily, involve processes other than those required to generate the intermediate representations. If we are to tap at all directly these intermediate representations—and given that they form the core of the comprehension system, we need to be able to do so — then the task cannot be one which requires any type of explicit decision about, or reflection upon, the properties of the representation. Thus, we have to use tasks which implicitly tap into the representations we are interested in.

A number of tasks, such as associative priming, word monitoring and lexical decision—if used appropriately—can satisfy the requirement of implicitly tapping mental representations. For example, the word monitoring task becomes an implicit measure of language function when the monitoring target word occurs *after* the relevant stimulus so that the listener's awareness of the properties of the target is not what is at issue. Rather, what we are interested in is how monitoring latencies to the target word are affected by what has been heard prior to that word. Similarly, in associative priming, where subjects hear a pair of words which may or may not be related in some way and they have to make a lexical decision (or naming) response to the second word, the subject's response is indirectly based upon his or her awareness of the relationship between the two words. The response provides an indirect measure of that relationship.

Furthermore, for a task to tap the intermediate representations which the listener constructs, it must also require the listener to produce a response which is closely tied in time to relevant stretches of the speech input. We have termed those tasks which tap into intermediate representations *on-line* tasks (Marslen-Wilson & Tyler, 1980; Tyler & Marslen-Wilson, 1982) and those which tap the properties of the final representation *off-line* tasks.

An on-line task can satisfy the requirement of a close temporal relationship between speech stimulus and response in one of two ways —either by requiring the listener to produce a fast reaction time response immediately after the critical part of the stimulus has been heard (as in the word monitoring task) or by stopping the input at a specified point and requiring the listener to make a response on the basis of partial information (as in the gating task). The more time that is allowed to elapse between stimulus and response (either because subjects are given plenty of time to respond, or because the word which they have to make a response to occurs a long time after the relevant stretch of speech input has been heard), then the more plausible it is that the response will be affected by those aspects of the representation of which they can become aware.

We can contrast these types of on-line task with off-line tasks. In general, off-line tasks share three characteristics. First of all, they rarely attempt to tie the response to particular aspects of the speech stimulus. This means that it is often unclear to what extent the listener's response is determined solely by the linguistic variables one is interested in. Take, as an example, the sentence–picture matching task. Here, subjects are presented with a sentence (either spoken or written) and a set of pictures. Their task is to match the sentence to the appropriate picture. Since they are under no time pressure to respond, other, non-linguistic, variables may also affect performance (cf. Black *et al.*, 1991). Second, all off-line tasks require the listener to be aware, in some way, of the utterance they have heard; they are all explicit measures of language comprehension. Third, they invariably access the final linguistic representation which the listener constructs.

Perhaps one of the surprising things about research into disorders of language comprehension is the extent to which it relies almost exclusively upon data from off-line tasks. This means that much of the data on aphasic deficits are restricted to telling us about those aspects of representations which the patient can explicitly reflect upon. They are unable to tell us about those representations of which the patient is unaware. And yet these, as we have argued elsewhere (e.g. Marslen-Wilson & Tyler, 1987), form the core of the comprehension system. To study only those aspects of linguistic representations of which the listener is aware undoubtedly gives a distorted view of aphasic deficits (see Tyler, 1988).

8.3. DIFFERENT KINDS OF EXPLICIT TASKS

So far I have been talking as though I assumed that all tasks which are used explicitly to tap linguistic representations in aphasic patients were of the same type. In fact, I want to claim that they are not. Tasks vary in a number of ways. In this chapter, I will focus on the way in which they differ with respect to conscious awareness. I believe that the tasks which are commonly used to test for comprehension deficits in aphasic patients fall into two broad categories.

First, there are tasks such as sentence–picture matching and acting out where the final product of the intermediate processes and representations can become available to conscious reflection when the task demands it. The point is that the listener has some degree of control over this. He or she can, in some sense, decide whether or not to reflect upon the representation in order to carry out the task. This is the more traditional kind of conscious awareness which has been discussed in terms of '...a mechanism of limited capacity which may be directed toward different types of activity'. (Posner & Snyder, 1975).

Second, there are explicit tasks which are based upon the patient's awareness that a linguistic procedure has not successfully run through its operations. The best example of this is *grammaticality judgements*— where the listener hears an utterance and has to say whether it is a grammatical/acceptable sentence of his or her native language. In this task, when there is an error in the operations of a procedure, this information percolates automatically to the listener's awareness. The subject has no control over whether or not to be aware that an error has occurred. [2] If it is indeed the case that errors in the operation of an automatic process automatically become available to consciousness, then the grammaticality judgement task potentially offers more insight into the nature of intermediate linguistic representations than tasks such as sentence–picture matching and acting out. Errors arise from the breakdown of processes and the resulting inability to construct intermediate representations. To the extent that subjects can accurately reflect upon the nature of the error, then the task can reveal something about the properties of intermediate representations. However this potential may be obscured by the processes involved in making the decision as to whether or not an error has occurred, and the time intervening between the occurrence of an error and the judgement response.

Let me elaborate upon the differences between these two types of task in more detail. The normal processes which translate the speech input into a meaningful representation are obligatory. They operate in a particular and fixed way upon the speech input. When these processes run through normally, we are not aware either of them or of their intermediate products. However, when they cannot—because there is some kind of error in the input which does not permit the normal procedure to run successfully—then the listener becomes aware of his or her inability to construct the correct representations. This does not mean that the listener necessarily knows what type of error has occurred, but only that the normal process has not been successful. The grammaticality judgement task is of this type. The listener can make the correct judgement on the basis of being aware that 'something has gone wrong'— i.e. a procedure has not been able to run through its normal operations. This is a very different task from those such as sentence–picture matching and acting out in that the listener has no voluntary control over whether he or she will become aware of the error.

These two types of tasks elicit different kinds of awareness on the part of the listener. In both cases, the listener becomes aware of linguistic representations, but the way in which he or she does so differs. Can we find evidence from aphasic patients for (a) the distinction between implicitly and explicitly accessed linguistic knowledge and (b) the distinction between different kinds of conscious awareness?

8.4. EVIDENCE FOR THE DISTINCTION BETWEEN THE IMPLICIT AND EXPLICIT ACCESS OF KNOWLEDGE

RH is a male patient who was born in 1920 and had a left hemisphere cardiovascular accident (CVA) in 1977. He has a significant degree of hearing loss (30 db) and is right hand dominant. His speech is fluent, containing relatively few content words, but many stereotypical phrases, as well as occasional verbal paraphasias. An example of his spontaneous speech is given below:

(*Experimenter asks RH about coming to the Speech Therapy Department after having his stroke.*)

HC: Yeah, and then you came to this place ...

RH: Yes ... well of course when they came there, I ... em ... he came there. I didn't know ... there and I didn't know anything for it, any ... I suppose we were there, when I went 1 2 3 4 5 and he looked there and said well so and so and so and so. Now if you look here and I see, and then he said right, the next one I went there, so this is right, then the next one I'm going, for him.

HC: What's this then? Is he teaching you to count or...

RH: Yeah ... 1 2 3 4 5 6. Before. But the first, when I first went there, went there, and I didn't know anything. I didn't know anything and then he started—he's trying something, and was trying that ...

HC: Trying to get you to say ...

RH: And I was OK and try. And then I ... you know, bad. [Laughs.]

On standard aphasia tests, such as the Boston Diagnostic Aphasia Examination (BDAE) and the Token Test, RH was diagnosed as having a severe comprehension deficit. On the Boston examination, which was administered in 1979, he was classified as a Wernicke with a poor auditory comprehension (z score = −0.05). His comprehension was also poor when measured by the Token Test (De Renzi & Vignolo, 1962; his score of 7/36 indicating that he had a severe aphasia. This diagnosis was confirmed in informal interaction, in which he appeared to have a severe comprehension deficit. This impression was, no doubt, partly due to his profound difficulty in producing coherent language.

His digit span (as measured on the BDAE) was only three. However, he was able to match four digits with 100% accuracy on a digit-matching task, and five digits with 66% accuracy, suggesting that he did not have a severe short-term memory deficit for digits. He completed the trail-making test in 205 s, indicating that he has severe brain damage, but his general intellectual abilities were above average as measured by the Raven Progressive Matrices.

When we first saw RH he had been tested on this range of standard tests and had been diagnosed as a typical 'Wernicke' with a severe comprehension deficit.[3] However, nothing further was known about the nature of this deficit, nor whether it was attributable to problems in the processes and representations involved in the on-line interpretation of the speech input or to problems with the final representation.

RH was tested on a battery of experiments designed to probe his ability to construct various types of linguistic representations. His performance on many of the tests of on-line processing was essentially normal. I will describe his performance on these tests in some detail.

First of all, RH had few problems with lexical processing. Whatever difficulties he did have were probably attributable to his profound hearing loss. In three studies we found that the processes involved in contacting the phonological form representation of real words were essentially unimpaired for both simple and morphologically complex words. In the first study he had to discriminate pairs of words which differed by one distinctive feature; in two studies using the gating task, he recognized both complex and simple words at the point at which they were recognized by unimpaired listeners; in an auditory lexical decision experiment with suffixed words and non-words, he was as sensitive (A' = 0.88) to the lexical status of a stimulus as all the other patients we have seen with a similar degree of hearing loss, but less sensitive than normal controls (A' = 0.99).[4,5]

RH also had no difficulty accessing lexically associated representations (syntactic, semantic and pragmatic) and using them immediately to construct structural representations of the speech input. This was shown in a word-monitoring experiment in which we had stimuli of the type shown in Table 8.1. RH was asked to press a response key as soon as he heard the target word ('guitar' in the example). Monitoring latencies were measured from the onset of the target word. The major assumption we make when using the word-monitoring task is that latencies to the target word reflect the successful processing of the prior linguistic material. So, in the present study, we assume that if listeners can access various types of lexical information associated with verbs and use them successfully to constrain possible verb–argument relations, then latencies to a target

TABLE 8.1

Example set of materials for verb experiment

1*a*. The crowd was waiting eagerly.
John carried the guitar.....
1*b*. The crowd was waiting eagerly.
John buried the guitar.....
1*c*. The crowd was waiting eagerly.
John drank the guitar.....
1*d*. The crowd was waiting eagerly.
John slept the guitar.....

---

word which follows the verb will be facilitated. However, when the appropriate verb–argument structure cannot be built (as in 1b, 1c and 1d) latencies to the target word will be slowed down.

In the sets of stimuli we used, the sequences were identical except for variation in the verb and in the argument frames associated with the verb. In sentence (1a) the relationship between the verb (*carried*) and the target (*guitar*) is fully acceptable on syntactic, semantic, and pragmatic grounds. The sub-categorization requirements of the verb allow for a nounphrase as direct object, a guitar has the appropriate semantics for the action of carrying, and carrying a guitar is a perfectly reasonable activity in the context of a standard model of the world. Monitoring response-times to targets in Normal contexts like (1a) formed the baseline condition.

Sentences (1b) and (1c) illustrate two grades of potential violation of the lexical representations evoked by the verb. In both cases the target noun phrase (guitar) remains categorically appropriate—the verbs are transitive and accept a nounphrase as direct object. Sentence (1b), however, constitutes a pragmatic anomaly, and contrasts with (1c), which constitutes a semantic anomaly. This, in effect, is the distinction between the linguistic and the non-linguistic aspects of the lexical representation of a verb. The anomaly—or the 'oddness'—of 'John buried the guitar' cannot be part of the linguistic specification of the semantics of the lexical items involved. It is something that we have to infer, given our knowledge of the world, and given what we know about guitars, the likely effects of burying them, and so on.

The second type of violation, in (1c), is a violation of the selection restrictions on the semantic properties of the items that can fill the argument slots made available by the verb's sub-categorization properties. The linguistic specification of drinking (that it involves liquids) and of guitars (that they are solid objects) is sufficient to make 'guitar' anomalous following 'drink' without having to invoke knowledge or operations outside the linguistic domain.

Finally, (1d) differs from the other two in violating the sub-categorization frame associated with a given verb. A verbform like 'sleep' is sub-categorized as an intransitive verb, and has no sub-categorized argument slot into which a nounphrase like 'guitar' can fit.

In the experiment, we found that the latencies of normal listeners to respond to the target were slower (compared to the baseline condition) when a sentence contained any kind of verb–argument violation. This suggests that they are accessing and using all types of verb information in the process of constructing an interpretation of an utterance. RH showed the same pattern.[6] His monitoring latencies to the target words were significantly slower for all three types of verb–argument violation compared to the appropriate condition. This shows that RH accesses the content of the verb as soon as he hears it and uses this information to constrain permissible verb–argument structures.

RH also had no difficulty developing the appropriate type of syntactic and semantic global representations spanning an utterance, as was shown by the pattern of his reaction-times in a second word monitoring study. In this study, we presented RH with three types of sentences—normal prose (where the utterance is semantically and grammatically normal), anomalous prose (where the utterance is grammatically normal but semantically meaningless) and scrambled strings (which have no semantic or grammatical structure)—as in the example set of stimuli in Table 8.2 (where the target word is 'church').

We placed target words at different word positions in each type of material in order to chart the processing of syntactic and semantic information as they become available over time. We found that RH performed just the same as unimpaired listeners. His latencies in normal prose were faster than those in anomalous prose and these in turn were faster than those in scrambled strings. More importantly, latencies got progressively faster across both normal and anomalous prose utterances (but not in scrambled strings), indicating that RH (as well as unimpaired listeners) was able to develop both syntactic and semantic

TABLE 8.2
Example set of materials for prose experiment

2a. Normal prose
Everyone was outraged when they heard. Apparently, in the middle of the night some thieves broke into the church and stole a golden crucifix.
2b. Anomalous prose
Everyone was exposed when they ate. Apparently, at the distance of the wind some ants pushed around the church and forced a new item.
2c. Scrambled strings
They everyone when outraged heard was. Of middle apparently the some the into the broke night in thieves church and crucifix stole a golden.

---

representations spanning an entire utterance. His ability to construct global structural representations across an utterance seems to be intact.

In another experiment we used the word monitoring task to assess whether he was able to access the syntactic and semantic properties of derived and inflected words and integrate them into the prior sentential context. The materials for these studies consisted of sentences which contained either a derived or inflected test word ('soften' in the example below) which was immediately followed by a target noun ('tissue' in the example below). The morphologically complex test word was either appropriate or inappropriate for the prior context. The example below illustrates the general structure of the sentences which we used (with test word emphasized):

> *The technique was very new. They claimed that it would soften tissue by a chemical reaction.*

Given the prior context, only certain morphological variants of the stem *soft* are contextually appropriate. In this particular case, the derivational forms *soften* and *softly* are permissible, whereas the form *softness* is not. On the basis of previous findings (Tyler & Marslen-Wilson, 1986), we would expect normal listeners to integrate rapidly an appropriate form (*soften*) into the context, and to be disrupted when they encounter an inappropriate form (*softness*). If this is the case, then in the present study, monitoring latencies to the target noun should be faster when the preceding complex word is contextually appropriate compared with when it is inappropriate. This is exactly what we found (see Tyler & Cobb, 1987).

RH showed the same pattern of results. When either the inflected or derived word was contextually appropriate, his monitoring latencies were significantly faster than when it was inappropriate. This suggested that he could access the syntactic and semantic properties of both derived and inflected words and immediately integrate them into the context.

The results of the on-line studies are clearly at odds with the results of the standard comprehension tests (e.g. Token Test, BDAE) on the basis of which RH was diagnosed as having a severe comprehension impairment. The most obvious explanation for the difference is in terms of the different ways in which the two kinds of tasks tap linguistic representations. However, before drawing this conclusion, we needed to make sure that the difference in results was not simply due to differences in the kinds of materials used. So we tested RH on the same materials we had used in some of the word-monitoring studies, but this time we used the grammaticality acceptability judgement task. RH listened to a sentence and, at the end of the sentence, judged whether or not it was an acceptable sentence of English.

In contrast to his performance in the monitoring studies, his performance on tasks requiring acceptability judgements was extremely poor.

This held for the acceptability judgement version of the verb–argument study (RH A' = 0.73; A' range for controls = 0.93–1) described above and the study involving morphologically complex words (RH A' = 0.58; A' range for controls = 0.92–1), using the same materials for which he had shown essentially the normal pattern of performance in the word-monitoring task.

One final possibility which we had to consider was that a short-term memory (STM) deficit was the underlying cause of his poor perform-ance on the judgement task and other standard tests of comprehension. In all these tests he was required to wait until the end of the sentence before making his response. We thought this memory explanation was unlikely for two reasons. First, we had tested his STM by means of digit span and digit matching tasks, and found that it was relatively unim-paired. Second, and perhaps more convincing, was his performance on a variant of the judgement task. Here he was asked to press a response key as soon as he detected an anomaly rather than waiting for the end of the sentence before making his decision. He also performed poorly on this version of the judgement task. This eliminated memory load as a possible factor affecting his acceptability judgements.

RH, then, shows a clear dissociation between relatively normal per-formance on tests of 'on-line' language processing, and significantly impaired performance on 'off-line' tests using tasks such as gram-maticality judgements, and sentence–picture matching. It appears that the intermediate representations and the processes involved in their construction remain unimpaired, while conscious access to the final rep-resentation which is constructed is impaired. The data suggest that RH can develop the appropriate representations of an utterance; his problem lies in being unable to gain access to them for the purpose of making explicit decisions about them.

RH is not the only patient whom we have encountered who exhibits this kind of implicit/explicit access distinction. We have seen a number of patients like this. One of the interesting points about these patients is that they do not have similar production deficits. JW, for example, is a patient who suffers from a profound production disorder. But in con-trast to RH, who is a fluent speaker, JW's speech is effortful and limited. He rarely produces more than single words and he does that with con-siderable difficulty, as the example of his spontaneous speech given below shows.

Sample of spontaneous speech:

E: Do you live in a house? Can you describe it?

JW: No, erm, a house, er .. 2 .. er .. 1, 2, 3 .. um ..

E: Are you trying to say what sort of house?

JW: Yes.

E: A semi, a terrace?

JW: Yes, and erm .. garden .. and erm .. lawn, lawn, lawn, and .. well ..

E: A long, thin garden?

JW: Shred, shed .. and er .. er

E: A vegetable garden?

JW: No .. er .. roses

JW was born in 1933 and had a stroke in 1981. He has a profound hearing loss (34 db) and on standard aphasia tests is diagnosed as a patient with a severe comprehension deficit. He scored 12/36 on the Token Test and his comprehension score was 0 on the BDAE. On the TROG (Bishop, 1983) which is a sentence–picture matching task, he scored 62% correct and on a two-picture sentence–picture matching task which we devised involving reversible passive, active and pseudo-cleft sentences, he scored 60% correct. Also, on a grammaticality judgement task involving various types of ungrammatical sentences (e.g. verb complement clauses, subject–auxiliary inversion, empty elements and passives) he performed poorly (JW $A' = 0.75$; A' range for controls $= 0.94–1$). On all of these tests of explicit access to linguistic representations, his performance was much worse than that of normal controls.

In contrast, his on-line monitoring performance, although showing some specific abnormalities, was very similar to normal. In spite of his hearing loss, he was able to access the phonological form of a word, as well as its syntactic and semantic implications, in much the same way as normal listeners. On the word-monitoring studies mentioned earlier, he also performed in many (but not all) respects like normal. In the verb–argument study, his RTs to target words increased significantly when he encountered all three types of verb–argument violations (semantic, pragmatic and syntactic). He also showed the word-position effect in normal prose (where RTs get progressively faster as more of a sentence is heard) which is typical of normal listeners. There was also evidence that he was somewhat sensitive to the contextual appropriateness of an inflected word. These results showed that many of the processes and representations involved in the on-line interpretation of the speech input were unimpaired. Unlike RH, however, he did differ from normal in one or two respects. First, he did not show the typical word-position effect in anomalous prose (which is grammatical but meaningless) and second, he was insensitive to the contextual appropriateness of derived words. These two may be linked in that they both rely, to a certain extent at least, upon form–class information being correctly used. He may, then, suffer from a functional deficit involving the use of syntactic information in the process of interpreting an utterance.

On the grammaticality judgement versions of the various monitoring studies, he performed much worse than the control group. In both the verb–argument study and the study involving morphologically complex words which I described earlier, his performance was outside the range of the normal controls. His results on these studies were consistent with his performance on the other off-line tests of comprehension described earlier.

JW and RH, then, show the same kind of dissociation between performance on implicit versus explicit tests of language comprehension. Many (although not all in the case of JW) of the processes involved in the on-line comprehension of spoken language appear to be unimpaired, whereas tasks which involve conscious access to representations produce severely abnormal performance. The fact that JW does not show the normal pattern in all of the on-line studies I have discussed does not undermine this claim. The important point is that, in a study where we use exactly the same materials and probe with two different tasks—one of which is implicit and the other which is explicit—we obtain normal performance in one case and abnormal in the other.

Although both patients show the same explicit/implicit dissociation in language comprehension, they differ markedly in their language production. RH produces fluent speech which is, essentially, semantically empty, whereas JW produces very little speech. What there is is mostly confined to single words. These two patients illustrate that the implicit/explicit distinction in language comprehension is not related to a patient's production deficit. Perhaps this is not surprising. We might plausibly expect that the comprehension processes and representations reflected in on-line tasks are those which might be more closely related to the processes and representations involved in language production. Both are automatic and not normally available to conscious awareness. However, when speakers try to consciously control what they say (as is the case in some kinds of experimental tasks and may be the case for some aphasic patients, cf. Kolk & van Grunsven, 1985), then we might find a closer correspondence between the explicit tests of language comprehension and the patient's production deficit.

8.5. EVIDENCE FOR THE DISTINCTION BETWEEN DIFFERENT KINDS OF EXPLICIT TASKS

I claimed earlier that there are different ways in which listeners can become consciously aware of linguistic representations. One way, exemplified by the grammaticality judgement task, is by virtue of the operations of an automatic procedure breaking down. When this happens, the listener automatically becomes aware that 'something has gone wrong' although he or she may not know what the error consists of. The other way is when the listener chooses to reflect upon the final linguistic representation, when the situation or task demands it.

There is some evidence in support of this distinction from existing studies of brain damaged patients. First, Cromer (1991) reports the case of a spina bifida girl (in her late teens) with arrested hydrocephalus who was diagnosed as suffering from the 'chatterbox' syndrome. Her performance on grammaticality judgements was far superior to her performance on sentence-picture matching tasks. Second, Linebarger *et al.* (1983) describe aphasic patients who also perform much better on a grammaticality judgement task than on a sentence-picture matching task. However, we do not know in either of these studies the extent to which the patients' on-line processing is intact.

We have also seen the same distinction in some of our own patients.[7] VS, for example, is a patient who has been diagnosed as nonfluent. She rarely produces more than single words and does that with considerable difficulty, as the example of her spontaneous speech given below shows.

Elicited conversation (14.4.89)

NG: Where did you used to live?

VS: Edge Road Edge Road I can't say that Mill Road Millweal Millwall like that Millwall Millweal like that footwall football.

NG: Oh football.

VS: Yeh Yeh not London Enchroad I ink it where Millwall

NG: It's a football team?

VS: Yeh yeh like that when Ised we we we Oh I can't say that (she's writing on a piece of paper with her left hand)

NG: Old Kent...

VS: ...Kent Road

NG: Oh Old Kent Road.

VS: Yeh yeh where we wer wer lived.

NG: Did you like it there?

VS: Yeh it's nice there but now I thought it's nice nice here. Harry said I like it ere like that. Yeh it's hot now in it?

VS had a slight hearing impairment (21.7 db loss). She was diagnosed as having a severe comprehension disorder on the basis of the Token Test (she scored 11/36 correct), but her comprehension score was +0.5 on the BDAE, indicating a less severe impairment. On a sentence–picture matching test involving pairs of pictures against which she had to match a spoken sentence, she scored 60% correct, and on the TROG (Bishop, 1983) she scored 50% correct. Although her scores on both the

TROG and the sentence–picture matching task are above chance, they are considerably worse than the control group's performance. Unimpaired subjects rarely make any errors at all on either of these tests.

In contrast, her performance on various on-line tests of comprehension was similar to normal in many respects. Just like normal subjects, her word-monitoring latencies increased in the presence of any type of verb–argument violation. In addition, she showed the typical word-position effect in normal prose (although not in anomalous prose).

When we tested her comprehension using the verb–argument materials in a grammaticality judgement task, she was less accurate than the controls but considerably better than chance (VS A' = 0.85; Range of control A' = 0.93–1). Her grammaticality judgements, then, are consistent with the results of the word-monitoring study and, in themselves, would suggest that VS does not have a severe comprehension deficit. However, the results of the other off-line studies described above paint a different picture; one which suggests that she does have a severe comprehension deficit. We see in VS, then, an example of a patient who shows much better performance when tested on a grammaticality judgement task compared to other explicit tasks which involve a different kind of conscious awareness.

If my hypothesis about the distinction between different kinds of conscious awareness is correct, then we should only expect to find patients who are better on grammaticality judgements than on tasks such as sentence–picture matching. The reason for this is as follows. Grammaticality judgements, I have argued, are a better reflection of on-line processes (although a less direct one than on-line tasks). To the extent that on-line processes are intact, then this should be better reflected in grammaticality judgements than in other explicit tasks where the relationship with on-line processes and representations is much more tenuous. This is certainly what I have found. I have not yet seen a patient where the reverse is true.

The final issue which I want to deal with in this context is the following. Given the discussion so far, what predictions would I have to make about patients whose on-line processes are impaired? The answer to this is complex because, to a large extent, it depends upon the nature of the on-line impairment. If a procedure is completely non-operational, then the grammaticality judgements which call upon that procedure should also be impaired. However, performance on grammaticality judgements may be better than the on-line data would suggest. This is because other metalinguistic and general cognitive processes can be recruited by the subject.[8] However, in general, it should not be possible for a patient to show *normal* grammaticality judgements in the presence of abnormal on-line processes—unless, as is the case with one of our patients, JG (see Tyler, 1991), on-line processes appear to be intact but slowed down. In JG's case, on-line processes and representations as measured by means of the word-monitoring task, are abnormal but his grammaticality judgements, although worse than those of the control group, are well above chance (JG A' = 0.87; Range of control A' = 0.93–1).

8.6. CONCLUSIONS

Most research in aphasia tells us primarily about one aspect of the comprehension system; about those processes and representations about which the listener can become aware. This means that an entire, and vital, aspect of the comprehension process—those processes and representations of which listeners are not normally conscious—remains largely unexplored in aphasia research. These are crucial properties of language comprehension because they form the core of the system. The current emphasis on off-line tasks obviously results in the development of theories of aphasia which are likely to give a distorted view of the kinds of the comprehension deficits which result from brain damage.

To understand the underlying causes of aphasic deficits and to use data from aphasic patients to generate theories about the structure and function of intact systems, we need to be able to determine the extent to which a patient's deficit is due to problems with conscious or nonconscious comprehension processes. This requires us to develop tasks which selectively tap into each kind of process. But to be able to do this, we need to relate the properties of each task to a theory of the process. We need to know what aspect(s) of the comprehension process are impaired.

The data described in this chapter suggest that consciousness (as it applies to language comprehension) is not a unitary phenomenon (cf. Allport, 1988). There are at least two types of awareness involved in language comprehension. What is important here is the claim that these two types of awareness come from different processes. One process which is automatic—the awareness which comes from a procedure not running through its normal operations; and one which is under voluntary control (at least to a certain extent) and which involves reflection upon the properties of the final representation. They can be selectively impaired in brain damage.

Finally, to end on a positive note, the data which I have discussed here suggest that notions of consciousness do have a concrete role to play in explaining aphasic deficits. What seemed like a confusing set of data to start with (at least to me) became coherent when reinterpreted in the light of qualitative distinctions between conscious and nonconscious processes. Initially, I was faced with a great deal of data on individual patients, all of which told me something about their comprehension abilities. But they told conflicting stories. A coherent pattern only emerged when I considered the data in the light of the conscious/nonconscious distinction.

We obviously need to know much more about this distinction and about the relationship between the different kinds of processes and representations. But what I hope I have demonstrated in this chapter is that we cannot develop an adequate understanding of comprehension deficits without taking the distinction into account.

FOOTNOTES

1 In Marcel's (1983, 1988) terms, I am making the non-identity assumption.
2 Freedman and Forster (1985) claim that only certain types of ungrammaticality affect performance (but see Crain & Fodor, 1987).
3 RH was tested at various times by myself and my colleagues, Howard Cobb and Naida Graham.
4 In the gating task, subjects are presented with increasingly larger fragments of a word and after each fragment, they say what word they think they are hearing (Grosjean, 1980; Tyler & Wessels, 1983, 1985)
5 For a discussion of the A' statistic, see Linebarger *et al.* 1983.
6 RH's mean latency was 413 ms whereas the mean latency of the control group was 353 ms. RH's longer latencies are most probably due to the general effects of brain damage, which frequently slows down psychomotor performance irrespective of the location of the damage (Benton & Joynt, 1959; Dee & Van Allen, 1973). Supporting this view is the RT data from a 65-year-old subject who has no detectable residual effects of a stroke she suffered in April 1986. She behaves normally on a variety of on-line tasks, but her latencies (a mean RT of 496 ms in the present study) are slower than normal and slower than RH's.
7 At various times these patients were tested by myself, Howard Cobb and Naida Graham.
8 In general, performance in an implicit task is less likely to be affected by metalinguistic and general cognitive processes.

ACKNOWLEDGEMENTS

My thanks to William Marslen-Wilson and Ruth Ostrin for reading an earlier draft of this chapter.

REFERENCES

Allport, A. (1988). What concept of consciousness? In A.J. Marcel and E. Bisiach (eds), *Consciousness in Contemporary Science*, pp. 159–182. Oxford: Clarendon Press.

Andreewsky, E. & Seron, X. (1985). Implicit processing of grammatical rules in a classical case of agrammatism. *Cortex,* **11**, 379–390.

Benton, A.L. & Joynt, R. (1959). Reaction time in unilateral cerebral disease. *Confinia Neurologica,* **19**, 247–256.

Bishop, D. (1983). TROG: Test for the Reception of Grammar. Abingdon, UK: Thomas Leach (for the MRC).

Black, M., Nickels, L. & Byng, S. (1991). Patterns of sentence processing deficit: Processing simple sentences can be a complex matter. *Neurolinguistics,* in press.

Cohen, N. & Squire, L. (1980). Preserved learning and retention of pattern-analyzing skill in amnesia: Dissociation of 'knowing how' and 'knowing that'. *Science,* **210**, 207–209.

Crain, S. & Fodor, J.D. (1987). Sentence matching and overgeneration. *Cognition,* **26**, 123–169.

Cromer, R. (1991). A case study of dissociations between language and cognition. In H. Tager-Flushberg (ed.), *Constraints on Language Acquisition: Studies of Atypical Children.* Hillsdale, NJ: LEA.

Dee, H.L. & Van Allen, M.W. (1973). Speed of decision making processing in patients with unilateral cerebral disease. *Archives of Neurology,* **28**, 163–166.

Dé Renzi, E. & Vignolo, L. (1962). The Token Test: A sensitive test to detect receptive disturbances in aphasics. *Brain,* **85**, 665–678.

Freedman, S. & Forster, K. (1985). The psychological status of overgenerated sentences. *Cognition,* **19**, 101–131.

Graf, P. & Schacter, D.L. (1985). Implicit and explicit memory for new associations in normal and amnesic subjects. *Journal of Experimental Psychology; Learning, Memory, and Cognition,* **11**, 501–518.

Grosjean, F. (1980). Spoken word recognition processes and the gating paradigm. *Perception and Psychophysics,* **28**, 267–283.

Hagoort, P. (1989). Processing of lexical ambiguities: A comment on Milberg, Blumstein & Dworetzky. *Brain and Language,* **36**, 335–349.

Kolk, H. & Van Grunsven, M. (1985). Agrammatism as a variable phenomenon. *Cognitive Neuropsychology,* **2**, 347–384.

Lahiri, A. & Marslen-Wilson, W.D. (1991). The mental representation of lexical form: A phonological approach to the recognition lexicon. *Cognition,* **38**, 245–295.

Linebarger, M., Schwartz, M. & Saffran, E. (1983). Sensitivity to grammatical structure in so-called agrammatic aphasics. *Cognition,* **13**, 361–392.

Marcel, A.J. (1983). Conscious and unconscious perception: An approach to the relations between phenomenal experience and perceptual awareness. *Cognitive Psychology,* **15**, 238–300.

Marcel, A.J. (1988). Phenomenal experience and functionalism. In A.J. Marcel and E. Bisiach (eds), *Consciousness in Contemporary Science,* pp. 121–158. Oxford: Clarendon Press.

Marslen-Wilson, W.D. (1973). Linguistic structure and speech shadowing at very short latencies. *Nature,* **244**, 522–523.

Marslen-Wilson, W.D. (1975). Sentence perception as an interactive parallel process. *Science,* **189**, 226–228.

Marslen-Wilson, W.D. (1987). Functional parallelism in spoken word recognition. *Cognition,* **25**, 71–102.

Marslen-Wilson, W.D. & Tyler, L.K. (1975). Processing structure of spoken language comprehension. *Nature,* **257**, 784–786.

Marslen-Wilson, W.D. & Tyler, L.K. (1980). The temporal structure of spoken language comprehension. *Cognition*, **6**, 1–71.

Marslen-Wilson, W.D. & Tyler, L.K. (1987). Against modularity. In R. Garfield (ed.), *Modularity and Knowledge Representations*. Cambridge MA: MIT Press.

Marslen-Wilson, W.D. & Welsh, A. (1978). Processing interactions and lexical access during word recognition in continuous speech. *Cognitive Psychology*, **10**, 29–63.

Marslen-Wilson, W.D. & Zwitserlood, P. (1989). Accessing spoken words: The importance of word-onsets. *Journal of Experimental Psychology: Human Perception and Performance*, **3**, 576–585.

Milberg, W. & Blumstein, S. (1981). Lexical decision and aphasia: Evidence for semantic processing. *Brain and Language*, **14**, 371–385.

Posner, M. & Snyder, C. (1975). Attention and cognitive control. In R. Solso (ed.), *Information Processing and Cognition: The Loyola Symposium*. Potomac, MD: Erlbaum.

Schacter, D., McAndrews, M. & Moscovitch, M. (1988). Access to consciousness: Dissociations between implicit and explicit knowledge in neuropsychological syndromes. In L. Weiskrantz (ed.), *Thought Without Language*. Oxford: Clarendon Press.

Schwartz, M., Saffran, E. & Marin, O. (1980). The word order problem in agrammatism 1. Comprehension. *Brain and Language*, **10**, 262–280.

Tyler, L.K. (1988). Spoken language comprehension in a fluent aphasic patient. *Cognitive Neuropsychology*, **5**, 375–400.

Tyler, L.K. (1992). *Understanding Misunderstanding: A Psycholinguistic Approach to Language Comprehension Deficits*. Cambridge, MA: MIT Press.

Tyler, L.K. & Cobb, H. (1987). Processing bound grammatical morphemes in context: The case of an aphasic patient. *Language and Cognitive Processes*, **2**, 245–263.

Tyler, L.K. & Marslen-Wilson, W.D. (1982). Speech comprehension processes. In J. Mehler, E.C.T. Walker and M. Garrett (eds), *Perspectives on Mental Representation*. Hillsdale, NJ: LEA.

Tyler, L.K. & Marslen-Wilson, W.D. (1986). The effects of context on the recognition of polymorphemic words. *Journal of Memory and Language*, **25**, 741–752.

Tyler, L.K. & Wessels, J. (1983). Quantifying contextual contributions to word recognition processes. *Perception and Psychophysics*, **34**, 409–420.

Tyler, L.K. & Wessels, J. (1985). Is gating an on-line task? Evidence from naming latency data. *Perception and Psychophysics*, **38**, 217–222.

Warren, P. & Marslen-Wilson, W.D. (1989). Cues to lexical choice: Discriminating place and voice. *Perception and Psychophysics*, **43**, 21–30.

CHAPTER 9

Consciousness and Awareness in Memory and Amnesia: Critical Issues

Daniel L. Schacter

9.1. INTRODUCTION

After a long period of neglect, the nature of the relation between memory and consciousness has become a major issue in neuropsychological and cognitive research (e.g. Jacoby, 1984; Tulving, 1985; Weiskrantz, 1986; Schacter, 1989, 1990b). As with various other phenomena discussed in the present volume, the roots of interest in this issue can be traced to a striking dissociation in a neuropsychological syndrome: the dissociation between implicit and explicit memory (Graf & Schacter, 1985; Schacter, 1987) in amnesic patients. The observation that amnesic patients can retain and express knowledge acquired during a specific prior episode, without any conscious or explicit recollection of that episode, was made initially in the nineteenth century (e.g. Dunn, 1845; Korsakoff, 1889; see Schacter, 1987), brought to the attention of contemporary students during the 1960s and 1970s (Milner et al., 1968; Warrington & Weiskrantz, 1968, 1974), and investigated intensively during the past decade (e.g. Cohen & Squire, 1980; Jacoby & Witherspoon, 1982; Moscovitch, 1982; Graf et al., 1984; Cermak et al., 1985; Graf & Schacter, 1985; Schacter, 1985; Schacter & Graf, 1986b). This finding has stimulated a large and ever-growing body of research on implicit memory in normal subjects (for reviews, see Schacter, 1987; Richardson-Klavehn & Bjork, 1988; Roediger, 1990) as well as studies that have attempted to elucidate properties and functions of conscious recollection (e.g. Gardiner, 1988).

While there is no denying the upsurge of interest in issues concerning aware and unaware expressions of memory, it is equally clear that

THE NEUROPSYCHOLOGY OF CONSCIOUSNESS
ISBN 0–12–498045–7

current understanding of the problem is rather modest: relatively few theoretical ideas and models have been put forward; the available proposals are all characterized by significant shortcomings; and there is considerable fuzziness and even confusion concerning basic terminology. The present chapter considers various types of experimental evidence pertinent to the memory/consciousness relation, attempts to clarify a number of conceptual and terminological issues, and assesses the empirical basis for two different types of explanatory approaches to the phenomena of interest.

9.2. VARIETIES OF CONSCIOUSNESS AND AWARENESS: TERMINOLOGY AND DATA

Definitional clarity is essential when dealing with an issue as difficult—and sometimes seemingly ephemeral—as the subject of the present chapter. Accordingly, it will be useful to summarize and expand on several definitional points I have made previously (Schacter, 1989, 1990b). First, the terms 'consciousness' and 'awareness' are used interchangeably to refer to what Dimond (1976) called 'the running span of subjective experience'—ongoing monitoring of subjective mental activities. With respect to memory, an 'aware' or 'conscious' expression of memory is characterized by a phenomenal quality of Jamesian 'pastness' (James, 1890; Tulving, 1985); that is, a subjective sense that a particular mental content represents an episode or episodes from one's personal past.

It is important to distinguish the foregoing sense of 'conscious recollection' from a related but quite different sense of the term that refers to whether a retrieval attempt is initiated intentionally or unintentionally. Because these two possible uses of the term 'conscious recollection' should not be conflated (Richardson-Klavehn & Bjork, 1988; Schacter et al., 1989; see also Jacoby & Kelley, Chapter 10, this volume), I will use the terms *intentional* and *unintentional* to refer to the manner in which retrieval is initiated, and reserve the terms *conscious* and *aware* for referring to the phenomenal or subjective experience associated with a retrieved mental content. Within this definitional context, the theoretical problem is to explain the origin of conscious/aware forms of remembering (explicit memory), and to understand how memory can be expressed in the absence of conscious recollection (implicit memory). These are formidable tasks. Moreover, they are made more difficult by the fact that it is possible to distinguish different types of aware and unaware expressions of memory: if awareness/unawareness of a prior experience can be manifest in different ways, then it is crucial to acknowledge and understand the nature of these differences. Upon reviewing relevant literature, I have been able to distinguish among five types of awareness/unawareness. Although they are undoubtedly related to one another at some level, each of the five types differ in specifiable and possibly important respects; I now discuss evidence bearing on each of them in turn.

9.2.1. Stochastic Independence and Item-level Unawareness

Consider first a finding that has been obtained in studies of normal, non-brain damaged subjects: priming effects on implicit memory tests frequently exhibit stochastic independence from conscious remembering. Thus, for example, in an experiment by Tulving *et al*. (1982) subjects studied a long list of low frequency words (e.g. ASSASSIN), and were then tested explicitly with a yes/no recognition task and implicitly with a fragment completion task (e.g. A—A-I-). Priming effects on the fragment-completion task were independent of recognition memory: the probability that subjects completed a fragment with a previously studied item was about the same for recognized and nonrecognized items. Similar demonstrations of stochastic independence between priming and recognition memory have been reported in a variety of experimental situations (e.g. Jacoby & Witherspoon, 1982; Hayman & Tulving, 1989a,b; Witherspoon & Moscovitch, 1989; Schacter *et al.*, 1990a). If we are willing to assume that a 'no' response on the recognition test indicates that subjects are not consciously aware of the prior occurrence of the item, then these data indicate that priming does not require or necessarily involve any conscious recollection.

9.2.2. Test Awareness and Unawareness

Although the data on stochastic independence suggest that implicit memory can be expressed independently of conscious recollection at the level of the *individual item*, they by no means indicate that priming occurs without any conscious recollection of the entire *study episode*. It is perfectly possible that during performance of a fragment completion or similar implicit test subjects occasionally become aware of the learning episode, perhaps because they unintentionally retrieve contextual information about a study list item. Nevertheless, the potential availability of such global awareness of the learning episode need not imply that it is present every time that subjects complete a fragment with a studied word; hence the possible co-existence of 'unawareness' at the individual item level (as indicated by findings on stochastic independence) and 'awareness' at the level of the global study episode.

This distinction can be brought into sharper focus by considering a recent study by Bowers and Schacter (1990) that provides pertinent experimental evidence. Noting that stochastic independence between priming and recognition need not imply that subjects are unaware of the study episode *throughout* a completion test, we examined whether priming is observed in those subjects who do not notice any connection between the study episode and completion test—a phenomenon that we refer to as *test unawareness*. Assessment of test unawareness presents some tricky methodological problems, because on-line queries about awareness/unawareness during completion test performance would necessarily induce awareness of the study episode. Accordingly, we used a post-test questionnaire to assess whether subjects were aware of the study episode at any time during test performance, despite the acknowledged pitfalls of a questionnaire procedure (e.g. Eriksen, 1960).

In the experiment, normal college students were shown a list of familiar words under either incidental or intentional encoding conditions, and performed a semantic orienting task for half the target items and a structural orienting task for the other half. After a delay, they completed a series of three-letter stems with the first word that came to mind. Half of the subjects were informed that they might complete some of the stems with study-list words, whereas the other half were not so informed. These latter, test-uninformed subjects were asked several questions at the conclusion of the test about whether they noticed any relation between the words that they had produced in response to the stems and the previously studied words. Subjects who indicated that they did not notice that any of the words that they produced on the completion test had been on the study list (approximately half of the subjects in the uninformed group) were classified as test unaware; the others were classified as test aware. The critical finding was that test unaware subjects showed robust priming—as much priming as the group who had been informed about the study-test relation—following both semantic and structural encoding tasks.

The Bowers and Schacter data indicate that only a sub-set of subjects remains unaware of the study episode throughout performance of a completion test. This type of unawareness is thus likely to be distinct from the sort of 'unawareness' indicated by stochastic independence between priming and recognition at the individual item level, in the sense that a subject could exhibit the latter type of unawareness and not the former.

9.2.3. Unawareness in Amnesic Patients

Although half of the college students in the Bowers and Schacter experiment met the criterion for test unawareness, it seems safe to assume that these subjects would easily be able to recollect consciously the study episode if they were asked about it. Indeed, the phrasing of the post-test awareness questions (e.g. 'While doing the stem completion test, did you notice whether you completed some of the stems with words studied in the earlier list?') pre-supposed an ability for conscious recollection of the study episode in response to a direct query. Test unawareness in college students does not imply an inability to recollect the study episode; it simply indicates that during completion test performance subjects did not *spontaneously* become aware of the study episode and its relation to the test.

Consider, by contrast, the case in which a severely amnesic patient exhibits implicit memory on an appropriate task. The striking phenomenon here is that a patient is *unable* to recollect consciously that there was a study episode. This observation was made in studies of preserved motor skill learning (Milner *et al.*, 1968) and priming effects (Warrington & Weiskrantz, 1968, 1974) that included patients with dense amnesia. My colleagues and I have reported similar observations in a variety of studies with a severely amnesic head-injured patient, KC. For example, KC showed robust priming effects that persisted over a 1-week delay on a task in which he was initially shown an ambiguous sentence (e.g. *The haystack was important because the cloth ripped*) followed by a disambiguating cue (e.g. *parachute*), and was then shown the sentence again after varying delays and asked to provide a word that would make the sentence comprehensible. KC provided the correct word much more frequently as a function of prior exposure to the sentence, but performed at the chance level on a yes/no recognition test of the sentences and indicated that he did not remember being shown any sentences previously (McAndrews *et al.*, 1987; see also Tulving *et al.*, 1991). Similarly, KC was also able to acquire complex new knowledge concerning the programming and operation of a microcomputer through a fragment cueing technique known as the method of vanishing cues (Glisky *et al.*, 1986a,b). Computer knowledge was acquired across several months of bi-weekly training sessions, and KC exhibited long-term retention with little forgetting across delays of up to 9 months (Glisky & Schacter, 1988). Nevertheless, when queried at the beginning of a session, KC could not remember any prior training episode and claimed that he had never worked previously on a microcomputer.

In this case and others like it, then, patients exhibit no awareness of prior study episodes or the items acquired during those episodes; and, unlike college students, patients were unable to achieve conscious recollection when queried directly. Thus, test unawareness in amnesic patients appears to differ substantially from test unawareness in college students.

9.2.4. Unawareness of Target Information During the Study Episode

Despite differences in the types of unawareness considered in the three preceding sections, all of the examples discussed share one feature in common: at the time of encoding, subjects were consciously aware of target information. Some studies of implicit memory (and explicit memory) have used incidental encoding procedures while others have used intentional encoding procedures, but in all cases subjects are perfectly aware of, and attend to, the target materials. Thus, the finding of a priming effect in the absence of conscious recollection does not imply a corresponding absence of conscious awareness of the primed material at the time of study. The question arises, then, as to whether implicit memory can be observed even when subjects are not consciously aware of target materials during the study episode.

Pertinent evidence is provided by studies in which a variety of procedures has been used to attenuate or block conscious awareness of target items during study. In a study by Eich (1984), for example, subjects were exposed to word pairs on an unattended channel that biased the low frequency interpretation of a homophone (e.g. taxi-FARE) in a dual-task auditory shadowing paradigm. Subjects were then given a spelling task that included previously presented homophones as well as nonpresented homophones. Eich found that the low frequency spelling was provided more often for the previously presented than nonpresented homophone—despite extremely low levels of recognition memory—thus demonstrating implicit memory for unattended target information. Forster *et al.* (1990) used a masked priming procedure developed by Forster and colleagues (e.g. Forster & Davis, 1984; Forster, 1987) to examine whether brief exposures to words that subjects did not consciously 'see' produced priming on subsequent stem- and fragment-completion tests. Subjects were given 60-ms exposures to familiar words (e.g. ELASTIC) with sufficient forward and backward masking to prevent conscious perception of the targets. After delays ranging from 500 ms to 20 s, subjects were then given either word stems (e.g. ELA   ) or fragments (e.g. E AS IC) and were told to complete them with the first word that came to mind. Significant masked priming was observed on both stem and fragment completion tasks, although the priming was short-lived and had dissipated almost entirely by the 20-s delay. Jacoby and Whitehouse (1989) used a somewhat different paradigm to demonstrate implicit memory for target information that subjects did not perceive consciously at the time of study (see also Jacoby & Kelley, Chapter 10, this volume).

The foregoing studies appear to show quite clearly that conscious perception is not necessary to produce implicit memory on a variety of tasks. Moreover, the type of 'test unawareness' exhibited by subjects in these studies appears to differ from the type of unawareness considered in previous examples. Because subjects either did not consciously perceive or did not consciously attend to target items, they could not recollect the prior occurrence of the items and in that sense resemble a severely amnesic patient. However, subjects in divided attention or masked priming studies would presumably have no difficulty remembering the episode in which the items were presented, and in that sense differ from a severely amnesic patient.

9.2.5. Unawareness of Target and Context During the Study Episode

Subjects in masked priming experiments are not aware of target information, but they are otherwise fully conscious and presumably attend to and process contextual features of the experimental situation normally. By contrast, consider a recent study by Kihlstrom *et al.* (1990) that examined whether implicit memory could be observed for information acquired by patients undergoing surgical anaesthesia. Although it seems clear that anaesthetized patients have no explicit memory for surgical events, there are conflicting reports concerning the evidence for implicit memory (for discussion, see Kihlstrom & Schacter, 1990). To investigate the matter, we studied 30 patients who were undergoing a variety of surgical procedures. Anaesthesia was induced by intravenous thiopental, accompanied by vecuronium to produce muscular paralysis, and maintained by isoflurane. While patients were unconscious, an audio tape consisting of 15 highly related paired associates was played repeatedly. Testing was conducted in the recovery room once patients were comfortable and ready to be interviewed. Implicit memory was assessed with a free association task in which the first word of previously presented pairs, as well as the first word of nonpresented pairs, was read aloud; patients were instructed to respond with the first word that came to mind. Explicit memory was assessed with free recall, cued recall, and recognition tests.

The critical result of the experiment was that a small but significant priming effect was observed on the free association test, despite an absence of conscious memory on any of the explicit tests. In this study, then, priming was observed in patients who not only lacked conscious recollection at the time of test, but were also unaware of both target words and experimental context—indeed they were fully unconscious—during the 'study' episode.

9.2.6. Varieties of Unawareness: Summary and Implications

The foregoing examples illustrate five different ways in which implicit memory can be expressed without awareness of a prior episode:

(1) Findings of stochastic independence indicate that subjects can show priming for an individual item even though they are not consciously aware that the item was presented previously in the study list.

(2) The phenomenon of test unawareness indicates that subjects who do not spontaneously become aware of the relation between the completion test and the study episode still show robust word priming.
(3) Studies with severely amnesic patients indicate that implicit memory occurs in subjects who cannot become aware of the study episode.
(4) Masked priming experiments indicate that implicit memory does not require conscious perception of target items.
(5) Preliminary evidence from surgical anaesthesia suggests that implicit memory can be expressed without awareness of the study episode in patients who were unconscious during the study episode.

An important implication of the foregoing is that careful attention must be paid to the use of such terms as 'memory without awareness', 'unaware expressions of memory' or 'unconscious memory', because each of these terms can refer to any one of the five phenomena that we have considered. Whether or not different mechanisms need to be postulated in each of these cases is an empirical matter; it is certainly conceivable that despite the different ways in which the various forms of unawareness are expressed, they are all explicable in similar terms at the level of mechanism or process. It does seem reasonable to suggest, however, that needless confusion can be avoided by specifying exactly what one has in mind when referring to an instance of 'memory without conscious recollection'.

One feature that is common to each of the five examples is that subjects in all cases fail to recollect consciously the prior occurrence of *individual items* in a prior study episode. Accordingly, when I use such phrases as 'memory without conscious recollection', I refer to cases in which memory for an individual item is expressed on an implicit test despite failure to remember that item on an appropriate explicit test. No further assumptions are made about test awareness versus unawareness or about conscious versus unconscious perception of the item at the time of study.

9.3. FIRST- AND SECOND-ORDER EXPLANATIONS OF IMPLICIT/EXPLICIT DISSOCIATIONS

9.3.1. Logic of First- and Second-Order Explanations

When an amnesic patient who lacks phenomenal awareness of the prior occurrence of target information none the less shows intact implicit memory for that information, what kinds of theoretical explanations are required to make sense of the phenomenon? I have found it useful to distinguish between *first-order* and *second-order* explanations of such dissociations (Schacter, 1990b). A *first-order* explanation seeks to explain an apparent awareness disturbance by postulating an impairment at the level of mechanisms or processes that are thought to underlie the generation of awareness itself. For example, several authors have speculated that the activation of specific neurophysiological systems and processes is necessary for, and supports the occurrence of, 'aware' experiences in different domains (cf. Dimond, 1976; Weiskrantz, 1986 and Chapter 1, this volume; Edelman, 1989; and Schacter, 1989). A first-order account of preserved implicit memory in amnesia might appeal to a disruption of a hypothetical awareness or monitoring system, or suggest a disconnection of that system from a memory system. That is, a first-order approach leads one to seek an explanation that is couched in terms of impaired awareness—rather than impaired memory—and thus is compatible with the notion that memory processes *per se* are not impaired in amnesia and that the crucial disturbance lies in the access of these processes to conscious awareness. A rather different, more functionally oriented first-order account is exemplified by Jacoby's (1984) idea that 'aware' experiences of remembering are based on the use of a fluency heuristic that enables one to make attributions about the source of retrieved information. Such an account would lead one to investigate the possibility that amnesic patients do not use the fluency heuristic normally, fail to make appropriate attributions about the source of retrieved memories, and hence lack a conscious experience of remembering.

In contrast to the foregoing, a *second-order* account of an unaware expression of memory does not invoke deficits in the processes or systems involved in the generation of awareness itself. Instead, it appeals to deficits in processes or systems that are necessary to make available certain types of domain-specific *information* that normally provide a basis for an aware experience of remembering. Consider, for example, the idea that the phenomenal experience of conscious remembering is associated with, and attributable to, access to contextual information about the time and place of an event. This notion might lead one to explain unaware expressions of memory in amnesic patients by postulating that (a) systems or processes involved in representing and gaining conscious access to contextual information are impaired in amnesia (e.g. Mayes *et al.*, 1985), and (b) systems or processes involved in implicit memory, which does not involve conscious access to contextual information, are spared.

An example of such a second-order explanation is provided by the idea that amnesic patients are afflicted by an impaired episodic or declarative memory system (which normally enables conscious access to contextual information and, hence, provides the informational basis for conscious remembering), but possess spared systems that support normal priming or skill-learning performance without conscious remembering (because these systems do not enable explicit access to contextual information). In such a second-order account, there is no reference to, or postulation of, mechanisms directly involved in the generation of awareness; conscious recollection is seen as a by-product of access to a certain type of retrieved information.

9.3.2. Evidence from Amnesic Patients

What sort of explanation—first order or second order—fits best with experimental data on implicit and explicit memory in amnesic patients? As discussed elsewhere (Schacter, 1990b), the phenomenon of preserved skill learning is readily accommodated by a second-order account that proposes that such learning is mediated by a preserved procedural or habit system (cf. Mishkin *et al.*, 1984; Squire & Cohen 1984) that depends on basal ganglia and related structures that are independent of the impaired limbic structures necessary for conscious recall and recognition. If the latter system normally enables explicit access to contextual information that supports the conscious experience of remembering, then it follows that amnesic patients can acquire skills despite impaired conscious recollection. For the present purposes, let us focus more closely on the phenomena of direct priming.

9.3.3. Priming of Familiar Words

There can be little doubt that even severely amnesic patients show intact priming of highly familiar, overlearned information—i.e. words (Warrington & Weiskrantz, 1974; Graf *et al.*, 1984, 1985; Cermak *et al.*, 1985), strongly related paired associates (Shimamura & Squire, 1984), and common idioms (Schacter, 1985). However, precisely because words, strongly related paired associates, and common idioms are already established in memory prior to the experiment, whereas contextual information about time and place of an episode is newly acquired during the experimental situation, it is rather easy to construct a second-order account of such priming phenomena; perhaps amnesic patients can activate or strengthen pre-existing memory representations, but cannot form new, context-specific representations that provide a basis for explicit remembering (cf. Graf, *et al.*, 1984; Shimamura & Squire, 1989). By this view, priming without conscious recollection does not require postulating impairments in the accessibility or functioning of systems/processes that are directly involved in awareness; an impairment in the hippocampally-based system necessary to establish new memories will suffice.

Of course, one could argue on the basis of evidence from the literature on normal, non-impaired subjects that priming of words and other kinds of familiar or overlearned information cannot be attributed solely to activation of pre-existing representations—such priming effects are frequently sensitive to study/test changes in specific surface features of target stimuli (e.g. Jacoby & Hayman, 1987; Roediger & Blaxton, 1987; Graf & Ryan, 1990), thereby suggesting that priming might reflect the acquisition of new, episode-specific memory representations. If so, then one might try to argue that priming without conscious recollection in amnesia demands a first-order explanation—i.e. that amnesic patients have intact an episodic/declarative memory system but are unable to gain conscious access to the products of this system. However, these kinds of specificity effects have not yet been observed in amnesic patients and, as we shall see shortly, even if such effects were to be observed a number of interpretations of them are possible.

9.3.4. Priming of New Associations

Consider next another type of evidence that is potentially more suggestive of a first-order interpretation than is the phenomenon of intact word priming—namely, priming effects that depend on the acquisition of contextually specific, novel associations between unrelated words. For example, Graf and Schacter (1985, 1987, 1989) and Schacter and Graf (1986a,b, 1989) developed a paradigm in which subjects study unrelated word pairs (e.g. WINDOW–REASON), and priming is later assessed with a word completion task in which stems are presented in one of three main experimental conditions: (a) a same context condition, where the stem of a previously studied word appears next to its study list cue (e.g. WINDOW–REA); (b) a different context condition, where the stem of a previously studied word appears next to some other cue (e.g. OFFICER–REA); and (c) a baseline condition where the stem of a non-studied word appears next to an unrelated cue (e.g. SHIP–CAS). The logic underlying the paradigm is that if more priming is observed in the same-context condition than in the different context condition, it can be inferred that this context-sensitive priming reflects the establishment, during the study episode, of a novel memory representation that links the two unrelated words.

In studies using this paradigm with non-amnesic student subjects, we found evidence of context-sensitive priming (more priming in the same- than different-context condition), but only when subjects engaged in some type of semantic study processing to link the two words (Graf & Schacter, 1985; Schacter & Graf, 1986a). We also found that priming of new associations could be dissociated from explicit memory for new associations through manipulations of degree of elaborative and organizational processing (Graf & Schacter, 1989; Schacter & Graf, 1986a), retroactive and proactive interference (Graf & Schacter, 1987), and sensory modality (Schacter & Graf, 1989).

The critical question for the present purposes concerns whether densely amnesic patients show this associative priming effect. If they do, such a finding could be taken as evidence to support a first-order interpretation of amnesia, inasmuch as it would suggest that amnesic patients can establish and retrieve new context-specific memories, but simply lack conscious awareness of them. The data, however, are equivocal. Graf & Schacter (1985) reported robust priming of new associations in amnesic patients, but subsequent analysis indicated that only patients with mild memory disorders showed the associative effect. Further experimentation confirmed that context effects are observed in mildly amnesic but not severely amnesic patients (Schacter & Graf, 1986b). Cermak *et al.* (1988a) and Shimamura and Squire (1989), both using the Graf and Schacter paradigm, found no evidence of associative effects in severely amnesic Korsakoff patients. Shimamura and Squire (1989) observed nonsignificant trends for associative effects in a group of anoxic and ischaemic amnesic patients whose memory disorders varied in severity. Cermak *et al.* (1988b), however, did observe some evidence of associative priming in a densely amnesic encephalitic patient (SS). Moscovitch *et al.* (1986) assessed priming of new associations with a different type of test (reading speed) than did Graf and Schacter, and found evidence for contextually sensitive priming in a mixed group of amnesic patients. However, this effect has not been replicated in subsequent research with different patients (Squire, personal communication).

In contrast to the robust evidence for priming of familiar words and word pairs, then, the data concerning priming of novel, context-specific associations in amnesic patients are mixed. Interestingly, results with college students indicate that whereas robust word priming effects are observed in what we have referred to as test-unaware subjects (Bowers & Schacter, 1990), associative priming effects appear to be observed only in test-aware subjects (Bowers & Schacter, 1990, experiments 2 & 3). Whatever the ultimate explanation of the data on associative priming, they do not support a first-order interpretation that holds that amnesic patients establish new, context-specific memories just like normal subjects and fail to exhibit conscious recollection because of a defective or disconnected awareness mechanism.

9.3.5. Priming of Novel Objects

In contrast to the foregoing, two recent studies have taken a rather different approach to examining priming of newly acquired information in amnesic patients. In both experiments, novel *nonverbal* materials were studied by amnesic patients, and priming was assessed with newly devised nonverbal implicit memory tasks. While it has been known for many years that amnesic patients show some priming effects when pictures of familiar objects are used (e.g. Milner *et al.*, 1968; Warrington & Weiskrantz, 1968; for review, see Shimamura, 1986; Schacter *et al.*, 1990b), little information exists concerning priming of novel nonverbal information.

Gabrieli *et al.* (1990) reported a case study of the well-known patient HM, who became severely amnesic after medial temporal lobe resection for intractable epilepsy. HM, as well as a group of control subjects, studied spatial arrangements of five dots from a 3×3 matrix that were connected to form a specific novel pattern. Priming was then assessed by presenting subjects with unconnected five-dot arrangements that could be completed in several different ways, asking them to draw any figure that connected the dots with straight lines, and determining whether subjects showed a significant tendency to complete the dots with previously studied patterns relative to a baseline condition. The key finding was that HM showed entirely normal priming effects on the dot completion test. By contrast, HM was severely impaired when asked to try to remember explicitly the prior occurrence of dot patterns on a four-alternative forced-choice recognition test.

A recent study in our laboratory (Schacter *et al.*, 1991b) used a rather different paradigm to investigate priming of novel nonverbal information in amnesic patients. In this paradigm, subjects are initially exposed to two-dimensional line drawings that depict unfamiliar three-dimensional objects and are asked to make a judgment about them, such as whether the object appears to be facing primarily to the left or to the right. Although unknown to the subject during this study phase, half of the objects are structurally *possible*—they could actually exist in the real world—whereas half are structurally *impossible*—they contain impossible relations among surfaces and edges that would prohibit them from existing in the real world. Priming was assessed with an object decision task in which subjects are given brief (i.e. 100-ms) exposures to studied and nonstudied objects, and are required to indicate whether each object is structurally possible or impossible. Experiments with normal subjects (Cooper *et al.*, 1990; Schacter *et al.*, 1990a; Schacter *et al.*, 1991a) have revealed that (a) significant priming is observed for possible objects—but not impossible objects—following encoding tasks that promote acquisition of information about global object structure; (b) whereas explicit memory (yes/no recognition) for the objects is improved by semantic encoding tasks and increasing numbers of study list repetitions, the magnitude of priming is not increased by either manipulation; and (c) object decision priming is unaffected by study-test changes in size and left–right orientation that significantly impair explicit memory.

To investigate object decision priming in patients with memory disorders, we first required subjects to make left/right judgements about target objects, next gave the object decision task (which included the studied objects plus an equal number of nonstudied objects), and then gave a yes/no recognition test for all objects in which subjects were instructed to say 'yes' if they remembered that an object had appeared during the left/right task. Three groups participated in the experiment: six patients with organic memory disorders (three ruptured anterior communicating artery aneurysm patients, two closed head injury, one with an uncertain diagnosis), six matched control subjects, and six college student controls (see Schacter *et al.*, 1991b, for details).

Results of the experiment showed significant priming in patients and controls: object decision performance was more accurate for studied than nonstudied objects, and the magnitude of this priming effect was virtually identical in the three groups. The amnesic patients showed significant priming of possible objects and no priming of impossible objects, just as has been observed with normal subjects in most experimental conditions. In contrast to their intact priming performance, patients were impaired on the explicit recognition test relative to both control groups.

Both the Gabrieli *et al.* (1990) and Schacter *et al.* (1991b) studies show intact priming of novel nonverbal information in patients with explicit memory deficits. These data are important for the present purposes because they indicate that amnesic patients are capable of establishing new memories of some sort in a relatively normal manner: the information about patterns and objects that provided the basis for priming did not exist in memory prior to the experiment and hence could not have been activated by a study-list presentation). Do these results, then, provide evidence for a first-order hypothesis that episodic memory is intact in amnesic patients and that their problem thus is attributable to defective or disconnected awareness mechanisms? Probably not.

To illustrate the point, consider the interpretation that we (Schacter *et al.*, 1990a, 1991a,b) have offered for priming of novel objects in normal subjects—namely, that such priming is mediated by a structural description system (Riddoch & Humphreys, 1987) that is dedicated to representing information about the form and structure of visual objects (the *structural description system* can be viewed as a sub-system of a pre-semantic *perceptual representation system* [Schacter, 1990a; Tulving & Schacter, 1990]). By this view, priming occurs on the object decision task because a recently stored structural description is activated during test performance, thereby facilitating the subject's ability to determine whether the test object is structurally possible or impossible. However, since the structural description does not contain information about the time and place that the object was encountered or elaborations that tie the object to semantic or associative knowledge, access to a structural description alone does not provide a basis for conscious recollection. Evidence in support of the structural description system hypothesis is provided by a variety of experimental findings concerning the properties of object decision priming noted earlier (Cooper *et al.*, 1990; Schacter *et al.*, 1990a; Schacter *et al.*, 1991a), and also by an independent line of investigation that has revealed dissociations between the representation of structural and semantic knowledge about objects in agnosic patients (e.g. Warrington, 1982; Riddoch & Humphreys, 1987).

With respect to amnesic patients, the idea is that priming in the structural description system, which may involve posterior cortical regions such as inferotemporal cortex (see Schacter *et al.*, 1991b), does not involve or depend on the limbic structures that are typically damaged in amnesia and that normally support explicit remembering (cf. Weiskrantz, 1985; Squire, 1987). Accordingly, amnesic patients may be able to form and gain access to novel structural descriptions of visual objects yet have difficulties consciously remembering the prior occurrence of these objects. Schacter *et al.* (1991b) offered this interpretation of the data on spared object decision priming in amnesic patients, and Gabrieli *et al.* (1990) have put forward a similar interpretation of their findings of normal priming of novel patterns in patient HM.

Although it is too early to say whether the structural description hypothesis is entirely satisfactory, the critical point for the present purposes is that a second-order interpretation of spared implicit memory for novel information in amnesic patients can be proposed and defended. An intriguing question in this regard concerns the contrast between the apparently robust evidence for priming of novel nonverbal information in amnesia, and the inconsistent results concerning priming of novel verbal associations discussed earlier (inconsistent results have also been observed in studies on priming of nonwords in amnesic patients; cf. Cermak *et al.*, 1985; Gordon, 1988; Smith & Oscar-Berman, 1990). Because of the numerous and substantial differences between the materials, study tasks, and tests that have been used in experiments concerning priming of novel verbal information and priming of novel nonverbal information, there is as yet no clear-cut answer to this question. Further investigation of the issue would be highly desirable.

9.4. RELATING THEORIES TO DATA

To return to the main issue at hand, what sort of data will be required to argue for a first-order interpretation of implicit memory in amnesia? As I have suggested elsewhere (Schacter, 1990b), critical support for such an account would be provided by an empirical demonstration that amnesic patients show intact implicit memory for the kinds of information that, when accessed explicitly, normally provide a basis for conscious recollection, e.g. spatial and temporal information about the global context of an event, or semantic elaborations that link an object or word to other components of an event or to pre-existing knowledge structures. If it were possible to show that these kinds of information are accessible to amnesic patients—albeit only on implicit tests—then one could no longer argue that amnesic patients are unable to acquire and retain the type of information needed to support conscious remembering. With such data in hand, it would be useful and perhaps necessary to argue that the outputs of episodic memory are disconnected from, and thus cannot serve as inputs to, the mechanism whose activation is necessary for the experience of aware or conscious remembering. However, there is as yet no strong evidence demonstrating implicit access to this type of 'recollection supporting' information in amnesic patients. To assess the issue empirically, it will first be necessary to develop appropriate experimental procedures and paradigms that yield evidence of implicit memory for global context or semantic elaborations.

Despite the lack of evidence that directly supports a first-order interpretation of implicit memory in amnesic patients, and the apparent ability of second-order explanations to accommodate existing results, the possibility of a first-order explanation should not be entirely discarded. The main reason for this stems from the apparent ubiquity of dissociations between implicit and explicit expressions of knowledge, as reviewed by Schacter et al. (1988) and discussed in other chapters in the present volume. As Schacter et al. (1988) argued in detail, studies of patients with a wide variety of neuropsychological impairments have provided evidence of spared implicit knowledge within the domain in which patients show deficits of explicit knowledge. Thus, 'blindsight' patients show implicit perceptual knowledge of stimuli that they do not consciously 'see' (e.g. Weiskrantz, 1986); prosopagnosic patients show 'implicit familiarity' with faces that are unfamiliar at the conscious level (cf. Bauer, 1984; Tranel & Damasio, 1985; De Haan et al., 1987); alexic patients are able to gain access to information about words that they cannot identify consciously (e.g. Shallice & Saffran, 1986; Coslett & Saffran, 1989); and similar kinds of dissociations have been observed in aphasia, neglect, and other syndromes (see Schacter et al., 1988). Despite differences among the various syndromes, the observed implicit/explicit dissociations are generally *domain-specific*—that is, patients do not exhibit a global disorder of awareness that affects performance in all cognitive domains; rather, the 'awareness deficit' is confined to the particular domain in which performance is impaired.

Because of the domain-specific character of the foregoing dissociations, it is not plausible to postulate that patients who exhibit implicit/explicit dissociations have simply suffered damage to an awareness system or mechanism; such damage would be expected to produce deficits in awareness across all domains. Nevertheless, it can be argued that domain-specific awareness deficits are produced by a *selective disconnection* between an awareness mechanism and particular processing or memory modules (Schacter et al., 1988; Schacter, 1989). Such a disconnection would produce the sort of domain-specific deficits that have been observed. Thus, the appeal of such a first-order account is that it can provide a parsimonious explanation of a variety of empirical observations. Second-order accounts, by contrast, involve postulating a separate explanation for each syndrome: the observed lack of awareness in a specific type of patient is attributed to an impairment of a specific process or system that is normally associated with, or provides a basis for, an 'aware' experience of perceiving, knowing, identifying, comprehending, or remembering.

While it seems clear that a first-order account that accommodates observations from a variety of neuropsychological syndromes has the advantage of parsimony over second-order accounts that differ with each syndrome, the evidence for a first-order account in any specific syndrome is weak. That is, there is little evidence that patients who show some preserved implicit knowledge carry out the same computations as normal subjects, and differ from normals only in the sense that they lack domain-specific conscious awareness. Rather, existing evidence is compatible with the idea that domain-specific failures of conscious awareness are associated with deficits in particular processes or systems that normally provide an informational basis for aware experiences of knowing, identifying, remembering, and so forth (see Schacter *et al.*, 1988 for discussion of pertinent evidence). Further exploration of issues that arise in relation to the distinction between first- and second-order explanations will likely provide important insights into the nature and functions of consciousness and cognition.

ACKNOWLEDGEMENTS

Preparation of this chapter was supported by a grant from the McDonnell-Pew Cognitive Neuroscience Program. I thank Terry Barnhardt for useful comments on an earlier draft of the manuscript.

REFERENCES

Bauer, R.M. (1984). Autonomic recognition of names and faces in prosopagnosia: A neuropsychological study. *Neuropsychologia*, **22**, 457–69.

Bowers, J.S. & Schacter, D.L. (1990). Implicit memory and test awareness. *Journal of Experimental Psychology: Learning, Memory, and Cognition*, **16**, 404–416.

Cermak, L.S., Talbot, N., Chandler, K. & Wolbarst, L.R. (1985). The perceptual priming phenomenon in amnesia. *Neuropsychologia*, **23**, 615–622.

Cermak, L.S., Bleich, R. & Blackford, S. (1988a). Deficits in the implicit retention of new associations. *Brain and Cognition*, **7**, 312–323.

Cermak, L.S., Blackford, S.P., O'Conner, M. & Bleich, R.P. (1988b). The implicit memory ability of a patient with amnesia due to encephalitis. *Brain and Cognition*, **7**, 145–156.

Cohen, N.J. & Squire, L.R. (1980). Preserved learning and retention of pattern-analyzing skill in amnesia: Dissociation of 'knowing how' and 'knowing that'. *Science*, **210**, 207–209.

Cooper, L.A., Schacter, D.L., Ballesteros, S. & Moore, C. (1990). Priming of structural representations of three-dimensional objects. Presentation to the Annual Meeting of the Psychonomic Society, New Orleans.

Coslett, H.B. & Saffran, E.M. (1989). Evidence for preserved reading in 'pure alexia'. *Brain*, **112**, 327–359.

De Haan, E.H.F., Young, A. & Newcombe, F. (1987). Face recognition without awareness. *Cognitive Neuropsychology*, **4**, 385–415.

Dimond, S.J. (1976). Brain circuits for consciousness. *Brain, Behavior, and Evolution*, **13**, 376–395.

Dunn, R. (1845). Case of suspension of the mental faculties. *Lancet*, **2**, 588–590.

Edelman, G.M. (1989). *The Remembered Present: A Biological Theory of Consciousness*. New York: Basic Books.

Eich, E. (1984). Memory for unattended events: Remembering with and without awareness. *Memory & Cognition*, **12**, 105–111.

Eriksen, C.W. (1960). Discrimination and learning without awareness: A methodological survey and evaluation. *Psychological Review*, **67**, 279–300.

Forster, K.I. (1987). Form-priming with masked primes: The best-match hypothesis. In M. Coltheart (ed.), *Attention and Performance*, Vol. 12. Hillsdale, NJ: Erlbaum.

Forster, K.I. & Davis, C. (1984). Repetition priming and frequency attenuation in lexical access. *Journal of Experimental Psychology: Learning, Memory, and Cognition*, **10**, 680–698.

Forster, K., Booker, J., Schacter, D.L. & Davis, C. (1990). Masked repetition priming: Lexical activation or novel memory trace? *Bulletin of the Psychonomic Society*, **28**, 341–345.

Gabrieli, J.D.E., Milberg, W., Keane, M.M. & Corkin, S. (1990). Intact priming of patterns despite impaired memory. *Neuropsychologia*, **28**, 417–428.

Gardiner, J.M. (1988). Functional aspects of recollective experience. *Memory & Cognition*, **16**, 309–313.

Glisky, E.L. & Schacter, D.L. (1988). Long-term retention of computer learning by patients with memory disorders. *Neuropsychologia*, **26**, 173–178.

Glisky, E.L., Schacter, D.L. & Tulving, E. (1986a). Computer learning by memory-impaired patients: Acquisition and retention of complex knowledge. *Neuropsychologia*, **24**, 313–328.

Glisky, E.L., Schacter, D.L. & Tulving, E. (1986b). Learning and retention of computer-related vocabulary in memory-impaired patients: Method of vanishing cues. *Journal of Clinical and Experimental Neuropsychology*, **8**, 292–312.

Gordon, B. (1988). Preserved learning of novel information in amnesia: Evidence for multiple memory systems. *Brain and Cognition*, **7**, 257–282.

Graf, P. & Ryan, L. (1990). Transfer appropriate processing for implicit and explicit memory. *Journal of Experimental Psychology: Learning, Memory, and Cognition*, **16**, 978–992.

Graf, P. & Schacter, D.L. (1985). Implicit and explicit memory for new associations in normal and amnesic subjects. *Journal of Experimental Psychology: Learning, Memory, and Cognition*, **11**, 501–518.

Graf, P. & Schacter, D.L. (1987). Selective effects of interference on implicit and explicit memory for new associations. *Journal of Experimental Psychology: Learning, Memory, and Cognition*, **13**, 45–53.

Graf, P. & Schacter, D. L. (1989). Unitization and grouping mediate dissociations in memory for new associations. *Journal of Experimental Psychology: Learning, Memory, and Cognition*, **15**, 930–940.

Graf, P., Squire, L.R. & Mandler, G. (1984). The information that amnesic patients do not forget. *Journal of Experimental Psychology: Learning, Memory, and Cognition*, **10**, 164–178.

Graf, P., Shimamura, A.P. & Squire, L.R. (1985). Priming across modalities and priming across category levels: Extending the domain of preserved function in amnesia. *Journal of Experimental Psychology: Learning, Memory, and Cognition*, **11**, 385–395.

Hayman, C.A.G. & Tulving, E. (1989a). Contingent dissociation between recognition and fragment completion: The method of triangulation. *Journal of Experimental Psychology: Learning, Memory, and Cognition*, **15**, 222–240.

Hayman, C.A.G. & Tulving, E. (1989b). Is priming in fragment completion based on a 'traceless' memory system? *Journal of Experimental Psychology: Learning, Memory, and Cognition*, **15**, 941–946.

Jacoby, L.L. (1984). Incidental versus intentional retrieval: Remembering and awareness as separate issues. In L.R. Squire and N. Butters (eds), *Neuropsychology of Memory*, New York: Guilford Press.

Jacoby, L.L. & Hayman, C.A.G. (1987). Specific visual transfer in word identification. *Journal of Experimental Psychology: Learning, Memory, and Cognition*, **13**, 456–463.

Jacoby, L.L. & Whitehouse, K. (1989). An illusion of memory: False recognition influenced by unconscious perception. *Journal of Experimental Psychology: General*, **118**, 126–135.

Jacoby, L.L. & Witherspoon, D. (1982). Remembering without awareness. *Canadian Journal of Psychology*, **36**, 300–324.

James, W. (1890). *The Principles of Psychology*. New York: Dover.

Johnson, M.K., Kim, J.K. & Risse, G. (1985). Do alcoholic Korsakoff's syndrome patients acquire affective reactions? *Journal of Experimental Psychology: Learning, Memory, and Cognition*, **11**, 27–36.

Kihlstrom, J.F. & Schacter, D.L. (1990). Anaesthesia, amnesia, and the cognitive unconscious. In B. Bonke, W. Fitch and K. Millar (eds), *Memory and Awareness in Anaesthesia*. Amsterdam: Swets & Zeitlinger.

Kihlstrom, J.F., Schacter, D.L., Cork, R.C., Hurt, C.A. & Behr, S.E. (1990). Implicit and explicit memory following surgical anesthesia. *Psychological Science*, **1**, 303–306.

Korsakoff, S.S. (1889). Etude medico-psychologique sur une forme des maladies de la memoire. *Revue Philosophique*, **5**, 501–530.

Mayes, A.R., Meudell, P.R. & Pickering, A. (1985). Is organic amnesia caused by a selective deficit in remembering contextual information? *Cortex*, **21**, 167–202.

McAndrews, M.P., Glisky, E.L. & Schacter, D.L. (1987). When priming persists: Long-lasting implicit memory for a single episode in amnesic patients. *Neuropsychologia*, **25**, 497–506.

Milner, B., Corkin, S. & Teuber, H.L. (1968). Further analysis of the hippocampal amnesic syndrome: 14 year follow-up study of HM. *Neuropsychologia*, **6**, 215–234.

Mishkin, M., Malamut, B. & Bachevalier, J. (1984). Memories and habits: Two neural systems. In G. Lynch, J.L. McGaugh and N.M. Weinberger (eds), *Neurobiology of Learning and Memory*. New York: Guilford Press.

Moscovitch, M. (1982). Multiple dissociations of function in amnesia. In L.S. Cermak (ed.), *Human Memory and Amnesia*. Hillsdale, NJ: Erlbaum.

Moscovitch, M., Winocur, G. & McLachlan, D. (1986). Memory as assessed by recognition and reading time in normal and memory-impaired people with Alzheimer's disease and other neurological disorders. *Journal of Experimental Psychology: General*, **115**, 331–347.

Richardson-Klavehn, A. & Bjork, R.A. (1988). Measures of memory. *Annual Review of Psychology*, **39**, 475–543.

Riddoch, M.J. & Humphreys, G.W. (1987). Visual object processing in optic aphasia: A case of semantic access agnosia. *Cognitive Neuropsychology*, **4**, 131–186.

Roediger, H.L. III (1990). Implicit memory: A commentary. *Psychonomic Society*, **28**, 373–380.

Roediger, H.L. III & Blaxton, T.A. (1987). Retrieval modes produce dissociations in memory for surface information. In D.S. Gorfein and R.R. Hoffman (eds), *Memory and Cognitive Processes: The Ebbinghaus Centennial Conference*. Hillsdale, NJ: Erlbaum.

Schacter, D.L. (1985). Priming of old and new knowledge in amnesic patients and normal subjects. In D.S. Olton, E. Gamzu and S. Corkin (eds), *Memory Dysfunctions. Annals of the New York Academy of Sciences*, **444**, 41–53.

Schacter, D.L. (1987). Implicit memory: History and current status. *Journal of Experimental Psychology: Learning, Memory, and Cognition*, **13**, 501–518.

Schacter, D.L. (1989). On the relation between memory and consciousness: Dissociable interactions and conscious experience. In H.L. Roediger and F.I.M. Craik (eds), *Varieties of Memory and Consciousness: Essays in Honor of Endel Tulving*. Hillsdale, NJ: Erlbaum.

Schacter, D.L. (1990a). Perceptual representation systems and implicit memory: Toward a resolution of the multiple memory systems debate. In A. Diamond (ed.), *Development and Neural Bases of Higher Cognitive Function. Annals of the New York Academy of Sciences*, **608**, 543–571.

Schacter, D.L. (1990b). Toward a cognitive neuropsychology of awareness: Implicit knowledge and anosognosia. *Journal of Clinical and Experimental Neuropsychology*, **12**, 155–178.

Schacter, D.L. & Graf, P. (1986a). Effects of elaborative processing on implicit and explicit memory for new associations. *Journal of Clinical and Experimental Neuropsychology*, **12**, 432–444.

Schacter, D.L. & Graf, P. (1986b). Preserved learning in amnesic patients: Perspectives from research on direct priming. *Journal of Clinical and Experimental Neuropsychology*, **8**, 727–743.

Schacter, D.L. & Graf, P. (1989). Modality specificity of implicit memory for new associations. *Journal of Experimental Psychology: Learning, Memory, and Cognition*, **15**, 3–12.

Schacter, D.L., McAndrews, M.P. & Moscovitch, M. (1988). Access to consciousness: Dissociations between implicit and explicit knowledge in neuropsychological syndromes. In L. Weiskrantz (ed.), *Thought Without Language*. Oxford: Oxford University Press.

Schacter, D.L., Bowers, J. & Booker, J. (1989). Intention, awareness, and implicit memory: The retrieval intentionality criterion. In J.C. Dunn and K. Kirsner (eds), *Implicit Memory: Theoretical Issues*. Hillsdale, NJ: Erlbaum.

Schacter, D.L., Cooper, L.A. & Delaney, S. (1990a). Implicit memory for unfamiliar objects depends on access to structural descriptions. *Journal of Experimental Psychology: General*, **119**, 5–24.

Schacter, D.L., Delaney, S.M. & Merikle, E.P. (1990b). Priming of nonverbal information and the nature of implicit memory. In G.H. Bower (ed.), *The Psychology of Learning and Motivation*, Vol. 26. New York: Academic Press.

Schacter, D.L., Cooper, L.A., Delaney, S.M., Peterson, M.A. & Tharan, M. (1991a). Implicit memory for possible and impossible objects: Constraints on the construction of structural descriptions. *Journal of Experimental Psychology: Learning, Memory, and Cognition*, **17**, 3–19.

Schacter, D.L., Cooper, L.A., Tharan, M. & Rubens, A. (1991b). Preserved priming of novel objects in patients with memory disorders. *Journal of Cognitive Neuroscience*, **3**, 118–131.

Shallice, T. & Saffran, E. (1986). Lexical processing in the absence of explicit word identification: Evidence from a letter-by-letter reader. *Cognitive Neuropsychology*, **3**, 429–448.

Shimamura, A.P. (1986). Priming effects in amnesia: Evidence for a dissociable memory function. *Quarterly Journal of Experimental Psychology*, **38A**, 619–644.

Shimamura, A.P. & Squire, L.R. (1984). Paired-associate learning and priming effects in amnesia: A neuropsychological study. *Journal of Experimental Psychology: General*, **113**, 556–570.

Shimamura, A.P. & Squire, L.R. (1989). Impaired priming of new associations in amnesic patients. *Journal of Experimental Psychology: Learning, Memory, and Cognition*, **15**, 721–728.

Smith, M.E. & Oscar-Berman, M. (1990). Activation and the repetition priming of words and pseudowords in normal memory and in amnesia. *Journal of Experimental Psychology: Learning, Memory, and Cognition*, **16**, 1033–1042.

Squire, L.R. (1987). *Memory and Brain*. New York: Oxford University Press.

Squire, L.R. & Cohen, N.J. (1984). Human memory and amnesia. In J. McGaugh, G. Lynch and N. Weinberger (eds), *Proceedings of the Conference on the Neurobiology of Learning and Memory*. New York: Guilford Press.

Tranel, D. & Damasio, A.R. (1985). Knowledge without awareness: An autonomic index of facial recognition by prosopagnosics. *Science*, **228**, 1453–1454.

Tulving, E. (1985). Memory and consciousness. *Canadian Psychology*, **25**, 1–12.

Tulving, E. & Schacter, D.L. (1990). Priming and human memory systems. *Science*, **247**, 301–306.

Tulving, E., Schacter, D.L. & Stark, H.A. (1982). Priming effects in word-fragment completion are independent of recognition memory. *Journal of Experimental Psychology: Learning, Memory, and Cognition*, **8**, 336–342.

Tulving, E., Hayman, C.A.G. & MacDonald, C. (1991). Long-lasting perceptual priming and semantic learning in amnesia: A case experiment. *Journal of Experimental Psychology: Learning, Memory, and Cognition*, **17**, 595–617.

Warrington, E.K. (1982). Neuropsychological studies of object recognition. *Philosophical Transactions of the Royal Society of London*, **B298**, 15–33.

Warrington, E.K. & Weiskrantz, L. (1968). New method of testing long-term retention with special reference to amnesic patients. *Nature*, **217**, 972–974.

Warrington, E.K. & Weiskrantz, L. (1974). The effect of prior learning on subsequent retention in amnesic patients. *Neuropsychologia*, **12**, 419–428.

Weiskrantz, L. (1985). On issues and theories of the human amnesic syndrome. In N.M. Weinberger, J.L. McGaugh and G. Lynch (eds), *Memory Systems of the Brain: Animal and Human Cognitive Processes*. New York: Guilford Press.

Weiskrantz, L. (1986). *Blindsight*, New York: Oxford University Press.

Witherspoon, D. & Moscovitch, M. (1989). Stochastic independence between two implicit memory tasks. *Journal of Experimental Psychology: Learning, Memory, and Cognition*, **15**, 22–30.

CHAPTER 10

Unconscious Influences of Memory: Dissociations and Automaticity

Larry L. Jacoby and Colleen Kelley

10.1. INTRODUCTION

The unconscious has long held fascination for the lay person as well as for psychologists. The lay person has viewed the unconscious as a potential threat because it represents a source of influence on behaviour that is beyond one's control. That threat has been intensified by sensationalistic claims of subliminal advertising and 'mind control'. Experimental psychologists, in contrast, have countered sensationalistic claims and sometimes have ended questioning the very existence of unconscious influences. Research on unconscious processes has been plagued by theoretical and methodological problems. Because of those problems, the unconscious along with its complement, consciousness, was banished by radical behaviourists and has only recently regained acceptance as a topic for research (see Hilgard, 1980 for a review of the history of consciousness). For most people, the term 'unconscious' brings the psychoanalytic tradition to mind. However, the unconscious that has recently gained prominence is cognitive rather than psychoanalytic (for a discussion of the differences see Eagle, 1987, and Kihlstrom, 1987). The cognitive unconscious and its association with attention owes more to James than to Freud.

Why the resurgence in interest in unconscious processes? Two recent developments in theory and experimental procedures made research on unconscious processes seem tractable in ways that it was not previously. Firstly, the distinction between automatic and controlled processing in theories of attention (LaBerge & Samuels, 1974; Posner & Snyder, 1975; Shiffrin & Schneider, 1977) led to a great deal of research

THE NEUROPSYCHOLOGY OF CONSCIOUSNESS
ISBN 0–12–498045–7

into processes that are unconscious by way of being automatic. As a function of extended practice, performance of a task becomes more efficient and seems to no longer require attention. This withdrawal of attention corresponds to James' (1890) description of the automaticity that accompanies the development of habit, and contrasts with the consciously controlled use of reason that would otherwise guide behaviour. Automatic processing is driven by the environment whereas controlled processing is controlled by the person via selective attention. Automatic processing has been defined as not requiring attention, and as occurring with neither intent nor awareness. By its list of putative characteristics, the automatic corresponds to unconscious processes and the controlled corresponds to conscious processes.

Secondly, exciting dissociations between direct and indirect tests of perception and memory reveal effects on indirect tests in the absence of direct report or awareness of those effects. Neurological deficits supply striking examples of perceptual analysis in the absence of conscious seeing and effects of the past in the absence of remembering. For an indirect test, people are not instructed to report on an event, but rather engage in some task that can indirectly reflect the occurrence of that event. For example, completing word fragments or identifying briefly presented words are indirect tests of memory because the probability of a correct response is influenced by earlier reading of the word whether or not people can remember the word.

As noted in other chapters in the present volume, dissociations between performance on indirect versus direct tests are common. In blindsight, patients can make visual discriminative responses without the subjective experience of seeing (Weiskrantz, 1986). In prosopagnosia, patients can make discriminative GSR responses to familiar faces, without the subjective experience of recognizing those faces (for a review see Young & De Haan, 1990, and Chapter 4 this volume). In Korsakoff amnesia, patients can give correct memory responses without the subjective experience of remembering (e.g. Warrington & Weiskrantz, 1974). Normal subjects also show dissociations between their performance on indirect versus direct tests of memory (for reviews, see Richardson-Klavehn & Bjork, 1988, and Hintzman, 1990). In unconscious perception (Marcel, 1983a), subjects show priming effects of briefly presented pattern-masked words in a lexical decision task, although they were unable to report that a word had been flashed when given a direct test of perception.

A direct test involves intention to report a particular event and awareness of having been influenced by that event, whereas an indirect test may not. Because of these differences, performance on an indirect test appears to be more under control of the stimulus environment (as structured by the indirect test) whereas performance on a direct test appears to be more under the control of the subject. This difference in control is partially captured by the use of the distinction between data-driven versus conceptually driven processing to account for dissociations between performance on indirect and direct tests of memory. Performance on indirect tests such as tests of perceptual identification or fragment completion seems to rely on prior data-driven processing of the perceptual characteristics of tested items, whereas performance on direct tests of memory appears to rely on prior conceptually driven processing of tested items (e.g. Jacoby, 1983; Roediger & Blaxton, 1987; Roediger, 1990).

It should be noted that we have used the distinction between direct versus indirect tests (e.g. Marcel, 1983a; Johnson & Hasher, 1987), rather than the implicit versus explicit distinction that is used by others contributing chapters to this volume. We prefer the indirect/direct distinction because the terms implicit and explicit have been used to refer both to the difference in instructions for the types of test and to the processes underlying performance on the two types of test (e.g. Richardson-Klavehn & Bjork, 1988). Distinguishing between tasks and underlying processes is important to us because we describe the processing differences between tasks in terms of the contrast between automatic and intentional processing. We argue that the difference in underlying processing is more fundamental than is the difference between the instructions given for the two types of test.

The distinction between automatic versus consciously controlled processing and that between direct versus indirect tests is more similar than is generally acknowledged (but see Klatzky, 1984). In the case of memory, it seems quite natural to say that performance on an indirect test reflects automatic processing whereby the indirect test automatically recruits and uses information from a prior episode without the subject's intention, without any extra expenditure of attention, and without any awareness of doing so. In this vein, at least some indirect tests of memory are unaffected by divided attention manipulations, whereas direct tests of memory show decrements when attention is divided (Jacoby *et al.*, 1989a). Neurological insult, ageing (Howard 1988) and depression (Hertel & Hardin, 1990) sometimes leave performance on indirect tests intact while disrupting performance on direct tests. Those same factors do not influence automatic processing but do influence consciously controlled processing (e.g. Hasher & Zacks, 1979; Weingartner, 1984, but see Hirst, 1982, for an opposite argument). There is also a parallel in level of control over responses: automatic processes are structured by the stimulus environment, as is performance on indirect tests, whereas controlled processes are structured by the subject, as is performance on direct tests.

Our goal in this chapter is to provide an overview of our research on unconscious influences of memory. We describe several experiments, and concentrate on the procedures used in those experiments as well as the results that they produced. The subjects in most of the experiments were undergraduates. Unlike others contributing chapters to this book, we have done very little work to examine the nature of the memory deficit produced by neurological insult. However, we think the procedures that we have developed to examine the memory performance of normal subjects will also prove useful for specifying the nature of the memory deficit suffered by various patient populations (see Mayes, Chapter 11, this volume). We argue that a major obstacle for advances in theory is that traditional testing procedures have not been sufficiently analytic to separate different functions of memory.

We begin by discussing the importance of subjective experience and by suggesting that the subjective experience of remembering is not identical to use of a corresponding memory trace. Most memory theorists have subscribed to a naïve realist view of the relation between memory representations and memory experiences. It is common to assume that our stock of theoretical constructs—memory traces, trace strength, access to traces—is identical to memory experience, albeit on different levels of analysis. We would like to call that assumption into question, and more precisely specify the basis for the subjective experience of remembering.

Memory for prior experience automatically influences the processing and interpretation of later events. One ubiquitous effect of past experience is to make processing more efficient, rapid, or fluent. Such fluent processing is then interpreted to give rise to a particular subjective experience. We present evidence to show that subjective experience is constructed and reflects an unconscious inference or attribution process. Next, we argue that consciously controlled processing does sometimes direct behaviour, and show that advantages can be gained by arranging a situation such that consciously controlled and automatic influences of memory act in opposition to one another. An important function of conscious control is to oppose unconscious influences of memory. Also, the opposition of unconscious and conscious influences of memory can be used as a methodological tool to provide a clear separation of the two in performance. More extensive discussions of the topics considered in those first two sections appear elsewhere (e.g. Jacoby & Kelley, 1987, 1990; Jacoby et al., 1989b; Kelley & Jacoby, 1990).

After discussing the advantages of opposition, we describe a procedure to separate the contributions to recognition memory performance of consciously controlled and automatic influences of memory (Jacoby, 1991). That *process dissociation procedure* yields an estimate of the probability of an item being called old because its prior presentation was recollected (a consciously controlled influence of memory) along with an estimate of the probability of the item being called old because of its familiarity (an automatic influence of memory). We discuss advantages of separating the contributions of automatic and consciously controlled processing within a task as compared to focusing on dissociations between tasks and identifying tasks with different types of processing. We argue that a problem for interpreting dissociations between tasks is that tasks are almost never process-pure. That is, people's performance on tasks that supposedly measure one process or system may actually be any mixture of processes. Finally, we discuss parallels between accounts of dissociations and theories of automaticity. We end by arguing that implicit memory should not be treated as a distinct area of research but, rather, the manipulations of direct versus indirect tests should be treated as one factor among many that influences the automaticity of processing.

10.2. THE CONSTRUCTION OF SUBJECTIVE EXPERIENCE

Dissociations between performance on indirect versus direct tests highlight the importance of subjective experience. What is most striking is the general absence of the subjective experience of remembering or perceiving on indirect tests. Without subjective experience, we are uncertain about the basis for our actions. Without the subjective experience of remembering, we may be unaware of how the past has influenced our current experience and so may misjudge current situations. It is important to understand what gives rise to subjective experience.

What could produce dissociations between indirect versus direct tests of memory? One approach explains dissociations in terms of separate memory systems with separate neuroanatomical substrates (e.g. Cohen & Squire, 1980; Tulving & Schacter, 1990): one system is capable of representing contextual and temporal aspects of an episode and is responsible for conscious recollection, whereas the other system does not preserve such memory for prior episodes and supports unconscious influences of the past. By that approach, the subjective experience of remembering reflects properties of the memory trace, so that having and using an episodic memory trace is necessary and sufficient to produce the subjective experience of remembering. For example, an amnesic's inability to have the subjective experience of remembering would be explained as resulting from the lack of ability to represent particular aspects of episodes, such as time and place.

However, the mapping between representation and subjective experience is far from perfect (e.g. Jacoby *et al.*, 1989b; Kelley & Jacoby, 1990). Even people with a normally functioning memory can use memory representations without experiencing remembering. Cryptomnesia or unconscious plagiarism is one example of the use of a memory representation without a corresponding subjective experience of remembering (e.g. Reed, 1974; Brown & Murphy, 1989). The contrasting case of 'remembering' without a corresponding memory representation also occurs. Patients who have suffered frontal lobe damage confabulate events when reporting on their past and seem to experience those confabulations as true memories (Baddeley & Wilson, 1986; Stuss & Benson, 1986; Moscovitch, 1989). Such confabulations are sometimes also produced by people with normal memory. Although representations obviously play a role in remembering, the presence of a memory representation is neither a necessary nor a sufficient condition for the subjective experience of remembering.

If having and accessing a memory representation does not necessarily produce the experience of remembering, what is the basis for the subjective experience of remembering? Along with others, we treat subjective experience as a construction based on inferences. In the domain of perception, Helmholtz (1867 republished in 1968) proposed that an unconscious inference process underlies subjective experience. He noted that memory can influence subjective experience of the physical present. Marcel (1983b) argued that conscious experience is constructed by a higher order representation that transforms the information from lower order sensory and cognitive processing. A conscious percept is said to result from the constructive act of fitting a perceptual hypothesis to the lower level data 'to make sense of as much data as possible at the highest and most functionally useful level possible (p. 248)'. By Marcel's account, subjective experience is better seen as an attribution or interpretation about cognitive and sensory processing than as a direct mirror of it. Gazzaniga (1988) also proposed that consciousness is not identical with processing but rather represents the work of an interpreter, and further suggested that the interpreter is primarily a left brain function. Schachter and Singer (1962) suggested that the subjective experience of emotion reflects an inference or attribution process.

We show that an inference process underlies subjective experience by showing errors of inference. First, we describe cases of unconscious influences of memory being misattributed to some source other than the past, and argue that measures of subjective experience can serve as valuable indirect tests of cognitive processes. Next, we describe illusions of memory, and discuss the importance of those illusions for uncovering the bases for the subjective experience of remembering.

10.3. MISATTRIBUTIONS OF MEMORY

As a function of prior experience, performance of a task becomes more fluent. Effects of prior experience can occur at any level of activity—reading a word more fluently, solving a problem more easily, or even generating a train of ideas more readily. Subjects can misattribute fluent processing that comes from prior experience to sources other than the past. As a commonplace example, when one is first learning a foreign language, the speech rate of native speakers of that language seems too rapid to comprehend. As one gains knowledge of the language, the speech rate of the native speaker seems to slow. That is, effects of the past (acquired knowledge of the language) are experienced as a change in the current physical stimulus (speech rate). Extensive practice is not always necessary to produce effects of this sort. A single prior presentation is sufficient to lengthen the apparent duration of a word that is flashed (Witherspoon & Allan, 1985) or lower background noise accompanying the presentation of a sentence (Jacoby *et al.*, 1988). Fluent processing may also be misattributed to a statement's being true, an argument's seeming to flow, or a problem's being easy (Jacoby & Kelley, 1987). The effect of 'mere exposure' in studies of aesthetic judgements may also be a case of the misattribution of fluent processing that is due to prior experience (Kunst-Wilson & Zajonc, 1980; Seamon *et al.*, 1983; Mandler *et al.*, 1987). People attribute effects on performance to whatever source is most obvious or plausible, which often depends on the judgements that they are asked to make.

The inference process is often an unconscious one. To show that this is the case, let us further consider the effects of prior experience on noise judgements. In one experiment, Jacoby *et al.* (1988) presented previously heard and new sentences against a background of white noise of varying loudness. Subjects judged the background noise as less loud when the sentences were old rather than new. The advantage in ease of perception of old sentences was misattributed to a lower level of background noise. That is, people were unable to separate out the contribution of memory to perception when judging noise level and so had the subjective experience of a change in noise level. Later experiments by a McMaster student, Jane Collins, have shown that this effect of prior experience on noise judgements is automatic in that people are unable to avoid the effect. Even when subjects were informed about the effect and told to avoid it, they continued to judge the background noise accompanying old sentences as less loud than that accompanying new sentences. She also found that this effect depends on the synchronous onset of the sentence and the background noise. If onset of the sentence precedes that of the background noise by a sufficient interval, the noise and sentence are perceived as separate 'streams', coming from separate sources, and effects of prior experience with sentences on noise judgements are no longer obtained. Sandra Huard, another McMaster student, has shown that the effects of hearing a sentence on later noise judgements persist over 24 h. These results indicate that effects of past experience on noise judgements reflect unconscious influences on subjective experience, rather than conscious processing carried out to satisfy demand characteristics of the task.

The subjective experience of amnesics is also affected by the past. Jacoby *et al.* (1989a) found that in normal subjects, prior presentation of names leads to an increase in the names' familiarity, and that familiarity can be misinterpreted as fame. Subjects read a list of names that included famous and nonfamous names; later, those old names were mixed with new names and presented to subjects in a fame judgement test. The familiarity of previously presented names was misattributed by subjects during the fame judgement test, so that both studied famous and studied nonfamous names were more likely to be judged famous than were new names. We refer to this effect of earlier reading names as a 'false fame' effect. The fame judgement task is an indirect test of memory, because subjects are not asked to judge whether a name had been read earlier, but having read a name earlier can influence later judgement of its fame. Squire and McKee (1991) found that the false fame effect is as large for amnesics as for normal subjects although, of course, amnesics are severely impaired in their ability to recognize names as previously presented when given a direct test of memory. Similarly, Johnson *et al.* (1985) showed that Korsakoff's syndrome patients acquire affective reactions although they are unable to report on the past experiences that produced those reactions.

Measures of subjective experience are useful as indirect tests of other processes in addition to memory. We have done preliminary research using noise judgements as an indirect test of categorization and as an indirect test of attitudes. For attitudes, the goal is to show that one's first reaction or 'gut feeling' about an issue is sometimes very different from the attitude that is expressed in response to a direct question. That is, we predict dissociations between performance on indirect versus direct tests of categorization and of attitudes, similar to those found for memory. In that vein, Greenwald (1989) used the fame judgement task as an indirect test of sexism. He found that for some people, only names of males gain false fame from their prior presentation, and argues that the lack of false fame for female names reveals a bias against females being famous.

For present purposes, the important point is that memory can automatically influence the interpretation of later events. Those automatic influences of memory can be misattributed to sources other than the past and thereby produce a misleading subjective experience. Effects of memory on subjective experience are automatic in that they require neither intent to use memory nor awareness of doing so. Use of a memory representation is not always accompanied by the subjective experience of remembering.

10.4. ILLUSIONS OF MEMORY

We argue that the subjective experience of remembering also relies on an inference or attribution. Effects of the past on current performance, such as increased efficiency or ease of processing may be correctly attributed to the past and so give rise to a feeling of familiarity. Fluent performance is generally a reliable cue to the past because past experience so often does facilitate later performance, and these transfer effects are remarkably specific (Jacoby *et al.*, 1989b). For example, previously reading a word facilitates its later perceptual identification and that fluent perceptual processing can be attributed to the past to produce a feeling of familiarity (e.g. Jacoby & Dallas, 1981). If ease of perceptual processing is a cue that serves as the basis for the experience of remembering, then experimental manipulations of perceptual processing should influence the subjective experience of remembering. That is, it should be possible to produce illusions of memory by manipulating perceptual processing by means other than past experience. Doing so would show that the subjective experience of remembering can occur without a corresponding memory representation. This is a particularly important line of argument, because such evidence argues against the notion that properties of a memory trace, such as strength, directly mediate the feeling of remembering.

Jacoby and Whitehouse (1989) manipulated the perceptual processing of words on a recognition memory test, independent of their actual status as old and new words, to produce a feeling of familiarity. Unconscious perception of a word flashed immediately prior to its presentation as a new word on a test of recognition memory produced an increase in the probability of false recognition. The flashed word produced more fluent perceptual processing of the new test word, which was interpreted as familiarity. We are confident that this effect is not due to conscious perception of the flashed words: when conditions were changed so that people could consciously see the flashed word, effects were *opposite* to those produced by unconscious perception. When people could see the flashed words, they interpreted the increased familiarity of the recognition test item that followed as due to its immediate prior presentation. That is, conscious versus unconscious perception of the flashed word produced different attributions of the subsequent fluent processing of the test word, as shown by opposite effects on recognition judgements. Placing the effects of unconscious versus conscious perception in opposition was a key feature of the design that allows us to be certain that the effects were due to unconscious perception, rather than conscious perception that was undetected by the experimenters. In a later section of this chapter, we discuss the advantages of placing unconscious and conscious influences in opposition.

More direct manipulations of the ease of perceptual processing produced by varying the perceptual characteristics of an item can also produce an illusion of memory. Whittlesea *et al.* (1990) rapidly presented brief lists of words to subjects, and followed each list with a recognition memory test word. Ease of perceptual processing was manipulated by varying the visual clarity of the test word within a narrow range that was not noticed by subjects (as assessed by reports at the end of the session). This produced an illusion of memory because subjects misinterpreted the variations in visual clarity as due to having read the word on the list. That is, words whose visual presentation was clearer were more likely to be judged old, although the manipulation of clarity was orthogonal to that of prior presentation. This illusion of memory was destroyed when subjects were informed that visual clarity was manipulated, and could correctly attribute variation in perception to variation in the physical stimulus.

The use of fluent processing as a cue that one is remembering is not restricted to perceptual processing. Lindsay and Kelley (1991) showed that the ease of producing an item during a recall attempt serves as a basis for experiencing that item as remembering. Lindsay and Kelley provided fragments of to-be-recalled words as cues. Some of the fragments were easy to complete and others were relatively difficult to complete. After generating an item for recall, subjects described their subjective experience as 'Clear Memory', 'Feels Familiar', or 'No Memory'. Unbeknown to subjects, a small proportion of the cues were fragments that could only be completed with a new word. Even for those new items, there were significantly more reports of 'Feels Familiar' and 'Clear Memory' for words produced given the easy cues than for words produced given the difficult cues. Thus ease of generating contributed to the subject's experience of remembering and produced an illusion of remembering. In a related vein, Ross (1989) found that memories can reflect people's theories as much as their past experience. We think that people's theories of what must have happened lead them to think readily of those outcomes when they attempt recall, and those constructions from theory are experienced as remembered even when they do not accord with the true past.

In summary, the subjective experience of remembering is not a property of a memory trace but instead relies on an inference. Normal subjects as well as amnesics sometimes use a memory representation without having the subjective experience of remembering. When the subjective experience of remembering is present, it is sometimes an illusion that occurs without a corresponding memory representation. The feeling of familiarity in recognition may be a particular interpretation of ease of processing—that it results from past experience. In a later section, we argue that familiarity is a relatively automatic basis for recognition memory judgements, in contrast to recollection, which is a consciously controlled basis for recognition. Amnesics may experience a feeling of familiarity, as suggested by Squire and McKee's (1991) finding that amnesics exhibit the false fame effect, but they may be unable to engage in the conscious recollection that is necessary to specify correctly the source of familiarity.

10.5. THE ADVANTAGES OF OPPOSITION FOR REVEALING UNCONSCIOUS INFLUENCES

We have described unconscious influences of memory on subjective experience and have shown that subjective experience is sometimes in error. Memory can automatically influence the interpretation of later events and those effects on interpretation can be misattributed to sources other than the past. Subjective experience is an important dimension because people usually act on the basis of their subjective experience. For example, one would behave differently if one concluded that difficulties in comprehension were because of the loudness of a background noise rather than because of a lack of relevant prior experience. Can people escape unconscious influences of memory?

Consciously controlled processing is often described as a prerequisite for intentional action (e.g. Kuhl, 1986; Shallice, 1988). However, consciousness also serves the equally important function of inhibiting action by opposing influences that would otherwise prevail. For example, we can use conscious recollection to avoid repeating our stories to the same audience, or to avoid plagiarism. In these cases, recognition in the form of conscious recollection allows one to avoid undesirable effects of the past. More generally, effects of misleading subjective experience can be avoided by abandoning subjective experience as a basis for responding and shifting to more analytic, consciously controlled processing (Jacoby & Kelley, 1987). Controlled processing in the form of monitoring one's performance can allow one to oppose undesirable unconscious influences of the past. The opposition of conscious and unconscious influences of memory can also be used as a methodological tool to separate clearly the two in performance.

Supposed demonstrations of unconscious perception and those of unconscious memory have been called into question on the grounds that the experimenter has mistakenly measured conscious rather than unconscious performance. Holender (1986) argued that because of problems in establishing a threshold, there is so far no convincing evidence of unconscious perception: reputed unconscious perception effects may actually be due to conscious perception that has gone undetected by the experimenter. Similarly, in studies of memory, performance on indirect tests of memory may be contaminated by conscious recollection (Richardson-Klavehn & Bjork, 1988). For example, the enhanced completion of word fragments for studied words relative to new may sometimes rely on intentional conscious retrieval of studied words. These problems for interpretation arise when unconscious and conscious influences would exert effects that are in the same direction. The problems can be avoided by arranging the situation such that unconscious and conscious influences produce opposite effects. Such a strategy of looking for opposite effects is a variant of methods that pit unintended processes against one's conscious intentions, as in the Stroop test, and is also a variant of the strategy of searching for qualitative differences in performance produced by conscious versus unconscious influences (e.g. Dixon, 1981; Jacoby & Dallas, 1981; Cheesman & Merikle, 1986).

To set conscious and unconscious influences of memory in opposition, we have used the 'false fame' effect described earlier (Jacoby *et al.*, 1989a, experiments 2 and 3). In the first phase of those experiments, people read a list of all nonfamous names, such as 'Sebastian Weisdorf'. In the second phase, they judged the fame of those old names mixed with new famous and new nonfamous names. We correctly informed subjects that all of the names they had read in the first list were nonfamous, so if they recognized a name on the fame test as from the first list, they could be certain that the name was nonfamous. Thus, conscious recollection of a name from the list opposed unconscious influences of the past on fame judgements. Given this arrangement, any increase in the probability of mistakenly calling an old, as compared with new, nonfamous name 'famous' must result from an unconscious influence of memory for its prior presentation. Conscious recollection of the prior presentation of a name would produce an opposite effect by allowing subjects to reject the name as nonfamous.

The attention to an event that is necessary to produce later awareness of memory for the event may differ from the attention that is necessary to produce unconscious influences (see Dixon, 1981 for a review). We placed conscious and unconscious memory in opposition to investigate differential effects of attention (Jacoby *et al.*, 1989a). Subjects in the false fame paradigm read a list of nonfamous names in the first phase under conditions of either full or divided attention. Dividing attention between reading the list of names and monitoring an auditory list of digits resulted in old nonfamous names later being more likely to be mistakenly called famous than new nonfamous names. The opposite occurred when full attention was given to reading the list of nonfamous names: subjects presumably could consciously recognize old names from the list, and so know that they were nonfamous. Further analyses of these studies showed that dividing attention reduced a person's ability to recognize a name as having been read earlier, but had no effect on gains in familiarity produced by that earlier reading.

Others (Grand & Segal, 1966; Koriat & Feuerstein, 1976; Eich, 1984) have shown similar dissociations between the effects of dividing attention on performance of indirect versus direct tests of memory. The opposition strategy that we used more clearly separates unconscious from conscious influences. In the experiments done by others, the situation was such that conscious and unconscious influences would produce effects in the same direction. Consequently, dissociations could arise even if the indirect and direct tests that were used did not measure different functions of memory but differed only in sensitivity. This possibility is ruled out by the opposition strategy. Our finding of opposite effects of prior presentation under conditions of full versus divided attention clearly reveals a qualitative difference between unconscious and conscious influences of memory.

Some types of neurological insult as well as normal ageing might produce a deficit in controlled processing while leaving unconscious influences of memory intact. Dywan and Jacoby (1990) found that aged subjects showed a larger false fame effect than did younger subjects. Aged subjects under conditions of full attention behaved similarly to younger subjects under conditions of divided attention. Hasher and Zacks (1988) suggested that because of a deficit in attention, older adults are less able to suppress their processing of and responding to stimuli that are to be rejected. This deficit produced by normal ageing may be due to a decline in frontal lobe functioning. Patients suffering frontal lobe damage are less able to monitor their memory performance than are normal people (e.g. Moscovitch, 1989). In that vein, Dywan (personal communication) has found that frontal lobe patients are severely impaired in their ability to use conscious recollection to avoid the false fame effect. As described earlier, Squire and McKee (1991) have found that amnesics show a false fame effect. In their experiment, names read in the first phase included both famous and nonfamous names, so conscious recollection was not placed in opposition to effects on familiarity. However, one would expect that amnesics would be unable to use conscious recollection to avoid the false fame effect.

Amnesics show near normal memory for the prior presentation of a word as measured by the indirect memory test of word fragment completion (e.g. Warrington & Weiskrantz, 1974). As argued earlier, a difficulty for interpreting effects of the past on fragment completion performance is that in addition to automatic influences of memory, performance may sometimes reflect subjects' intentional retrieval of the earlier studied words. To avoid this difficulty, the opposition strategy can be applied to a word fragment completion test by instructing subjects that they must complete word fragments with words that were not presented earlier. Under those instructions, any advantage of old over new words in fragment completion performance must be due to an unconscious influence of memory. Cermak (personal communication) has used such instructions and found that amnesics were very likely to complete fragments with old words although they were instructed to avoid doing so. Normals used conscious recollection to avoid using words from the studied list. The advantage of placing conscious recollection and unconscious influences of the past in opposition is that one's measure of unconscious effects is not contaminated by conscious effects.

The problem of separating bases for judgements is a more general one than simply separating conscious from unconscious influences. In particular, some memory deficits might result in people being unable consciously to recollect memory for a prior experience, but leave them able to use familiarity as a basis for memory judgements (e.g. Mandler, 1980; Johnson, 1988). To determine whether this is indeed the case, one needs some way of separating recognition memory judgements based on familiarity from those based on conscious recollection. In the next section, we describe a procedure devised to separate those two bases for recognition memory judgements.

10.6. SEPARATING AUTOMATIC FROM CONSCIOUSLY CONTROLLED BASES FOR JUDGEMENTS: THE PROCESS DISSOCIATION PROCEDURE

Performance on indirect tests of memory may rely more heavily on automatic forms of processing than does performance on direct tests of memory. However, there is not a one-to-one mapping between the direct versus indirect test distinction and the automatic versus consciously controlled processing distinction. Automatic forms of processing play a role in performance on direct as well as indirect tests. With regard to performance on direct memory tests, the distinction between automatic and controlled processing has been applied to both differences in encoding and differences in retrieval. Hasher and Zacks (1979) suggested that whereas the encoding of some attributes of an event is automatic, the encoding of other attributes requires effort and is consciously controlled. In regard to retrieval, dual-process theories (e.g. Atkinson & Juola, 1974; Mandler, 1980; Jacoby & Dallas, 1981) hold that both conscious recollection and familiarity serve as bases for recognition memory decisions. Conscious recollection may depend on more controlled processing at retrieval, whereas familiarity may be relatively automatic in that it is generally faster, less effortful, and less reliant on intention.

We will next describe an experiment done to gain evidence of automatic versus consciously controlled bases for recognition memory judgements by showing differential effects of dividing attention during the prior presentation of items. The results from that experiment further illustrate the advantages of placing automatic and controlled processes in opposition as compared with a situation in which the two types of processing produce effects in the same direction. Then we will show that comparisons of effects in the opposition case with those in the same-direction case can provide separate estimates of the contributions of recollection and of familiarity to recognition memory judgements. Therefore, it is possible to investigate the effects of variables such as divided attention and meaningfulness of encoding on familiarity versus recollection. The *process dissociation* procedure described there serves as an alternative to other procedures that have been used to separate automatic from consciously controlled processes. Furthermore, the process dissociation procedure can be used to separate different bases for judgements in categorization and perceptual tasks, as well as memory tasks.

We will end this section by discussing the relation between types of processing and tasks. Many explanations of dissociations between performance on indirect versus direct tests identify the types of test with different types of processing. For example, Graf and Schacter (1989, experiment 1) showed that use of a story to organize words presented at study enhanced performance on a direct test but not on an indirect test of memory. They concluded that relating items with a story influences grouping and that grouping facilitates performance on direct tests, but that performance on indirect tests relies on unitization rather than grouping. However, one could probably produce a dissociation between two direct tests of the same form as the dissociation Graf and Schacter found between an indirect and a direct test of memory. For example, if subjects were required to respond prior to a short deadline on a direct test of memory, they would not have time to engage in the consciously controlled processing that is probably necessary to remember a story to aid retrieval of studied items. Consequently, performance on a direct test that required rapid responding would rely heavily on automatic processing (as does performance on an indirect test), and so should dissociate from performance on a direct test that allowed ample time for responding. That is, the dissociation might better be thought of as being between automatic versus consciously controlled bases for responding rather than between indirect versus direct tests of memory. Rather than searching for task dissociations and identifying tasks with types of processing, it would be better to separate the contribution of different types of processing to performance of a single task.

10.7. DIFFERENTIAL EFFECTS OF DIVIDING ATTENTION DURING STUDY

In our fame judgement experiments (Jacoby *et al.*, 1989a) described in the last section, we found that divided as compared to full attention to reading the names in the first phase reduced subjects' ability to recollect reading a name later, but did not influence the gain in the name's familiarity that was produced by its being read. That study placed the effects of recollection and familiarity on fame judgements in opposition, so that we could separately study the two. We have used a similar opposition procedure to separate recollection and familiarity as bases for recognition memory judgements. We begin by describing the effects of divided attention when the situation was such that recollection and familiarity would produce effects in the same direction, and then contrast the conclusions that can be drawn from those results with conclusions that can be drawn when effects of the two types act in opposition.

We were particularly interested in how variation in the processing of meaning has its effect on recognition memory performance (cf. Craik & Lockhart, 1972). We predicted that processing meaning aids recollection rather than familiarity. Processing was varied by having subjects judge whether word pairs were related or not, for both related and unrelated pairs. The meaningful processing that results from judging the relatedness of a pair could benefit later recognition memory for a word from that pair by increasing the probability of recollection rather than familiarity. Subjects might later be better able to recollect reading a word earlier that had been in a related pair of words as compared with in an unrelated pair of words (cf. Gardiner, 1988).

Jacoby (in preparation) examined the effects of dividing attention during study on the later use of recollection and familiarity as bases for recognition memory judgements. An outline of the procedure appears in Table 10.1. In Phase 1 of that experiment, subjects were asked to judge whether pairs of words presented visually were related or unrelated. Attention to that task was either full or divided by requiring subjects to monitor simultaneously a string of digits presented auditorially. In Phase 2 of the experiment, subjects in both the full- and divided-attention conditions *heard* a list of words that they were told to study for a later test (both groups studied this list with full attention). In Phase 3, subjects were given a visually-presented, forced-choice recognition memory test. Each pair of recognition test words consisted of a new word paired with an old word from either the Phase 1 word pairs or from the list heard in Phase 2. Fifty test pairs contained a word that was earlier heard, 15 test pairs contained a word from a related pair presented in Phase 1, and 15 test pairs contained a word from an unrelated pair presented in Phase 1.

Subjects in a condition referred to as the inclusion condition (we will

TABLE 10.1
Procedure for separating recollection and familiarity as bases for recognition memory

		PHASE 1	
40 pairs	20 Related		Visually presented
	20 Unrelated		for judgement
			task
Full vs divided attention			

	PHASE 2	
60 single words		Aurally presented
		to be remembered

	PHASE 3	
80 pairs	50 Phase 2 (Heard)-New	Visually presented
	15 Phase 1 (Related)-New	for recognition
	15 Phase 1 (Unrelated)-New	task

Inclusion vs exclusion force-choice recognition

	Subject to respond	
	Inclusion	Exclusion
Phase 2 (Heard)	Old	Old
Phase 1 (Related)	Old	New
Phase 1 (Unrelated)	Old	New

elaborate on this term later) were instructed to pick the word from each pair that had earlier been presented in *either* Phase 1 or Phase 2. In the inclusion test condition, as in most recognition memory tests, subjects could use either recollection or familiarity as a basis for recognition memory judgements, and use of the two bases would produce responses in the same direction. In line with results reported earlier for the fame judgement experiments, divided as compared to full attention to judging whether words in a pair were related was expected to reduce later recollection but to leave gains in familiarity intact. Furthermore, because of their more meaningful processing, words presented in related pairs were predicted to hold an advantage in recollection over words presented in unrelated pairs.

Results for the inclusion test conditions are shown in the top two rows of Table 10.2. Our main interest was in recognition memory performance for words presented in related versus unrelated pairs, and it was only for those words that attention was manipulated. The results show that words presented in related pairs were more likely to be recognized as old than were words that were presented in unrelated pairs. For both related and unrelated pairs, divided as compared with full attention to judging relatedness reduced later recognition memory performance. One could argue that the effect of divided attention was to reduce subjects' ability to use recollection later as a basis for recognition memory judgements. However, surprisingly, there was no interaction of relatedness of pairs and attention condition, and therefore the results do not provide support for the suggestion that the advantage for words presented in related pairs was specific to recollection.

Although the above results are consistent with the claim that dividing attention during study affected later recognition by its influence on recollection, the results are not conclusive. This is because recollection and familiarity would produce results in the same direction, so a reduction in either or both could be responsible for the poorer recognition

TABLE 10.2
Probabilities of calling an item 'old'

| | Probability of responding 'Old' | | |
	Related	Unrelated	Heard
Inclusion test			
Full attention	0.83	0.70	0.79
Divided attention	0.75	0.61	0.77
Exclusion test			
Full attention	0.31	0.38	0.70
Divided attention	0.47	0.49	0.70

memory performance following divided attention. What is needed is a means of placing familiarity and recollection in opposition to more clearly separate effects on the two bases for judgements.

To separate familiarity and recollection, subjects in an exclusion test condition were instructed to pick a word as old on the recognition memory test only if the word was one that they had heard in Phase 2. Subjects in this condition were warned that some of the tested words had been presented in Phase 1 but they should not be picked as old. Subjects were told that if they could recollect having earlier encountered a word as a member of either a related or an unrelated pair presented in Phase 1, they could be certain that the word was not one that they had heard earlier, and consequently should not be picked as old. That is, whereas subjects in the inclusion test conditions were to include words presented in related and unrelated pairs as words that were to be called old for the test of recognition memory, subjects in the exclusion test conditions were to exclude those words. These differences in test instructions were the only differences between the inclusion and exclusion test conditions.

In the exclusion test condition, presentation of a word in Phase 1 was expected to increase its familiarity and thereby increase the probability of its being falsely recognized as having been heard earlier. Any such increase would necessarily reflect an automatic influence of memory. This is true because conscious recollection would have an opposite effect. If subjects recollected having earlier encountered the word as a member of either a related or unrelated pair, they could be certain that the word had not been heard, and so they should not pick it as old. In Phase 1, judgements of the relation between words in a pair were made under conditions of full or divided attention. Dividing attention was expected to reduce later recollection and thereby leave effects of familiarity due to presentation in Phase 1 largely unopposed.

The effect of divided attention and the effect of word-pair relatedness on recollection are shown in the results from the exclusion test conditions (see the bottom two rows of Table 10.2). Dividing subjects' attention when they were judging whether words in a pair were related reduced later recollection, and so increased the probability of those words later being falsely recognized as heard. Words presented in related pairs in Phase 1 held some advantage in recollection over words presented in unrelated pairs. The increase in false recognition produced by divided attention was slightly larger for words from related compared to unrelated pairs, as would be expected if words from related pairs held a larger advantage in recollection when attention was full rather than divided.

Looking at results for 'heard' words in Table 10.2, it can be seen that those words were more likely to be correctly recognized in the inclusion test conditions than they were in the exclusion test conditions. One possible reason for that result is that subjects may have sometimes been unable to recollect earlier hearing a word and confused words that were heard with words that were earlier presented in related or unrelated pairs. Confusion of that sort would result in words that were heard being mistakenly rejected in the exclusion test conditions but not in the inclusion test conditions.

Results from the exclusion test conditions are sufficient to allow the conclusion that dividing attention during the presentation of items reduces later recollection. However, those results do not allow one to conclude that dividing attention had no effect on familiarity. To draw that conclusion, one needs some way of separately estimating the effects on recollection and the effects on familiarity. We describe how the results of the inclusion and exclusion conditions can be combined to allow a process dissociation of familiarity and recollection.

10.8. SEPARATELY ESTIMATING AUTOMATIC AND CONSCIOUSLY CONTROLLED INFLUENCES

If responding is under conscious control, people should be able to follow instructions to respond differentially to items of a given class. For example, in the inclusion test conditions in the experiment described above, conscious recollection allowed subjects to select for earlier presented items and increased the probability of correctly calling words old. In the exclusion test conditions, conscious recollection allowed subjects to select against words that were earlier presented in related or unrelated pairs and decreased the probability of those words being falsely recognized as heard earlier. In contrast, automatic influences of memory do not support such selective responding. Familiarity increased the probability of responding old to words earlier presented in related or unrelated pairs, regardless of whether those words were to be called old (inclusion test conditions) or new (exclusion test conditions).

Typically, recognition memory tests tap a mixture of consciously controlled recollection and automatic familiarity. However, given that only recollection can allow subjects to selectively respond to items (select for or select against those items), it should be possible to estimate the separate contributions of recollection and familiarity to recognition memory judgements. To do so, a process dissociation procedure was developed. The rationale underlying the process dissociation procedure is that consciously controlled processing or recollection can be measured as the difference between the likelihood of responding to an item of a given class when people are attempting to select *for* items of that class as compared with when they are attempting to select *against* items of that class.

To illustrate, consider the case in which conscious control of responding is complete so that the probability of recollection is 1.0. In that case, a word read earlier in Phase 1 would always be called old in the inclusion test condition and never be called old in the exclusion test condition. The difference between the probabilities of calling an item of the particular type old between the two conditions would then be 1.0, the probability of recollection. In contrast, consider a case where the probability of recollection is 0 and words are called old solely on the basis of their familiarity. In that case, the probability of calling an item old would not be controlled by instructions. Rather, the probability of calling an item of a particular type old would be the same in the inclusion and the exclusion conditions. More generally, the difference between the probabilities of calling an item old in the inclusion and the exclusion conditions can be used to estimate the probability of recollection.

Following others (e.g. Mandler, 1980), it is assumed that recollection (R) and familiarity (F) serve as two independent bases for calling an item old on a test of recognition memory. In the *inclusion* condition, the probability of saying old to a word earlier presented in a related pair (O_{IR}) can be written as

$$O_{IR} = R_R + F_R - R_R F_R \tag{1}$$

In the *exclusion* condition, an item earlier presented in a related pair would be called old (O_{ER}) only if the item was familiar and its presentation as a member of a related pair was not recollected.

$$O_{ER} = F_R(1 - R_R) = F_R - R_R F_R \tag{2}$$

The probability of recollection can then be estimated as

$$R_R = O_{IR} - O_{ER} \tag{3}$$

Of course, the same equations hold for words that were presented in unrelated pairs as for words presented in related pairs. As can be seen by comparing Equations 1 and 2, when recollection equals 0, the probability of calling an item old is the same in the inclusion and exclusion test conditions, and totally reflects familiarity. By simple algebra, F can be estimated given an estimate of R and the observed probability of calling items old (e.g. O_{IR}).

The process dissociation procedure can be applied to the data in Table 10.2 to estimate separately the effects of dividing attention on recollection and familiarity. The difference between the inclusion and the exclusion conditions in the probability of selecting an item as old can be used to estimate the probability of recollection as a function of attention, separately for words presented in related and unrelated pairs. Those estimated probabilities of recollection can then be used to estimate the probabilities of selecting an item as old on the basis of its familiarity. Estimated probabilities are shown in Table 10.3.

Words presented in related pairs held an advantage both in recollection and in familiarity over words presented in unrelated pairs. The

TABLE 10.3
Estimates of recollection and of familiarity

| | Estimated probabilities | |
	Related	Unrelated
Recollection		
Full attention	0.52	0.32
Divided attention	0.28	0.12
Familiarity		
Full attention	0.646	0.558
Divided attention	0.652	0.557

effect of relatedness on familiarity is surprising and intriguing, and has not been revealed by previous methods of separating the two bases for recognition memory judgements (e.g. Mandler, 1980). For words previously presented in either a related or unrelated word pair, dividing attention during their prior presentation reduced subjects' ability later to use recollection as a basis for recognition memory judgements. In contrast, dividing attention during the earlier presentation of words had no effect on familiarity-based judgements. Results reported by Jacoby *et al.* (1989a) also showed that dividing attention during study had no effect on the use of familiarity as a basis for fame judgements, but did have an effect on recollection. The procedure used in that paper for separating effects of recollection and effects of familiarity on fame judgements was based on a rationale that is similar to that underlying the process dissociation procedure.

Other experiments (Jacoby, 1991) have examined the effects of dividing attention at test. In those experiments, subjects made yes/no recognition memory judgements either under conditions of full or divided attention. Inclusion and exclusion conditions were as described for the above experiment. The process dissociation procedure was used to separate the effects of dividing attention at test on recollection and on familiarity as bases for recognition memory judgements. Results showed that dividing attention at test almost totally eliminated subjects' ability to use recollection, but had no influence on familiarity-based judgements. Again, the effects were similar to those earlier found for fame judgements (Jacoby *et al.*, 1989a).

The results of our experiments have changed the way that we think about familiarity. First, it is clear that familiarity does not depend only on the perceptual characteristics of a tested item, but, rather, also depends on the prior processing of the item (e.g. relatedness of a pair). Although, as described in an earlier section, ease of perceptual processing contributes to the subjective experience of familiarity, the processing of meaning also influences familiarity. This is shown by the finding that words from related pairs were more familiar than were words from unrelated pairs.

Second, the results reinforce our belief that familiarity is not simply a correlate of some characteristic of a memory trace, such as strength. We predict that the estimated values of familiarity of words read in Phase 1 would change if the list of words presented to be remembered in Phase 2 are read rather than heard. That is, familiarity is better described as arising from relationships among items, in the same way that similarity is traditionally described, rather than as an absolute characteristic of memory for an item. We believe familiarity is context dependent in a way that results in its changing across tasks and situations. The view of familiarity that we are developing is in some way similar to the treatment of familiarity in global memory models (e.g. Gillund & Shiffrin, 1984; Hintzman, 1988). In a related vein, the issue of whether dissociations arise from a difference in memory representations or a difference in retrieval processes will be discussed in the final section of this chapter in conjunction with theories of automaticity.

We have gone into a good deal of detail describing the process dissociation procedure because we think it is likely to be useful for better specifying the nature of the memory deficits produced by neurological insult. For example, frontal-lobe patients might suffer a deficit in recollection but show normal use of familiarity. Also, variants of the process dissociation procedure are useful for separating automatic from consciously controlled influences in categorization and in perceptual performance as well as in memory performance. The use of rules for categorization relies on consciously controlled processing, as does recollection, whereas categorization on the basis of similarity to earlier-presented instances relies on more automatic forms of processing, as does the use of familiarity for recognition memory judgements. For perception, a corresponding distinction is that between perception above the subjective threshold and perception below the subjective threshold (e.g. Reingold & Merikle, 1990). Preliminary experiments using the process dissociation procedure to separate unconscious from conscious perception and to separate the use of rules from categorization on the basis of similarity have produced promising results.

10.9. TASKS AND PROCESSES

The strategy of attempting to separate different functions of memory by estimating their effects within a task contrasts with the strategy of searching for dissociations between tasks. Some have suggested that indirect tests typically rely on prior data-driven processing, whereas direct tests typically rely on prior conceptually driven processing (Jacoby, 1983; Roediger & Blaxton, 1987; Roediger et al., 1989). Others (e.g. Cohen & Squire, 1980; Tulving & Schacter, 1990) have suggested that performance on indirect tests reflects the use of a memory representation that is anatomically distinct from the memory representation that is responsible for performance on direct tests of memory.

A difficulty for identifying processes with tasks is that tasks are probably never process-pure (e.g. Dunn & Kirsner, 1989; Reingold & Merïkle, 1990). For example, consider the conditions that have been said to give rise to responses based on automatic processes. The use of an automatic basis for responding is more likely when subjects must respond rapidly, when attention is divided, and when an indirect test is given. However, it is doubtful that any of those conditions produce responding that is purely automatic. Likewise, it is doubtful that allowing ample time to respond along with full attention for a direct test insures a pure measure of consciously controlled processing. Indeed, Jacoby and Hollingshead (1990) have shown that subjects given a direct test under those conditions do sometimes use an automatic basis for responding just as they would had they been given an indirect test of memory. The process dissociation procedure described here allows one to avoid treating tasks as process-pure by providing a means of separating effects of different types of processing within a task. By using the process dissociation procedure, one need not assume that an indirect test relies only on automatic processes. Rather, effects of task instructions at test on automatic and consciously controlled bases for responding can be separately observed in a manner parallel to the studies of the effects of full versus divided attention.

The goal of the process dissociation procedure used here is the same as that motivating others' attempts (e.g. Mandler, 1980) to estimate separately the influence of different bases for recognition memory decisions. However, the process dissociation procedure is very different from other procedures: it is the difference between separating processes within a task and identifying processes with tasks that is important (see Jacoby, 1991, for a discussion). The intent of separating processes within a task is the same as in signal-detection theory (e.g. Swets *et al.*, 1961). It is meant to separate different bases for responding and to reveal invariance in one basis for responding across variance in the other.

The emphasis on differences in processing that accompanies the search for task dissociations has obscured the importance of finding invariance (cf. Stevens, 1951). To be certain that a variable does not influence a particular basis for responding, one must have a means of separating bases for responding within a task. Extending the analogy with signal-detection theory, identifying types of processing or memory representation with tasks makes no more sense than it would to identify sensitivity and bias with separate tasks. Both sensitivity and bias contribute to performance of any particular judgement task so it would not be reasonable to claim that one task measured only sensitivity whereas a different task measured only bias. The same can be said for consciously controlled versus automatic processing, and can probably also be said for other contrasts that have been used to account for dissociations between performance on indirect and direct tests.

10.10. PARALLELS BETWEEN ACCOUNTS OF DISSOCIATION AND THEORIES OF AUTOMATICITY

Identifying dissociations between performance on indirect versus direct tests with the contrast between automatic versus consciously controlled processing reduces the number of problems that are to be solved only by virtue of the fact that problems for explanations of dissociations are the same problems as encountered by theories of automaticity. That is, there are parallels between theorizing about automaticity and theorizing about dissociations.

One parallel is that awareness and intentionality are often confounded in discussions of dissociations just as they are in the definition of automaticity (e.g. Bargh, 1989). The relation between awareness and intentionality is an asymmetric one: when people are unaware of the stimuli controlling their responses we conclude that the responses are unintentional, but when they are aware of the stimuli, the responses are not necessarily intentional. In fact, awareness of a stimulus may follow the response, rather than be responsible for initiation of a response. Performance on the Stroop test (1935) illustrates this point. Subjects are aware of the colour words that interfere with their naming of the colour of the words, although they clearly do not intend to read the colour names. Reading the colour words seems to be driven by attention to the stimulus even though it is counter to the intention to name the colour of the words. Similarly, the false fame effect in our experiments seems to result from stimulus-driven processing that makes a name seem familiar. Use of memory for the prior presentation of names when making fame judgements is unintentional, and for the false fame effect to occur, any awareness of earlier reading of the name in the list of nonfamous names must follow responding. Freudian slips and actions slips are cases where awareness immediately follows responses that happen unintentionally. One interpretation of these cases is that the interference is an automatic, unintentional result of processing environmental stimuli. In other cases, facilitation has been attributed to automatic processing, as in the case of priming in lexical decisions (e.g. Neely, 1976).

Both priming and interference effects have been interpreted as resulting from automatic processes happening without awareness or intention. The automatic processes are controlled by stimuli whereas consciously controlled processes are controlled by intentions (LaBerge & Samuels, 1974; Posner & Synder, 1975; Shiffrin & Schneider, 1977; Hasher & Zacks, 1979). Automatic processing has been modelled as activation spreading among abstract representations such as nodes in a network that can be primed by mere exposure to stimuli. The abstract representations that are responsible for automaticity are distilled from extensive prior experience and differ from the memory representations upon which the novice relies. In contrast to the reliance of automaticity on the spread of activation, conscious control is treated as due to the operation of a control system of limited capacity (Shiffrin & Schneider, 1977; Shallice, 1988). The association of control and phenomenal awareness has been developed further by Johnson-Laird (1983, 1988).

Is the separation between control by stimuli versus conscious intentions ever really the case? After extensive learning, automatic responses are said to become as encapsulated and uncontrolled as reflexes. However, even reflexes can be modified by attention (see review by Anthony, 1985). Neumann (1984) argued that automaticity is not a characteristic of processing controlled by stimuli, but rather is an emergent property of the exercise of specific skills in an environment. When all the parameters of the task are specified by the combination of memory for the skill and the environment, then the task is automatic. He suggests that automaticity cannot be driven by stimuli separately from skills that are brought into play by intentions. For example, priming in lexical decision is not a result of seeing the prime which then automatically activates the target, but is due to the exercise of the skill of predictive reading. That is, stimulus-driven processing is integrated with, and done in the context of, the goals and intentions set by consciously controlled processing, rather than being invariant across contexts. Models of the sort proposed by Neumann describe interference as arising from problems in co-ordinating tasks rather than from a limited-capacity processor (Allport, 1989).

Logan (1988) has described automaticity as relying on memory for instances, rather than on the development of an abstract representation (cf. Schneider & Shiffrin, 1977), and has pointed out parallels between performance on indirect tests of memory and automaticity (Logan, 1990). By Logan's view, automaticity comes about when people change over from computing responses algorithmically to relying on memory for a past episode. He models the decrease in speed of responding that reflects the development of automaticity by assuming that instance-based responding is faster than is algorithm-based responding, and by also assuming that experience with a task makes reliance on instances more likely by increasing their number.

Abstractionist (e.g. Schneider & Shiffrin, 1977) and instance (Logan, 1988) theories of automaticity are paralleled by accounts of dissociations. Like abstractionist theories of automaticity, multiple memory system accounts of dissociations hold that performance on indirect tests relies on a memory representation that is different from that responsible for performance on direct tests (e.g. Cohen & Squire, 1980; Tulving & Schacter, 1990). In contrast, processing accounts of dissociations (e.g. Jacoby & Brooks, 1984; Roediger *et al.*, 1989) and the instance theory of automaticity hold that memory for prior episodes contributes to performance on both indirect and direct tests of memory. Elsewhere (e.g. Jacoby & Brooks, 1984; Jacoby & Kelley, 1987), we have described how dissociations can arise although both indirect and direct tests rely on memory for episodes, and have given reasons for preferring a processing account over an abstractionist or memory systems account of dissociations.

The concern with the integration of stimulus-driven with consciously controlled processing described for theories of automaticity also has its parallel in accounts of dissociations. Accounts of memory dissociations in terms of data-driven and conceptually driven processing (e.g. Roediger *et al.*, 1989) require that the two types of processing not be terribly interactive. Otherwise, it would not be meaningful to claim that some tests rely primarily on data-driven processing whereas other tests rely primarily on conceptually driven processing. Similarly, accounts of dissociations in terms of separate memory representations require that the use of the different representations not be so interactive as to rule out identifying memory representations with types of test. However, akin to the relation between stimulus-driven and consciously controlled processing in automaticity, memory for data-driven and memory for conceptually driven processing appear to be integrated in their contribution to performance on indirect tests of memory (e.g. Levy & Kirsner, 1989; Jacoby *et al.*, 1991). Returning to a point made earlier, tests cannot legitimately be treated as pure with regard to either processes or memory representations.

One can describe the integration of data-driven and conceptually driven processing in terms similar to Neumann's (1984) by describing skill as relying on memory for prior episodes (cf. Logan, 1988): memory on an indirect test is not simply processing controlled by stimuli, but rather reflects the use of memory for prior episodes used in an 'environment' that includes the indirect test cues. When all of the parameters of the task used as an indirect test are specified by the combination of memory for prior episodes and the environment, then the effects of memory on an indirect test will automatically emerge. Neumann argues that conscious control is made necessary by a poor fit between skill and the environment. Similarly, when engaged in a task whose performance can benefit from memory for prior episodes, awareness of the past may spontaneously arise only when the mismatch is such that performance is not sufficiently well served by unconscious memory.

10.11. SUMMARY AND CONCLUSIONS

Let us end by briefly summarizing the main points that we have made. We began by suggesting that dissociations between performance on indirect and direct tests of memory can be understood in terms of the contrast between automatic and consciously controlled processing. Memory for past experience automatically influences the ease of processing and the interpretation of later events. Subjective experience is constructed and reflects an unconscious attribution or inference process that attributes effects to a source. Because of errors in the attribution process, measures of subjective experience are valuable as indirect tests of memory. However, tests are not process-pure. That is, indirect tests cannot be treated as pure measures of automatic processing nor can direct tests be treated as pure measures of consciously controlled processing. To be certain that effects are produced by unconscious influences of memory, it is necessary to arrange a situation such that automatic and consciously controlled influences are placed in opposition. Doing so allows one to separate clearly the two types of effect, but does not allow one to estimate their magnitude.

Next, we described a process dissociation procedure that can be used to separately estimate effects of variables on consciously controlled and automatic processes. That procedure estimates consciously controlled processing as the difference between performance under conditions in which consciously controlled and automatic processes produce effects in the same direction as compared with performance under conditions in which the two processes act in opposition. Use of the process dissociation procedure to estimate effects showed that dividing attention, either at test or during study, reduced subjects' ability to use conscious recollection as a basis for recognition memory judgements, but had no effect on familiarity-based judgements. It seems likely that variants of the process dissociation procedure will be useful for specifying the nature of memory deficits, and for separating automatic and consciously controlled processes in categorization and perceptual tasks as well as in memory tasks.

Accounts of dissociations parallel theories of automaticity. We hold that performance on both indirect and direct tests of memory relies on memory for prior episodes, just as Logan (1988) argues that automaticity reflects memory for instances. Although we lacked sufficient space to describe the relevant evidence, we concluded that memory revealed by indirect tests is not a characteristic of processing wholly controlled by the present physical stimuli (cf. Roediger *et al.*, 1989), nor is it a characteristic of a memory representation of present physical stimuli (cf. Tulving & Schacter, 1990). Processing is too interactive to allow types of processing or types of memory representation to be isolated by mapping them on to tasks. Although our interest in unconscious influences began with the finding of dissociations between performance on direct and indirect tests (Jacoby & Dallas, 1981), we have moved away from relying on dissociations between tasks and have developed techniques to separate the contribution of different types of processing within a task. Following Neumann's analysis of automaticity (1984, who in turn describes his approach as following Wundt's), we believe that memory revealed on an indirect test reflects the fit between memory for prior episodes and the requirements of the present task.

In a commentary on research in decision making, Estes (1980) made a distinction that seems pertinent to memory research, i.e. the distinction between a task orientation and a process orientation. He noted that work in problem solving and decision making at that time primarily had a task orientation. For example, psychologists had studied water-jug puzzles, missionaries and cannibals, and the Tower of Hanoi, rather than more abstract processes that might cut across areas. He noted that two consequences of such a task orientation are a lack of citations across research areas and an attempt to construct taxonomies of tasks. Estes urged researchers in decision making and problem solving to take a more process-oriented approach (and he warned that 'theoretically significant classifications more often follow than precede the development of process-oriented models (p. 269)...'). We think much can be gained from adopting a process orientation in memory research, and in particular from relating dissociations to the contrast between automatic versus consciously controlled processing.

REFERENCES

Allport, A. (1989). Visual attention. In M.I. Posner (ed.), *Foundations of Cognitive Science*. Cambridge, MA: MIT Press.

Anthony, B.J. (1985). In the blink of an eye: Implication of reflex modification for information processing. In P.K. Ackles, J.R. Jennings and M.G.H. Coles (eds), *Advances in Psychophysiology*, Vol. 1. Greenwich, CT: JAI Press.

Atkinson, R.C. & Juola, J.F. (1974). Search and decision processes in recognition memory. In D.H. Krantz, R.C. Atkinson, R.D. Luce and P. Suppes (eds), *Contemporary Developments in Mathematical Psychology, Vol. 1, Learning, Memory and Thinking*. San Francisco, CA: Freeman.

Baddeley, A. & Wilson, B. (1986). Amnesia, autobiographical memory, and confabulation. In D.C. Rubin (ed.), *Autobiographical Memory*. Cambridge: Cambridge University Press.

Bargh, J.A. (1989). Conditional automaticity: Varieties of automatic influence in social perception and cognition. In J.S. Uleman and J.A. Bargh (eds), *Unintended Thought*. NY: Guilford Press.

Brown, A.L. & Murphy, D.R. (1989). Cryptomnesia: Delineating inadvertent plagiarism. *Journal of Experimental Psychology: Learning, Memory, and Cognition*, **15**, 432–442.

Cheesman, J. & Merikle, P.M. (1986). Distinguishing conscious from unconscious perceptual processes. *Canadian Journal of Psychology*, **40**, 343–367.

Cohen, N.J. & Squire, L.R. (1980). Preserved learning and retention of pattern-analyzing skill in amnesia: Dissociation of knowing how and knowing that. *Science*, **210**, 207–210.

Craik, F.I.M. & Lockhart, R.S. (1972). Levels of processing: A framework for memory research. *Journal of Verbal Learning and Verbal Behavior*, **11**, 671–684.

Dixon, N.F. (1981). *Preconscious Processing*. Chichester: John Wiley.

Dunn, J.C. & Kirsner, K. (1989). Implicit memory: Task or process? In S. Lewandowsky, J.C. Dunn and K. Kirsner (eds), *Implicit Memory: Theoretical Issues*. Hillsdale, NJ: Erlbaum.

Dywan, J. & Jacoby, L.L. (1990). Effects of aging on source monitoring: Differences in susceptibility to false fame. *Psychology and Aging*, **5**, 379–387.

Eagle, M.N. (1987). The psychoanalytic and the cognitive unconscious. In R. Stern (ed.), *Theories of the Unconscious and Theories of the Self*. Hillsdale, NJ: Analytic Press.

Eich, E. (1984). Memory for unattended events: Remembering with and without awareness. *Memory and Cognition*, **12**, 105–111.

Estes, W.K. (1980). Comments on directions and limitations of current efforts toward theories of decision making. In T.S. Wallsten (ed.), *Cognitive Processes in Choice and Decision Behavior*. Hillsdale, NJ: Erlbaum.

Gardiner, J.M. (1988). Functional aspects of recollective experience. *Memory and Cognition*, **16**, 309–313.

Gazzaniga, M.S. (1988). Brain modularity: Towards a philosophy of conscious experience. In A.J. Marcel and E. Bisiach (eds), *Consciousness in Contemporary Science*, Oxford: Clarendon Press.

Gillund, G. & Shiffrin, R.M. (1984). A retrieval model for both recognition and recall. *Psychological Review*, **91**, 1–67.

Graf, P. & Schacter, D.L. (1989). Unitization and grouping mediate dissociations in memory for new associations. *Journal of Experimental Psychology: Learning, Memory, and Cognition*, **15**, 930–940.

Grand, S. & Segal, S.J. (1966). Recovery in the absence of recall: An investigation of color-word interference. *Journal of Experimental Psychology*, **72**, 138–144.

Greenwald, A.G. (1989). What cognitive representations underlie social attitudes? Paper presented at the meetings of the Psychonomic Society, Atlanta, GA.

Hasher, L. & Zacks, R.T. (1979). Automatic and effortful processes in memory. *Journal of Experimental Psychology: General*, **108**, 356–388.

Hasher, L. & Zacks, R.T. (1988). Working memory, comprehension, and aging: A review and a new view. In G.K. Bower (ed.), *The Psychology of Learning and Motivation*, Vol. 22. New York: Academic Press.

Helmholtz, H. (1968). Concerning the perceptions in general. In W. Warren & R. Warren (eds), *Helmholtz on Perception: Its Physiology and Development*. NY: Wiley.

Hertel, P.T. & Hardin, T.S. (1990). Remembering with and without awareness in a depressed mood: Evidence of deficits in initiative. *Journal of Experimental Psychology: General*, **119**, 45–59.

Hilgard, E.R. (1980). Consciousness in contemporary psychology. *Annual Review of Psychology*, **31**, 1–26.

Hintzman, D.L. (1988). Judgements of frequency and recognition memory in a multiple-trace memory model. *Psychological Review*, **95**, 528–551.

Hintzman, D.L. (1990). Human learning and memory: Connections and dissociations. *Annual Review of Psychology*, **41**, 109–139.

Hirst, W. (1982). The amnesic syndrome: Descriptions and explanations. *Psychological Bulletin*, **91**, 435–460.

Holender, D. (1986). Semantic activation without conscious identification in dichotic listening, parafoveal vision, and visual masking: A survey and appraisal. *Behavioral and Brain Sciences*, **9**, 1–23.

Howard, D.V. (1988). Implicit and explicit assessment of cognitive aging. In M.L. Howe and C.J. Brainerd (eds), *Cognitive Development in Adulthood: Progress in Cognitive Development Research*. NY: Springer-Verlag.

Jacoby, L.L. (1983). Remembering the data: Analyzing interactive processes in reading. *Journal of Verbal Learning and Verbal Behavior*, **22**, 485–508.

Jacoby, L.L. (1991). A process dissociation framework: Separating automatic from intentional uses of memory. *Journal of Memory and Language*, in press.

Jacoby, L.L. & Brooks, L.R. (1984). Nonanalytic cognition: Memory, perception and concept learning. In G.H. Bower (ed.), *The Psychology of Learning and Motivation: Advances in Research and Theory*, Vol. 18. NY: Academic Press.

Jacoby, L.L. & Dallas, M. (1981). On the relationship between autobiographical memory and perceptual learning. *Journal of Experimental Psychology: General*, **3**, 306–340.

Jacoby, L.L. & Hollingshead, A. (1990). Toward a generate/recognize model of performance on direct and indirect tests of memory. *Journal of Memory and Language*, **29**, 433–454.

Jacoby, L.L. & Kelley, C.M. (1987). Unconscious influences of memory for a prior event. *Personality and Social Psychology Bulletin*, **13**, 314–336.

Jacoby, L.L. & Kelley, C.M. (1990). An episodic view of motivation: Unconscious influences of memory. In E.T. Higgins & R.M. Sorrentino (eds), *Handbook of Motivation and Cognition: Foundations of Social Behavior*, Vol. 2. NY: Guilford Press.

Jacoby, L.L. & Whitehouse, K. (1989). An illusion of memory: False recognition influenced by unconscious perception. *Journal of Experimental Psychology: General*, **118**, 126–135.

Jacoby, L.L., Allan, L.G., Collins, J.C. & Larwill, L.K. (1988). Memory influences subjective experience: Noise judgements. *Journal of Experimental Psychology: Learning, Memory, and Cognition*, **14**, 240–247.

Jacoby, L.L., Woloshyn, V. & Kelley, C.M. (1989a). Becoming famous without being recognized: Unconscious influences of memory produced by dividing attention. *Journal of Experimental Psychology: General*, **118**, 115–125.

Jacoby, L.L., Kelley, C.M. & Dywan, J. (1989b). Memory attributions. In H.L. Roediger and F.I.M. Craik (eds), *Varieties of Memory and Consciousness: Essays in Honour of Endel Tulving*. Hillsdale, NJ: Erlbaum.

Jacoby, L.L., Levy, B.A. & Steinbach, K. (1991). Episodic transfer and automaticity: the integration of data-driven and conceptually-driven processing in rereading. *Journal of Experimental Psychology: Learning, Memory, and Cognition* in press.

James, W. (1890). *Principles of Psychology*. NY: Henry Holt.

Johnson, M.K. (1988). Discriminating the origin of information. In T.F. Oltmanns and B.A. Maher (eds), *Delusional Beliefs: Interdisciplinary Perspectives*. NY: John Wiley.

Johnson, M.K. & Hasher, L. (1987). Human learning and memory. *Annual Review of Psychology*, **38**, 631–668.

Johnson, M.K., Kim, J.K. & Risse, G. (1985). Do alcoholic Korsakoff's syndrome patients acquire affective reactions? *Journal of Experimental Psychology: Learning, Memory, and Cognition*, **11**, 22–36.

Johnson-Laird, P.N. (1983). *Mental Models*. Cambridge, MA: Harvard University Press.

Johnson-Laird, P.N. (1988). A computational analysis of consciousness. In A.J. Marcel and E. Bisiach (eds), *Consciousness in Contemporary Science*. Oxford: Clarendon Press.

Kelley, C.M. & Jacoby, L.L. (1990). The construction of subjective experience: Memory attributions. *Mind and Language*, **5**(1), 49–68.

Kihlstrom, J.F. (1987). The cognitive unconscious. *Science*, **237**, 1445–1452.

Klatzky, R.L. (1984). *Memory and Awareness*. New York: Freeman.

Koriat, A. & Feuerstein, N. (1976). The recovery of incidentally acquired information. *Acta Psychologica*, **40**, 463–474.

Kuhl, J. (1986). Motivation and information processing: A new look at decision making, dynamic change, and action control. In R.M. Sorrentino and E.T. Higgins (eds), *Handbook of Motivation and Cognition: Foundations of Social Behavior*, Vol. 1. NY: Guilford Press.

Kunst-Wilson, W.R. & Zajonc, R.B. (1980). Affective discrimination of stimuli that cannot be recognized. *Science*, **207**, 557–558.

LaBerge, D. & Samuels, S.J. (1974). Toward a theory of automatic information processing in reading. *Cognitive Psychology*, **6**, 293–323.

Levy, B.A. & Kirsner, K. (1989). Reprocessing text: Indirect measures of word and message level processes. *Journal of Experimental Psychology: Learning, Memory, and Cognition*, **15**, 407–417.

Lindsay, D.S. & Kelley, C.M. (1991). Ease of generation during recall induces a feeling of remembering. Poster presented at the American Psychological Society, Washington DC, June 1991.

Logan, G.D. (1988). Toward an instance theory of automatization. *Psychological Review*, **95**, 492–527.

Logan, G.D. (1990). Repetition priming and automaticity: Common underlying mechanisms? *Cognitive Psychology*, **22**, 1–35.

Mandler, G. (1980). Recognizing: The judgment of previous occurrence. *Psychological Review*, **87**, 252–271.

Mandler, G., Nakamura, Y. & Van Zandt, B.J.S. (1987). Nonspecific effects of exposure on stimuli that cannot be recognized. *Journal of Experimental Psychology: Learning, Memory, and Cognition*, **13**, 646–648.

Marcel, A.J. (1983a). Conscious and unconscious perception: Experiments on visual masking and word recognition. *Cognitive Psychology*, **15**, 197–237.

Marcel, A.J. (1983b). Conscious and unconscious perception: An approach to the relations between phenomenal experience and perceptual processes. *Cognitive Psychology*, **15**, 238–300.

Moscovitch, M. (1989). Confabulation and the frontal systems: Strategic versus associative retrieval in neuropsychological theories of memory. In H.L. Roediger and F.I.M. Craik (eds), *Varieties of Memory and Consciousness: Essays in Honour of Endel Tulving*. Hillsdale, NJ: Erlbaum.

Neely, J.H. (1976). Semantic priming and retrieval from lexical memory: Evidence for facilitatory and inhibitory processes. *Memory and Cognition*, **4**, 648–654.

Neumann, O. (1984). Automatic processing: A review of recent findings and a plea for an old theory. In W. Prinz and A.F. Sanders (eds), *Cognition and Motor Processes*. Berlin: Springer-Verlag.

Posner, M.I. & Synder, C.R.R. (1975). Attention and cognitive control. In R.L. Solso (ed.), *Information Processing in Cognition: The Loyola Symposium*. Hillsdale, NJ: Erlbaum.

Reed, G. (1974). *The Psychology of Anomalous Experience: A Cognitive Approach*. Boston, MA: Houghton Mifflin.

Reingold, E.M. & Merikle, P.M. (1990). On the inter-relatedness of theory and measurement in the study of unconscious processes. *Mind and Language*, **5**, 9–28.

Richardson-Klavehn, A. & Bjork, R.A. (1988). Measures of memory. *Annual Review of Psychology*, **39**, 475–543.

Roediger, H.L. (1990). Implicit memory: Retention without remembering. *American Psychologist*, **45**, 1043–1056.

Roediger, H.L. & Blaxton, T.A. (1987). Retrieval modes produce dissociations in memory for surface information. In D.S. Gorfein and R.R. Hoffman (eds), *Memory and Cognitive Processes: The Ebbinghaus Centennial Conference*. Hillsdale, NJ: Erlbaum.

Roediger, H.L., Weldon, M.S. & Challis, B.H. (1989). Explaining dissociations between implicit and explicit measures of retention: A processing account. In H.L. Roediger and F.I.M. Craik (eds), *Varieties of Memory and Consciousness: Essays in Honour of Endel Tulving*. Hillsdale, NJ: Erlbaum.

Ross, M. (1989). Relation of implicit theories to the construction of personal histories. *Psychological Review*, **96**, 341–357.

Schachter, S. & Singer, J. (1962). Cognitive, social and physiological determinants of emotional state. *Psychological Review*, **69**, 379–399.

Schneider, W. & Shiffrin, R.M. (1977). Controlled and automatic human information processing: I. Detection, search and attention. *Psychological Review*, **84**, 1–66.

Seamon, J.G., Brody, N. & Kauff, D.M. (1983). Affective discrimination of stimuli that are not recognized: Effects of shadowing, masking, and cerebral laterality. *Journal of Experimental Psychology: Learning, Memory and Cognition*, **9**, 544–555.

Shallice, T. (1988). Information-processing models of consciousness: Possibilities and problems. In A.J. Marcel and E. Bisiach (eds), *Consciousness in Contemporary Science*. Oxford: Clarendon Press.

Shiffrin, R.M. & Schneider, W. (1977). Controlled and automatic human information processing: II. Perceptual learning, automatic attending, and a general theory. *Psychological Review*, **84**, 127–190.

Squire, L.R. & McKee, R. (1991). The influence of prior events on cognitive judgements in amnesia. *Journal of Experimental Psychology: Learning, Memory, and Cognition*, in press.

Stevens, S.S. (1951). Mathematics, measurement, and psychophysics. In S.S. Stevens (ed.), *Handbook of Experimental Psychology*. NY: John Wiley.

Stroop, J.R. (1935). Studies of interference in serial verbal reactions. *Journal of Experimental Psychology*, **18**, 643–662.

Stuss, D.T. & Benson, D.F. (1986). *The Frontal Lobe*. NY: Raven Press.

Swets, J.A., Tanner, W.P. & Birdsall, T.G. (1961). Decision processes in perception. *Psychological Review*, **68**, 301–340.

Tulving, E. & Schacter, D.L. (1990). Priming and human memory systems. *Science*, **247**, 301–305.

Warrington, E.K. & Weiskrantz, L. (1974). The effect of prior learning on subsequent retention in amnesic patients. *Neuropsychologia*, **12**, 419–428.

Weingartner, H. (1984). Psychobiological determinants of memory failures. In L.R. Squire and N. Butters (eds), *Neuropsychology of Memory*. NY: Guilford Press.

Weiskrantz, L. (1986). *Blindsight: A Case Study and Implications.* Oxford: Oxford University Press.

Whittlesea, B.W.A., Jacoby, L.L. & Girard, K.A. (1990). Illusions of immediate memory: Evidence of an attributional basis for feelings of familiarity and perceptual quality. *Journal of Memory and Language,* **29,** 716–732.

Witherspoon, D. & Allan, L.G. (1985). The effects of a prior presentation on temporal judgements in a perceptual identification task. *Memory & Cognition,* **13,** 101–111.

Young, A.W. & De Haan, E.H.F. (1990). Impairments of visual awareness. *Mind & Language,* **5,** 29–48.

CHAPTER 11

Automatic Memory Processes in Amnesia: How Are They Mediated?

Andrew R. Mayes

11.1. INTRODUCTION

Organic amnesics show impaired recognition and recall for both post-traumatic and pre-traumatic information about facts and events. In other words, they are impaired at consciously identifying information that they have retrieved or with which they have been confronted as coming from memory. It is not that they are unconscious of the information. Rather, the information lacks familiarity either in a specific sense ('I do not remember experiencing this on a particular occasion') or in a vaguer sense ('I do not feel that I have experienced this on one or more occasions' or 'I do not have any feeling of knowing this fact'). In contrast, it is often claimed that amnesics show good memory for information even though they are unaware that they are remembering (see Mayes, 1988 for a review). This claim is interesting and important because if it can be shown that amnesics have *completely preserved* memory for *all* those kinds of information for which they show impaired recall and recognition, then it becomes plausible to argue that their problem is one of acting upon normally stored memories so as to make them feel familiar.

In this chapter, I shall be assessing the evidence for this claim and its implications. I shall also briefly consider what the pattern of functioning shown by amnesics may reveal about how recognition and recall are achieved by people with intact brains. In order to do this, I shall first outline some contemporary views about the nature of what is usually referred to as priming, then I shall consider several major hypotheses about what kind or kinds of functional deficit underlies the memory deficit shown by amnesics. The predictions that these hypotheses make about the preservation or non-preservation of priming for various kinds of information will then be discussed with particular attention being paid to the effect on these predictions of the different views about the nature of priming. Evidence about amnesic priming will then be reviewed paying particular attention to largely unpublished work that has been carried out in my laboratory. The concluding section will discuss what needs to be done to help clarify unresolved issues in the field.

11.2. PRIMING AND INDIRECT TESTS OF MEMORY

Amnesics have been found to show normal simple classical conditioning (Weiskrantz & Warrington, 1979; Daum et al., 1989) and a preservation of the acquisition and retention of motor, perceptuomotor and even perhaps cognitive skills (see Shimamura, 1989). These forms of preserved memory contrast with the improverished recall and recognition that amnesics have for the learning experience and for the material used during learning. Nevertheless, the dissociation is not particularly surprising because there is evidence that at least certain forms of classical conditioning depend on the integrity of the cerebellum (Lye et al.,1988), and other evidence points to a role for the basal ganglia in skill memory (Mishkin et al., 1984). It therefore seems likely that these forms of memory are dealt with by very different brain systems than the ones that are damaged in organic amnesics.

Amnesics have, however, been shown to perform normally on certain item-specific indirect tests of memory. This is important not only because the preserved memory is item-specific, but also because it is for kinds of information (for example, about words or complex figures) that are almost certain to be largely represented and presumably stored in association neocortex. It is exactly this kind of information that amnesics are unable to recognize or recall. An indirect test of memory is one in which subjects are typically not informed that memory will be or is being tested in order that they do not intentionally try to retrieve or identify an item as coming from memory. An indirect memory test that taps item-specific memory is often referred to as a test of priming. Hence, priming is a form of item-specific indirect or unintentional memory. It is displayed when an item is processed differently or more efficiently as a result of having been previously encountered. The term is unfortunate because it implicitly presupposes a theory of how indirect memory tests are performed, according to which performance depends on the relatively prolonged activation of a memory trace. In brief, the encounter with an item primes its memory representation and this changes the way in which the item is subsequently processed. To avoid this presupposition it would be safer to use the expression 'item-specific indirect or unintentional memory', but this is cumbersome so, with some misgivings, the term 'priming' will be used here.

As Jacoby and Kelley indicate in this volume (Chapter 10), priming tasks are probably not process pure in the sense that they depend solely on unintentional or automatic memory processes, and recall and recognition tasks are also probably not process pure because they not only depend on intentional and effortful memory processes, but also on more automatic and unintentional memory processes. Nevertheless, performance on recall and recognition tasks depends on intentional memory processes to a much greater degree than does the typical priming task, and it may even be that performance on some priming tasks depends entirely on unintentional automatic memory processes. The issue is important: amnesics may fail to show preservation of performance on a particular priming task because normal subjects partially mediate their performance via intentional and effortful memory processes at which the patients are impaired, despite the fact that their unintentional automatic memory processes may be preserved. The issue may be even more difficult to resolve because it is possible that normal subjects sometimes use effortful memory processes unintentionally (Schacter, Chapter 9, this volume).

Therefore, if subjects are given a priming task in which everything is done to encourage them to use unintentional, automatic memory processes, at least three things may happen. First, subjects may not do what the experimenter wants and instead use intentional and effortful memory strategies. Second, subjects may be unable to stop themselves using such strategies even though they do not intend to do so. Third, subjects' performance may be largely mediated by unintentional and automatic memory processes. Attempts to eliminate the first possibility have sometimes reached Machiavellian proportions—for example, no reference is made to any kind of memory test, at test target items are intermixed with a far higher proportion of foil items, and the response required of subjects is either speeded or is apparently unrelated to memory (for example, judging how loud white noise is or for how long a word has been presented). In order to ascertain whether these measures have been successful various criteria have been proposed for distinguishing intentional effortful memory processes from unintentional, automatic ones. If subjects are not using conscious memory, then, it is argued, priming effects should be no different for unrecognized items than for recognized ones. Although this seems plausible at first sight, recognition and priming are not only measured on separate occasions, but testing one may influence performance on the other. Even if the second problem can be discounted, stochastic independence of memory performances on two occasions does not necessarily indicate that distinct processes are involved. The same processes may be at work, but rather noisily, so that they produce different results on the two test occasions.

Schacter *et al.*, (1989) have proposed a retrieval intentionality criterion to check whether performance on a priming task is being mediated by intentional and effortful retrieval. If this possibility is to be discounted, then subjects need to be tested with identical cues under two conditions. The first condition involves telling subjects to use the cues to remember target items and the second condition involves giving indirect memory instructions to inhibit the intentional use of memory. If a variable can be found that influences performance on one test but not the other, then it can be argued that the indirect memory test does not depend on intentional memory. For example, a word stem like 'sta—' can be shown to subjects in two test conditions. In one condition, subjects are told to try and remember the word shown earlier beginning 'sta—', and in the other condition they are told to produce the first word that comes to mind beginning with those three letters. Performance on the first condition only is improved by giving a semantic rather than a structural orienting task during learning (Graf *et al.*, 1982). Schacter *et al.*, (1989) would take this as strong evidence that subjects are not intentionally using effortful memory processes in the word completion condition. Even if they are correct however, it is still possible (as they concede) that performance in the word completion condition involves an unintentional kind of effortful memory.

One might have some confidence that performance on an item-specific indirect memory task was not appreciably influenced by either intentional or unintentional effortful memory processes provided that performance was not worsened by dividing attention at the time of test (something that is known to disrupt recognition and recall). But even if a task satisfied this test, one would still have learnt very little about the nature of the unintentional, automatic processes that mediate performance. Furthermore, when amnesics fail to show normal performance on a priming test, one wants to know whether this is because of a deficiency in an automatic memory process or merely in effortful memory processes. Jacoby and Kelley (Chapter 10, this volume) discuss an important new procedure that may allow one to estimate the contribution of both automatic and effortful processes to memory performance. This will be considered at the end of this chapter in relation to the performance of amnesic and normal subjects on certain priming tasks.

Whether or not one can estimate the contribution of automatic and effortful processes to memory performance it is important to have clear and testable ideas about their detailed nature. Three questions should be addressed. First, can automatic memory processes give rise to aware memory (the feeling of familiarity that underlies recognition)? Second, and relatedly, do the automatic memory processes that give rise to priming constitute a sub-set of the processes that are necessary for recognition, or are some of these automatic processes unique to priming? If the former possibility holds, then it should be impossible for brain damage to disrupt priming without also disrupting recognition or recall. If the latter possibility holds, however, it should be possible to find a double dissociation between impairments of priming and those of recognition and recall. Third, exactly what processes constitute automatic and effortful memory?

With respect to the first question, priming is most usually understood to occur even in normal people in the absence of awareness, and the fact that severe amnesics appear to show preserved priming in some indirect memory tasks seems to be an argument against the possibility that the automatic processes underlying priming are sufficient to produce recognition. This argument is based on the assumption that such amnesics can show normal priming whilst having chance levels of recognition for the primed items. But as will be discussed below, recognition may depend on dual processes working in parallel, and only one of these may be drastically affected in amnesics. And although the bare feeling of familiarity may depend on automatic processes that are not completely co-extensive with those that underlie at least some forms of priming, it may be that it is impossible to show some preservation of priming without also showing above chance levels of recognition. Priming often involves increases in the speed or accuracy with which critical items are processed, but it may also involve making automatic attributions on the basis of such improvements in processing efficiency (for example, see Witherspoon & Allan, 1985). Perhaps priming of this latter kind does not occur normally in patients whose recognition is strictly at chance. The question of whether the automatic processes underlying priming are ever sufficient to produce recognition is not easy to answer. Priming could occur quite independently of the processes that lead to recognition, even if reliably associated with it, and this possibility is very hard to eliminate. In summary, certain concatenations of automatic processes may lead to a feeling of familiarity. Most forms of priming may depend on only some of these automatic processes. Other forms may depend on very similar processes to those that lead to familiarity. It is a question of considerable interest whether amnesics have sparing of these latter kinds of priming.

Even if the processes underlying priming are insufficient to produce recognition, they may, nevertheless, contribute to it. Obviously, the processes underlying priming and either cued recall or recognition are likely to be the same early in processing, but in the later stages of processing several possibilities obtain. The first possibility is that priming and recognition (or cued recall) depend on different representational systems located in different brain regions. For example, many forms of priming may depend on activity in perceptual representation systems (see Tulving & Schacter, 1990; Schacter, Chapter 9, this volume) whereas recognition that these items are familiar, particularly on the basis of recent experience, may depend on a parallel representation within an episodic memory system that also contains contextual information specifying the episodes in which perceptual items were encountered. If this possibility holds, then it should be possible not only to find patients with preserved priming and impaired recognition for the *same* items, but also patients with impaired priming and intact recognition for the *same* items. Although Alzheimer patients have been reported to show impairments of word completion priming (Shimamura *et al.*, 1987), they are also impaired at cued recall and recognition of recently shown words. There is currently no convincing evidence for the existence of patients who have impaired priming in the face of intact recognition and cued recall.

The second possible relationship between the processes underlying priming and those underlying recognition depends on a dual processing view of recognition that has been associated both with Jacoby (for example, see Jacoby and Kelley, Chapter 10, this volume) and Mandler (1980, see also Mandler *et al.*, 1990). One set of these processes is automatic, and this is postulated to work in parallel with another, effortful, set. According to Jacoby and Kelley the automatic processes can give rise to a feeling of familiarity whereas the effortful processes, referred to as recollection, give rise to a contextually richer aware memory. With face recognition this might be illustrated by the difference between recognizing that a face is familiar and recognizing that it is the butcher's face. The automatic processes responsible for familiarity are very similar to the ones that lead to priming, but it might be argued that there are some automatic processes unique to priming and some unique to familiarity. Recollection, being effortful, shares few processes with either priming *or* familiarity. Once again, this possibility predicts that there should be patients who are impaired at priming, but show normal recognition (and probably cued recall). Not only this, but if, as Jacoby and Kelley argue, recollection and familiarity can be independently measured, then patients should exist who are impaired at both.

There is a third possibility according to which the automatic processes of priming are subsumed by those that lead to familiarity, but additional automatic processes are required to produce the feeling of familiarity. As with the previous possibility, recollection, being effortful, shares few processes with either familiarity or priming. This possibility seems to accord well with the failure to find patients who are impaired at priming, but who are normal at recognition, because it predicts that familiarity cannot be preserved when the processes leading to priming are disrupted. It does, however, allow that recollection can be preserved in the face of disrupted priming so patients might be found with severely impaired priming and perhaps only mildly impaired recognition. If valid, the procedure of Jacoby and Kelley provides a means of identifying whether there are any patients who show preserved recollection in the face of impaired priming.

There has still been very little specification of the automatic processes that underlie priming and familiarity, and of the effortful processes that lead to recollection. This is the third question raised above. Broadly speaking, priming seems to involve a change in the way that previously encountered items are processed. Jacoby and Kelley (Chapter 9, this volume) provide examples that make it clear that priming may be indicated either by the more rapid and accurate processing of previously encountered items, or by the unconscious inferences that are based on this more rapid processing. Examples of the first kind might be perceptual identification priming, in which previously encountered items are perceived more accurately when briefly exposed, or any kind of repetition priming in which a response is faster with previously encountered material. Examples of the second kind have been provided by Jacoby and his colleagues, and include the tendency to judge that previously shown words have been displayed for longer than new words in perceptual identification and duration judgement tasks, and the tendency to judge that white noise presented simultaneously with spoken sentences is less loud if the sentences have been previously presented (see Jacoby and Kelley, Chapter 9, this volume). It is argued that these tendencies arise because the repeated words and sentences are processed more rapidly and efficiently. Because of the context in which these tasks are presented, this leads to the false unconscious inference that the words were shown for longer (rather than that they are familiar) and that the white noise was quieter (rather than that the sentences were familiar). Although these unconscious (and automatic) inferences are false, they provide clear evidence that subjects are showing some item-specific memory. In a similar vein, Jacoby and Kelley argue that the feeling of familiarity derives from an unconscious inference based on the more fluent processing of remembered items.

If this account is correct, then certain forms of priming share with the process that generates familiarity not only increased fluency for remembered items, but also a very similar kind of unconscious inference. One might expect, therefore, that if amnesics were to show preserved 'attributional priming' for a particular item, then they should also show a preserved feeling of familiarity for that item. This would leave them with some ability to be aware that items have been previously encountered, but without the ability to identify in what context. Although it was suggested earlier that severe amnesics are likely to be impaired at both attributional priming and familiarity judgements, this idea has not been rigorously tested. It might be that only very severe amnesics show this combination of impairments, whereas milder amnesics show preservation of both attributional priming and familiarity. If so, severe amnesia might involve an additional impairment that affects the automatic processes required for attributional priming and the production of feelings of familiarity. In contrast, even severe amnesics may show preservation of those kinds of priming that depend only on increased efficiency of processing previously encountered items.

One would not, however, expect amnesics to show normal recognition because, on the dual processing account, recognition also depends on the intentional and effortful processes that underlie recollection. In contrast to the feeling of familiarity, recollection enables subjects not only to remember items, but also to identify in what context they were previously experienced. Both cued recall and recognition must surely depend in part at least on the intentional, effortful processes that recollection requires, although the precise retrieval processes involved may differ. Just as Jacoby and Mandler have each argued that recognition depends on two processes acting in parallel so has Jones (1983) argued that cued recall can be mediated by two distinct processes. One mechanism, referred to as generate–recognize, is similar to a recollective process and is contingent on successful recognition. The second depends on the cue directly accessing the target item. In Jones' model this process is estimated as the probability of recall when recognition fails. This process seems to have much in common with the automatic process that leads to priming and possibly also familiarity in recognition. It is possible that the argument might be extended to free recall if this can be seen as a case of implicit cued recall with the context acting as the cue.

There seem to be two extreme views about the kinds of representation on which priming is based. One view is that perceptual priming depends on the activation and sometimes the creation of representations in a perceptual representation system (PRS). Tulving and Schacter (1990) believe that the information supporting priming is hyperspecific, so that if two sets of priming cues are used for the same items, performance for the two priming conditions will show stochastic independence. For this and other reasons, they believe that the representations that mediate priming are separate from those that mediate aware episodic memory. More semantic kinds of priming also occur, and this view would hold that these depend on the activation and perhaps creation of representations within a semantic memory system that is also distinct from episodic memory. It remains a moot point whether the PRS and semantic systems are completely independent of episodic memory or whether they are components of it. The latter would apply if episodic representations comprise components from the PRS and semantic memory system plus contextual markers which define particular events. Whichever is the case, this view seems to imply that priming occurs when experience activates, or creates and activates, representations in either the PRS or the semantic memory system, and this activation facilitates subsequent processing of primed items. Perceptual and semantic priming should not be sensitive to contextual change between initial encounter and test because such priming does not involve the automatic retrieval of contextual information. Priming of contextual information may occur, but this would involve the episodic memory system.

The other view of priming is that like aware memory it depends on the use of the episodic memory system, but that unlike aware memory it depends solely on the automatic use of this system (see Jacoby and Kelley, Chapter 10, this volume). In other words, perceptual and semantic priming, as well as contextual priming, probably rely in part on the automatic retrieval of contextual information. In support of this view, Allen and Jacoby (1990) have reported that perceptual identification priming is enhanced when the test list contains a high as opposed to a low proportion of target words. They found that this effect was as great for poorly recognized words as it was for well recognized words. Thus they argued that it could not be explained in terms of subjects' use of intentional and effortful memory processes, but depended on the sensitivity of priming to contextual change. The general issue is far from resolved, however. For example, Lewandowsky *et al.* (1989) have reported that context-dependent forgetting effects do not occur in priming unless the contextual change involves what Baddeley (1982) referred to as interactive context, affecting the meaningful interpretation of the target items. There is no published evidence that priming is sensitive to changes that include the spatiotemporal location of items and their manner of presentation (independent context; Baddeley, 1982). But the view that priming depends on automatic memory processes acting on episodic memory requires that it should be sensitive to changes of independent context just as much as it is to interactive context. Interestingly, Ellis *et al.* (1990) have described a long-lasting form of face repetition priming in which subjects become faster at recognizing previously seen famous faces. This form of priming seems to be sensitive to changes of the room used for the experiment between initial exposure and test (Ellis, personal communication). The problem is that it is unclear whether this change affects the meaningful interpretation of the faces.

It should be clear from this section that although there has been much experimentation on priming, our understanding of what processes mediate it and how they relate to the processes of recognition, cued recall and free recall is still far from adequate. The relevance of this becomes apparent in considering the predictions of theories of amnesia about the kinds of priming that should be shown by patients.

11.3. THEORIES OF AMNESIA AND THEIR PREDICTIONS ABOUT PRIMING IN PATIENTS

If amnesics show completely preserved priming for all forms of information for which they have impaired recognition and recall, then it becomes plausible to postulate that their ability to acquire and retain new episodic and semantic memories is intact, but that the system(s) that subserve such memories is disconnected from awareness. In Schacter's (1990) terminology, amnesics may have an intact declarative/episodic memory system, but this system is disconnected in both directions from a conscious awareness system. One problem with this hypothesis is that it provides no insight into how recognition and recall of particular items is achieved in addition to unaware memory of the same items. It is unclear whether the feeling that a particular memory is familiar is produced by the same processes that lead to awareness of the thing that is actually being remembered. There may be several conscious awareness systems and amnesics' intact declarative/episodic memory system may only be disconnected from the one that produces the conscious awareness that something has been experienced before. If there is a conscious awareness system that is specific to the production of aware memories, then it is possible that some amnesics have suffered direct damage to this system. It is of interest to note that abnormal feelings of familiarity (both *déjà vu* and *jamais vu*) can occur as part of the aura in temporal lobe epilepsy. The neural systems that produce awareness of pastness may therefore be located in the medial temporal lobe structures or the immediate connections of these structures. It seems unlikely that these structures are involved with the production of all kinds of awareness.

The disconnection hypothesis of amnesia has to explain why these patients show normal immediate memory, and also why their recall and recognition of remote memories is generally less impaired or not impaired at all. The obvious explanation that short-term and very remote memories are held in a declarative/episodic memory system which is not disconnected from either a general or memory-specific awareness system is arbitrary, and requires justification. The disconnection also cannot be complete except in the severest amnesics, because most patients show aware memory for some things from their recent past. There is therefore a need to postulate why some information can be recalled and recognized, but other information cannot.

The prediction that leads most clearly from the disconnection hypothesis is that amnesics will show completely normal priming for *all* those kinds of information they have difficulty recalling and recognizing. But as the hypothesis postulates that declarative/episodic memory is intact, then patients should also show preservation of long-lasting priming, at least of certain kinds of information. This should be expected on the grounds that, according to the hypothesis, both aware and unaware memory are drawn from the same remembered representations. Of course this does not mean that aware and unaware memories should be equally long-lived, but one would expect there to be a rough correspondence. For example, if recognition was still above chance in normal subjects 2 months after training, the hypothesis would be embarrassed if perceptual identification priming never lasted longer than a couple of hours. Furthermore, there is evidence that some forms of priming are very long-lasting (if anything longer lasting than aware memory, for example, see Mitchell & Brown, 1988), so the hypothesis should predict that amnesics will be normal at these kinds of priming. If amnesics only show preserved priming in tasks where priming lasts for a few hours at most, this would suggest that the unaware memory that they can show depends on a different kind of memory representation from that which underlies aware memory. According to the disconnection hypothesis, patients should show not only long-lasting priming for information encountered post-traumatically, but in principle, they should also show priming for information encountered pre-traumatically.

All versions of the hypothesis that amnesia is caused by the inability to access a conscious memory system are specifically designed to account for amnesic priming. It is not clear that they make any other specific predictions. In general, if this kind of hypothesis is correct, then amnesics should be equally impaired at the recall and recognition of all kinds of information. There is, however, evidence that amnesics are more impaired at free recall of recently shown words than they are at the recognition of such words (Hirst *et al.*, 1986, 1988). In unpublished work, we have usually, but not always, replicated this finding so the precise conditions under which it occurs need to be carefully investigated. We also have evidence that amnesics are more impaired at the cued recall of certain kinds of independent and interactive context than they are at recognition of related target information to which they paid attention during learning (see Mayes, 1988 for a review). For example, Pickering *et al.* (1989) found that Korsakoff patients were more impaired at remembering whether words had been presented to them visually or auditorily than they were at recognizing the words, and that this impairment correlated with severity of amnesia but not signs of frontal lobe damage. Shoqeirat (1989) has confirmed these findings in a larger group of amnesics of mixed aetiology and found a similar disproportionate impairment for memory of the spatial location of target items. In unpublished work, we have shown that disproportionate deficits are not only found in memory for independent context, but also in memory for words, presented at the periphery of attention, that affect the meaningful interpretation of other words at the focus of attention (interactive context).

In order to avoid floor and ceiling effects, and scaling problems, all the above studies used a procedure in which target recognition levels were matched between amnesics and their controls by testing the patients under easier conditions (shorter delays, longer learning exposures, etc.), and then determining whether the two groups are still matched on target free recall or on various forms of context memory. If it is assumed that the matching manipulation does not have a greater effect on recognition than other memory measures, thereby producing the appearance of a disproportionate amnesic deficit artefactually, then a disconnection hypothesis cannot readily explain these results. The hypothesis is far too imprecise to see how a partial disconnection between an intact declarative/episodic memory system and a conscious awareness system can affect target free recall, and memory for independent and interactive context, more than target recognition memory.

Just as disconnection accounts of amnesia are purpose-built to explain preserved priming, so is the context-memory deficit hypothesis (see Mayes et al., 1985 for a review) purpose-built to explain disproportionately severe deficits in context-memory and, to a lesser extent, target free recall. The hypothesis states that amnesics have a primary, severe deficit in remembering contextual information and that this causes a secondary, less severe problem in the recognition of target information. As there is evidence that amnesics can encode at least certain kinds of context normally (Shoqeirat, 1989), poor memory for context probably arises because of a failure of consolidation or recollective retrieval. In contrast, the hypothesis implies that target information that was attended to during learning is consolidated into memory, but cannot be recognized because recollective recognition (although not the familiarity process postulated by Mandler (1980)) requires it to be associated with its independent and interactive contextual markers. Disproportionate free recall deficits in patients can be explained by analogy with context-dependent forgetting in normals, which typically occurs for free recall, but not recognition (Baddeley, 1982). The assumption is that contextual cues are important in accessing target information for recall, but that it is less important to associate targets with their contextual markers for recognition. Impaired recognition in amnesics can be explained because normal subjects' target recognition is disrupted by changes of interactive context between learning and test (Tulving & Thompson, 1973). Severe deficits in target recognition as well as recall may seem surprising on this account, but it should not be forgotten that the unavailability of aware memory for contextual information is postulated to be orders of magnitude worse in amnesics than it is in normal subjects who are being tested after a contextual shift.

Schacter (1990 and Chapter 9, this volume) has considered what he terms a second-order account of the unaware memory found in amnesia which seems equivalent to the context-memory deficit hypothesis. He supposes that aware memory for previously experienced items depends on the ability to associate those items with the time and place of their occurrence, and/or background semantic and associative information. The implication is that patients have a disrupted declarative/episodic memory system in which contextual information is not available, and that this causes a problem in remembering not only episodes, but also facts. Hirst (1989) has also argued that amnesics encode (presumably in the sense 'register and consolidate') content or target information, but not the 'larger context' in which this content falls. This failure affects free recall particularly badly because amnesics cannot relate different contents to each other and so cannot retrieve the desired content. The effect on recognition is less severe because the recognition cue minimizes any such search. Even recognition should be disrupted in patients, however, because items cannot be so readily related to their contexts. But priming should be preserved because it does not require any reference to be made to the episodic context in which targets occurred.

The sense in which context is used in these different expositions varies. Thus, whereas I have suggested that amnesics' primary problem may be in remembering all kinds of independent and interactive context, Schacter seems to focus more on spatiotemporal varieties of independent context and on information that may possibly correspond to interactive context, and Hirst believes that patients can manage to 'encode' context provided it falls within one 'snapshot' of psychological time, but cannot remember 'cross-snapshot' contextual features that help to define such things as list membership. It is hard however to see how Hirst's view can account for amnesics' disproportionate impairment in memory for the sensory modality via which recognized words were presented, because such information is processed within one 'snapshot'. Our evidence suggests that amnesics have disproportionate difficulties with both independent and interactive context, which seems to be more consistent with the accounts offered by Schacter and myself.

If any version of the context-memory deficit hypothesis of amnesia is correct, what implication does this have for amnesic priming? This will depend on what account of priming is correct and on what version of the context hypothesis is correct. First, if it is supposed that amnesics consolidate contextual information but have an impairment of intentional, effortful, memory processes so that they cannot recall or recognize context, then amnesic priming for all kinds of information should be normal regardless of whether priming requires the automatic retrieval of context or not. The predictions about priming made by this version of the context hypothesis do not therefore differ from those of the disconnection hypothesis. But the two hypotheses can be discriminated in terms of what they predict about disproportionate impairments for target recall and context memory.

Second, if amnesics fail to consolidate contextual information, and if perceptual and semantic priming do not depend on the automatic retrieval of contextual information, then one should expect amnesics to show normal priming for all kinds of previously familiar and previously novel target information, but not for contextual information. In contrast, if all kinds of priming depend on the automatic retrieval of contextual information, then amnesics should not be completely normal at any kind of priming. They should, however, be more impaired at priming to contextual information than they are at priming to target information. These predictions are, however, difficult to make precisely because it is not completely clear what is implied by the claim that priming depends on automatic retrieval from episodic memory. The implications depend on how, when and to what extent the automatic retrieval processes call on contextual information in order to produce normal perceptual and semantic priming.

Many researchers do not find it plausible that normal recall and recognition are so dependent on accessing the context of target information that an impairment of the ability to recall and recognize context could cause the severe deficits in target recall and recognition seen in some amnesics. Instead, they believe that amnesia is caused by failure to consolidate *all* those kinds of information which patients cannot readily recall or recognize. The most strongly supported variant of this hypothesis postulates that information critical to episodic and semantic memory is initially stored in structures damaged in amnesics, such as the hippocampus (Squire *et al.*, 1989; see Mayes, 1988 for a review). In time, this information, or something equivalent to it, is transferred to the association neocortex (Zola-Morgan & Squire, 1990). This means that amnesics will fail to store new information and will show retrograde amnesia for all information that has not already been transferred to association neocortex. Protagonists of this view either discount evidence of disproportionate impairments in target free recall and context memory in amnesics as artefactual, or they believe that their hypothesis can predict these impairments along the lines that target recall and context memory require more information to be stored per unit of time than does target recognition, and that this increased demand will cause the damaged 'consolidation' system to collapse, whereas a lighter load will not.

What does the general consolidation hypothesis of amnesia predict with respect to amnesic priming? Once again this depends on the correct account of priming. If priming does not depend on automatically accessing contextual information, then amnesics should show preserved priming for information that was familiar prior to the priming experience. This should occur because a memory representation already exists for this information, which merely needs to be reactivated in some way to produce normal priming. Information that was previously novel should not, however, show priming because amnesics are *ex hypothesi* unable to consolidate new information into long-term memory. In contrast to this, if all priming depends to some degree on the automatic retrieval of contextual information, then the general consolidation failure account of amnesia predicts that patients should not show preserved priming for either familiar or novel information.

All the predictions made in this section about amnesic priming by the different hypotheses of what causes the syndrome should be viewed with some caution. For example, it is implausible, but possible, to advance a view of priming which would allow it to be normal even when based on partially degraded memory traces. This might lead to the prediction that mild amnesics will show preserved priming of all kinds of information even if they suffer from a partial failure of consolidation. Nevertheless, the predictions constitute a 'best bet' given the current unarticulated state of theorizing about amnesia and priming. The next section will outline what is known about amnesic priming in order to determine how well the predictions of the different hypotheses are met. This should throw light both on the causes of amnesia and on the mechanisms that underlie priming.

11.4. CHARACTERISTICS OF AMNESIC PRIMING

A brief summary of the available evidence would state that amnesics appear to show preserved priming of target information that was previously familiar, show much less clear evidence of priming to previously novel verbal target information, and show relatively good evidence of preserved priming to novel nonverbal target information. Priming of various kinds of contextual information has been relatively untested and it remains unclear to what extent this kind of priming can be demonstrated even in normal subjects. This summary of current knowledge corresponds to that of Schacter (Chapter 9, this volume), but seems inconsistent with all current views of amnesia and priming, and indeed with any plausible view of these phenomena. This suggests, therefore, that it is a blurred reflection of the truth, and that a more detailed examination of available data may illuminate the nature of the blurring.

Priming for previously highly familiar and overlearned verbal information has often been shown to be preserved in amnesics. There is, for example, good evidence that word-completion priming (Graf *et al.*, 1984), free association priming with strongly related paired associates (Shimamura & Squire, 1984), and perceptual identification priming with words (Cermak *et al.*, 1988a,b) are completely preserved in amnesics. We have also found evidence that prior reading of lists of words facilitates subsequent reading of the lists to the same extent in amnesics with mixed aetiologies and controls, even when patients' baseline reading speeds are the same as those of their controls (Mayes *et al.*, in press).

All these examples are compatible with the idea that automatic access to target items is facilitated, so that they are processed more rapidly and fluently. But there are forms of priming of familiar verbal information that involve not only an increase in the ease of automatic access, but also an automatic attribution that is based on this increased fluency. One example of this kind of priming has been reported by Witherspoon and Allan (1985). They found that when words were shown twice, and very briefly on the second occasion, then subjects not only identified the words more accurately, but also tended to judge that they had been shown for longer than words seen only once. It seems likely that because of the context in which the judgement was made, subjects misattributed the greater ease of identifying repeated words to their having been shown for longer rather than to their familiarity. We have now tried this task with a group of amnesics of mixed aetiology and their matched controls, and found that the patients not only show preserved perceptual identification priming, but also preservation of the tendency to overestimate the exposure time of repeated words (Paller et al., in press). This is interesting because it suggests that, for certain kinds of material, patients both process repeated items more efficiently, and base an automatic attribution upon this to the same extent as do normal subjects. Jacoby and Kelley (Chapter 10, this volume) have argued that a very similar kind of automatic attribution underlies the familiarity process that can lead to recognition.

Although there have been several demonstrations of preserved amnesic priming of familiar verbal information, there have, to my knowledge, been no convincing demonstrations of normal priming of familiar non-verbal information. This is probably because it is hard to find instances of hard-to-verbalize yet highly familiar information. One exception is faces. We have recently adapted a task developed by Young and Roberts (see Roberts, 1988), which involves judging whether pairs of face pictures are of the same person or of two different people. The pairs comprised either two views of one famous person, or views of two different famous people. The famous peoples' faces were highly familiar to patients and their controls alike. It had been established previously that when these familiar face pairs were shown for a second time, then subjects made their 'same' or 'different' judgements faster than equivalent judgements that had not been primed. We found that amnesics were facilitated to the same extent as their controls even when the measure of priming was proportional (see Moscovitch et al., 1986), to allow for the fact that the amnesics' baseline rate for making the judgements was considerably slower.

The priming of familiar information in amnesics may throw some light on the question of whether they are more susceptible than normal subjects to proactive interference, and also on the role of contextual retrieval in such priming. Mayes et al. (1987) confirmed Shimamura and Squire's (1984) finding that amnesics show normal free association priming to strongly related word pairs. That is, when shown pairs like 'soldier–rifle' and later given the first word of the pair and asked to free associate to it, then patients tend, as much as controls, to produce the word that was earlier paired with it. Mayes et al. (1987) modified this task so that it involved an A–B, A–C combination using pairs like 'soldier–rifle' and 'soldier–army', with each list being presented five times before free association priming was tested. Korsakoff patients were found to show normal priming for list A–C as well as A–B. However, both groups showed proactive interference and primed much less to list A–C, producing intrusions from the A–B list. But when memory instructions were given, the controls showed no proactive interference for list A–C, whereas the amnesics showed as much as before, even though they were given five trials to the controls' one in order to match cued recall for list A–B. This suggested that the amnesics' greater susceptibility to proactive interference under memory instructions arises because they have to rely mainly on the same automatic processes that mediate priming, and these do not access the contextual information that distinguishes the A–B and A–C lists. In contrast, normal subjects can use recollective processes that access the contextual information that discriminates between the two lists.

In unpublished work, we have replicated these findings with a group of amnesics of mixed aetiology using a 20-min delay between the presentation of the two lists. In this second experiment, subjects were either trained on the two lists in a standard environment or in a distinctive one (the room had red walls illuminated by a red light, incense was burning, Indian music was playing and the word pair cards were written strikingly and presented on a lectern). The intention was to test an idea, derived from the work of Winocur and his colleagues (Winocur & Kinsbourne, 1978; Winocur *et al.*, 1987), that amnesic memory performance should be better when they learn in a distinctive context. If the idea was correct, then amnesics should retain contextual and other details of the A–B list better over the 20-min delay and this should mean that they show less interference with list A–C. There was no indication from our results that this was happening either with free association (priming) or cued recall instructions. There was, however, one significant interaction. Although the overall level of priming in the amnesics and their controls was the same, the control subjects showed more priming when learning in the distinctive environment whereas the amnesics tended to show (very) slightly more priming when learning in the ordinary environment. This suggests that background context interacts differently with the automatic processes that underlie priming in amnesics than it does in normal people. It could be that amnesics fail to store distinctive contextual information such that their priming can benefit from it. The possibility is important and needs to be more thoroughly investigated.

All the kinds of priming of familiar information that have been described, and for which amnesics show preservation, involved testing at delays of 2 h or less. If it is to be argued that priming is based on the same memory representation as aware memory, then it needs to be shown that priming of familiar information is preserved in amnesics at delays where aware memory is beginning to fade. Long-lasting priming tasks such as that of Mitchell and Brown (1988) therefore need to be tried with patients. There is another feature of priming that is also relevant to the issue of whether it and aware memory are based on the same memory representations. This relates to the relative amount of memory that is shown when memory for the same information is tapped by direct and indirect tests. The amount is more or less the same in amnesics, but with normal subjects far more is remembered with direct memory tests. For example, normal subjects remember far more words when given cued recall than word completion instructions whereas amnesics show little difference. The comparison is harder to make when the priming measure is one of speed of response, but the point is much the same. Amnesics show far less item priming than normal subjects show aware memory. This does not provide good evidence that amnesics have stored as much target information as normal people.

In unpublished work from my laboratory, Diamond has recently found evidence that amnesics may store information about recently encountered words to levels approaching those of normal people. Six amnesics with mixed aetiologies were compared with six matched controls on a task in which subjects heard 20 words being spoken, performed other tasks for 30 min, and were then given a Yes/No recognition test comprising the 20 old words and 20 foils. Skin conductance and heart rate was monitored in both the learning and test phases. The subjects' autonomic responses to the words at test were examined in order to determine whether there was significant autonomic discrimination between old and foil words. When significant discrimination occurred, the number of old and foil words to which an autonomic response was made was estimated, and a 'guessing corrected' score for autonomic discrimination was calculated. A guessing corrected score for overt recognition of the old words was also calculated in the same way. Autonomic discrimination of items has been used by several workers as a means of measuring indirect memory (for example, see Bauer, 1984). In Diamond's study, whereas the amnesics were very impaired at recognizing the old words, their autonomic discrimination was actually non-significantly better than that of their control subjects. More importantly, their autonomic discrimination of the old words was non-significantly worse than the control subjects' recognition judgements. It would appear that when priming of familiar material is measured in this way amnesics remember as much as normal people, irrespective of whether the normals' memory is measured directly or indirectly. Thus it could be that behavioural priming tasks significantly underestimate memory strength. The autonomic measurement procedure should therefore also be applied to tasks that involve the learning of *novel* material in order to determine the generality of the effect found by Diamond.

As Schacter (Chapter 9, this volume) indicates, evidence of preserved priming for novel verbal information in amnesics is not good. Schacter mentions the study by Moscovitch *et al.* (1986), which found that amnesics displayed a normal degree of reading speed-up for new associations between words, but mentions that an unpublished study by Squire fails to replicate this effect. It is difficult to assess this conflict without more detailed information, but we have found that amnesics' reading speeds up to a normal degree when they repeatedly read lists of pronounceable non-words (Mayes *et al.*, in press). This effect was found even with amnesics whose baseline reading speeds for the non-words were as fast as those of their controls. It is plausible to argue that this preserved priming shown by the patients was for information that had been novel prior to the training. If it is harder to find preserved priming in amnesics for novel associations between words, this might be because the facilitation in normal subjects is partially mediated by the use of recollective memory processes unavailable to the patients.

In further studies, we have failed to find evidence of priming in amnesics using two tasks in which performance depends on memory for new associations between words. In the first study, Paller (unpublished) compared the performance of 12 amnesics with mixed aetiologies with that of 12 matched control subjects on a perceptual identification priming task. In this task, subjects encoded novel word associates such as 'Baby–Bishop', both by rating the imageability of sentences such as 'The plump BABY was sick on the BISHOP' and by judging which of the objects named by the associated words was bigger. In the test phase, subjects were asked to read the two words that were presented in alternation with three stimulus masks (for example, Mask–Baby–Mask–Bishop–Mask). Presentation durations were adjusted so that identification of the first word was easy, but that of the second word was difficult. In young subjects and in the amnesics' control subjects, identification of the second word was significantly better when it was preceded by the word with which it had been studied (same condition) rather than by a word that had been paired with another from the study list (different condition). The amnesics were tested twice, several months apart, on this task. On neither occasion did they show significantly more priming in the same condition than the different condition, although they did show normal levels of perceptual identification priming for the repeated words themselves (familiar information priming). With this task, the question again arises of whether the amnesics are failing to show normal levels of priming to new verbal associations, or whether normal subjects' perceptual identification in the 'same' condition is partially mediated by recollective processes linked to aware memory. Although the aspects of the task related to memory are disguised, and the identification responses are made rapidly, this latter possibility is hard to exclude.

In the second study, Mayes and Gooding (1989) used the word-completion priming task developed by Graf and Schacter (1985). This task was designed to test the possibility that there is an enhancement in word-completion priming produced by pairing the word-stem cue with a word associated with it during learning (for example, 'BABY–BIS—'). Unlike Graf and Schacter (1985) and Cermak *et al.* (1988b), but like Shimamura and Squire (1989) and Cermak *et al.* (1988a), we found no evidence that our mixed-aetiology amnesic group of 17 patients showed any enhancement of word-completion priming as a result of memory for the new verbal associations. There was, however, some evidence that the degree of enhancement shown by individual patients correlated with how good their cued recall was for critical words. Once again, this raises the possibility that any enhancement of 'word-completion priming' shown by normal subjects (we found a significant improvement in our control group) may be mediated by aware memory for the associations. Although application of the retrieval intentionality criterion of Schacter *et al.* (1989) makes it unlikely that normal subjects are deliberately using recollective processes, the possibility that they occasionally use recollection unintentionally is a serious one. The fact that test unaware (see Schacter, Chapter 9, this volume) normal subjects fail to show any enhancement of word-completion performance is also consistent with any such enhancement effect being mediated by unintentional recollective processes. If all effects that apparently reveal normal priming to novel verbal associations actually depend on unintentional recollection, then amnesics will not have been shown to be impaired at such priming. Instead, one would have to explain why automatic memory processes are unable to operate on this kind of material.

There has been less exploration of priming of novel hard-to-verbalize materials, but with the tasks that have been used there is better evidence that amnesics show normal levels of priming. Given that amnesics have very little aware memory, this suggests that performance on these tasks must be mediated largely by automatic memory processes. In addition to the task involving judging whether drawings are of possible or impossible three-dimensional objects (Schacter, Chapter 9, this volume), we have, in currently unpublished studies, examined two tasks that seem to depend on the priming of novel nonverbal information.

The first of these tasks is the one used by Gabrieli *et al.* (1990) to show normal priming in the severely amnesic patient HM. This task can be viewed as a nonverbal equivalent of word-completion priming. Subjects were first shown a series of five dot arrays, derived from a nine dot matrix, and asked to join the dots in the first way that came to mind in order to get a baseline. Following a delay, drawings, produced by joining the dots, were studied and subjects were asked to copy them. After a 3-min delay subjects were once more asked to join the dots in the first way that came to mind. Using this procedure, Gooding (unpublished) examined the performance of 10 amnesics with mixed aetiologies and found that, unlike HM, they just failed to reveal significant priming when priming was scored as the number of drawings they completed 'correctly' above their baseline levels. However, when priming was scored as the number of 'correct' lines minus the number of incorrect lines, then the patients showed significant priming, and to the same degree as their matched control subjects. Interestingly, there was a suggestion that patients with more severe amnesia did better on this task, so aware memory may have actually been hampering performance in the milder amnesics. Although this relationship did not apply to the normal subjects, the possibility that even *their* priming performance was hindered by aware memory cannot be discounted. If the level of automatic memory as well as the level of recollection could be directly calculated, as Jacoby and Kelley (Chapter 10, this volume) argue can be done, then comparison between amnesics and normal subjects on this task would be greatly helped.

The second task we have used is the one already described that requires subjects to judge whether face pairs belong to the same or different people. In addition to testing subjects with famous faces we also tested them with unfamiliar ones. Although response time did not decrease as much on re-exposure as it did with the famous faces, the amnesics still showed as much priming as their control subjects with the unfamiliar faces. As with many priming tasks, the effects were small and the amnesics did show slightly (although non-significantly) less priming than their controls. This relates to a general concern about the whole field. One would be happier if more priming effects were not only robust, but large, and amnesics showed, if anything, larger effects than their controls.

Section 11.3 placed considerable stress on the importance of determining whether or not priming of contextual information is preserved in amnesia, and indeed, whether such priming occurs in normal subjects. Evidence of automatic access to contextual information can either be gained directly or more inferentially. An example of the latter approach was provided earlier in this section when I described the free association priming task set in both ordinary and distinctive environments. More generally, attempts can be made to reduce priming by changing contextual features between learning and test. Unfortunately, it is unclear that a change of independent context without a concomitant change in interactive context is sufficient to have any effect on priming. Until such an effect is found robustly in normal subjects, one cannot ask whether amnesics show the effect to the same degree. For example, in my laboratory, Gooding has developed a speed copying task in which subjects copy shapes similar to those used by Gabrieli *et al.* (1990). In both amnesics and controls copying is faster on the second occasion that the shapes are copied, although the speed-up may not be completely normal in all amnesic patients. The shapes are embedded in object drawings, and these can either be changed or left the same between first and second copying. Contextual change significantly reduces the amount of facilitation found in young subjects, and, to a lesser extent, in amnesics and their controls.

There have been two groups of studies of preserved priming in memory-impaired patients of what appears to be contextual information. First, Vakil *et al.* (1991) showed that the ability of closed head-injury patients to reproduce the order of a list of 15 words was impaired when subjects were given the words and explicitly told to put them in the correct order. However, when subjects were simply told to recall as many words from the list as possible, then they tended to recall them in the same order as that used during learning presentations. This effect, which presumably depends on automatic access to temporal order information, was significant and as large in the closed head-injury patients as their controls. Nevertheless, one cannot exclude the possibility that the normal subjects' performance was inhibited by the use of other retrieval strategies to a greater extent than was the patients' performance. In the second group of studies, Nissen and Bullemer (1987), and later Nissen *et al.* (1989), gave subjects a serial reaction time task comprising a 10-trial stimulus sequence. Korsakoff patients became faster at reacting to repeated sequences even though they failed to recognize that they had seen them before. Furthermore, the patients appeared to retain quite normally their ability to react faster to the repeating sequences over a period of 1 week. Performance on this task would seem to depend on automatic access to some kind of spatiotemporal memory about the order in which stimuli are presented. Even if the task depends on automatic access to information about independent context, however, it is unclear that this information is being stored in association cortex. It might, for example, be represented in the basal ganglia because it requires the formation of perceptuomotor links (see Willingham *et al.*, 1989), in which case its relevance to the hypotheses about the causes of amnesia, discussed in the previous section, is unclear.

11.5. CONCLUSIONS

The simplest conclusion from the above results is that amnesics do seem to show normal levels of automatic memory to certain kinds of information for which they have very impaired recognition and recall. It is too early, however, to claim that they show preserved automatic memory for all kinds of information, and particularly for novel targets and context. It is also unclear how long their automatic memory lasts relative to normal peoples' effortful memory. Finally, it is uncertain whether amnesics store as much information as do normal people.

To resolve these issues two things need to be done. First, more tasks need to be developed that tap automatic memory for novel kinds of target and contextual information. These tasks should show robust, long-lasting priming in normal people. Second, the procedure proposed by Jacoby and Kelley (Chapter 10, this volume), or equivalent procedures, need to be applied in order to get independent estimates of the influence of automatic and effortful memory in patients and controls, using modifications of the priming tasks that have already been examined in these subjects. This is important wherever there is doubt about whether a 'priming' task depends only on automatic memory processes (this includes just about every task!). In principle, the procedure discussed by Jacoby and Kelley can be applied to any priming task where the measure is accuracy of response. Where the measure is speed of response the procedure cannot be used in any straightforward fashion.

Application of the procedure can be illustrated by two tasks. The first was adapted for use with amnesics by McAndrews *et al.* (1987) and is of considerable interest because it demonstrates memory for novel verbal target information in severe amnesics after a delay of 1 week. Their memory was not as good as that of milder amnesics or normal control subjects, however, because performance in the subjects with the better memories probably depended on recollective processes more than automatic ones. The task involved asking subjects to interpret incomprehensible sentences like 'The person was unhappy because the hole closed' and if they failed, supplying them with an explanatory phrase ('pierced ears' with the example here). Subjects were later presented with the sentences again, intermixed with new ones, and once more asked to supply an interpretation. Amnesics were able to provide interpretations for the old sentences even though their aware memory for these sentences was minimal. The contribution of an automatic familiarity process to this ability might be assessed by asking subjects to throw out an interpretation quickly, and then to indicate whether they had remembered this or generated it for themselves. This would enable an inclusion and exclusion score to be calculated, from which levels of automatic memory and recollection could be derived.

The second task that can be used to illustrate the application of the procedure outlined by Jacoby and Kelley is the word completion priming task involving new associations, as used by Graf and Schacter (1985). An inclusion procedure for this task simply asks subjects at the test stage to try and remember the words shown to them during learning and if they cannot, to have a guess (i.e. produce the first word that comes to mind). For the exclusion condition, subjects are told to produce the first word that comes to mind provided they do not remember it as the one they were shown earlier. Gooding (unpublished data) has run a preliminary version of this task with a group of 12 amnesics of mixed aetiology and their matched controls. The levels of automatic memory for the words themselves were estimated for the patients and their controls and found to be identical. Neither group showed any automatic memory enhancement based on the new verbal associations, however, although the control subjects did show considerably more *recollection* based on the new associations. The validity of these estimates depends on several assumptions, one of which is that subjects do not change their recognition criteria between the inclusion and exclusion conditions. We are currently checking this possibility. If the estimates are valid, this would mean that enhanced word completion in this task depends on aware memory and not automatic, unaware, memory.

Jacoby and Kelley illustrate their procedure by estimating the relative strengths of familiarity (automatic) and recollection (effortful) processes. These are discussed with respect to aware memory and, in particular recognition. The examples I have employed use the procedure to estimate an automatic unaware kind of memory that I have dubbed somewhat inappropriately as priming. If automatic processes are sufficient to yield recognition (and even perhaps cued and free recall under certain circumstances), then one would expect amnesics to be less impaired in the familiarity component of recognition than they are in the recollective component (or even, in the case of mild amnesics, not impaired at all in the familiarity component). If amnesics do show preservation of 'attributional priming', then the views of Jacoby and Kelley carry an important implication. This is that it may be possible, through the use of feedback, to train amnesics to make attributions of familiarity on the basis of more fluent processing of previously experienced items.

Before doing this however, it is important to determine whether the familiarity process is indeed less impaired than recollection in amnesia. If this is the case, then one might expect amnesics to show less disruption of their recognition than do normal people when memory is tested under divided attention conditions. This would be expected because (as Jacoby and Kelley discuss) recollection is disrupted by the division of attention whereas familiarity processes may not be. As Gardiner and Java (1990) have produced evidence to show that the normal recognition advantage for low frequency words depends solely on the ability to recollect such words better than common words (thus identifying where they were encountered), one would also expect amnesics to show much less recognition advantage for low frequency words than do their control subjects. It is, however, the procedure outlined by Jacoby and Kelley that provides the 'royal road' for determining whether or not amnesics are less impaired (or even unimpaired) at familiarity processes than they are at recollection. By applying this procedure to both recognition and priming tasks in patients and controls it should also be possible to determine the relationship between the automatic processes that mediate performance in both kinds of task.

REFERENCES

Allen, S.W. & Jacoby, L.L. (1990). Reinstating study context produces unconscious influences of memory. *Memory and Cognition*, **18**, 270–278.

Baddeley, A.D. (1982). Domains of recollection. *Psychological Review*, **89**, 708–729.

Bauer, R.M. (1984). Autonomic recognition of names and faces in prosopagnosia: A neuropsychological application of the guilty knowledge test. *Neuropsychologia*, **22**, 457–469.

Cermak, L.S., Bleich, R.P. & Blackford, S.P. (1988a). Deficits in the implicit retention of new associations by alcoholic Korsakoff patients. *Brain and Cognition*, **7**, 145–156.

Cermak, L.S., Blackford, S.P., O'Connor, M. & Bleich, R.P. (1988b) The implicit memory ability of a patient with amnesia due to encephalitis. *Brain and Cognition*, **7**, 145–156.

Daum, I., Channon, S. & Canavan, A.G.M. (1989). Classical conditioning in patients with severe memory problems. *Journal of Neurology, Neurosurgery and Psychiatry*, **52**, 47–51.

Ellis, A.W., Young, A.W. & Flude, B.M. (1990). Repetition priming and face processing: Priming occurs within the system that responds to the identity of a face. *Quarterly Journal of Experimental Psychology*, **42A**, 495–512.

Gabrieli, J.D.E., Milberg, W., Keane, M.M. & Corkin, S. (1990). Intact priming of patterns despite impaired memory. *Neuropsychologia*, **28**, 417–427.

Gardiner, J.M. & Java, R.I. (1990). Recollective experience in word and nonword recognition. *Memory and Cognition*, **18**, 23–30.

Graf, P. & Schacter, D.L. (1985). Implicit and explicit memory for new associations in normal and amnesic subjects. *Journal of Experimental Psychology: Learning, Memory and Cognition*, **2**, 501–518.

Graf, P., Mandler, G. & Haden, P. (1982). Simulating amnesic symptoms in normal subjects. *Science*, **218**, 1243–1244.

Graf, P., Squire, L.R. & Mandler, G. (1984). The information that amnesic patients do not forget. *Journal of Experimental Psychology: Learning, Memory and Cognition*, **10**, 164–178.

Hirst, W. (1989). On consciousness, recall, recognition, and the architecture of memory. In S. Lewandowsky, J.C. Dunn & K. Kirsner (eds), *Implicit Memory: Theoretical Issues*. Hillsdale, NJ: Erlbaum.

Hirst, W., Johnson, M.K., Kim, J.K., Phelps, E.A., Risse, G. & Volpe, B.T. (1986). Recognition and recall in amnesics. *Journal of Experimental Psychology: Learning, Memory and Cognition*, 445–451.

Hirst, W., Johnson, M.K., Phelps, E.A. & Volpe, B.T. (1988). More on recognition and recall in amnesics. *Journal of Experimental Psychology: Learning, Memory and Cognition*, **14**, 758–762.

Jones, G.V. (1983). Structure of the recall process. In D.E. Broadbent (ed.), *Functional Aspects of Human Memory*, London: The Royal Society.

Lewandowsky, S., Kirsner, K. & Bainbridge, V. (1989). Context effects in implicit memory: A sense-specific account. In S. Lewandowsky, J.C. Dunn and K. Kirsner (eds), *Implicit Memory: Theoretical Issues*. Hillsdale, NJ: Erlbaum.

Lye, R.H., O'Boyle, D.J.O. Ramsden, R.T. & Schady, W. (1988). Effects of a unilateral cerebellar lesion on the acquisition of eye-blink conditioning in man. *Journal of Physiology*, **403**, 58P.

Mandler, G. (1980). Recognizing: The judgement of previous occurrence. *Psychological Review*, **87**, 252–271.

Mandler, G., Hamson, C.O. & Dorfman, J. (1990). Tests of dual process theory: Word priming and recognition. *Quarterly Journal of Experimental Psychology*, **42A**, 713–739.

Mayes A.R. (1988). *Human Organic Memory Disorders*. Cambridge: Cambridge University Press.

Mayes, A.R. & Gooding, P. (1989) Enhancement of word completion priming in amnesics by cueing with previously novel associates. *Neuropsychologia*, **27**, 1057–1072.

Mayes, A.R., Meudell, P.R. & Pickering, A.D. (1985) Is organic amnesia caused by a selective deficit in remembering contextual information? *Cortex*, **21**, 313–324.

Mayes, A.R., Pickering, A.D. & Fairbairn, A. (1987). Amnesic sensitivity to proactive interference: its relationship to priming and the causes of amnesia. *Neuropsychologia*, **25**, 211–220.

Mayes, A.R., Poole, V. & Gooding, P. (1991). Increased reading speed for words and pronounceable nonwords. *Cortex*, in press.

McAndrews, M.P., Glisky, E.L. & Schacter, D.L. (1987) When priming persists: long-lasting implicit memory for a single episode in amnesics patients. *Neuropsychologia*, **25**, 497–506.

Mishkin, M., Malamut, B. & Bachevalier, J. (1984). Memories and habits: Two neural systems. In J.L. McGaugh, G. Lynch and N. Weinberger (eds), *The Neurobiology of Learning and Memory*. New York: Guilford Press.

Mitchell, D.B. & Brown, A.S. (1988). Persistent repetition priming in picture naming and its dissociation from recognition memory. *Journal of Experimental Psychology: Learning, Memory and Cognition*, **14**, 213–222.

Moscovitch, M., Winocur, G. & McLachlan, D. (1986) Memory as assessed by recognition and reading time in normal and memory-impaired people with Alzheimer's disease and other neurological disorders. *Journal of Experimental Psychology: Learning, Memory and Cognition*, **115**, 331–347.

Nissen, M.J. and Bullemer, P. (1987). Attentional requirements of learning: Evidence from performance measures. *Cognitive Psychology*, **19**, 1–32.

Nissen, M.J., Willingham, D. & Hartman, M. (1989). Explicit and implicit remembering: when is learning preserved in amnesia? *Neuropsychologia*, **27**, 341–352.

Paller, K.A., Mayes, A.R., McDermott, M., Pickering, A.D. & Meudell, P.R. (1991). Indirect measures of memory in a memory duration-judgement task are normal in amnesic patients. *Neuropsychologia*, in press.

Pickering, A.D., Mayes, A.R. & Fairbairn, A.F. (1989). Amnesia and memory for modality information. *Neuropsychologia*, **27**, 1249–1259.

Roberts, J. (1988) A new method of testing implicit memory in normal and amnesic subjects. MSc Thesis, University of Lancaster.

Schacter, D.L. (1990). Toward a cognitive neuropsychology of awareness: implicit knowledge and anosognosia. *Journal of Clinical and Experimental Neuropsychology*, **12**, 155–178.

Schacter, D.L. Bowers, J. & Booker, J. (1989). Intention, awareness, and implicit memory: The retrieval intentionality criterion. In S. Lewandowsky, J.C. Dunn and K. Kirsner (eds), *Implicit Memory: Theoretical Issues*, Hillsdale, NJ: Erlbaum.

Shimamura, A.P. (1989). Disorders of memory: the cognitive science perspective. In F. Boller and J. Grafman (eds), *Handbook of Neuropsychology*, Vol. 3. Amsterdam: Elsevier.

Shimamura, A.P. & Squire, L.R. (1984). Paired-associate learning and priming effects in amnesia: a neuropsychological study. *Journal of Experimental Psychology: General*, **113**, 556–570.

Shimamura, A.P. & Squire, L.R. (1989). Impaired learning of new associations in amnesia. *Journal of Experimental Psychology: Learning, Memory and Cognition,* **14**, 763–769.

Shimamura, A.P., Salmon, D.P., Squire, L.R. & Butters, N. (1987). Memory dysfunction and word priming in dementia and amnesia. *Behavioral Neuroscience,* **101**, 347–351.

Shoqeirat, M. (1989). Contextual memory deficits and rate of forgetting in amnesics with different aetiologies. PhD Thesis, University of Manchester.

Squire, L.R., Shimamura, A.P. & Amaral, D.G. (1989) Memory and the hippocampus. In J. Byrne and W. Berry (eds), *Neural Models of Plasticity.* New York: Academic Press.

Tulving, E. & Schacter, D.L. (1990) Priming and human memory systems. *Science,* **247**, 301–306.

Tulving, E. & Thompson, D.M. (1973). Encoding specificity and retrieval processes in episodic memory. *Psychological Review,* **80**, 352–373.

Vakil, E., Blachstein, H. & Hoofien, D. (1991). Automatic temporal order judgment: The effect of intentionality of retrieval on closed-head injured patients. *Journal of Clinical and Experimental Neuropsychology,* in press.

Weiskrantz, L. & Warrington, E.K. (1979). Conditioning in amnesic patients. *Neuropsychologia,* **17**, 187–194.

Willingham, D.B., Nissen, M.J. & Bullemer, P. (1989). On the development of procedural knowledge. *Journal of Experimental Psychology: Learning Memory and Cognition,* **15**, 1047–1060.

Winocur, G. & Kinsbourne, M. (1978) Contextual cueing as an aid to Korsakoff amnesics. *Neuropsychologia,* **16**, 671–682.

Winocur, G., Moscovitch, M. & Witherspoon, D. (1987). Contextual cuing and memory performance in brain-damaged amnesics and old people. *Brain and Cognition,* **6**, 129–141.

Witherspoon, D. & Allan, L. G. (1985). The effects of a prior presentation on temporal judgments in a perceptual identification task. *Memory and Cognition,* **13**, 101–111.

Zola-Morgan, S. & Squire, L.R. (1990). The primate hippocampal formation: evidence for a time-limited role in memory storage. *Science,* **250**, 288–290.

CHAPTER 12

Conscious and Unconscious Processes in Language and Memory—Commentary

Michael D. Rugg

12.1. INTRODUCTION

The distinction between conscious and unconscious influences on behaviour has, in one form or another, been central to neuropsychological research on memory for some considerable time. In contrast, the distinction has received little attention in studies of the breakdown of auditory and written language following brain damage, despite the huge literature on these subjects reaching back well into the last century. This imbalance is reflected in the preceding four chapters—whereas the three contributions on memory are firmly rooted in an extensive empirical and theoretical literature, that on language disorders presents and discusses new empirical findings in the context of a very much sparser background.

The present chapter attempts an overview of some of the issues raised by the preceding four contributions. Whenever possible, a distinction has been maintained between types of task and types of process. In line with many others (e.g. Richardson-Klavehn & Bjork, 1988; Humphreys et al., Chapter 3, this volume; Jacoby & Kelley, Chapter 10, this volume; Young & De Haan, Chapter 4, this volume), a division is drawn between direct and indirect tests: in a direct test the instructions make specific reference to the need to exercise a given ability, and performance is dependent on that ability. In an indirect test assessment is incidental, using a task on which performance will be influenced by, but is not directly dependent upon, the ability in question. The two types of process that (it is hoped!) are differentially tapped by these tasks have been given a variety of dichotomous labels: explicit versus implicit, aware versus unaware, conscious versus unconscious, overt versus covert, to name but a few. All of these are intended to capture the distinction between processing of which the subject is in some sense aware, and about which he or she can frame a verbal report, and processing that is reflected in behaviour in the absence of a corresponding change in the content of awareness. In the following sections the terms *explicit* and *implicit*, arguably in widest use at present, will usually be employed to denote these two types of processing.

It is worth noting that the foregoing definition of explicit processing does not differentiate between awareness of a process, and awareness of its *outcome*, although this seems, at least in principle, to be a meaningful distinction. In practice, the term would appear to be used mainly to refer to awareness of the outcome of processing. For example, in saying that a face has been recognized explicitly, no implication is usually intended that the perceptual/cognitive processes that underlie face recognition form part of the phenomenal experience of that face.

12.2. DISORDERS OF LANGUAGE

Tyler (Chapter 8, this volume) redresses the lack of attention paid in the past to distinctions between the different ways that tasks can tap language competence. Whereas the distinction she draws between implicit (i.e. indirect) and explicit (i.e. direct) tasks is framed in a conventional, relatively atheoretical way, other task distinctions are more closely tied to a particular class of theory of language processing. An important theoretical division is drawn between the 'intermediate' and 'final' representations that are formed in the course of the processing of an utterance, only the latter being directly available to awareness. Intermediate representations and the processes leading to their formation can be studied in two ways: (a) with indirect *on-line* tasks—tasks in which responses to target features are made so rapidly that slower-acting conscious processes, reliant on the formation of final representations, have no influence, and (b) with direct tasks that are sensitive to 'interrupts' generated when the automatic processes producing intermediate representations fail to run to completion (as with some kinds of grammatical anomaly). Tyler provides evidence that dissociations can be found between performance on both types of task and that on more conventional tests of linguistic competence (*off-line* tasks). These dissociations are interpreted as evidence that the processing leading to the formation of intermediate linguistic representations can be normal or near normal in at least some severely aphasic patients.

The classification of tasks put forward by Tyler has the merit of being integrated with a well-articulated theory of normal language processing. But even within the context of the theory, it is not obvious how dissociations between performance on on-line as opposed to off-line tasks should be interpreted. Although intact on-line performance may be possible on the basis of intermediate level representations only, this does not rule out the possibility that final representations are also created normally, but that conscious access to them cannot be achieved. Such data therefore do not distinguish between comprehension deficits caused by the inability to fully process linguistic input to the highest level, and deficits resulting from the inability to access the end products of normally processed input. Distinguishing between these alternatives will require the development of tasks that tap implicit processing dependent on final rather than intermediate level representations.

The theory outlined by Tyler predicts that while normal implicit processing of speech input can co-exist with deficits in explicit processing, the reverse dissociation cannot occur (other than for the reasons noted in her chapter). This is because according to the theory, the representations supporting explicit processing are causally dependent on those responsible for implicit processing. Therefore, to the extent that the theory is correct, 'classical' double dissociations between performance on on-line and off-line tasks will never be found. But single dissociations between tasks are susceptible to the criticism that the tasks merely differ with respect to difficulty or sensitivity (indeed, even 'classical' double dissociations are not necessarily immune from such criticisms). [1] In the present context for example, it might be argued that on-line tasks require less processing resources than off-line ones, or are simply more sensitive to residual linguistic abilities. While the co-occurrence of normal on-line performance and grossly abnormal off-line performance might make this explanation unlikely, it does not rule it out; the precise relationship between performance on two tasks will depend on the tasks' respective 'performance-resource functions' (Shallice, 1988). A possible way forward is to parametrically vary the difficulty of each type of task, and thus to 'sample' performance at more than one point on the relevant performance-resource functions (cf. Dunn & Kirsner, 1988a). If performance remains normal over wide variations in difficulty in one kind of task, but is never normal on the other, it is unlikely that the dissociations between the tasks result from what Shallice (1988) has termed 'resource artefacts'.

Dissociations between conscious and unconscious processing of linguistic input have also been described in cases of the acquired reading disorder pure alexia (also referred to as letter-by-letter reading, alexia without agraphia, and word-form dyslexia). In this syndrome, patients are able to read words aloud only by the serial identification of individual letters (letter-by-letter reading), having seemingly lost the ability to rapidly process letter strings in parallel (e.g. Warrington & Shallice, 1980; Patterson & Kay, 1982). The reading speed of these patients is therefore very slow, and increases linearly with word length. The functional locus of the impairment in pure alexia is uncertain: by one account (Warrington & Shallice, 1980), the syndrome arises when the 'visual word form system' is damaged, forcing the patient to identify letters one at a time and then to employ a 'reverse spelling' procedure. An alternative explanation (Patterson & Kay, 1982) proposes that the locus of the impairment is not in the visual word form system, but in the transmission of letter identities to that system. Whereas the normal mode of transmission is parallel, in letter-by-letter readers it is serial.

The first detailed description of implicit word processing in pure alexia came from a single case study by Shallice and Saffran (1986; see that paper and Coslett & Saffran, 1989 for reviews of earlier work). Their patient took on average almost 4 s to read aloud three-letter words, and at an exposure duration of 2 s, he could correctly report three out of 12 four-letter words, three out of 12 six-letter words, and none out of 12 eight-letter words. Yet at the same exposure duration his lexical decision performance (between words and non-words that differed by one or two letters from real words) for items of five or more letters was reliably above chance, and occurred in the virtual absence of explicit identification of the items. In other experiments, the patient was found also to perform above chance on a variety of forced-choice tests of semantic categorization. In a subsequent study, Coslett and Saffran (1989) described a very similar pattern of performance in a further four cases of pure alexia. Coslett and Saffran demonstrated that unlike their oral reading, these patients' lexical decision performance was un- affected by word length (at least over the range of three- to five-letter words), and further showed that performance on forced choice semantic categorization was unlikely to reflect guessing strategies based on identification of the words' initial letters. Coslett and Saffran empha- sized the disparity between the patients' behaviour and reported sub- jective experience while performing forced choice tasks; reminiscent of 'blindsight' patients (Cowey & Stoerig, Chapter 2, this volume), all felt that they were merely guessing, and expressed 'surprise and consternation' (Coslett & Saffran, 1989, p. 337) when informed that their performance was above chance.

Shallice and Saffran (1986) considered two alternative explanations for their patient's ability to recognize words without awareness. Implicit word recognition might be mediated by the same or a sub-set of the pro- cesses that also mediate explicit reading but in a manner that prevents the products of such processing from entering awareness (e.g. because of sub-threshold activation of lexical representations). Alternatively, implicit word recognition might reflect the function of a second reading system, independent of the one underlying explicit reading. In the view of Shallice and Saffran (1986), a promising candidate in this respect is the reading system of the right hemisphere.

Discussion of these alternative explanations was continued by Coslett and Saffran (1989). They noted that of the three patients whose explicit reading showed some recovery, all showed patterns of reading consis- tent with what might be expected of a right hemisphere reading system (see Baynes, 1990 for a review), for example, better reading of high than of low imageability words. These observations led Coslett and Saffran to suggest that recovery in these patients was based on the increasing capacity of their right hemispheres to support explicit reading, and that this capacity evolved from processes that initially supported only implicit processing. Thus by this view, not only does implicit word recognition in pure alexia rely on a system neuroanatomically and functionally distinct from the one supporting residual explicit reading (at least initially), but in some circumstances the functioning of this system can become accessible to awareness.

The 'right hemisphere' hypothesis of implicit reading in pure alexia is consistent with the classical neurological account of this syndrome (Déjerine, 1892), which proposes that the alexia arises because of a disconnection between an intact right hemisphere and a 'reading centre' in the posterior region of the left hemisphere. However, the hypothesis has difficulty explaining why evidence of implicit word recognition is not found in all cases of pure alexia who have intact right hemispheres (e.g. the four patients described by Patterson & Kay [1982] were all at or near chance for lexical decisions on briefly presented items). Coslett and Saffran suggest two possible reasons: first, not all individuals possess competent right hemisphere reading systems and second, implicit word recognition may depend critically on the strategy adopted to perform the task—patients may need to be strongly encouraged to forsake any reliance on their residual explicit reading skills, and instead just to 'guess'. Clearly, few findings could refute the combination of these two hypotheses! (see also Baynes, 1990). A further problem with the 'right hemisphere hypothesis' is that it is based to a large extent on the pattern of *explicit* reading performance exhibited by recovered patients. Even if recovered explicit reading is mediated by a right hemisphere system, it is not clear that this must also be true of implicit reading prior to recovery.

One way this question might be resolved is by further characterization of what letter-by-letter readers can and cannot read implicitly; do they, for example, show imageability or part of speech effects, as would be predicted by the right hemisphere hypothesis? Another way to address the question would be to use priming procedures to investigate whether the systems mediating implicit and explicit reading interact. Using a procedure in which prime words were exposed for as long as it took the patient to read them, Schacter *et al.* (1990) demonstrated that letter-by-letter reading can benefit from repetition priming. By modifying the procedure to include prime durations too short for explicit identification, it should be possible to determine whether the implicit processing of a word can prime its subsequent explicit recognition. If it can, this would arguably pose problems for the hypothesis that implicit word recognition in pure alexia relies on a system independent of the one mediating explicit reading in these patients.

Studies of pure alexia with indirect tests would also be of interest because they would allow the functional properties of implicit word recognition to be more closely compared with those of implicit face recognition in prosopagnosia. Behavioural evidence for implicit face recognition in prosopagnosic patients has come almost entirely from their performance on indirect tasks, the same patients performing at chance on forced choice tasks ostensibly tapping the same knowledge (e.g. discriminating familiar from unfamiliar faces; Young & De Haan, Chapter 4, this volume). This contrasts with the situation in pure alexia in which evidence for implicit processing comes almost exclusively from findings of above-chance performance, without acknowledged recognition of the test stimuli, on forced choice tasks such as lexical decision. If divergences are also found between the performance of pure alexic and prosopagnosic patients on comparable indirect tests, this would suggest that implicit recognition in the two disorders depends on qualitatively different kinds of mechanism.

If correct, Coslett and Saffran's (1989) hypothesis that the processes supporting implicit word recognition can over time come to support explicit reading might have important general implications. The elucidation of the changes that underlie the evolution from unaware to aware reading might offer important clues as to what it is that allows the products of any cognitive process to enter awareness. And establishing that a transition from unaware to aware processing can occur for one cognitive ability would offer hope that similar transitions could be induced in others, with potentially important consequences for the rehabilitation of a range of cognitive disorders (see also Young & De Haan, Chapter 4, this volume).

12.3. MEMORY AND AMNESIA

The three chapters on memory leave little doubt about the relative maturity of the work in this field, and of the success with which research on normal subjects has been integrated with that on amnesic patients. One dominant theme that emerges is how best to interpret the dissociations, demonstrable both in amnesics and normals, between performance on direct and indirect tests of memory.[1] This issue is currently focused on whether these dissociations should be taken as evidence for the existence of multiple memory systems, with differing principles of operation, differing levels of access to awareness, and different functional roles (a 'second-order account'; Schacter, Chapter 9, this volume), or rather as being indicative of the separability of memory processes from systems that interpret and use the products of such processes in the conscious control of behaviour (a 'first order account'; Schacter, Chapter 9, this volume).

Whether memories for different kinds of material, or expressions of memory on different tasks, rely on different *neural* systems is not at issue; there is neuropsychological evidence both for material-specific deficits on direct memory tests (e.g. Smith, 1989), and for dissociations between performance on different indirect tests thought to tap implicit memory equally 'purely' (e.g. Heindel *et al.*, 1989). But are these neurologically dissociable systems also *functionally* dissociable, in the sense that they exhibit qualitatively different principles of operation in respect of properties such as contextual specificity, access to awareness, etc? Schacter favours a qualitative distinction between memories reliant on modules or sub-systems of the 'perceptual representation system', and memories represented by a more general episodic system, largely on the grounds that the two types of system are differentially sensitive to contextual factors. By contrast, the framework of Jacoby and Kelley (Chapter 10, this volume) assumes that *all* experience is represented in an instance-based, contextually specific fashion, and that distinctions should be drawn not between functionally distinct memory systems or stores, but between the different modes by which memories can be retrieved, and the uses to which the products of retrieval can be put (see also Masson, 1988; Roediger *et al.*, 1989; Roediger, 1990).

As is evident from the contributions, the 'systems versus processes' debate has yet to be resolved. The contributions point to two main lines of evidence relevant to the debate: the ability of amnesic patients to demonstrate implicit memory for novel information (that is, material such as nonwords, for which no memory representation would have existed premorbidly), and the sensitivity of implicit memory to contextual factors. If amnesics are unable to show implicit memory for novel items, this could be regarded as damaging for the view that, other than for a deficit in conscious recollection, amnesic memory operates similarly to that of normal subjects. In fact the evidence points in the opposite direction, in that amnesic subjects do show implicit retention of at least some kinds of novel information (i.e. visually presented nonverbal stimuli; see Chapters 9 and 11, this volume, by Schacter and Mayes). This does not however necessarily cause embarrassment for the position advocated by Schacter (Chapter 9, this volume). The perceptual representation system is conceived of as being able to create new representations on the basis of a single instance of a novel item, provided the item conforms to the computational constraints of the relevant sub-system (e.g. orthographic legality in the case of the word form system, possible real-world object in the case of the structural description system, etc.). This flexibility allows such systems to exhibit implicit memory for at least certain kinds of novel information.

As discussed in detail by Mayes, a more critical factor in deciding whether memories expressed on direct and indirect tests are functionally equivalent might be their relative sensitivity to context. In Schacter's framework, the information represented in the perceptual representation system, and responsible in large part for implicit memory, is context free; indeed, independence from spatio-temporal context is a major factor preventing such information from being consciously accessible. In contrast, Jacoby and Kelley (Chapter 10, this volume) view the issues of the context dependence of a memory, and awareness of it, as independent. Memories for prior episodes *always* preserve context, and hence the retrieval of all information, be it by direct or indirect means, is potentially subject to contextual variables. In view of the different predictions that can be derived from these opposing viewpoints, it seems clear that the influence of context on performance on indirect tests, by both normal and amnesic subjects, will continue to be a theoretically important issue (see also Lewandowsky *et al.*, 1988).

One aspect of the amnesic syndrome not addressed in detail in any of the contributions is retrograde amnesia. Research on memory for information acquired premorbidly is methodologically difficult, even in patients in whom the event causing their amnesia can accurately be dated. It does appear however that patients with similar degrees of anterograde impairment can differ in the degree and temporal extent of their retrograde deficits, with occasional patients showing apparently normal memory for events occurring more than 1 or 2 years premorbidly (Zola-Morgan *et al.*, 1986; Squire *et al.*, 1989). The apparent lack of a strong relationship between the severity of anterograde and retrograde impairments (although see Shallice, 1988) has been taken as evidence that pre- and postmorbid memory rely on partially distinct brain systems, damage to which can vary independently (Squire *et al.*, 1989). As noted many times previously, the co-existence of a marked anterograde deficit and a temporally limited or graded retrograde impairment is problematic for explanations of amnesia framed purely in terms of a retrieval deficit—why should premorbid memory be immune from such a deficit?

The invariable existence of some degree of retrograde impairment, even in cases of amnesia with relatively circumscribed pathology, has been accounted for neurologically (Squire *et al.*, 1989; Zola-Morgan & Squire, 1990) with the proposal that over time, episodic memories become progressively less dependent on the brain structures implicated in anterograde amnesia. Thus the abrupt loss of functioning of these structures will cause more disruption to premorbid memories formed just before the trauma than to those formed some time before. The functional concomitants of this time-dependent change in the neurological basis of memory remain to be determined, but should help to elucidate the difference(s) between memories (other than when they were acquired) that amnesic patients can and cannot gain awareness of. For example, memories may perhaps become less context-bound with time, so that their retrieval becomes less dependent on the kinds of contextual information that amnesics have difficulty processing and/or storing (see Schacter, 1988 and Mayes, Chapter 11, this volume, for further discussion).

Because of uncertainties about the functional equivalence of normal and amnesic remote memory, and indeed about how normal memories evolve with time (see for example Shallice, 1988; MacKinnon & Squire, 1989), differing accounts of amnesia have plenty of room for manoeuvre when tackling the relationship between anterograde and retrograde deficits. None the less, the current level of knowledge provides some constraints (however weak), and as more is learned these can only become stronger.

As things stand presently, is not clear how the account of amnesia put forward by Jacoby and Kelley (Chapter 10, this volume) can deal with the co-occurrence of severe anterograde and temporally limited retrograde amnesia. Discussed only briefly, this account seems to propose that amnesic patients retain a normal capacity to acquire information, but are unable to make use of it when this requires conscious recollection (cf. Baddeley, 1982). But, as noted before, some patients appear to be able to recollect information learned quite recently before their trauma. Other accounts of amnesia that seem easier to reconcile with the existence of graded/limited retrograde deficits are less easy to integrate with the position advocated by Jacoby and Kelley. For example, one alternative is that amnesia arises from an inability to represent some critical attribute or attributes of new and recent premorbid events (certain contextual attributes, for example) that ordinarily provide the retrieval pathways for conscious recollection, but which are less important for implicit memory (cf. Mayes, Chapter 11, this volume). From this perspective, amnesia results not from a deficiency in recollection, but from the inadequacy of the representations on which recollective processes operate. Another, related, possibility is of course that amnesia reflects the loss of a specific memory system dedicated to the acquisition and storage of new and recent episodes in a consciously accessible form, and that intact implicit memory reflects the functioning of other memory systems, such as those underlying the acquisition of perceptual representations and motor skills (see for example Squire, 1987).

Another important issue in the study of conscious and unconscious memory, especially evident in Jacoby and Kelley's contribution, is how to investigate the relative influences of different kinds of memory without the need to assume that different tasks are, in the words of Jacoby and Kelley, 'process pure' (the 'transparency assumption' of Dunn & Kirsner, 1988b). That is, how can one circumvent the criticism that performance on a task chosen to reflect only implicit memory is 'contaminated' by explicit memory (and vice-versa)? Jacoby and Kelley's solution is to devise experimental situations in which the two kinds of memory are placed in opposition. The critical feature of this general approach is that an experimental task is arranged so that implicit and explicit processes will have *opposite* effects on behaviour, thereby allowing their relative influences to be assessed directly, and neatly sidestepping the issue of whether the task exclusively taps only one form of memory (see Merikle & Reingold, 1991, for a description and demonstration of a complementary approach to the problem of separating the influences of implicit and explicit memory in normal subjects).

As Jacoby and Kelley point out, the 'opposition' methodology, and the quantitative development of it described in Chapter 10, is applicable outside the field of memory research. It will be of interest to see whether it can be adapted to the investigation of any of the other areas covered in the present volume. If it can, it might provide a new means of independently characterizing the processes responsible for implicit and explicit processing in these areas, and of dealing with the perennial problem of devising tests sensitive to only one or the other kind of processing.

Jacoby and Kelley convincingly demonstrate how opposition methodology can play an important role in investigating the respective roles of what they refer to as familiarity and recollection in recognition memory. *Dual-process* models of recognition memory propose that judgements about past occurrence are based on two independent sources of information: the outcome of a consciously controlled search of memory (recollection), using the test item as a retrieval cue, and the ease (or *fluency*) with which the test item is perceived. Perceptual fluency serves as a guide to prior occurrence because it is enhanced by repetition (the well-known phenomenom of repetition priming). Thus test items that are perceived most fluently are, all other things being equal, the ones that are likely to have been encountered most recently. Jacoby and Kelley persuasively argue that for perceptual fluency to serve as a basis for recognition memory, its effects must unconsciously be attributed to past experience, rather than to variables such as stimulus clarity. They further argue that the outcome of this attribution process is the experience of familiarity. This process is held to be intact in amnesia, and to provide the basis for whatever performance amnesic patients can muster on direct memory tests. However, as Mayes discusses in Chapter 11, it is presently unclear whether the processes that underlie priming effects in amnesia allow such patients to experience familiarity; this may require more than just an intact capacity for priming.

'Raw' familiarity (familiarity based solely on ease of processing; Mandler, 1980) is in any case likely to be an ineffective basis for recognition memory. Much more effective is *relative* familiarity—the difference between the raw familiarity of an item, and the level of familiarity that would be 'expected' given its history of past occurrence (Mandler, 1980; Mandler *et al.*, 1982; Humphreys *et al.*, 1989; Rugg, 1990). For example, it is well known that the recognition memory (but not the recall) of words with a low normative frequency of occurrence in the language is better than that of otherwise comparable high frequency words (see Rugg, 1990 for a review). One possible explanation for this is that recognition judgements are determined in large part by raw familiarity—when this is above a certain criterion level, a 'yes' response is given, when below criterion, a 'no' response is made. Given the (not unreasonable) assumption that the magnitude of a word's raw familiarity is inversely proportional to the time since it was last encountered, it follows that the raw familiarity of 'old' and 'new' low frequency words will differ by a greater extent than will that of equivalent high frequency ones. Hence old and new low frequency words will be better discriminated. However, on the assumption that the same criterion is adopted for both classes of word, this explanation predicts that the word frequency advantage in recognition memory will arise not as a consequence of a higher hit rate for old low frequency items, but from a lower false positive rate for new ones. This is because the raw familiarity of a low frequency word may, as a function of repetition, approach that of a comparably repeated high frequency item, but it cannot exceed it. By contrast, the raw familiarity of an unrepeated low frequency word will on average always be lower than that of an otherwise comparable high frequency item.

In fact, the word frequency advantage arises because low frequency words attract both a lower number of false positives, *and* a higher hit rate (e.g. Mandler *et al.*, 1982; Glanzer & Adams, 1990). This finding is difficult to reconcile with the idea that recognition judgements in such studies are based solely on raw familiarity (or an any other unidimensional, 'strength-like' attribute; Glanzer & Adams, 1990). It is, however, compatible with the notion that recognition judgements are based on an index akin to relative familiarity; that is, on the outcome of a process which compares the raw familiarity of an item with what would be expected on the basis of past encounters with it (Mandler *et al.*, 1982).

Thus familiarity-based recognition memory judgements in normal subjects may not (always) be made on the basis of raw familiarity. Instead, a more complex index—familiarity relative to some baseline—might be employed. Could it be that, in the absence of conscious recollection, the phenomenal experience that an item has recently been encountered depends critically upon evaluation of its relative rather than its raw familiarity?

If this speculation is correct, raw familiarity may provide a means of making above-chance recognition judgements in the absence of conscious recollection, but these judgements will not be accompanied by a *feeling* of familiarity for correctly detected old items. In other words, successful performance on a direct memory test might occur without any concomitant awareness that performance is accurate (a possibility that reinforces the importance of separately specifying tasks and processes). The capacity of an amnesic patient to experience 'pastness' might therefore be dependent not merely on the ability to make above-chance recognition judgements, but on the ability to do so on the basis of relative familiarity. If the reasoning in the foregoing paragraphs is correct, this ability could be assessed by testing amnesics' recognition memory for low- and high-frequency words. For the reasons discussed previously, reliance on raw familiarity should lead to a low frequency advantage in false positive responses only, whereas if relative familiarity is used, an advantage should exist for hit rate also. (Either way, amnesics would be expected to show a recognition memory advantage for low frequency words, in contradiction to the prediction made by Mayes [Chapter 11, this volume] from the results of Gardiner & Java [1990]).

Relevant data come from a study of five Korsakoff patients by Huppert and Piercy (1976). These patients showed a normal recognition memory advantage for low frequency words, but this was attributable entirely to an excess of false positive responses to high frequency items, suggesting that their recognition judgements were based on raw rather than relative familiarity. Unfortunately, no description is given of the patients' reports of their subjective experience while carrying out this task. It also remains to be seen whether a similar finding occurs in amnesic patients of other aetiologies. If it does, this would suggest that the processes underlying 'familiarity-based' recognition memory in amnesic and normal subjects are qualitatively different, and would add weight to the view that the deficit in amnesia involves more than the inability to engage in conscious recollection.

12.4. CONCLUDING COMMENTS

On reading the different contributions to this book, it is impossible not to be struck by the ubiquity (necessity?) of verbal reports as the means of deciding whether performance on some task is or is not accompanied by awareness. This raises two problems. First, unless awareness of an event is to be *defined* as the ability to frame a verbal report about it, why should what people *say* be thought to have a more transparent relationship with the contents of phenomenal experience than what they *do*? We seem quite willing to accept that behaviour such as button-pushing can occur without concomitant awareness; why is this not also possible for language?

The second difficulty is that the contents of awareness may sometimes be inaccessible to the language system. For example, commissurotomized patients may deny the occurrence of stimuli presented to the left visual field, but demonstrate extensive processing of these stimuli when appropriately tested (reviewed in Springer & Deutsch, 1989). Few however believe that this disparity between behaviour and reported experience is sufficient reason to assume that the right hemisphere of these patients is unaware of left-lateralized stimuli; the alternative, that the contents of awareness in the right hemisphere are not accessible to the left-lateralized speech system, seems more plausible (Sperry, 1984).

Commissurotomy is of course an extreme case, in which the neuro-anatomical basis of the proposed disconnection between a system putatively capable of awareness, and the system capable of reporting it, is clear. But by what criteria should a similar 'disconnection account' be rejected in cases which are less clear-cut neurologically, but who manifest equally dramatic dissociations between motor and verbal behaviour? For example, what distinguishes the *behaviour* of a commissurotomy patient reacting to a stimulus in his/her left visual field, and a blindsight patient doing the same for a stimulus presented in his/her scotoma, such that we are more willing to assume visual awareness on the part of one than the other?

A final question, brought sharply into focus from reading the contributions in this book, is *why* do we have phenomenal experience? What benefits are derived from being aware of the products of cognitive processing? Within the discipline of psychology this question is usually addressed in cognitive/functionalist terms, by appeal to the need for some kind of executive or supervisory system (or systems), which can override automatic determinants of behaviour and select and maintain goal-directed activities (e.g. Jacoby & Kelley, Chapter 10, this volume; Posner & Rothbart, Chapter 5, this volume; and see Shallice, 1988 and Schacter, 1989, for reviews). Such accounts address the question of the possible functions of the processes thought to be associated with consciousness, but they leave open the issue of *why* they should be associated—why should a conscious supervisory or monitoring system be more effective than an unconscious one? One is left with the suspicion that cognitive and neuropsychological methods will continue to allow steady progress in specifying both the necessary conditions for phenomenal experience to occur, and the functional role(s) of the cognitive processes that accompany such experience. But the reason why it exists might prove more elusive.

FOOTNOTE

1. It should be pointed out that the 'dissociative approach' has been called into question as a means of providing evidence for the existence of qualitatively different kinds of memory process. According to Dunn and Kirsner (1988a), even 'classical' double dissociations between two pairs of independent variables (e.g. crossover interactions between two tasks and two manipulations, or two tasks and two classes of subject), are a logically insufficient basis from which to argue for the existence of independent processes or systems—such conclusions can only be based on what Dunn and Kirsner refer to as patterns of 'reverse association'.

It is also worth noting that a second line of evidence for the independence of memory processes, 'stochastic independence' of performance on items common to more than one memory test (e.g. Tulving *et al.*, 1982, and Schacter, Chapter 9, this volume), has also been called into question. Hintzmann and Hartry (1990) have argued strongly that whether or not stochastic independence occurs between two tests depends to too great an extent on the idiosyncracies of individual test items to be of theoretical significance.

ACKNOWLEDGEMENTS

The comments of Andrew Mayes and David Milner on an earlier version of this chapter are gratefully acknowledged.

REFERENCES

Baddeley, A.D. (1982). Domains of recollection. *Psychological Review*, **89**, 708–729.

Baynes, K. (1990). Language and reading in the right hemisphere: Highways or byways of the brain? *Journal of Cognitive Neuroscience*, **2**, 159–179.

Coslett, H.B. & Saffran, E.M. (1989). Evidence for preserved reading in 'pure alexia'. *Brain*, **112**, 327–359.

Déjerine, J. (1892). Contribution à l'étude anatomo-pathologique et clinique des différentes variétés de cécité verbale. *Comptes Rendus Hebdomadaires de Séances et Memoires de la Société de Biologie, Ninth Series*, **4**, 61–90.

Dunn, J.C. & Kirsner, K. (1988a). Discovering functionally independent mental processes: The principle of reversed association. *Psychological Review*, **95**, 91–101.

Dunn, J.C. & Kirsner, K. (1988b). Implicit memory: Task or process? In S. Lewandowsky, J.C. Dunn and K. Kirsner (eds), *Implicit Memory*. Hillsdale, NJ: Erlbaum.

Gardiner, J.M. & Java, R.I. (1990). Recollective experience in word and non-word recognition. *Memory and Cognition*, **18**, 23–30.

Glanzer, M. & Adams, J.K. (1990). The mirror effect in recognition memory: Data and theory. *Journal of Experimental Psychology: Learning, Memory, and Cognition*, **16**, 5–16.

Heindel, W.C., Salmon, D.P., Shults, C.W., Walicke, P.A. & Butters, N. (1989). Neuropsychological evidence for multiple implicit memory systems: A comparison of Alzheimer's, Huntington's, and Parkinson's disease patients. *Journal of Neuroscience*, **9**, 582–587.

Hintzmann, D.L. & Hartry, A.L. (1990). Item effects in recognition and fragment completion: Contingency relations vary for different subsets of words. *Journal of Experimental Psychology: Learning, Memory, and Cognition*, **16**, 955–969.

Humphreys, M.S., Bain, J.D. & Pike, R. (1989). Different ways to cue a coherent memory system: A theory for episodic, semantic and procedural tasks. *Psychological Review*, **96**, 208–233.

Huppert, F.A. & Piercy, M. (1976). Recognition memory in amnesic patients: Effects of temporal context and familiarity of material. *Cortex*, **12**, 3–20.

Lewandowsky, S., Kirsner, K. & Bainbridge, V. (1988). Context effects in implicit memory: a sense-specific account. In S. Lewandowsky, J.C. Dunn, and K. Kirsner (eds), *Implicit Memory*, Hillsdale, NJ: Erlbaum.

MacKinnon, D.F. & Squire, L.R. (1989). Autobiographical memory and amnesia. *Psychobiology*, **17**, 247–256.

Mandler, G. (1980). Recognizing. The judgment of previous occurrence. *Psychological Review*, **87**, 252–271.

Mandler, G., Goodman, G.O. & Wilkes-Gibbs, D.L. (1982). The word-frequency paradox in recognition. *Memory and Cognition*, **10**, 33–42.

Masson, M.E.J. (1988). Fluent reprocessing as an implicit expression of memory for experience. In S. Lewandowsky, J.C. Dunn, and K. Kirsner (eds), *Implicit Memory*. Hillsdale, NJ: Erlbaum.

Merikle, P.M. & Reingold, E.M. (1991). Comparing direct (explicit) and indirect (implicit) measures to study unconscious memory. *Journal of Experimental Psychology: Learning, Memory, and Cognition*, **17**, 224–233.

Patterson, K.E. & Kay, J. (1982). Letter-by-letter reading: Psychological descriptions of a neurological syndrome. *Quarterly Journal of Experimental Psychology*, **34A**, 411–441.

Richardson-Klavehn, A. & Bjork, R.A. (1988). Measures of memory. *Annual Review of Psychology*, **39**, 475–543.

Roediger, H.L. (1990). Implicit memory: A commentary. *Bulletin of the Psychonomic Society*, **28**, 373–380.

Roediger, H.L., Weldon, M.S. & Challis, B.H. (1989). Explaining dissociations between implicit and explicit measures of retention: A processing account. In H.L. Roediger and F.I.M. Craik (eds), *Varieties of Memory and Consciousness*. Hillsdale NJ: Erlbaum.

Rugg, M.D. (1990). Event-related potentials dissociate repetition effects of high- and low-frequency words. *Memory and Cognition*, **18**, 367–379.

Schacter, D.L. (1989). On the relation between memory and consciousness: Dissociable interactions and conscious experience. In H.L. Roediger and F.I.M. Craik (eds), *Varieties of Memory and Consciousness*. Hillsdale NJ: Erlbaum.

Schacter, D.L., Rapscak, S.Z., Rubens, A.B., Tharan, M. & Laguna, J. (1990). Priming effects in a letter-by-letter reader depend upon access to the word form system. *Neuropsychologia*, **28**, 1079–1094.

Shallice, T. (1988). *From Neuropsychology to Mental Structure*. Cambridge: Cambridge University Press.

Shallice, T. & Saffran, E.M. (1986). Lexical processing in the absence of explicit word identification: Evidence from a letter-by-letter reader. *Cognitive Neuropsychology*, **3**, 429–458.

Smith, M.L. (1989). Memory disorders associated with temporal-lobe lesions. In L. Squire and G. Gainotti (eds), *Handbook of Neuropsychology*: Vol. 3. Amsterdam: Elsevier.

Sperry, R.W. (1984). Consciousness, personal identity and the divided brain. *Neuropsychologia*, **22**, 661–673.

Springer, S.P. & Deutsch, G. (1989). *Left Brain, Right Brain*, 3rd edn. New York: Freeman.

Squire, L.R. (1987). *Memory and Brain*. New York: Oxford University Press.

Squire, L.R., Haist, F. & Shimamura, A.P. (1989). The neurology of memory:

Quantitative assessment of retrograde amnesia in two groups of amnesic patients. *Journal of Neuroscience*, **9**, 828–839.

Tulving, E., Schacter, D.L. & Stark, H.A. (1982). Priming effects in word fragment completion are independent of recognition memory. *Journal of Experimental Psychology: Learning, Memory, and Cognition*, **8**, 336–342.

Warrington, E.K. & Shallice, T. (1980). Word form dyslexia. *Brain*, **103**, 99–112.

Zola-Morgan, S. & Squire, L.R. (1990). The primate hippocampal formation: Evidence for a time-limited role in memory storage. *Science*, **250**, 288–290.

Zola-Morgan, S., Squire, L.R. & Amaral, D.G. (1986). Human amnesia and the medial temporal region: Enduring memory impairment following a bilateral lesion limited to field CA1 of the hippocampus. *Journal of Neuroscience*, **6**, 2950–2967.

INDEX

Absorption spectrum, 23
Abstract representations, 124, 125, 224, 225, 228
Accessory optic nuclei, 13
Achromatopsia, 31, 42, 149, 151
Activation, 64, 65, 70, 84, 85, 94–99, 102, 103, 124, 147, 152, 187, 189, 194, 224, 225, 242, 266
Agnosia, 2, 43, 50, 52, 61, 62, 81, 140, 141, 144, 151, 152, 154
Akinetic mutism, 94, 107
Alexia without agraphia, 265
Alexia, 2, 81, 126, 194, 265–268
Alzheimer patients, 240
Amblyopic, 26
Amnesia, 2, 80–83, 152, 179, 183, 187–190, 193, 202, 235, 241–249, 255–258, 268, 270–272, 274
Anomalous, 17, 133
Anomalous pictures/sentences, 2
Anomalous location, 16
Anosognosia, 2, 80–83
Anterior attention network, 93–98, 101, 102, 105
Anterior cingulate, 7, 93–99, 102, 107, 108
Aphasia, 2, 4, 7, 159, 165, 171, 175, 194
Association neocortex, 236, 248
Associations, 50–53, 55, 84, 94, 97, 99, 125, 189, 190, 193
Associative priming, 72–74, 162, 190
Attention deficit disorder, 107
Attention without awareness, 99, 141
Attributional priming, 241, 258
Automaticity, 74, 161, 201–205, 214, 215, 222–227
Automatic processing, see Automaticity
Automatic memory processes, 235, 237, 238, 243, 254

Autonomic responses, 2, 60, 72, 96, 252

Backward masking, see Masked priming
Basal ganglia, 102
Binding problem, 6, 7,
Binding, 6, 7, 93
'Blind touch', see Unfeeling touch
Blindsight, 2–5, 7, 8, 11–31, 39, 119, 140, 141, 202, 266, 275
Blobs, see Cytochrome oxidase histochemistry

Cell assemblies, 116, 124
Cerebellum, 236
Chromatic opponency, see Colour opponency
Classical conditioning, 236
Clearing of consciousness, 91, 98, 108
Collaterals, 17
Colour opponency, 15, 20, 22, 24
Colour perception, 43, 55, 60–65
Colour processing, 42–44, 55, 60–65, 150
Commissurotomy, 153, 274, 275
Completion, 2, 123, 126, 130, 133, 181–186, 189, 191, 203, 211, 213, 238, 240, 249, 252–255, 258, 264
Comprehension, 160, 161, 172, 175
Conceptually driven processing, 5, 203, 222, 226
Conditioning, 8, 236
Confabulation, 130, 205
Confidence rating, 56, 57, 60, 64, 152, 153
Conscious control, 69, 91, 101, 106–108, 204, 219, 225, 268

Conscious perception, 29, 144, 184,
    186, 209, 211, 222
Conscious recollection, 179–190, 193,
    205, 210–214, 218, 219, 227,
    269, 271, 273, 274
Contents of phenomenal experience,
    124, 125, 274
Context memory, 2, 142, 146, 150,
    167, 169, 171, 174, 180, 181,
    185–190, 193, 194, 205, 222,
    225, 239, 240–251, 255, 256,
    264, 265, 269–271
Controlled processing, 201
Correlated oscillations, 7
Cortical microstimulation, 30
Covert attention, 97, 129
Covert processing, 39–44, 48, 51, 52,
    62, 63, 78, 150, 264
Covert recognition, 71
Cross-integration of phenomenal
    experience, 123
Cytochrome oxidase histochemistry,
    25, 41–43, 58–59, 63, 64

Data-driven processing, 5, 202, 203,
    222, 226
'Deaf hearing', 2, 31
Declarative memory, 4, 187, 189,
    244, 243, 246
Depth of processing, 5
Diachronic structure of conscious
    experience, 120
DICE model, 6
Direct and indirect tests, 39, 55,
    60–65, 76–78, 141, 151,
    202–209, 214, 215, 223–227,
    244, 251, 263, 264, 268–273
Directional hypokinesia, 118, 119,
    134, 146
Disconnection hypothesis of
    amnesia, 244
Dissociations, 2–9, 81, 97, 99, 101,
    106, 122, 139, 140, 144–148,
    153, 187, 193, 194, 202–205,
    208, 212–215, 222–228, 264,
    265, 268, 269, 275
Divided attention, 100, 184, 203,
    212–218, 223, 258
Dopamine, 102, 107

Dorsal lateral geniculate nucleus
    (dLGN), 5, 7, 12–20, 23, 25,
    30, 31
Dorsal stream, 149, 150
Double dissociations, 3, 4, 265, 275
Dreams, 122–124
Dual-process theories, 214, 272
Dyslexia, see Alexia

Electrical stimulation, 31
Emotional expression, 52, 70
Encoding, 76, 182–184, 191, 214
Episodic memory, 5, 6, 192, 194,
    205, 239, 242–248
Equiluminance, 57, 59, 62–64, 149
Event-related potentials, 1, 8, 60, 72
Evoked potentials, see Event-related
    potentials
Excitation, 30
Explicit knowledge, 2–4, 77, 84, 100,
    134, 152, 159–165, 170–174,
    179–181, 184–194, 203, 241,
    244, 249, 254–257, 261–268,
    271, 272
Explicit memory, 100, 152, 179, 180,
    184, 185, 188–192, 271, 272
Explicit task, 159, 160, 163, 164, 172,
    174
Extinction, 120, 129
Extra-striate cortex, 17, 22, 29, 31, 40

Face matching, 52, 53, 77, 81
Face processing system, 41, 52–54,
    61, 70, 71, 81
Face recognition, 4, 40–45, 64, 65,
    69–72, 75–86, 159, 240, 264,
    268
False fame effect, 208, 210–213, 224
Familiarity, 40, 53, 54, 65, 70, 75, 77,
    79, 151, 152, 194, 204,
    207–209, 212–222, 227, 235,
    238–242, 244, 246, 250, 257,
    258, 272–274
Field defect, 11–15, 22–28, 43, 141
First-order explanations, 187–195
Fluency, 152, 187, 206–210, 241, 249,
    258, 272
Forced-choice tests, 2, 4, 8, 23, 29,

40, 61, 64, 73, 75, 78, 79, 141, 148, 191, 216, 266
Fragment completion tasks, 44, 48, 50, 52, 54, 181, 183, 184, 203, 213
Free association, 185, 249–251, 255
Free recall, 185, 242–248, 258

GABA-immunohistochemistry, 19, 30
Geniculostriate pathway, 16, 40
Global shapes, 48
Grammaticality judgement task, 160, 164–176
Guilty Knowledge Test, 72
Gut awareness, 4, 208

Hemineglect, *see* Neglect
Hippocampus, 102, 248
Homunculus, 120, 123
HRP, 16, 19, 21, 37, 38

Illusions of memory, 206–209
Imaging, 1, 9, 92–98, 103–108, 112
Implicit knowledge, 1, 4, 7, 8, 77, 84, 99–101, 139–142, 145, 148–152, 159–162, 165, 170, 172, 176, 195, 203, 236, 242, 263–268, 272
Implicit memory, 77, 152, 179–194, 205, 269–271
Implicit task, 159
Independent context, 243, 245, 247, 255, 256
Indirect tests, 39, 40, 44, 60–65, 76–78, 141, 148, 151, 202–208, 211, 214, 215, 222, 223
Infancy, 96, 103–106
Inhibition, 30, 74, 99, 100, 103, 104, 133, 147
Intentional retrieval, 213
Intentionality, 224, 237, 254
Interactive context, 243–247, 255
Interference tasks, 73
Intermediate and final representations, 161
Interneurons, 16, 19, 25
Introspection, 115, 116

Ishihara test, 60–64, 149, 151
Isoluminance, *see* Equiluminance
Item-specific indirect memory, 236, 238, 241

Laevophobia, 131
Language disorders, 263
Lateral geniculate nucleus, *see* Dorsal lateral geniculate nucleus
Lateralization, 96
Learning, 40, 50–53, 61, 64, 72, 74–81, 99, 100, 206, 225, 236, 238, 245, 246, 251–257
Letter-by-letter reading, 43, 265–267
Lexical decision, 2, 160, 162, 166, 202, 224, 225, 266–268
Line bisection, 146, 148
Locus coeruleus, 95, 96
Long-delayed forced-choice recognition, 2

Magnocellular system, 15, 20, 41, 59, 62, 149
Masked priming, 2, 43, 59, 63, 117, 120, 125, 147, 184–186
Memory, *see* Mental unity
Mental unity, 121, 122, 179–200, 201–233, 235–261, 263–264, 268–274
Midbrain, 7, 38, 40, 93, 143
Minimal on-time, 8
Misoplegia, 131
Monkeys, 4, 13–16, 21–23, 26–28, 129, 130, 143–146, 149
MT, 5, 20, 29, 30, 145, 149
Multiple memory systems, 225, 268

Neglect, 2, 7, 20, 29–31, 77, 107, 113–120, 125–140, 145–148, 154, 179, 194
Nucleus of the optic tract, 13

Object recognition, 44, 48, 75, 81, 96
Object decision task, 191, 192
Object-centred representations, 75, 150

Off-line tasks, 4, 162, 163, 170, 172,
    174, 176, 264, 265
Olivary pretectum, 13
On-line tasks, 4, 7, 95, 162, 163, 166,
    169–176, 182, 264, 265
Optic ataxia, 144–146, 238
Orienting, 84, 91, 93, 95, 97, 98,
    101–108, 142, 143, 182
Overt recognition, 48, 72, 74, 78,
    83–86, 252
Overt processing, 8, 9, 42, 48, 50,
    61, 64, 72–78, 83–86, 142, 264

Parietal cortex, 7, 29, 93–96, 107,
    112, 145–149
Parvocellular system, 15, 20, 22, 63,
    149, 150
Perceptual identification priming,
    149, 203, 208, 240–244, 249,
    250, 253
Perceptual representation system,
    192, 239, 269, 270
Performance-resource functions, 265
Personification, 131
PET, *see* Imaging
Phenomenal experience, 6, 30, 98,
    113–118, 121–126, 129–132,
    135, 180, 186, 187, 225, 264,
    273, 274
Photopic curve, 23
Picture completion, 2
Pα ganglion cells, *see* Retinal
    ganglion cells
Posterior attention network, 93–101,
    103–108, 112
Priming, 2, 3, 8, 11, 29, 72–74, 99,
    115, 125, 126, 142, 153, 161,
    163, 181–194, 202, 224, 225,
    235–258
Priming of contextual information,
    255
Priming of new associations,
    189–191
Procedural memory, 4, 189
Process orientated approach, 228
Projection neurons, 16, 19, 22, 25, 37
Prosopagnosia, 2, 4, 7, 29, 39–43,
    52, 61, 64, 65, 70–72, 76, 79,
    81, 84–86, 151–153, 194, 202,
    268

Psychopathology, 91
Pβ, *see* Retinal ganglion cells
Pulvinar nucleus, 13–16, 20, 23, 93,
    96, 146
Pure alexia, 265–268
Pγ, *see* Retinal ganglion cells

Qualia, 115
Quantum effects, 7

Raw familiarity, 272–274
Reaction times (RT), 25–28, 50, 54,
    73–75, 85, 93, 95, 100, 142,
    162, 168, 176, 256
Recognition, 2–4, 29, 39–42, 44, 46,
    48, 50–55, 61–65, 69–86, 96,
    141–144, 151, 152, 181–185,
    188, 191, 192, 204, 209–223,
    227, 234–248, 250, 252,
    256–258
Recognition memory, 151, 181, 184,
    204, 209, 210, 213–223, 227,
    246, 272–274
Recollection, 82, 123, 179–181,
    183–186, 188–190, 192–194,
    205, 210–222, 227, 240, 242,
    254–258, 272
Rehabilitation, 22, 268
Relative familiarity, 272–274
Remote memory, 271
Repetition priming, 2, 243, 267, 268,
    272
Resource artefacts, 265
Retinal ganglion cells, 7, 15, 16,
    19–25, 30, 38, 40, 211,
    213–215, 222
Retrieval, 70, 79, 80, 83, 142, 180,
    214, 237, 238, 242, 243,
    246–248, 250, 254, 256
Retrograde amnesia, 248, 270, 271
Retrograde neuronal degeneration,
    16, 19, 20, 37, 270
Reverse association, 275
Right hemisphere, 96, 153, 166, 274
Right hemisphere hypothesis of
    implicit reading, 267

S-layers, 15
Schizophrenia, 107, 122, 123
Scotoma, 14, 25, 142, 275

Scotopic vision, 22, 23
Secondary cortical areas, 29, 31, 37
Second-order explanations, 154,
 186–188, 193–196, 246, 268
Selective attention, 6, 30, 91, 92,
 147, 202
Semantic memory, 79, 242, 243, 247,
 248
Semantic priming effects, 160, 242,
 243, 247, 248
Semantic versus episodic memory, 4
Sentence arrangement, 2
Sentence-picture matching task, 160,
 163, 164, 170–174
Sequence learning, 99, 100
Shadowing in dichotic listening, 2
Shape discrimination, 42
Signal-detection theory, 223
Single dissociations, 3, 4, 265
Skills, 2, 145, 151, 188, 236, 267, 271
Skin conductance, 13, 72, 252
Sleep, 1, 96, 105, 168
Somatoparaphrenia, 130, 131
Spatial perception, 146
Spatial opponency, 15
Stem completion tasks, 2, 182, 184
Stimulus-driven processing (*see also*
 Automaticity), 224–226
Stochastic independence, 181, 182,
 185, 237, 242, 275
Striate cortex, 5, 6, 7, 11–13, 16–22,
 25–31, 37–42, 59, 64, 103, 145,
 147, 150, 151
Stroop, 3, 94, 98, 105, 107, 211, 224
Structural description system, 192,
 193, 269
Subjective experience, 56, 93, 97, 98,
 106, 113, 114, 130, 180,
 202–207, 211, 221, 227, 266,
 274
Subjective threshold, 3, 152, 222
Subliminal perception, 2, 4, 114, 115,
 125, 126, 131, 133
Superior colliculus (SC), 5, 7, 12–14,
 19, 20, 25, 26, 29, 40, 93, 103
Supplementary motor area, 93, 94,
 102, 107, 112
Surgical anaesthesia, 185, 186

Target detection, 94–99

Test unawareness, 182–186
Theory of other minds, 8
Transneuronal retrograde
 degeneration, 20
Two visual systems, 4

Unawareness and denial of
 neurological disorders, 131
Unconscious inference, 206
Unconscious influences, 201–204
Unconscious perception, 64, 65, 140,
 143, 147, 186, 202, 209, 211,
 222
Unfeeling touch, 2, 31
Unilateral neglect. *see* Neglect

Visual area 1 (V1), *see* Striate cortex
Visual area 2 (V2), 5, 22, 23, 150
Visual area 3 (V3), 5, 42
Visual area 4 (V4), 5, 19, 22, 23, 37,
 42, 147–151, 275
Visual area 5 (V5), *see* MT
Ventral lateral geniculate nucleus
 (vLGN), 12
Vigilance, 5, 91–98, 108, 112
Visual agnosia, 42, 152
Visual awareness, 12, 28, 143, 145,
 150–153, 234, 275
Visual form agnosia, 144, 152
Visual orienting, 98, 104
Visual pathways, 4, 12, 40, 117, 143
Visual word form system, 112, 266
Visuomotor processing, 141–145,
 149–154
Volition, 101, 106, 107

Wavelength discrimination, 14, 15,
 20–24, 38, 142, 151
Word completion task, 189, 238, 240,
 252, 258
Word frequency, 273
Word monitoring, 162, 163, 166–171,
 174
Word-completion priming, 240, 249,
 253, 257
Word-form dyslexia, 265